- I am not responsible f
  but I can change my thoughts
- Let the feelings rise and fall
- Temper is sabotage
- Self-appointed expectations produce
  self-induced frustrations
- Endorse for the effort; not the results
- Endorse for part acts; not the total effort
- Endorse, endorse, endorse
- I can move my muscles
- Be objective
- Start with the weakest link
- Handle problems in a cultured manner
- This is a test; this is just a test.
  If this were a real emergency, you would be notified

Definition of Spotting

Turn the spotlight on one's mental activities to discover the unrealistic thinking that had slipped in and was creating the turmoil. Once spotted, it could be corrected by exchanging it for a more realistic appraisal

MANAGE YOUR FEARS
MANAGE YOUR ANGER

A Psychiatrist Speaks

Abraham A. Low, M.D.
Founder of Recovery, Inc.

Willett Publishing Co.
Glencoe, Illinois 60022

Other books by Abraham A. Low, M.D.:

Mental Health Through Will-Training

Peace Versus Power in the Family:
Domestic Discord and Emotional Distress

Mental Illness, Stigma and Self-Help:
The Founding of Recovery, Inc.

The above books are published by Willett Publishing Co.,
Glencoe, IL 60022

Selections From Dr. Low's Works (1950 – 1953) is published by
Recovery, Inc., 802 N. Dearborn St., Chicago, IL 60610

Library of Congress Catalog Card Number: 95-60989

ISBN 0-915005-05-0

*To the potential in each of us
to break the grip of fear and anger*

TABLE OF CONTENTS

INTRODUCTION

This book contains transcriptions from audio tapes of lectures made by Abraham A. Low, M.D., in 1953 and 1954, during the two years preceding his death.* The concepts expressed remain as current today as they ever were. The ongoing presence of crippling fear and uncontrolled anger in modern life calls for effective methods of managing these disruptive forces. Abraham Low's comprehensive system of self-help techniques addresses this ever-present issue. Its effectiveness is demonstrated by the thousands of people who have benefited from the training offered by Recovery, Inc., the organization Low founded in 1937.

These tapes were made by a man of special background. For those who listen to the tapes while reading this book, his European accent will be evident. So, too, will be his grounding in earlier twentieth-century technology: One rides streetcars and places calls through telephone operators. The role of women in the mid-1950s had yet to be influenced by the attitudes that have evolved since then; nevertheless, Low's concepts and techniques impart an equally powerful inner strength to both women and men.

The tapes record extemporaneous talks given by Low to his patients on Saturday afternoons and Tuesday evenings. Their spontaneous character is evident in the sentence struc-

---

* *The seventy lectures on tape, as well as Dr. Low's books, can be ordered from Recovery, Inc., 802 N. Dearborn St., Chicago, IL 60610, or from the Abraham A. Low Institute, 550 Frontage Road, Northfield, IL 60093.*

ture, idiomatic expressions and momentary grammatical lapses. Occasionally he announces one subject and then talks about another. The lecture titles in this book reflect the subject actually discussed. Every effort has been made to preserve the accuracy of the spoken word. Minor changes have been made to facilitate the reader's understanding.

The richness and clarity of these talks demonstrate Low's ability to render complex subjects understandable to the layman, even to people preoccupied with fear and anger. What emerges is Low's complete identification with the suffering that fear and anger create, his sense of humor and his deep concern for those who sought his help.

EDITOR'S NOTE

For those who are listening to the tapes while reading, deletions have been made where Dr. Low corrected his own words or phrases as he spoke, and words have been inserted occasionally to facilitate the reader's understanding.

REFERENCES TO OTHER PUBLICATIONS

Low's references to "the book" denote his text *Mental Health Through Will-Training.*

Low's references to "articles" and *Recovery News* concern a periodical published by Recovery, Inc., and edited by Phil Crane from August, 1947, to September, 1954, following the discontinuance of the *Recovery Journal* (June, 1946, to June, 1947). Forty-eight issues of the *Recovery News* were published.

ACKNOWLEDGEMENTS

The editors wish to thank Mary Spalding for her able transcriptions of the tapes; Nancy L. Bryan and Patricia L. Reband for their editorial skills; and the Board of Directors of Recovery, Inc., for its enthusiastic cooperation in this project.

Marilyn Low Schmitt
Phyllis Low Berning
EDITORS
CHICAGO, 1995

LECTURE 1

THERE ARE TWO CHOICES: SECURITY AND INSECURITY

27 Minutes
Recorded Saturday, August 22, 1953

Again we have the experience of listening to our patients who sat on the panel, and, as usual, they talked shop, which they should. They did not talk about pressing issues. They did not talk politics or art. They did not talk about war. But you will understand that they are not taught and not meant to speak of grave issues, but of everyday life. And it is the everyday life in which my patients bungle their job of living. They don't bungle it in the political field, not in the economic field, and not in any other field, but daily living. And daily life consists of trivialities, and the two patients on the panel dealt with trivialities; this means with vital, pulsating life.

So you heard that Ann, sitting here, told you of a very trivial affair. She thought that people talked about her. I have seen plenty of persons who just itch to be talked about. The trouble with them was that they were afraid nobody would notice them. They wanted publicity, social publicity, neighborhood publicity. They wanted to be talked about. And if Ann thought that somebody talked about her, what was the calamity? Suppose two people get together and say, well, Ann is an excellent person. That would be nothing dishonorable, nothing harmful. Why does Ann think that if somebody talks about her, it will be something uncomplimentary? I hope you grasp this issue.

There is no doubt that while I am here with you, a great number of you have thoughts about me, and after the meeting will be over, you will express the thoughts, and you will

1

talk about me, at least some of you. I could now make assumptions, and there are mainly two assumptions that one can make about certain issues, two assumptions which touch me when I view these issues. Anything that I view is either harmful to me or useful, when we leave out the indifferent things. I don't think there are such. If you view them, then they are not indifferent. I'll repeat. Whenever you form a view about a thing that interests you, then that thing either gives you security or insecurity. It either is considered to be harmful or useful, and there are no other two ways of judging things that we are interested in, about which we form a view. Then they are either spelling security or insecurity.

If this is so, then Ann had a choice. She could have chosen to think that if people talk about her, they are complimentary. Or, she could have chosen the other possibility, that people talking about her are uncomplimentary. And I make these choices. And if I know that certain people talk about me, I am almost certain they talked about me in a favorable sense. And about other people, I am just as certain that they might have or did talk about me in terms of unfavorable comment. So, I choose, and sometimes I choose this alternative and sometimes the other. But my patients never choose. They are always sure. They are always sure that they are talked about unfavorably—that if somebody talks about them or thinks about them, that the thought or the talk are not friendly or not complimentary.

If this is so, then we say our patients—as I will now draw on this blackboard—our patients have a mind that goes straight at a certain choice. The alternative choice is ruled out. There are two choices, security or insecurity, and if my patients begin to make the choice, it aims straight and undeviatingly toward the notion of insecurity. You see, if I have a choice, then I may naturally choose either the one or the other element, or thing, or item. And if I leave the choice open, then my mind is open, open to possibilities, and that's what we call *the open mind.*

I will again tell you, at the risk of repeating myself unduly, there are only two things in this world to choose, provided you think of something personal, of something that is either good or bad to you. Among gloves in a department store you can have ten thousand choices, but that's hardly much of a personal issue. Among any kind of merchandise that you want to purchase, there you have endless choices perhaps, but if you are involved in a situation which is strictly personal, for instance, whether to strike your child or not, there are naturally only two choices. Whether to be friends with somebody or not, there are two choices. Whether to be suspicious or not, two choices. And if your mind is open, then you don't know which way you will choose. You will have to decide.

If your mind is closed, then there is no choice. You have already determined what to choose. And once you are determined, there is no choice, and your mind is closed to the choice of alternatives. And that's what I deal with. With my patients, as long as they are patients, [they] keep their minds automatically closed. They don't want to open it. If I treat them and train them, that means if I endeavor to open their minds, I wanted to say then they jump at me (of course, only if I permit them to do that, but that's what they would like to do). They immediately think that I accuse them of something, that I wish to disturb them, and then they sabotage me, and they shut their minds more closely yet, and we get the resistance of the patients.

You will understand now that my task is to open the patient's closed mind. You should think that a patient wants to get well, so he should listen to me. He should accept the choice which I offer him, and he should not insist on retaining the choice which he has selected.

Then the question arises: What does the patient choose? You have heard me say frequently, and I repeated it just a few minutes ago, that in that department of life which we call personal, there are always two choices to be made. Well, essentially they can all be reduced to the choice between security beliefs and insecurity beliefs.

But there is something else, although it belongs to these two choices very intimately, and yet it will have to be discussed separately. And I will quote one choice that is of extreme importance to you with regards to symptoms.

If a patient has had difficulty sleeping for years or he had bowel trouble for years or he had palpitations for years, and now I train him, then he has the choice either to stand the palpitations and not to work himself up about them or to become temperamental; that means to work himself up over the symptom.

Now there are two things, and you know them. The human body is so constituted that it takes care of simple disturbances. Everybody can leave it to his organization, to his organs, to take care of palpitations, of headaches, of numbness, of any kind of symptom, provided it is not a protracted physical disease. Nature bungles physical diseases that have developed to some extent, but nature is the highest authority for curing simple disturbances. And if I diagnose you as a nervous patient, then be certain that all your symptoms are simple disturbances and nothing else. No sickness. And simple disturbances can be corrected by the body.

The body itself is a self-repairing machine. I have told you that repeatedly. Now, if you have palpitations, wild palpitations, and you have had them for years, if you relax here, the heart will relax, provided the heart is not ill. Even then, it may do it under very frequent circumstances. But it will not relax in a second. The habit of producing palpitations cannot be sideswiped in a second, perhaps not in a minute, perhaps not in five minutes. It could if your certainty here in the brain would be without any doubt. And many of you have experienced this sudden stoppage of symptoms that have been very wild, once you are really certain that they are nervous and nothing to fear. But if the symptom does not disappear instantly on your relaxing, then it goes on and gives you, what? No danger, but torture. No danger, but torture.

If now you make up your mind there is no danger, it is only torture. Only! Don't laugh when I say that. Everybody can stand torture for a good purpose. If you are certain that it is merely torture—let me say discomfort, all right—then you are sure, and the heart will gradually or suddenly stop being a disturbance. What does that require? That requires mental courage, or we can call it *mental effort,* and too many people don't like effort. You see, when you have palpitations, it's very easy and no effort whatever to run to the phone and call the doctor. That's easy. That's comfort, or the prospect of comfort. Here in this organization you are trained to stand discomfort and to make a strenuous effort. And a supreme effort for a nervous patient is to stand his symptoms, not to run to the phone to call the physician, and it's remarkable what you do when you decide to stand the discomfort of the symptom.

[handwritten margin note: stand]
[handwritten margin note: Discomfor]

What you have done, then, is to make a decision, and no matter what decision you make, a decision always steadies you. It calms you. I don't know how many of you have had this common experience: that they wanted and should have visited a neighbor or somebody that they should have visited, and they put it off, and put it off, and could not get themselves to make the visit because for some reason the person they had to visit was disagreeable, perhaps, or the situation had some element of disagreeableness. And people like this may go on for hours and days and months, and postpone an unpleasant task, a task that they think will give them torture. All of a sudden they make the decision to go, and they go, and they are calm.

Plenty of people have experienced the fact that for years or for months they have dreaded the prospect of asking their employer for an increase in salary. And the wife was after them, urging them to be a man and have the courage, and that only made it worse. Now, they not only fear the prospect of approaching the employer, but they fear going home because the wife would bawl them out, and fears multiply, and they develop another fear which we call *shame.* They became ashamed of themselves, and in a situation like this all kinds of uncertainties and insecurities pile up, and an individual and his life is miserable.

Once he makes the decision to walk up to the boss and ask for the raise, all the anxiety is gone. Mark it: Any decision will steady you. And I have seen patients who reported to me that once they made up their minds, this means they made the decision to stand the torture of any kind of symptom, the symptom was gone, in many cases in an instant. So you have the choice between effort, particularly the effort of the decision, and the comfort of running for help—that's comfort—either to the doctor or somewhere else. And while you're running for help, you must tell the story, and while telling the story, you work yourself up and become temperamental and emotional, and that makes the symptom worse. If you shun the effort of standing your discomfort, you are in trouble. If you make the decision to stand it, then you may dispose of your symptom in a fraction of a second, or at some longer interval.

All of it, you will understand, can be explained to you, and you then think you understand what you have been told, but understanding means very little, although it is necessary, too, but what actually counts is training. And I told you already, this organization does not stand for any kind of particular philosophy, except that it emphasizes what is called *common sense*. But it stands for effort and for the principle—well, the principle I guess—to have the will to bear discomfort, which I will now change and give it another phrasing, and you should have the will to stand torture. This is the road to health if the tolerance of torture is gained through persistent training.

Thank you.

LECTURE 2

THE PASSION FOR SELF-DISTRUST

14 Minutes

Recorded Saturday, August 22, 1953

The panel will discuss today the subject of "The Passion for Self-Distrust." Now, distrust is what you usually call *a suspicion*. And a suspicion is fear, the fear that something may happen—of course, something unpleasant, disagreeable, dangerous. And if somebody has fear, well, that may be a salutary fear, a necessary fear, a useful fear. For instance, if I worry, I may do very well to worry. This means worry may be very useful because if I worry in a real danger, in a realistic danger, well, then I'll take the necessary precautions, and a fear of this kind is useful.

Even if a fear turns into a scare, it may still be useful, and frequently is. Suppose I have neglected my work, and then something happens that gives me a shock. I get scared. That scare is useful. It will presumably make me pay more attention to my work.

But when the patient is given to fear, there is nothing useful about it. He fears all the time. He develops the habit of fearing. Now, look here: Fear, or distrust, or suspicion, should naturally arise only when there is a danger. And I have yet to see the average person that is always in danger for weeks, and months, and years. Yet my patients, once they conceive a fear, are fearful all the time.

Environment changes and therefore dangers come and go, but the patient's fear is permanent for days, weeks and years, so *that* fear certainly does not serve any useful purpose.

The patient's fear, as I told you, develops into a habit, and a habit may be with you all your life. If the habit grows stronger, then, of course, it becomes an addiction. And that's what we mean by saying the patient's fears and the patient's distrust [are] in the order of a passion, the passion to self-distrust.

If a person is not in fear, then he feels secure. It's a remarkable thing that once you feel secure, every part of your body feels secure. That means that the body is a total. If you feel secure, then the stomach feels secure, and the heart feels secure, and the rectum feels secure, and the brain feels secure. Then there is no tenseness. But if you are in fear, or in a suspicion, in a state of distrust, that's the reverse of security. Then you feel insecure.

But environment is not constantly threatening. Environment changes. And if you feel constantly insecure, that cannot refer to any reality or any real danger in [the] environment. That can only be a sense of [in]security that has developed into a senseless habit apart from any danger in environment.

If you have this passion for fear, then you are constantly insecure. Then your stomach feels insecure, your brain is insecure, and every organ of the body is insecure. And this type of insecurity, that settles on the individual organs, we call commotion, or disorder, or ailment. We'll better call it *disorder*. Fear disorders the organs and creates symptoms. And once the patient has a symptom, then, since he fears it all the time, he makes it stay all the time.

The other day I saw a patient who has a very distressing symptom, an obsession. An obsession that when she touches something, she may become infected. So, she can't touch anything. Or if she touches something, if she touches the table, for instance, she has to run to the bathroom and wash and scrub. And while the touching lasted only a second, the scrubbing and washing is bound to last quarters of hours and sometimes solid hours. And this person is completely incapacitated for any job, for doing housework or for doing anything, because she has the fear of touching.

And she asked me, "How can I get rid of this fear?" And she has come to meetings, has read my book, and I told her, simply, fear can only be eliminated through its opposite, and the opposite is to know there is no danger. But you must know it; you must not merely repeat a sentence: "There is no danger." The repetition of sentences does not count in the matter of making persons feel secure.

And how are you going to acquire this knowledge that there is no danger? It must be a certain knowledge. It must not be a knowledge vitiated by doubt. And you have to see to it that you incorporate into yourself that type of knowledge which cannot be doubted. If you doubt the knowledge that was given you, then you are again insecure. Then you don't know that there is no danger.

Briefly, I'll tell you, such a certain knowledge can only be acquired if you practice it and listen to it and think about it continually till it is settled. And if you consider this necessity for continuous practicing till you really incorporate a certain knowledge in your brain that nervous symptoms are not dangerous, then you will understand to get well takes time, time filled in with continuous practice. If anybody, any one of you, has the infantile idea that you just can manage to hear that there is no danger, and then you think you understand it, and therefore it will be settled in your brain, well, that is wish thinking. I hear plenty of things, and I understand them, and then I go ahead and still practice the habits that I have acquired, although I know now that they are not of the best. That happens to everybody because everybody has harmful habits.

For instance, the harmful habit of temper, which disturbs family life, which disturbs friendship, is a disturbance to neighborhood relationships, may disturb and ruin the job. The ones that are addicted to temper can easily be told the sentence, "Temper is harmful." And while they are told how harmful temper is, they understand, but in the next minute they explode again, or *may* explode again.

Understanding alone will not help and has not helped any patient that has developed a long-term nervous problem.

The only thing that will help the patient is training, persistent training. And how this training is done, I am not going to tell you, but that's what this organization has been built for. And if you want to know how this training is done, my advice is to come and undergo the training, not to get it explained. But once you undergo the training, keep in mind a day's training, or a week's training, is insufficient. And if you only want to spend a limited time on this training program, you better stay out of it.

Thank you.

LECTURE 3

WILL VERSUS FATE

27 Minutes
Recorded Saturday, August 29, 1953

. . . He lowered his voice to the point where I didn't hear much, but I caught one phrase of his, and I'm going to discuss it. What I mentioned is no criticism of Bill because ordinarily I do understand him when he sits on the panel, but today I didn't. Maybe I have something in my ears that he couldn't penetrate. Well, I don't know. Bill said that he had some trouble with the purchasing agent in the office where he works, and although I don't remember what precisely he reported as the difficulty, but finally he launched out into a statement asking the question, "Why was I chosen by fate to suffer this and that?" He didn't say that he asked the question. He said in former days he would have asked it. Is that correct? In former days he would have asked the question, "Why was I chosen by fate to suffer some iniquities?" or whichever wording he gave his question. I know that many of my patients recall, before they improved or recovered, ask[ing] themselves this question, and the question can be worded simply and in general terms to read: Why is fate against me? Why must I have all the bad luck in the world?

And whenever a patient either asks such a question, or thinks about it, he does the following thing: Here is the patient—you know I mark the patient as a circle on this blackboard—and that patient, or that person, views himself. He reflects on himself. And you see that I drew here a loop of

11

something that starts within the body of the patient, and moves outside the body, and then goes back to the body, and that's what we call *reflection*. And the patient begins to think. That means, essentially, he directs his thoughts outside his body and then reflects [them] again into his body. And what a patient, or a person, reflects about is done in certain terms, and these terms are usually generalizations, and my patients have a way of generalizing in their own manner.

Now, you will understand that the word *fate* is a generalization. Fate is something that covers the destiny of everybody of the whole world, and what more evidence do you want that this is a generalization? Everybody that has ever lived was subject to the effect of fate. For instance, he went out on the street, and there came a pouring rain and got him wet. That was done by fate, naturally. Or he ran his leg against a crickety, rickety chair, and since it was a lady, she got a run in the hose. Fate! And you stub your toe against some object, that's fate. And you die, and you get sick, it's all fate.

But there is something else in this life. It is true that I can stub my toe against a sharp edge, and that may be fate, but it may be something else. It may be that I was negligent, careless. It may be that if I had exercised my will, I would have paid proper attention to things around me, and I would have avoided kicking against the sharp edge. You will now understand one and the same accident that happens, or event that happens, may be due to fate, but it may also be due to a lagging will, to the will that lags in the matter of attention. And it will be good for you to know that these are the main forces in this world. We call them *fate*, which is thoroughly impersonal, and *will*, which is thoroughly personal. And when Bill explained that in former days he used to ask himself, "Why was I chosen by fate to suffer this and that?"— when he did that, he was perfectly human. And everybody would like to credit calamities and misfortune to fate, but it may be that the will is also involved.

Now let me tell you, when you develop a poor resistance in your nervous system, whether you develop it or whether it is born with you does not matter, but if you have a poor resistance, that was done by fate. You simply don't know, yourself, how to arrange it that you create a poor resistance. If you have poor resistance, that is done to you, or given to you, by fate. You did not want to have poor resistance, by no means. And so all of you, when you had your first symptoms, or your first break, or your first decline in nervous reactions, you had it as a heritage from fate. You were not responsible for what happened to you. [None] of my patients has any reason to blame themselves for their nervous or former mental condition, whatever it is. But once you become my patient, then things change. You are not responsible for your nervous reactions, and you are not responsible for handling them properly or improperly as long as nobody has shown you how they can be handled properly. But once somebody has shown you how you can handle your nervous system so that it gets a bigger share of resistance, and you don't apply what you have been given in technique and training, then—and now the symptoms get worse, or when the symptoms don't get measurably better—then you are responsible.

That means you don't apply wholeheartedly the techniques and the training that [have] been given to you, and that's what my patients do if they don't improve properly. I don't say that they are responsible if they don't improve quickly. I don't say that. Anybody must exert effort. You have been trained to discipline yourself, and if you apply yourself, even if you apply yourself inefficiently, if you apply yourself at all, if you make any reasonable effort, then you are not responsible whether the effort is successful or not. But you must make an effort. You can't disclaim responsibility if you don't show any improvement for years and years and years. Then you are responsible somehow. But if a patient improves and adds more improvement as he goes along the route of recovery, and a little improvement again and again, although he does not reach the goal of health quickly, but if he improves measurably, then I know he has done his part, although not efficiently, but he has done it.

And you will understand that you are not responsible, first, for the fact that you have weak nerves. Second, you are not responsible for the fact that somebody else gets well more quickly than you do. Nobody will be fair if he holds that against you, because there are so-called individual differences. And just like somebody is a more glib speaker than you may be, and somebody is more aggressive and perhaps more successful in business than you are, nevertheless, these are individual differences for which fate is responsible and not you and your will.

So I don't want to be misunderstood to mean that all my patients must get well in a short space of time. That would be unfair to demand. And you will understand why it is unfair, because there are individual differences in the intensity of reactions, in the speed of reactions, and in the energy of reactions. The individual differences are dispositions with which you have been born, and they should be credited to fate and not to your will.

And on this occasion, I just remembered that I am discussing Bill. That fellow Bill has an attraction for me. His character, his manner of doing things attracts me. And if I am not mistaken, I have discussed him here from this platform perhaps half a dozen times already, and there will perhaps be another half dozen times. Some of you have not heard what I may have said about Bill a half a year or a year or five years ago. Bill, who tells you that before being trained in Recovery, he used to blame fate for his inefficiencies, for his symptoms, for his calamities, has done a job which serves more than anything else that any patient has done to convince me that will can really be opposed to fate and can conquer fate.

When I saw Bill about eight or nine years ago—I don't remember exactly when it was, but that's not a marked mistake if I say it's eight or nine years ago—he had a history of some half dozen of readmissions to the Elgin State Hospital. And if you know what happens to patients if they go and go and go to state hospitals, then you will know how Bill reacted in those days. For one thing, when I saw him and got busy

14

with him, he said, "Well, I want to go back to the hospital." There he had peace. All day he could sit on a bench and nobody bothered about him, and he got used to this matter of having peace, that nobody should bother about him. But I have a perverse tendency to bother about patients, and so I bothered about Bill, too. And I got him to be active, and he improved, but very little.

Well, one of his particular deficiencies was that he could not open his eyes. He always held them a quarter or at least half closed, but closer to a quarter or one-tenth of the width of the lid. I tried to instill into him the notion that he can break this defect of the gaze by exercising his will. Be certain that it was fate that gave him this compulsion to keep his lids closed, and I wanted to train him to oppose his will against fate, but fate had done a terrific injury to Bill.

In state hospitals, patients can actually sit for years and close their eyes, and if they exercise only a little pressure on their lids, in the course of time, they develop a cramp in the lids. And when Bill came here, it was painful for him. It was physical pain to open and widen the lids of his eyes. And I look at him today, and you could have looked at him three years ago, and he has no longer any trouble opening his lids and keeping them open. I have never seen a patient, in all my experience of over thirty years, I have never seen a patient that has performed this feat, but I have seen plenty of such patients in state hospitals. I have seen some of them in my private practice, but with none of them did I have success, because they did not cooperate. Fate had struck them, and they did not learn to oppose their wills against fate.

Now let me tell you that I speak to you as your doctor. I speak to you as the one who trains you back from sickness to health. Mine is a voice crying in the wilderness, except in Recovery. And it's unfortunate that it is so, because outside, in the wilderness of cities and towns, I call this *an oasis,* and the other *a wilderness.* In this wilderness of modern life, they try to teach you that everything is fate, not will. They try to teach you that once you have been frustrated in your childhood, you are doomed, unless some expert steps in and treats you for three or four or five years at a certain fee, which is, of course, considerably extended as the period of treatment is extended likewise. Why people should constantly be dragging their youth behind them, I have not been able to realize after I drifted away from this modern teaching.

I was a victim of modern teaching, too. Twenty years ago I still was a victim, but I gradually wiggled out of the embrace of modernism. And modernism thinks that the human body is a machine and nothing else, and if in a machine something goes wrong, you must have a mechanic to fix it. And modernism has discarded a view that has been valid for centuries and millenniums: That the human body is a machine, that's correct, but a self-repairing machine. And unless you fracture your leg or you contract an honest-to-goodness organic disease, nature, or the self-repairing tendency of the body, can cure any complication that is not a far-gone sickness or accident. Minor complications the body can repair expertly; and doctors are, well, tyros compared to the body in minor ailments. No doctor has ever cured a cold, to my knowledge. Nature cures them all. Many doctors have prescribed for colds. I have done that, too, but I was so uncertain as to what I should prescribe, that I felt I didn't know what to prescribe. And take it for granted, nature is the only thorough authority for curing minor ailments, not severe diseases. There, nature bungles. The machine does not well repair a fracture. It does by no means well repair a pneumonia, but penicillin does much better than nature in pneumonias. And there are many other things that do much better than nature in severe ailments. But nervous conditions have never been severe ailments. They are minor complications, unless you work them up to major complications, but even then, they are only complications. Even if you have been a nervous patient for thirty and thirty-five and forty years— and I have seen them—even then, once you learn how to relax and to throw off fears, nature is certain to repair the complication even after thirty and thirty-five years. I have

16

seen that done among my patients. I train them to drop their fear, and then nature went on the job and did it, and that's what I wanted to tell you. And Bill is evidence of the efficiency of our method, of the truth of our statements. Our statements concern, and our method is built on the principle that in minor complications like nervous symptoms—even if they are severe they are only minor complications—in minor complications you must set your will against fate, and once you set your will against fate, you relax, and nature has then an opportunity to correct the complication because our body, this means nature, is a self-repairing machine.

Thank you.

*Set your will against Fate
There are minor complications,
(Nervouse conditions) are
Minor until they are worked up,

— Our body's are self
repairing machines,

— IF you relax, nature has
an opportunity to correct
the complication,

LECTURE 4

EXCEPTIONALITY

15 Minutes

Recorded Saturday, August 29, 1953

The panel will discuss today the subject of "Exceptionality." Well, I see patients frequently who tell me stories, apparently very innocently and in good faith, and the stories are unbelievable. And yet let me add, they are stories that anyone, nervous patient or not nervous patient, could tell. So, they are common stories that represent common fallacies.

A patient, for instance, comes to me and tells me, "Well, of course, I developed a depression. Why shouldn't I? I lost my mother." Now then I ask myself, what goes on in the mind of this patient? The average person certainly loses a mother once in his or her life. Do they all develop depressions?

And another patient tells me, "Of course, I developed a severe nervous reaction because I couldn't meet my payments on the mortgage." Then I ask myself again, does really the average person who loses his home, or loses a mortgage, develop a depression or a severe reaction? If that were so, then half the farmers of this country in 1931 would have developed depressions. They practically lost their farms [at] the rate of about half of all of them.

And all this gibberish means the patient wants a cause, a reason for his going down with a depression, or a panic, or an hysterical reaction. It's about time that my patients should know that nervous conditions are merely an indication that your nerves have little resistance to the stress of life.

18

But there are very few people that have good resistance all round. Millions of people have poor resistance from their nervous system, others from their sinus system, others from their digestive system. I doubt whether there are many people in this world that have good resistance all round. And you happen to be people whose digestion has fairly good resistance, whose sinuses have fairly good resistance, whose eliminating system has fairly good resistance, but your nervous system has no good resistance. So, you are perfectly average compared to patients who have just as little resistance as you have, but in another system.

(I still have the floor, and I don't want anybody to talk. I don't share the floor with anybody when I am here.)

I hope you will understand that all of you have committed a sin against logic because all of you have assumed that you are rare exceptions. And once you are my patient, it is about time that you acquire a better logic, that you acquire the logic of what is called *average limitations*. And people are always limited in their resistance. As I mentioned, the one has a poor resistance with regard to the nervous system, the other with regard to the digestive system, and so forth. I have patients whose nerves sometimes are so lacking resistance that they produce very severe reactions, but that's still average. There are people with a poor resistance in their digestive system, and they develop very severe pains and cramps and deficient secretion in their digestive system without having an actual organic disease of the stomach.

But some people come to me—and the other day a patient did that—and tell me, "Well, I don't have a condition as you usually describe it in your meetings and as you have described it in your book. I have a different condition." So that man naturally thought he certainly is an exception. And mind you, the different condition that he quoted was stammering. I have never heard that this is so exceptional, and I have treated hundreds of patients who suffered from stammering, and I once even conducted a clinic at a research hospital for stammerers. And if we had a special clinic for them, be sure they are not exceptional cases. A stammerer, I want to

19

tell you, suffers from self-consciousness. That's all that I have been able to find in the overwhelming majority of stammerers, and nobody will be able to convince me that self-consciousness is an exceptional condition. I am self-conscious. Put me into a certain situation where I become flustered, and I'll be self-conscious. Fortunately, I don't let my reactions go to extremes, and I am self-conscious only on some occasions.

But the patient who is extremely self-conscious once was mildly self-conscious, and if he is now extremely self-conscious, that means he has worked up his reaction to a point where it is extreme. But be certain that average persons develop extreme reactions in some field of life. At times, they develop them.

And patients come to me and tell me, "Well, I did very well for so-and-so many months, but today I have symptoms again." And I ask myself, is that so exceptional, that a man who has done well gets symptoms again? Has he never heard of the setback that is very common and average with people who suffer?

When I ask[ed] this man, "What kind of symptoms did you get?" he said, "I sneeze and cough." I asked him, "Since when have you been sneezing and coughing?" and he said, "For the past four days." So I told him, "I don't want to hear anything about the sneezing and coughing. The advice that I'll give you [is] either you stop it, because it is merely a habit"—by the way, I examined him—"or you ignore it, and it will disappear. But if you worry about it, if you worry about a nervous symptom, then, of course, you will work it up so that it will become extreme. But it's no exception."

And in conclusion I want you to know I have lived more than most of you, I mean *longer* than most of you. And perhaps I can say that there are very few people that have lived more than I did. This means more intensely, and I have not shirked strain and stress. Nevertheless, I get practically all the reactions that patients tell me about. The only difference between me and my patients is that if I notice a cramp, and a spasm, and a palpitation, and a headache, and a numbness, and whatever else I notice, I know these are average reactions of an average individual that nobody can escape, and that I notice so frequently only because I want to study them. Ordinarily they are so mild that I would not notice them at all. I only turn my attention to my body precisely with a view to studying how my sensations and my reactions are. And in the course of the years I have developed a habit of constantly studying my body, unless my attention is grossly involved in some important task, and so I notice my reactions almost every minute. And I'm very proud then of myself because I know that I can pay close attention to my reactions, both mental and physical, and yet they don't do me any harm. I never work them up to a pitch of excitement. I never let them grow, and so I feel that I am stronger than everything that goes on in my body, and I have full control over my body, and that gives me what is actually and really needed for life: That gives me self-confidence and self-assurance. And the more I work up my self-assurance, the less severe reactions [I have].

I will give you just one example. I used to get colds two and sometimes three times a year. In the past five years, if I remember correctly, I didn't have one single cold any more. I am in full control of my body because I don't view my symptoms with any—not even the slightest—degree of anxiety. They are all average manifestations, and why should I bother about average manifestations? Why should I view them as exceptional happenings?

Now I don't expect you to reach the degree of self-control that I have reached. That's a matter of continuous practice for decades, not only for months and years, but I want you to acquire a trifling part of this self-discipline. And if you do that, the reward will be not perfect health, not exceptional health, but a good average health.

Thank you.

LECTURE 5

THE GROUP OF THE PATIENT AND THE DOCTOR FORM A WHOLE

32 Minutes
Recorded Saturday, September 12, 1953

You remember that Gertie, sitting here to my right, told you about her encounter with her husband. The husband came home late, quite late, and when he came home, Gertie, I guess, had every right to be provoked, but she shelved her provocation. And when she reported this episode here, she said, "Well, I learned in Recovery to control my impulses." I don't remember whether she used this verbiage, but [she said] something of this sort.

You see, Gertie had here two choices: She could have exploded and could have controlled the explosion that might have happened. Now she chose to control and not to let her impulses explode. What would have happened if she had exploded? Well, of course, you may say, well, there would have been an explosion, no more.

But there was a husband, and the husband and the wife formed a group, the marital group. And Gertie would not only have exploded against the husband, but against the marital group; this means against the husband and against herself. And it's remarkable how people are likely to forget this relationship as it exists when two persons meet and form a group.

There are all kinds of groups. I may meet somebody in the streetcar, on an airplane, or plainly on the outside on the street. If a man comes to me and asks me the time, for this second or few seconds in which he asks a question and I answer, we form a group. And a group, once it has formed, creates obligations. Even if it is merely the group of my person and the person who asks about the time, for the time being we have formed a group, and I am, for instance, now under obligation to return a courteous answer. I could, for instance, tell him, "Well, mind your own business," or, "Leave me alone," or, "I don't want to have any dealings with you." Then I would have exploded against the group which is not personally close to me. That would be very rude, but it would be no calamity to our group life because we don't live a group life.

But between a husband and a wife, the group life is very personal, very close, extremely important, presumably to both of them. You see, when the man on the street meets me and wants to know what is the time, we form a group, I have no doubt about that, but this group is loose, not close. It is impersonal, not personal. But once I get married, then my partner and I form, well, one of the closest groups there are in this world, a very personal kind of a group, a very important kind of a group. And once this group is formed, everybody should presume that this group will be something that we call *a whole*.

And I want you to know something about this matter of the whole as a group arrangement. You see, your body is a whole, a whole thing. It enjoys wholeness, and it will be good for you to know what that means. The body, including naturally the mind, is the closest whole we know. For instance, there are no separate parts in that body and, as I said, I throw in the mind, too. If you have a pain in a tooth, you should think the tooth hurts, but that's nonsense. The body hurts, not the tooth. The tooth is only an incidental, but your body is upset. You feel uncomfortable, not only around the tooth, but all over. And then your thoughts begin to function, and you get fearful ideas, ideas of insecurity, that you may have to go to the dentist, and he may have to drill your tooth, and you will spend a miserable hour or two hours in his chair. And then perhaps [ideas] come up: Well, maybe it is a tooth abscess and there is danger of infection. It's not your tooth that thinks of infection. It's not your tooth that becomes scared and feels insecure. It's the whole body.

And now people meet one another, not in the fashion that I described of a stranger coming up to you and asking the time. That's an insignificant group, and it is not whole. There is no wholeness in that group. But a man marrying a woman is an entirely different situation, but I don't want to discuss the marriage group. I merely started out from it because it was mentioned.

There is another group that is equal in importance to anything that is important, and that's the group of the patient and the doctor. And from what I told you, you will realize the patient and the doctor form a whole, not a loose group, and in a whole, there are certain laws that must be observed.

First, the law, if one minor part of the whole is injured, the entire body suffers, as I mentioned in the instance of the tooth. You can't have a headache and think that your head suffers. You suffer. The whole suffers. Here is the table, and some people somehow have an idea that the table is a whole. Let me tell you immediately there is nothing of this kind. You knock off a piece of this table, let me say a corner, and the remainder of the table doesn't feel anything. Be sure it doesn't. The table is a total, not a whole. It's a total. It has parts, but it is not a whole.

Now, Gertie and her husband behaved in a manner in which I might have behaved with this man who asked the time. We were not a whole. We were a total of two members. And in a total, remove the one part, for instance, remove the drawer from the table, and the other parts don't suffer. If you chop off a piece from the table, the other parts don't suffer. And if I meet somebody on the street who asks the time, and then, for some reason, he falls and injures himself, I don't suffer. You see, we were not a whole. We were merely a sum, a sum of two, which you may call a total if you wish.

Gertie and her husband acted as a sum of two people, not as a family whole, the whole of a family. Yet they were a whole. And if the one suffered, the other was bound to suffer, too. And why did they act like a sum and not like a whole?

24

And why do the patients, when they see me, when they come to me in the beginning, consider themselves separately from me and me separately from themselves? In Gertie's and her husband's case, in this instance that she reported, I don't mean otherwise, they acted like the parts of a sum. I know that. And they share and live together in a very fine and intimate way, but sometimes, as in every married life, the marriage falls apart for a few minutes or a few hours, and the two are a sum and not a whole.

In a whole, there must be respect, mutual respect. Just as I, if I have a headache, I have respect for my head, and I try to get rid of it, not merely to help my skull but to help myself. I have respect for every part of my body and mind, and they are equals. Whether I have a pain in the leg or in the head does not matter. The whole of the body shares the woe, and the grief, and the suffering. And, likewise, if I feel relaxed in my head, then be certain my stomach relaxes, my liver relaxes, my thoughts relax. There is all-out sharing in a whole, not in a sum. And if an argument develops between two marital partners, they fall apart into a sum for that time. For the time being, they are not a whole.

And my patients come to me, and I try to convince them that I now formed a whole with them. And during the first examination that I give them, I think most of them accept this concept of the whole, although neither I nor they use the word. And before long, the patient turns against me. I am sure that I don't turn against him. And now the whole falls apart and is a sum for some time; and in a sum, the parts of the sum share neither joy nor grief.

Once they fall apart, there is temper. And in temper, the one temperamental person turns against the other and there is a fight. We call it *the disruption of the whole*. You understand, I constantly shift the theme on[to] the whole between the patient and the doctor, and the one between husband and wife. I shall resume the disruption that forms in that particular whole that is made by doctor and patient.

A whole has something that we call *function*. It functions or does not function. This means it functions success-

DISRUPTION OF THE Whole

fully or unsuccessfully. If it functions successfully, there is order. In such a whole, order means the one member knows what to do in order to maintain the whole, the other member knows, and everybody knows his place.

In a marital whole, the husband usually knows that his place is not in the kitchen. I hope he knows. And the wife knows that that's precisely her place. And this one mention of two items will, I hope, illustrate to you that as a whole there must be order, and every member must know what is his or her place.

When I meet a patient, I try to form a whole with the patient, and I think I know my place in this whole, but the patient apparently doesn't know that. He thinks I am out of place. He thinks I ask too much of him, I don't consider him enough, and he turns against me, well, you know, only temporarily, but at any rate, as long as he turns against me, the whole is disrupted. It falls apart. And why does the patient think that I am against him? He never says that, by the way. He still keeps coming to my office. He still cooperates, but he doesn't accept what I tell him. And incidentally, also, he does not know he thinks I am wrong, I ask the wrong thing of him. He thinks I don't understand his particular case, I don't know how much he suffers.

Well, let's go back to the marital scene, and you will see in every whole either the members of the whole cooperate, but then they must accept one another, or they fall apart. Then they are a sum. In order to accept, one must first know that the one who talks knows his business, that he is competent to make the statements which he makes. Second, that in making a statement or doing something, he has no ill-will. He is not troublesome. He has no intentions to harm you, or to balk you, or to frustrate you. And unless you have this implicit trust in the other member of the group, there will be dissension.

And my patients approach me with distrust. At the lowest denominator, they think I ask too much of them. I should make it easier for them. In other words, I neglect cer-

[margin handwritten note: no ill will and no trouble]

tain items that are of interest to group life and to the life of the whole. The patients approach me with distrust. And you can draw the parallel to the marital scene. And, in other words, I want to state the issue as follows: In every whole, there should be order, but the order requires that the members of the whole trust one another and particularly avoid assumptions that the other partner neglects the one partner, or distrusts the one partner, or tries to domin[ate] him.

And my patients come to me, and they think I neglect certain aspects of their suffering, that I don't understand what they actually need. I ask them to get well through self-control, but the patient thinks, and some of them tell me, "Well, why are you my doctor if I have to help myself? Can't you help me?" Patients have told me that. That's an unfair statement. There is no doubt that if I ask a patient to exercise self-control, self-discipline, and to help himself, that does by no means [mean] that I am not ready to do my part in helping him.

And in the marital scene, the same situation. When Jack (that was Gertie's husband) came home late and Gertie became provoked inside, she became provoked because she had the idea that Jack permitted this bit of misdemeanor because he doesn't care for her, because he was indifferent to her comfort. In other words, he did what he did from ill-will. And in a whole, Gertie concluded, there should be no ill-will.

My stomach, for instance, has no ill-will against the brain, and the brain no ill-will against the stomach. They all try to act jointly and cooperatively. What did Gertie do then? She immediately noticed that such an impulse to tell the husband that he acted like a so-and-so—she wouldn't have said any more than that—would have disrupted the marital whole, and Gertie there and then decided, "I am not going to provoke my husband." This means I am not going to disrupt the marital whole. And so the husband came a trifle too late, according to my taste, and Gertie kept quiet. She merely asked him the question, and the husband answered it in a pretty flippant manner, and Gertie might have felt another impulse to explode, but she didn't. She kept the whole together. She did not permit the whole to fall apart into a sum.

And let me tell you that in life in general, where everybody craves a life in the group, and everybody is unhappy if he can't live in a group, what is of the utmost importance is to keep maintaining the wholeness of the group. This matter that we call the *marital whole*, or *the medical whole*, the *patient-physician relationship*, as we call it, or the wholeness of an office in which one works, the wholeness that should somehow prevail among neighbors, and so forth, now you must decide which is the most important whole for you, which gives you the finest and greatest sustenance. Marital life is, of course, a most beautiful and most important whole, but don't forget that you are patients. You can have your marital wholeness, and that will certainly not interfere with the other whole that you entered into, the whole relationship between patient and physician. And what does that require to maintain this wholeness of the relationship? Again, hold down your impulses, as Gertie did. Gertie felt provoked. This means she felt the impulse to fight her husband, but she held it down, and the whole of the marital relationship was preserved.

Will you kindly try to do me the favor to help me [in] maintaining this delightful relationship between patient and doctor, which, as I told you, constitutes another extremely valuable group relationship, the relationship of the whole and its members. And in this whole, you may be assured I respect you and your needs and your aspirations. And I am certain that you respect me and my needs and my aspirations. And, further, you want to maintain this group and its wholeness. You want to benefit by it. I want to maintain it and benefit by it. And if this relationship cannot be maintained, it cannot give you the benefit that it should give you unless you control that thing that will explode if you feel provoked. I can't tell you not to feel provoked. I may tell you that I have a great capacity for feeling provoked about every few minutes, but I hope I have an equally great capacity, and perhaps a trifling greater capacity, to hold down the feeling of being provoked.

Well, if you have learned from the remarks that I made here one thing, that there are two relationships in which people can meet, the one is the sum of two or more people that congregate somewhere, and the other is the whole of two or more people that become integrated into one another, not merely congregated, and it's this whole that must be preserved. That whole is constantly in danger of falling apart and being disrupted by nothing more than temper, and if you grasp that, then you will realize, finally, and perhaps for good, the reason why I stress this matter of temper.

* Hold down the angry or fearful impulses, to save the efforts the whole's and relationships

* The whole is constantly in danger of falling apart & being disrupted by nothing more then temper
  - & if you grasp that, then you will finally realize why I stress temper

LECTURE 6

THE VANITY OF KNOWING BETTER

20 Minutes
Recorded Saturday, September 12, 1953

The panel will discuss the subject of "The Vanity of Knowing Better." Now, it is of extreme importance for the patient not to be confused. And confusion means that one has two conceptions, two thoughts, two ideas, about the same situation, or about the same person, or about the same circumstance. You cannot have the thought [that] a person may be your enemy and yet think he is your friend. If you definitely are convinced—this means you firmly believe—that he is your friend, then you are secure with regard to him.

If now the thought creeps in that he may be an enemy, well, how can you be secure with regards to him? If you now knew that he is an enemy, then you could again feel a measure of security and take precautions. The precautions will tell you, well, he is not friendly towards you. He is perhaps even hostile to you, but you can now look out and take your precautions. Now you can sit back and wait. But if you can't hold either view and you don't know whether he is your friend or whether he is your enemy—in other words, if you have two contradictory views about the same person—then you are confused. You don't know what is what.

Now, the patient should know how to hold views apart and how to arrange it that they don't become confused. The reverse of confusion is discrimination. This means keeping views apart. And the patient must, for instance, keep apart the views about vanity. The reverse of it is pride. You may

Discrimination – keeping views apart.

Confusion – discrimination

Vanity – Pride.

perhaps be in doubt whether this manner of contrasting pride with vanity is correct. Let me tell you here immediately that the patient has every right to be proud of him[self], but then he becomes vain and becomes ashamed of himself. And I will tell you something about pride. I am, for instance, proud, in dealing with a patient, that I have been able to cure him or to get him improved. What does that mean? That I feel proud after I did something constructive and helpful for a patient. Well, I'll give you a bird's-eye view about what that thing of helping a patient involves.

Well, I have to struggle with the patient. I have actually to engage in a scuffle with him each time I see him until he is really improved. And what I am proud of, in this matter of finally helping the patient, is that I scored a victory, and people are proud if they are victorious. But the term *victory* and *victorious* does not express the situation. I should say if I have helped a patient, then I have scored an accomplishment, but that is really a victory. If you accomplish something, for instance, if you are one of those patients that in the morning feel limp, devitalized, tired, exhausted—and you know I have quite a few of these patients—and then you make up your mind, regardless of how tired you are, how limp you feel, how lifeless you are, regardless of all of this, you will jump out of bed and do things, then you have scored a victory. Or, let me again say, you can chalk up an accomplishment. Then you can be proud of yourself.

Now, whether you call it *victory* or *accomplishment* does not matter much. The point is that you can always be proud of yourself if you have conquered either an enemy outside or an enemy within. And if you stay in bed and fret and feel you are lifeless, then this fact, this feeling of being lifeless, chains you to the bed, and it is your enemy, the enemy within. If now you conquer this enemy, well, why shouldn't you have every right to be proud of yourself?

But you have read this article that we are going to discuss this afternoon, and what did you read there? I didn't read it, but I remember that article [is] about Ada and her sister. Is anybody denying that? No. And what did they scuffle about? The question was whether a certain dish was a wall plate or an ashtray. And finally Ada's sister scored a victory over Ada because of an ashtray. You understand an ashtray or a wall plate is a trifling thing, and why to start a fight about such a trifling thing, I and you will most likely not understand well. But these are the matters that people fight about in families, among friends, among neighbors, and we call these matters *trifles*. And if Ada's sister scored a victory over Ada, well, she was victorious, but could she be proud of that? Did she accomplish anything? To try to score victories, or to chalk up accomplishments with trifles, this we call *vanity*. You can be vain about such an accomplishment, but not proud of it.

And my patients who don't improve come to my office, and if I tell them something, they contradict me. Well, they start a fight with me. Whether I score a victory in this fight, or the patient scores, it is a fight about a trifle. And if the patient begins to fight with me, he is vain. He has the vanity of knowing better. You know how far he can get with me. I can always tell him that the interview is finished, and [he] can now leave the room. I can tell him that, and he can't tell me the same thing. I grant you that I am usually more courteous than that, and I don't turn out my patients in this high-handed manner, but I could.

You will realize that when my patients argue with me and contradict me, they cannot accomplish anything but what will harm them. If later on they should be proud of having told me off, then, of course, it would be a victory gained in the field of trifles, and that is vanity. But you remember I told you my patients have every right to be proud of themselves. And I mentioned the example of the patient lying in bed and feeling unable to jump from the bed and to get started with his work. And you will understand that if a patient does that, he has definitely gained a victory over a formidable enemy, that is, his incapacity. Why is he not proud of himself?

And then I see patients, and they come to me with complaints, and some of them complain not so much about their symptoms but about something that has only indirectly to do with their suffering and their symptoms. They complain that they are self-conscious. They meet a boss, and they can't look him in the eye. They meet a friend, and they['d] rather shy away from him and [act] as if they didn't see him, and pass him up. And this self-consciousness we call *the stigma of nervous and mental conditions*. And the patient is in the very deplorable and regrettable habit of feeling stigmatized. This means he feels ashamed of the fact that his nervous system is weak. This is, again, vanity. That patient is vain enough to expect that all his systems must be perfect. I have yet to see a human being that has nothing but perfect systems. The one person has an imperfectly working digestive system, and, believe me, a weak digestive system can cause endless troubles. It does not have to be a sickness but just a weakness. Like all of you have no sicknesses but weaknesses of the nervous system. Some of you have had a mental sickness, but now you are out of it, and your nervous system is either strengthened—perhaps quite strong—or if it is still weak, what of it? A weakness of the nervous system can certainly be taken care of here. If you expect that everything within you should be perfect, well, that's vanity. That's again vanity.

I wish only to repeat again, and I hope you will heed what I am telling you. Any one of you who has conquered one set of symptoms, or more symptoms and some sets of symptoms, has accomplished something that is by no means common. Indeed, it's very rare, except here in Recovery, where it is not rare. And once you have accomplished a conquest over a nervous symptom, your victory is astounding. Ordinarily people don't do that. Ordinarily if people have nervous symptoms, these nervous symptoms set up vicious cycles, and in time they grow worse and worse, not better. And mark it: you have accomplished your victory over your nervous troubles, not by tricks, not by somebody pulling a trick on you, or you pulling a trick on yourself, but by exercising your will power by means of a method that I have taught you. You owe the conquest over the symptom to your own strength, not to my strength, not to my tricks or stratagems. And why you should not finally get to the point where you acquire pride because of what you have accomplished in your handling of your symptoms—well, I don't know why you don't acquire this pride.

But some patients come to me and tell me again the story of the stigma, and when I go into a little detail, I find out that the patients are afraid that other people notice that they have a weak nervous system. Well, these patients credit the other people with a penetrating insight that I have not noticed in ordinary people. I have not noticed it even in many instances where I met very learned professors. They haven't got that insight either. And if you think that untrained people on the outside can look into your face and say, "Well, he or she has a weak nervous system," well, you are very optimistic about the capacities of the human race. I must tell you that.

I have described that in an article in the *Recovery News* that was written several months ago. I will advise you to get up to the desk and ask for the article and read it. I shall look up the *Recovery News* and I will leave a slip at the desk, putting down the issue of the *Recovery News* in which it was published, and reading it will help you very successfully to distinguish and to discriminate between vanity and pride. And in the same article I also mention the fact, that I mentioned here, about patients developing [a] sense of shame from their vanity of wanting to have perfection in all their systems and functions.

Thank you.

* a sense of shame from their vanity of wanting to have perfection in all their systems and functions.

* It's vanity to think your nervous system should be perfect.

34

LECTURE 7

TEMPER AND TEMPERAMENT

18 Minutes
Recorded Saturday, October 3, 1953

The panel will discuss the subject of "Temper and Temperament." It is remarkable that in textbooks, psychiatric or sociological or psychological, you will seldom, if ever, find the word *temper*. It is simply not discussed. You know that I distinguish between feelings; second, sentiments; third, emotions, into which both feelings and sentiments can be worked up; and finally temper. My colleagues only use the word *emotions* for this whole spectrum of reactions. But, of course, they sometimes also use the word *feeling*. But in the main, they speak of emotions, of emotional conflicts. They hardly ever—if they mention it at all—they hardly ever mention the word *temper*. But you know that in Recovery the word *temper* dominates practically every discussion of ours. We do not speak much of temperament because with patients, temperament is almost always worked up into temper, just as patients are in the habit [of] work[ing] up their feelings and sentiments into emotions. If you want to know more about these matters, read up in my book, and you'll find it explained. It is in the third part of the book under the heading "Sabotage."

Today I'll tell you something about temper and temperament, and I will best, perhaps, choose an example. If you have a family in which there is a baby, then the following thing may happen. The baby may begin to cry and, as babies do, the crying develops into yelling. Now how will the mother react, how will the father react, and how will or may, perhaps, the maid react? The answer is: That depends on their temperament.

The mother, the moment she hears the yell of the child, will immediately jump up and go, or run, to the nursery. Her temperament has been touched or stirred, and now it develops feelings, the feeling of sympathy or the feeling of apprehensiveness; mainly, of course, of sympathy.

Now the father may react differently. I don't say he will always react the way I want to describe. I will only say that some fathers may at times react as I will point out. He may become angry because there he was sitting reading, and his temperament was even, peaceful, and now this baby dares yell. And he may become angry that his peace is disturbed, that his temperament has been stirred up while previously it was calm, relaxed and even. And he may make some unpleasant remarks. He may, at any rate, ask the temperamental question, "Can there never be any peace in this home?" I hope you will understand the meaning of such a statement. With the father, we'll say the temperament that had been even, placid and calm while he was reading and the baby was sleeping, now his temperament has been stirred up, and it has risen to anger, to an emotion, anger. How the emotion then develops into temper, I'll mention later on.

Now the maid. The maid may hear the baby's yell and not be stirred by it. She may be indifferent to the baby, and her temperament will remain even, calm and placid if it was calm and placid before. We say that the maid is indifferent. This means her temperament is not stirred by anything the baby might do. I do not say that maids generally are like that, but they may be reacting in this manner. In these three examples, we will say the maid, the maid's temperament rests placidly on its resting level and is not stirred.

The mother's temperament, with regard to the baby, is sunny, always ready to enjoy the baby, even if it yells. The mother, with regard to the baby, has a sunny temperament. With regard to others, she may be anything else. She may be very sullen, temperamental, contentious, belligerent. But with regard to the baby, the average mother has a warm, sunny temperament. The father has at this moment—not regularly, I presume—developed a temperamental reaction of anger, of resentment.

And let me tell you that temperament is of these three types. Either it cannot be moved or stirred at all because the person is indifferent, stolid. Or it is stirred, in the mother's case, into a reaction of warmth, of warm feelings, of joy, particularly of seeing the baby. In the father, it has been raised to dark feelings. He is angry, and he may also be fearful. He may be fearful that if the mother can't pacify the baby, he will be in trouble and wouldn't be able to read and rest.

And you know that I distinguish between angry temper and fearful temper and that's all. The mother's reaction does not fall into the category of temper at all. Joy doesn't become temperamental. It arises from temperament, but is—as far as I know—never worked up into temper. So, if you will understand that there is a certain thing in us that is ordinarily placid, calm, restful, and that's what we call *our temperament.* But if something happens on the outside or inside that disturbs the situation, then temperament is aroused. Then it develops feelings or sentiments, and the feelings and sentiments may be worked up into temper. And I will merely tell you, and the rest you can read up in the book, that temper is either fearful: then it is linked up to the belief that there is danger. Or it is angry: then it is linked up to the belief that somebody did wrong.

Now the father, who became resentful and made this stinging remark, developed temper. He thought the baby was wrong or the mother was wrong in not pacifying the baby, and he had also the fearful temper because he was afraid that now his peace will be disturbed. But he was angry and fearful only for a minute, for two minutes, for a short period of time. And then we call that *an emotion.* An emotion always rises and goes down the moment the disturbance is gone. An emotion lasts only as long as the disturbance lasts. It may still have an aftereffect, but if the aftereffect goes on for hours and days and weeks, then it's held up by temper. Temper has duration. Emotions have very little duration. I hope you understand that, and, assuming that you do, I will now tell you that essentially I am not interested in the relationship between the ordinary father and his baby and the ordinary mother and her baby, and certainly I am not interested in the relationship of the maid to the baby. I am interested in patients, and I want you to know how you develop your temper and how you give it duration.

You see, in the case that I mentioned, something outside—the baby—was yelling and disturbing mother and [raising] her into joy and disturbing father and [raising] him into anger and fear. With my patients, I am not interested [in] whether they are disturbed by a baby or by somebody making noise or by somebody insulting them. I am not interested in that. I am only interested in the fact that they may be disturbed by their nerves inside, by fatigue, by dizziness, by palpitations, by pains and pressures that are caused inside by their nervous system, and then they become temperamental. This means they add to their disturbance the idea, "There is danger," or the idea, "I am angry at myself. I do wrong. I ought to be able to control my body, and I don't do it, and that's wrong." Then you become disgusted with yourself, and you become discouraged about yourself, and that is temper directed against yourself.

We are not interested—not primarily interested—in Recovery whether you develop temper against somebody else. We are interested in that, too, but not primarily. We are mainly interested in the fact that our patients are likely to develop temper against themselves when they experience nervous disturbances. And if my patients conceive the idea that they do wrong, then they ordinarily make a habit of continuing this idea or this belief, and so their temper gains duration. As long as they are disgusted with themselves, as long as they are ashamed of themselves, or fear themselves (or fear their symptoms, in other words), as long as they do that, the reaction is maintained. And you know that patients are likely to have fears for days, for weeks, for months, even for years. Even for decades, I have seen patients maintaining fears almost continuously.

Well, you will understand that if a patient has developed temper, if he has permitted his temperament to rise to the height of temper, then we must devise means of getting him rid of it.

The father and the mother that I quoted developed reactions but only for a short period of time. And outside in life you see temperamental reactions of this short nature, of this short duration, all over. We are not interested in short-living emotions or temper. We are interested in that temper that the patient develops and that has duration, usually for years, or months. And if it has duration, that means that the patient has developed a habit, a deep-seated habit, of constantly worrying and constantly being disgusted with himself. And such a habit of long standing develops strength. That habit becomes deeply rooted in the patient's temperament. And that habit, being of long standing and gaining strength, is easily precipitated, easily aroused. And the more it is aroused, the more it gains strength, the deeper it roots itself into the ground. And you will understand that a habit of this kind will take a long time to be uprooted by the doctor who treats you. And if you think there is a short circuit around the disease towards health, well, you are mistaken, painfully mistaken. And on this occasion I want to remind you again that your habits of temper, of fear, anger, disgust, discouragement, and disappointment are deep-rooted and require a long period of time to be uprooted through treatment.

Thank you.

Deep Rooted Disturbances are what we do not want. Longstanding ill thoughts of one self.

LECTURE 8

NERVOUS PATIENT VERSUS NERVOUS PERSON

18 Minutes
Recorded Saturday, October 3, 1953

You remember that Elizabeth told you today about an experience she had had in the cafeteria. If I remember correctly, she was self-conscious, tense, either for some particular reason or because she is a nervous patient and has not received very much training yet, although she has responded magnificently. Well, she was self-conscious, and, if I understood correctly, she walked out of the restaurant or was ready to walk out of the restaurant without paying her check. And so she was stopped by the cashier telling her, "You can't get away with that here," as if she could get away with it somewhere else. She apparently meant to tell her, "Well, if you want to do it somewhere else, I have no objection, but don't do it here in my place."

Well, I think if I heard such a remark shouted at me, I would feel embarrassed, and so did Elizabeth. That's perfectly natural, to feel embarrassed [in] such a situation. But then you remember that Elizabeth went on to tell you that instantly she felt trembling, shaking, palpitations, presumably sweat, racing of thought, and a few other symptoms. Being as disturbed as she was, we do not expect her to furnish a complete list of the symptoms because so-and-so many she did not notice in her excitement. But be sure she had plenty of similar symptoms. Well, but it took her, I presume, quite a while to calm down.

You heard, for instance, that Paul told you how he spoke to his superior and forgot himself and mentioned a remark that might have been objectionable or insulting, and then it took him a full hour to get rid of the symptoms that he developed, which is not a bad record, but it could be better. And my assumption is that Elizabeth felt the aftereffect of her scare for some time. I may be mistaken, but it is only an assumption of mine. If so, then we will say Elizabeth carried forward some of her symptoms, and maybe all of them, into a fairly prolonged aftereffect. At any rate, I can only say that patients do that.

Why should that temper, the excitement, the commotion, last longer than the insulting element in [the] environment had lasted? If somebody irritates me, then my temper rises, but once the man is out of sight, I presume my temper will go down, and it will do that very quickly. And why have my patients an aftereffect of some length and most of them of great length? You can say that symptoms—shaking, trembling, palpitations, pressures—are bound to have an aftereffect. They must die down, and the dying down takes time. I don't doubt it.

But if I have a pain, or if people in general have pains and pressures or palpitations—for instance, because a dog jumps up at them suddenly—the palpitations take their time to disappear, but the time is measured in seconds or minutes. Why then did Elizabeth's palpitations and sweats and tremblings and shakings not disappear in a minute or two? You understand that this is an important question, and that it is bound to throw light on the reaction of our patients. Let me tell you briefly that there are simply two kinds of reactions that cause disturbances or discomfort.

The reactions may be due to physical disturbance, to physical discomfort as it is caused by palpitations and shakings and sweatings and tremblings. Elizabeth had physical symptoms, and the discomfort which they caused was physical discomfort. But Elizabeth has also a mind—and by the way a very good one as far as I know—and so she began to think about the symptoms and about the discomfort they caused. And when she began to think, she didn't think calmly, but emotionally—or better, temperamentally. And she thought with fearful temper and angry temper. She was afraid that she had compromised herself, and she was angry with herself that she had done so. Therefore, being moved by the fear that she had compromised herself, she became embarrassed. She was ashamed of herself. And what we call *shame, embarrassment,* the feeling that you made a fool of yourself, is very uncomfortable, indeed. But this is now mental discomfort, not physical comfort.

Will you try to understand that my patients, and other persons, too, may develop symptoms suddenly, and these symptoms will cause physical discomfort. But when they begin to think about their misdemeanor, about what happened to them or what they did, then they become ashamed of themselves, and this causes mental discomfort. And with a patient who has not improved yet—different from Elizabeth, who has made a good improvement—with such a patient, the more ashamed the patient is of himself, the more severe grows the physical discomfort. And the severer the physical discomfort grows, the more ashamed does the patient become of herself. And so a vicious cycle develops between the physical discomfort and the mental discomfort. Fortunately, Elizabeth has learned already, and practices very successfully, the art of not developing a vicious cycle. Therefore, her reaction presumably died down fairly soon. Well, look here. If somebody develops mental discomfort— and you will understand that that means embarrassment, sense of shame, feeling stigmatized, all of this goes by the name of mental discomfort—and if a patient develops this, what does he do? He accuses himself, he blames himself, he condemns himself.

And now there can develop another vicious cycle because my patients are in the habit [of] not just feeling ashamed and condemning themselves for one minute or ten minutes. To the contrary, when my patients begin to lash out against themselves, to accuse themselves, to condemn themselves, they do something that gives the self-condemnation duration. They make their feeling of self-condemnation, or the act of self-condemnation, endure. And they do it in the following manner: They say, "What a fool did I make of myself!" And then they begin to think about themselves, and, in thinking of themselves, naturally they think of how they acted previously. They think of their past. They reminisce. They retrospect. And now, of course, in the past anybody can find occasions where he made a fool of himself, occasions when he did something that was embarrassing, that made him lose face. That's the easiest thing to do.

If I should look back into my past, which I do very frequently, well, don't ask me what I find there. I wouldn't tell you, but be sure what I find is not all complimentary. Some of it is extremely uncomplimentary, but that's private, and you can't share my private secrets with me. So, I shall only speak in generalities and tell you that when I look back into my past, I could easily exclaim, "Oh, what a rascal have I been!" Well, what of it? So, I have been a rascal numerous times. And then I add, "Well, what of it?" So, I am an average person. I am like everybody is.

And I have yet to see saints in this life. I haven't seen any saint yet. What I see is always average people, sinners, delinquents, people who are frequently careless, frequently reckless, frequently—well, you can say anything you want. If you have had any reaction that you might be ashamed of, be certain I had it and all humanity had it, except the saints. But, you know, saints don't live in a human group. They live among divines, saintly people, not in an ordinary, average human group. I hope they don't. Why should they do that?

Will you keep this in mind? Elizabeth created symptoms, and with the symptoms physical discomfort. Then she began to think about her reaction and with this she created the feeling of embarrassment, of shame, of self-accusation, self-blame, guilt feelings, and all of this created what we call *mental discomfort.* But fortunately she did not work herself up to any length of time and did not develop the vicious cycle, so she could come here and recount her experience and laugh at it. She has given up the habit of being ashamed of herself, the habit of feeling stigmatized, the habit of self-blame and guilt-feeling, and at present she has reached the stage where she is no longer habitually stigmatized but only occasionally.

And if a person reaches the stage where he only develops symptoms occasionally, where he develops physical discomfort occasionally, and mental discomfort occasionally, then he is practically well. He has become an average nervous person and is no longer an average nervous patient.

And I want to tell you, Elizabeth is one of those of my patients who somehow, I don't know how to give a reason for it, but she is somehow fast in shedding her nervous reactions—this means the reactions of a nervous patient—and in exchanging them [for] the habits or reactions of a nervous person. But most of you take more time to graduate from the status of a nervous patient to the status of a nervous [person], and therefore most of you have to wait longer than Elizabeth had to wait. And that means that you cannot persuade yourself, and you certainly should not persuade yourself, that you can slip out of your nervous ailment in that speedy manner that Elizabeth has demonstrated to you. To develop from the status of a nervous patient to that of a nervous person usually takes time. There are miracle cures that happen once in a while, and I don't like them, because usually after a few weeks or a few months, if I see the patient again who had staged a miracle cure, and if that happens, the thing is very discouraging. The patient then draws the conclusion, "Well, I am hopeless. Even when I get well, I slip back again." And that makes for discouragement, and that's the reason why I don't like miracle cures.

Elizabeth has worked hard, and if she gains a quick result, well, the way she has worked is guarantee that her results will not be fleeting. The results as she has accomplished them will have duration.

Thank you.

LECTURE 9

FRUSTRATIONS, EMERGENCIES AND BELIEFS

27 Minutes
Recorded Saturday, October 10, 1953

You heard Anna tell you that she had lost some of her belongings, some documents if I remember correct[ly], in the bus. And then one of her friends in the office, not very friendly indeed, told her, "Well, that has never happened to me." And what that means, you know. It meant to point out to Anna that she is not an average person but exceptionally clumsy or forgetful or unskillful, perhaps exceptionally dumb.

You will understand if somebody is confronted with a remark like this, then his or her feelings are hurt, and we call that *frustration.* Particularly if the person, insulted and her feelings hurt, cannot come back for some reason, cannot begin a fight or an argument.

Then we deal with this matter of frustration, and from here I'll immediately pass on to what Mary told you. It was this delightful story about her husband not doing his part. Well, I have heard that of very many husbands, and perhaps my dear wife could tell you a story of such things, too. But my wife handles it approximately as Mary handled it. She does not blame me and does not work herself up over the fact that I don't do much in the house. She turns the tables on me and says, "You must not do anything in the house because you are a doctor, and you need your fingers. If you cut them, what will happen?" Well, I don't know. I doubt whether she means that. But it's, of course, a nice explanation of the fact that she is frustrated and doesn't mind, and I appreciate it.

45

Well, you remember that Mary got an oven that she cherished, that was particularly serviceable and suitable for her needs, and then the oven didn't light. That's frustration. There is no doubt about it. And then she tried to get help, and her husband was not available in this world. He was sleeping, so he was out of contact. And when she awoke him, he didn't awaken. And if he did, he didn't give any sign of it except making a remark that might have been made in sleep, so apropos was it.

So Mary was triple-frustrated, and perhaps ten times frustrated, till finally she worked up a temper and thought of throwing the turkey. I thought she wanted to throw it at her husband, but she claims she wanted to throw it in the garbage can, maybe, I believe.

Well, she was frustrated, and the story had a happy ending for Mary, at least, not so much for her husband, when she lit the stove. She didn't relish the idea that her husband should get away with it without any penalty, and so you remember she turned on the radio, most likely not too low, precisely, but most likely a little at a high pitch, so that at least her husband shouldn't be able to sleep on, and there she got her revenge. It's, of course, a very amusing story, and the frustration was pretty severe and the revenge very mild.

Now, you understand that all of you have frustrations, and that I have frustrations, and I have frustrations perhaps every minute of my life. For instance, I am, like other people, practically never satisfied with what I am doing. I always feel I could have done better. You wouldn't believe it, perhaps, but I assure you that this is the case. And I cannot imagine any human being that would be satisfied with his existence, with his work, with his conduct, with his accomplishments. If he were, he would be a remarkable person. It is simply not human to be satisfied most of the time. Naturally, nobody can ever be satisfied all the time, but it is extremely difficult to be satisfied most of the time, or a great length of time.

So, everybody is frustrated, so frustration is certainly average. It's not only average, it is common, continuous, more or less, only interrupted by some fleeting moment, sometimes by a fleeting hour, sometimes by an afternoon in which there is great excitement—a wedding, a child born, or any excitement. Or you sit at a very interesting play, and for hours you may be carried away from yourself. Then you may be satisfied with these one, two, or three hours of diversion. Then you might be honestly relaxed. But this is rare, and all a human being can do is to hold the continuous series of frustrations down to a low level. In other words, he cannot avoid the millions of frustrations that are awaiting for him in the course of a certain time. Let me say, within a few weeks or months or years, you have millions of frustrations, and you can't escape them. So the number of frustrations can hardly be reduced. Everybody's exposed to them practically all the time, but the intensity of frustration, the severeness of frustration, can be handled.

And you will now understand that if my patients are constantly or almost constantly frustrated, that's average. Nobody can escape it. That's the duration, the frequency of frustration, that everybody is subject to, as far as I know, because I know it from my own case. I presume [there are] not too many people in this world that relax better than I do. I doubt that. But the intensity of the frustration, the severeness of the frustration can be held down. And I want to tell you something about the method with which frustrations can be held down to a low intensity, without raising their number and their duration.

It is a simple prescription that I will offer to you. The prescription reads, "If you deal with everyday life, with routine work or routine existence, if you deal with the trivialities of the daily round, don't believe that they are emergencies." Then you will be frustrated on every step because at one time the plumbing goes wrong, at another time a stove doesn't

47

light, and at a third time a co-worker makes a slurring remark, and a husband is impatient, and so forth. But you will only have severe disturbances of your equilibrium at some time, very seldom, because emergencies happen very seldom in the existence of the average person.

Now you will understand that my patients are of a different cast. To them, a palpitation is an emergency. A headache, that naturally with my patients comes on with great intensity because it's an old, long-range headache that has gained momentum, that headache to my patients becomes an emergency. And if they are depressed—which I am very frequently, I may tell you—they think it is an emergency because naturally having been worked up for weeks and months and sometimes for years, it strikes the patient very vehemently right in the morning when the patient wakes up. And therefore, my patients think of their troubles—of their frustrations, especially the frustrations that come from symptoms, and they are indeed sharp and severe—they think of them as emergencies.

And if you think of an event as an emergency, then what happens is clear. You work yourself up over it, you become panicky, you become hopeless, and the frustration reaches proportions that are overwhelming, and life is no longer worth living.

And it [is] about time for my patients to realize that frustration is average, universal. It is there practically all the time and just to be faced as average events. But that if you don't face your frustrations, your palpitations, your pressures, your numbnesses, your depressions, your fatigue as average events, if you believe they are emergencies, then, of course, you'll get dismal ideas into your head. How long can you stand a life that is full of emergencies?

And so you begin to diagnose, to diagnose either that this thing will kill you yet, or that you will never get rid of it, which is another dire diagnosis or prognosis, or that your nerves will become exhausted, and all these thoughts come to you. And you know that my patients have an extraordinary talent for working themselves up and for self-diagnosing. And so they are always living in that dreadful psychology, which means that their life is full of danger, of the dangers of emergencies. I, for one, cannot imagine a more dreadful sort of life. And you know how dreadful your life has been, and sometimes still is.

So why don't you do something? What I ask you to do is to change your beliefs, the belief that your life is steeped in emergencies, in extreme danger, and everybody can either accept a belief or refuse to believe. Every child can do that. Every imbecile can do that. Why don't my patients do what everybody can do? I will not give you the answer to this question because I have discussed it repeatedly in my book and in the *Recovery News*. And if you want to know why my patients insist on keeping their beliefs while they could certainly refuse to keep them, read *Mental Health Through Will-Training* and the *Recovery News* after the book was issued, and you will find out. If you don't know where to find it, you can ask me.

But in the meantime, I ask myself, why does a person who suffers acutely, why does this person not resort to such a simple expedient as to drop beliefs? I drop beliefs right and left, and everybody does. But there are certain beliefs that I do not drop. These are the so-called *values* in life. Of course, I hope I don't drop them. I hope I don't just shed them. And you know that I have concluded if the patient refuses to drop a belief, then he must have conceived of that belief as a value, and a high value. The patient does that, and for the following reason—and that's only one reason. I have all kinds of other reasons in the book, where you can read it.

Our patients have suffered for endless months and years, and during this time they have established ideas about what they suffer from. And they have decided that what they suffer from—whether it's nerves or not nerves doesn't count—but what they suffer from is something that they can't help. So, they have declared themselves a victim of the ailment, of the nervous ailment, and a victim is helpless. At any rate, once you think of yourself as being a victim, you will not try to seek help from your inner environment, from yourself. You will assume that you can't conquer this condition. And then you come to Recovery and there you are shown a method which enables you to practice self-help, and there you can't help seeing all kinds of patients that get well mainly through self-help, and that disturbs you.

You see, my patients only get well through self-help if they do certain things. For instance, so many of my patients have the impulse to talk and talk and talk, and they feel they have to talk, they have to express themselves, they say. Well, if somebody talks about a certain condition all the time, ten or twelve hours a day, every day of the week, every week of the month, finally that patient should realize that he has expressed himself already. Why does he go on constantly talking and talking and again expressing himself and again? Obviously, the patients don't express very much. They merely babble and chatter with vehemence, with temper, but it is temper and gossip about themselves. What I have heard of patients expressing was not worth expressing, and certainly not worth listening to. Some of what the patient says— and this he has only to tell once, maybe another time, but certainly not 500 times—some of what he expresses is worth listening because it is a report about symptoms, about suffering, about adjustments, improvements, hopes, and so forth. But if such things are constantly repeated and constantly dished out to anybody who cares to listen, if it is repeated a thousand times, two thousand times, maybe five thousand times, that should be plenty of expression by now, and why does the patient keep on expressing himself?

Well, there are many people today that say, "Get everything off your chest. Express what is stirring within you." Well, maybe they are right. I can't tell you. But this ideal of self-expression is very harmful to my patients. If coeds do that, let them do it, but my patients should practice self-discipline and not self-expression.

Well, will you understand now, if somebody for months and months and years and years has constantly assured the husband and the father and mother and the employer and the co-workers and anybody who knows the person, that he or she is a victim, that she can't do anything to help herself, and then this person comes to Recovery and sees that there is a help, and she could employ it, then a very dark thought crowds into the brain of this person. She becomes apprehensive (I say *she*—it is naturally just as well a *he*, too). She becomes apprehensive that if now she gets well, people will tell her, "Didn't I tell you that it was up to you?"

And that's a dreadful prospect of being told that somebody, through her own fault, because she didn't want to make an effort, has dragged on for months and years, ruining or injuring her family and herself, losing valuable time in which she could have been a boon to her children, to her friends, to the community. And the person, realizing that he or she could get well through the Recovery techniques, shrinks from the task. She's afraid that people will blame her for the great waste that she has established in her life. And do you understand now that if somebody does not drop this belief that he can['t] get well, that belief has value. It prevents disgrace. It prevents the disgrace of being told, "Didn't I tell you that it is up to you to get well, and why didn't you listen? If you had listened, we would now be so much better off. The family would not have needlessly suffered. The children would not have been exposed to the agony of not having a mother take care of them."

And so there is a premium on the patient's refusing to accept my beliefs about nervous conditions and to shed his or her beliefs. This is a tragedy, but unfortunately the tragedy is endlessly prolonged by patients, and the tragedy is permitted endlessly to wreak havoc on families and on the patient himself or herself. And I hope that today I was able to demonstrate to you, along with this example of Mary and Anna who have demonstrated to you that beliefs can be changed. And I may tell you here that Mary, particularly, had her disastrous belief that everything is an emergency and that she could not help herself. She has had this belief, as far as I know, for many, many years before she finally came to Recovery.

And yet, today she told you that on that morning she was frustrated. And I must say, while the frustration was not in the nature of an emergency, it was a severe frustration, and how elegantly did she handle it. Well, she handled that frustration elegantly and successfully because she had dropped her beliefs that life is full of emergency, and that frustrations are intolerable and never average, they are always exceptional. That was Mary's belief about her life. She dropped these beliefs and turned around and accepted my beliefs, which naturally know nothing about emergencies in average life.

Thank you.

LECTURE 10

EXTERNAL AND INTERNAL ENVIRONMENT

12 Minutes
Recorded Saturday, October 10, 1953

The panel will discuss the subject of "External and Internal Environment." Patients are fond of thinking that their condition was caused by something external, something in an external environment. And so they have an idea that perhaps if they change environment, it will help them. And I see so many patients who have been with me for months, or perhaps for weeks, and have improved, but they become impatient. The improvement doesn't go fast enough. And then they come to my office, and on one nice day, they direct the question to me, "Don't you think, Doctor, that if I go to Florida that will help me?" Well, the one patient says Florida, the other California, the third Canada, and so it goes.

Now many of these patients have had their trouble for endless years, and they have gone to Florida, perhaps several times, and they know it does not help them. They come back and are as bad as they used to be and perhaps a little worse. And yet their mind is after a change of environment. They don't believe that their nervous trouble comes from inner environment. They try to persuade themselves that it comes from outer environment. And some of them go to Florida. Some of them go to California or to Canada, and, well, they feel better when they are there, while they are there. But once they come back to Chicago, their old trouble starts again, and now it is worse because they were disappointed. And I try to persuade my patients that if they want to go anywhere for pleasure, they have my blessings. But if they want to go for health, I call their attention to the fact that so many patients write to me from Florida, from California, from Canada, from all over, and ask whether they could come to Chicago and get help.

So, apparently, change of environment, naturally, does not help any patient who has suffered for a long time from his nerves, or her nerves. Then I ask myself, why don't the patients learn? They have made trips, and they know they haven't helped them. Why don't they learn? And the answer, I think, is this: Patients of mine have complained for endless years, or at least for many months, and home life has become a dreary scene. The children are all upset because the mother is never cheerful. The husbands have to listen to their wives and constantly get a running stream of complaints, and they become sick and tired of these constant complaints, and they develop temper and return sharp remarks to the questions or statements of the wife, and home life is a shambles. When the husband becomes ever more provoked by the wife's disturbing him, then, of course, he makes remarks which are very disturbing to the wife. And he loses whatever affection he has shown before, whatever attention he has given the wife, and instead of giving her attention, he tries to keep away from her, and he comes home late. And he is angry at the wife because the moment he has any engagement, she develops a head pressure, and he can't go. He has to stay home. And so-and-so many husbands have to take off from their work in order to stay with their wives [at] home if she has a particularly severe day, and family life is completely disturbed, or almost completely.

The wife hasn't got the patience to sit with the husband at a card game, she doesn't like to accept social engagements, invitations, and you understand, the home life of a long-term nervous patient is the dreariest locality one can imagine, at any rate, in those cases where the husbands react as I have pictured to you.

There are naturally quite a number, and perhaps many husbands, that don't answer to this description. They are patient and loving and attentive and try to be helpful. There is no doubt that there are many such husbands.

I may tell you here that wives are much more numerous, compared to husbands, who try to stick with their husband and show an enormous amount of patience and keep up their affection for the husband no matter how long he may have been a patient. But wives are notorious, this means women are notorious for a capacity of suffering without saying much. Wives, or women in general, can suffer much better than men. I don't mean men who are nervous patients. I mean men in general. Too many men, when they only have a cold, go berserk. They can't stand it. They immediately think they have a pneumonia and call the doctor immediately. Then they take their temperature, and they are so excited that they can't read it, so they read upward, and they find they have a temperature of 110 or 115, you know. Men don't take kindly to suffering.

Naturally, there are many men who do that, who do take kindly to it, but as a general rule, they don't know to suffer as beautifully as many, very many women can. And there is a reason, especially if the woman is a wife, which means if she's married and has children. She doesn't, she may not take care of her husband, but she is eager to take care of the father of her children, which is not bad at all. That's no indictment of [the] woman.

Well, at any rate, it will be good for you to know that a nervous patient who has suffered endless months or years, then at some time begins to suffer particularly, not just from her symptoms, but from the destroyed home life. And the home becomes agony to this woman patient. And so you will understand if this has developed, if that woman patient can't find a home in her own house, in her own family, then, of course, there is a premium of accusing external environment and then to crave a change of environment. And this woman patient wants to go to Florida or to California, not because she has any idea that Florida or California will help her, but she wants to escape the dreariness of home life. And I don't blame her. But here in Recovery there should not be any such situation because that woman now knows that in Recovery she is almost certain to restore her health, and she should [now] look into the future and not at the present dreary situation.

Previous to these patients coming to Recovery, there has been no such institution that could raise their morale and their hopes and strengthen their personal disposition. But now that they are in Recovery, I will advise you, if one of you has thoughts of moving elsewhere in order to escape the climate of Chicago, I will advise you if you have this desire, then you don't escape the climate of Chicago but the dreary climate of your family life. And if you know that, then there is just a good chance that you give up your wild dreams of getting a cure from external environment, and you will come back to Recovery and take part in our activities and expect health from what you learn in Recovery.

And in Recovery you are told that if you want to get well, you have to influence your internal environment—your internal environment that consists mainly of impulses, sensations, obsessions, that must be controlled as you learn here. And, second, of your beliefs, that must be changed according to the standards that you are taught here.

Thank you.

LECTURE 11

THE PATIENT IS AN APPRENTICE

29 Minutes
Recorded Saturday, October 17, 1953

You heard the panel members, and, as usual, what they told you was a message. And it would be very important to find out what was the message they conveyed to you. If I say it was a message, then I mean it was one message, but there were three panel members here. How could they join in concert and convey one message?

Now those of you who are not new to these meetings know that this has been done by training—by continuous, laborious training—so that each panel member has learned to produce thoughts, concepts, beliefs, that are Recovery's beliefs, not the panel member's. They have been trained to think in a certain direction with regard to health—of course, with regard to health only. Otherwise, my patients are naturally free to think as they wish, or as they ought to, regardless of whatever they may have learned in Recovery. But in point of health they must have one conception only, and that is naturally the conception of their physician.

Now, you will remember that Frances told you about a shower: Both she and her sister received an invitation to attend this shower, and the invitation read, "money preferred." Well I guess that's a very sensible suggestion, but Frances' sister became provoked, and she raised a fuss about somebody wanting to tell her what to do, and she thought that was an imposition. And you will now remember that

Frances told you that if that had happened years ago, she would not have been able to stand up to the sister, and the sister would have confused her. And that happens to too many of my patients. They become confused so easily, by a simple argument, by the simple fact that somebody opposes them.

And Frances went on to state that now if such a thing happens—as in the given example it did happen—that means, now if somebody frustrates her, she doesn't permit them to confuse her any longer.

And you remember that Fanny told you about her drawing school, drawing class experiment, and she was put before a board and she was to draw and she didn't know how to draw. So that was confusion, frustration. And what all the patients here tell you is how, in the past, they were frustrated and became confused, and today they are just as frustrated, but they no longer become confused.

And we ask ourselves how they learned, how they learned to eliminate confusion when they are frustrated. And I hope you will realize that this is the common fate of patients. The moment they are frustrated, or they think they are frustrated, they become confused and perhaps something worse happens to them. They become panicky, and then, naturally, all rational thought and rational reaction is side-tracked by the panic. And then the patients actually are confused and do the wrong thing and say the wrong thing. And how have these patients that have been sitting here on the panel learned to avoid confusion and to avoid panic? I guess they told you they received training. And, of course, one would like to know how this training works. But I'm not going to tell you that. That would take too much time to explain how the Recovery training works. But I'll tell you about something else.

Training cannot be done in ten minutes. Those of you that have done some training of any kind on others—even if it was only a pet, a dog—those of you who have done that know that this cannot be in ten minutes, that it cannot be in two weeks, and not in three months. It takes time, in terms of months and longer, but at least of months. And during this time that the training goes on, during the weary months in which it proceeds, the patient, or the dog in dog training, is an apprentice, *is an apprentice,* and I want you to know what that means.

An apprentice is naturally unschooled as a rule when he begins his apprenticeship. And so Fanny began her apprenticeship in a drafting course, or an art course, and what did she do? She was placed before a board and was to draw lines or figures, and she didn't know how to do that job. She had never learned it. And she became discouraged. What would happen to our workers—to our craftsmen—if, when they begin their apprenticeship, they should become discouraged the first day? We would have no craftsmen. And yet that is what our patients do. They have a passion for becoming discouraged. They have a passion to be discouraged, and that means they don't consider themselves apprentices.

If Fanny meant to say that she should have been able to handle the drafting job the first time that she attended the course, will you realize that she did not think of herself as one that wishes to learn, as one that undergoes apprenticeship. But, whether she knew it or not, she thought that she should have been able to do the job without learning it. Well, Frances* told you, "Look here, the others did it, and I didn't." The others took to the drafting immediately, and it's quite possible. But how could they? How is it that they could do it and Frances couldn't? (Uh, Fanny. Pardon me.) There must be a reason.

Now you could say perhaps some of the others were perhaps trained already. But Frances went with her sister, who apparently had no training, and she did a tolerably good job. So Frances had, first, to learn how to draw, but, second, she had to learn something else. Her sister went ahead and tried without any fear, and Frances became paralyzed when she thought that now she had to do something which was strange to her. But why did her sister immediately chip in?

* *The names Fanny and Frances are confused throughout this section. All further references should be to Fanny.*

And the answer is that my patients are paralyzed by the fear of making mistakes. They are just as good—and in many instances much better—than the average person, but they are afraid to make mistakes.

And once Frances went over to the board and took the chalk into her hand and began to draw, she discovered she could do a pretty good job. So, do you understand, with her it was the fear of making mistakes that kept her from doing the job properly and not the inability to do the job. And that describes every patient of mine. My patients are a capable lot. They have the capacity to do a good job, but they are afraid of making mistakes. And if now you ask what is the heart of Recovery training, then I'll tell you it is to learn how to make mistakes with courage, with the courage to make them.

Doesn't it sound very simple? Well, stop fearing mistakes, and you will go ahead and do the job, whatever it is, with courage, with initiative, with no trouble. And then you'll bring out everything that you can do. Indeed, a very simple formula for nervous health. And you know the formula works. But it works, yes, but then sometimes it doesn't work. And then it works again, and then, again, it does not work. And what happens? What happens is that the patient then becomes discouraged, and he says, "Look here. This formula may work with everybody else but not with me." And the patient gives up practicing and is no longer an apprentice. The patient drops the apprenticeship

Now perhaps with this little example you may realize what the training process consists of. The training process in Recovery—both with the formula that I mentioned and with dozens of other formulas that I will not mention—the training process consists in a simple phrase, in making the patient realize that he is in apprenticeship. You notice Fanny didn't know it. Now that I reminded her of it, she naturally realized that that was her mistake. She forgot that she was still in apprenticeship—as a matter of fact, with her, in the first days of apprenticeship.

Now if the patient realizes, if it is drummed into his head that he is an apprentice and is expected to go through apprenticeship for months, then he understands the task expected of him, and he understands how the road towards improvement proceeds and where it leads. It proceeds through apprenticeship and leads to health, to mental and nervous health. Well, I have had plenty of apprentices working under me, and not only patients. I had to train nurses. I had to train social workers. I had to train resident physicians. I had to conduct research projects and had to train plenty of people. And there I had to tell my charges, "Go ahead and make mistakes." This means first start out by yourself, then submit the paper that you have worked out, and I'll correct it. And when I read the papers on many occasions, my spirits fell. They were awful at times, at least as bad as what my patients may do at any time. And I had to correct the paper and return it, and the poor chap had to work it over, and he sweated plenty. And then he submitted the now redone paper, and I had to correct again and amend and change and then to turn over the paper again to the young gentleman. And he was made to sweat again, and that could not be helped if the training was to be effective. Of course, you can break in people without giving them thorough training, but if you want to train them so that they could really handle a job, no breaking in will do. It must be training.

Now you will realize that training imposes all kinds of difficulties, both on the one who does the training and the one who takes it, on the teacher and on the pupil. And as far as I am concerned, I presume that I have done a fairly good job in training people. But I was a hard taskmaster, and some of my previous resident physicians, and social workers, and interns have perhaps not the kindest feelings towards me. But I hope they have because they realized it was for their best.

And with patients I am a strict taskmaster. Patients come, and what do they want? They don't want to engage in this arduous task of undergoing apprenticeship. Apprenticeship takes time until you learn something, something that you can really manipulate effectively. And the patient comes as a sufferer, as a person who suffers agonies, and how can you tell a person in agony that he will have to wait months and months until he finally learns how to drop his agonies? It is inhuman. It simply can't be done.

And, of course, you know here in Recovery the patient gets relief soon, but he is not cured. He is not markedly improved in the beginning. But he gets relief soon because coming here and coming to the family meetings, joining a social—as it was announced to you for tomorrow—he gets encouragement, not from me, but from my patients. And that is a kind of encouragement that comes from the heart and has a warmth of feeling and is given to the patient from one who has suffered likewise, and that is a telling variety of relief.

Let me tell you that I have never been able to give patients quick relief if they merely came to my office. Perhaps there was a remarkable case here and there that responded quickly. But if they fell back after a day or two, or a week or two of relief, and were in torture again, then they had lost faith. And I couldn't do anything with them in my office alone if they refused to join this group. But here I have assistants by the dozens, and almost by the hundreds, and my patients get their relief, their initial relief, from these assistants of mine—this means my patients, my former patients, those patients that have already "graduated." And there is no finer exhibit and specimen of relief than that given by one patient to the other, and so my patients get relief very soon. They don't have to wait for months and months till they finally will get relief. And after they have received their initial relief, then they think, as they express it, "Well, I got it licked." But when a patient says, "Well, I got it licked," what does that mean? This means he thinks he doesn't need apprenticeship any longer. He thinks he is cured, and then the trouble begins.

The patient stops cooperating fully. He cooperates only half, by halves, and then the apprenticeship is not only an imposition on the patients but on me. Then I have difficulty to arouse the patient from his pessimism, from his discouragement. The patient then forms the idea, "Well, even

Recovery can't help me," and now the discouragement is deep. That was about the last resort that the patient thought of—Recovery.

And will you now understand—and I don't think I have to tell you much more about this subject—all along, when I try to get my patients to enter their apprenticeship, there come up obstacles. First, the patient gets setbacks, and, naturally, as I have told you, setbacks are unavoidable. Now, if the patient were working in the spirit of an apprentice, he would take it for granted that he is in for setbacks. An apprentice can never be a master in the beginning. He must go through his training. And now perhaps you will realize that the training is heartbreaking for the doctor—for the patient, too—but believe me it is heartbreaking for the doctor, too. And there are many other things that are in the way of this prolonged apprenticeship. The patient not only gets setbacks, but he has real troubles.

The patient may be the mother of three children. How are you going to get a mother of three children to come regularly to meetings? Here, in other words, I touch on environmental difficulties which are, of course, very important in the case of a mother of little children. But other patients who are not mothers—some of them are not even fathers—come to me and tell me about their troubles out in environment. Well, they have to pay off a mortgage, they tell me, so they have to work hard and can't come here. And then some other person tells me, "Well, I had a severe cold, and that kept me from coming." Why, I think I have had colds by the hundreds during my lifetime, and I don't remember that any cold has kept me from my work even one single day. But if somebody looks for excuses, he can find them galore.

And all I want to tell you in this respect is that the patient comes up with all kinds of excuses that made him miss meetings, this means lay off on the apprenticeship. But the only environmental difficulty that I really honor and respect is the difficulties that are in the way of a mother with three children. I will even admit that the mother with two children, and one child, has my sympathy if she has to undergo training in terms of apprenticeship.

Now the patients who have sat here on the panel and told you their beautiful stories of how they handled themselves vigorously with regard to their symptoms and got rid of them by means of the Recovery training, told you precisely the story of Recovery. It is training. And what I wanted to add, that the story of Recovery must be supplemented by the statement that training requires long, drawn-out apprenticeship. And will you do me the favor not to forget that it is not only training that you are offered in Recovery, but the training is enforced by making you know that you are apprentices. If you retain what I told you now and keep in mind the fact that you are in apprenticeship, it will be so much easier for you and more easy, or easier yet, I am afraid, for me.

Thank you.

INTELLECTUAL VALIDITY AND ROMANTIC VITALITY

17 Minutes
Recorded Saturday, October 17, 1953

The panel will discuss today a subject that is phrased and entitled in rather high-flown language. It is "The Intellectual Validity and the Romantic Vitality." Well, if you have read the book, you will know what that means. If you have not read the book, well, I'll try to explain the terms. You see, in this life of ours, every minute, every second, I try to be right. I try to pronounce right—correct—statements, and I try to have correct conceptions, notions, ideas. So, everybody tries to be right in simple things. It is understood that everybody tries to be right in morals and ethics and legally, but in simple things everybody has the ambition to be right. And, second, everybody has the ambition to be valid and vital. And what do these terms mean? What does it mean to be right, to have the right idea?

I will explain it to you by referring to patients. I will explain the questions, What is right? and What is vital? You see, if somebody has a depression—and practically all my patients drift into one at this time and then some other time—if they have a depression, mild or severe, they think they don't think right, and they think they have lost their vitality. It is not true that they have done so. They merely believe or suspect—this means think—they can't speak and think right any longer, and they have no vitality in the pursuance of their daily routine (not morally and ethically and legally). I wish that my patients were a trifle less concerned about their ethics and morals and legality. They are far too concerned about these matters. Instead of having an average concern, they have an extreme concern about them.

Now, such patients who suffer from a depression think that whatever they do is wrong. They think whatever they have done in the past is wrong, and they recount past misdemeanors and so-called delinquencies, which have perhaps some basis in fact but are monstrously exaggerated. And you understand that such patients categorically deny that there is anything right in their thinking.

And then the patients notice certain things that are really distressing. They notice that when they want to dress in the morning, it is so difficult to slip into a sleeve. They notice it is difficult for them to get out of bed. It is difficult for them to take a look at their children. And when they take a look at the children, then they are overwhelmed with the fear that the children don't mean anything to them. They are just young persons. They remember that in former days, before they had the depression, just looking at the children, just thinking of them, gave them some glow and warmth of feeling, and now everything is cold inside. And they look at the children, and they might just as well look at a strange boy that has no relation to their inner life. And you will understand that such a situation is extremely discouraging and disheartening.

And then the patient, who is perhaps a housewife, knows that she should now prepare breakfast for the children and perhaps for the husband, and her energies give out. She can't make up her mind. She can't make a decision. When she wants to fetch the eggs and prepare a dish or a frying pan for them, everything is delayed, everything is slowed down. She has no decision, no initiative, no impetus. And you will understand that this means lack of vitality. And if a patient like this comes to my office and she is steeped in pessimism, things don't mean anything to this patient anymore. She—I say *she*, but this naturally applies to a *he* just as well—she goes, or she is to go, let me say, to an office where she may have some sort of a job, and the job used to stimulate her and now all the stimulation is gone.

And patients of this kind say, for instance, "I eat, but I have to force myself to eat. And while I am chewing, while I am swallowing, there is no feeling, no appetite. Things are mechanical. The whole body feels like a machine, like a mechanical something." Some patients have told me, and it is correct, "Well, you can stick me with a pin and perhaps with a knife, and I don't feel anything." And patients have told me, when for some reason I gave them an injection, they say, "Now I feel the pain. Isn't that heavenly." The pain came back. And that is heavenly for a person of this kind.

And these patients say they have lost their vitality, and they have lost their power for decision, for prompt action, for taking the initiative, for making up their mind, and they have lost the power of thinking. They are among people, and thoughts don't come. They are asked a question, and they have difficulty return[ing] an answer. And I ask some of these patients a simple question. "How is your appetite?" I ask. And if they have not improved yet, the answer is standard, and it runs, "I can't eat breakfast." And these patients usually have given up breakfast, unless they are forced to take something in the morning. "And at noon, the luncheon has to be pushed down forcefully, otherwise I wouldn't eat. I have to force myself to swallow the morsels." And then I ask, "Well, how is it in the evening?" Then the patient usually says, "Well, isn't that strange. In the evening I can eat with appetite." So, I tell the patient, "Well, if your vitality is gone and dead, and it comes back in the evening, who brings it back? That's a miracle." And I tell them, "In ordinary life, miracles don't happen. And if your vitality comes back in the evening, then it was there but somewhere in hiding." And some patients tell me they can't eat anything with appetite, neither breakfast nor lunch nor dinner. So, with them it seems the vitality is definitely gone, not merely hiding. Then I ask them a simple question again, and it runs as follows, "How, if you go out to a restaurant in the evening, do you eat? Or

don't you eat? Do you have to force yourself or don't you?"
And too many patients answer, "Well, if I am invited out, I do
much better." And some clearly state, "Well, outside, in a
restaurant or in some place where I don't have to cook, everything is lovely."

Well, you know, that is nothing laughable, although it
sounds laughable. What these patients have difficulty [doing]
is to get the initiative to get something started, and in a
restaurant nothing has to be gotten started. So, the thing
sounds ridiculous, but it isn't. It has a good meaning. And
then I tell the patients, "The first thing you have to do is to
crowd out of your brain the idea that your vitality is gone and
dead. What is neither gone nor dead is, first, the vitality and,
second, your capability for making a decision, for making up
your mind to something. None of it is dead, but all of it is difficult to handle in your present state."

And so I will advise you, don't go on constantly discouraging yourselves by thinking that your vitality is gone
and dead. It is merely dormant. It hibernates. It is not active.
And now you can activate it or reactivate it [if you stop main-
taining] the idea that anything in your body is dead. Nature
works differently. There is nothing dead in the body if you are
alive. The only things that are half dead are such structures as
hair and nails, but everything else is alive. But it may be dormant, it may be asleep, inactive.

And if patients of this kind who think they have lost
their vitality and perhaps their being right—this means their
validity—[they] should consider what I have told you: that
nothing is ever dead as long as you live. But many things in
a nervous patient are depressed and crowded out of the
stream of life. They are in life but don't "stream." And in
order to make the stream flow again, the stream of feeling, the
stream of interest, the stream of mental reaction and emotional reaction, what is required is for the patient not to discourage himself. And in order not to discourage himself, the
patient must be trained, trained to develop courage, trained
to develop the capacity for braving discomfort—even if you

call it torture, but it's still discomfort. And once you learn that, after due training, there is no difficulty to have both validity and vitality restored to its former function, which is then as lively as it ever was.

And don't listen to anybody who will tell you once you have had a severe nervous or mental condition that you will never come back. That's, of course, arrant nonsense, and don't listen to such prophets of doom.

Thank you.

SELF-BLAME, EXCEPTIONALITY
AND AVERAGENESS

27 Minutes
Recorded Saturday, November 14, 1953

Now, the three members, as usual, have presented you with examples from their own life, as usual, from their daily life: daily life in which mothers have to take their children to a parade, and people go out to the street to buy a newspaper, and other people discover a mouse in their flat. And these were the three facts that the patients mentioned here. They are trivial, be sure, very trivial. Even the mouse is trivial. And yet the patients bring them as examples of what? Of how they conquered their nervous conditions. Keep that in mind.

A condition as complex as a nervous ailment is—and there can be no question about its being complex—can be taken care of by the simple formulas that the patients offered you. And should you think that this is mere talk—which you of course will not think, I am sure—should you think so, should you particularly refer to a statement made by Vickie that she thought she was dying, you might be inclined to call this an exaggeration, but it is not so.

I don't mean to say that Vickie has been dying, but she was thoroughly convinced for years and years that she has been dying away by inches. This means that thought of being in a state of decay has possessed Vickie's mind for many years, every day, all day. So, if she mentions that she felt she was dying, she actually felt it. It is, of course, an obsession with her, and now it comes over her only occasionally. But when I met her first, years back, this condition dominated her life every day, all day, for years. So, in quoting this symptom, be certain the symptom was there, whatever it is. And she felt, she thought, you may say she imagined—I have no objection to this designation either—she imagined that she was now dying away. I don't care whether you call it *a belief,* or *a feeling,* or *an imagination.*

I wish that no human being ever gets such an imagination. Even if an imagination, if it dominates life, then let me tell you, life is no longer worth living. [There's] an imagination of this kind that the patient cannot throw off, and she could not without help. Fortunately, she got help.

You remember that Vickie told you that when she noticed that she was late for the appointment at the parade, she tried to speed up her work and then got herself into trouble. The heart began to kick up, and, of course, she had all kinds of fears, sweats, and tenseness, and I don't remember what else she mentioned. Well, one thing she might have mentioned, and I might have missed the item, but maybe she did not mention it: She felt guilty. She certainly did. She has always done that, and I have yet to see the numbers of patients that do not blame themselves for not being able to get well. I have yet to see the numbers of patients—some of them I have seen—but the numbers of patients who avoid this dreadful thing that we call *self-blame, guilt feelings.*

And I listened to Mary, who told you how she went out on the street to buy a paper—the paper that you all know, the *Chicago Sun Times*—and she went back and read it. She added that she is fond of reading papers. Well, I am not, I can tell you. I read papers because I have to, not because I like to. But Mary is different from me, so she likes to read papers, which is all right. But then she felt she hadn't read enough yet, and she went out on the street to get another paper, the *Examiner,* and she came back with the *Sun Times* again. She bought the paper that she had read already. She said in former days, before she had her Recovery training, she would have worked herself up, and she would have blamed herself for not paying more attention to things. And then Mary went on to mention that in former days, she had before her mind's eye the fate of her sister, who is in a state hospital and has been there for years. And blaming herself and feeling guilty, of course, the thought would have come to her that she might land in a state hospital. And why? Because she did not tend to her activities and her functions, because she was negligent and forgot things that she [couldn't] remember, and perhaps there were all kinds of other reasons for her blaming herself. And what does that mean, this guilt feeling, that self-blame?

My patients have learned to avoid it after they have received their training in Recovery, and the question arises: What is this feeling, and how should it be avoided? You see, I never blame myself, let me say, for stumbling and falling. Some people do blame themselves even for this, but I don't think I blame myself if I stumble and fall. Why not? Well, there was a stone, and I hit it, and I fell. If I blamed myself for this fall, that would mean I would tell myself I should have avoided it. I should have avoided falling. This means I should have avoided getting in touch with the stone, and I grant you it can be done. If a person does do nothing but constantly be careful, looking around where there might be a stone on the path that he treads, maybe he can avoid falling over the stone. But I refuse to spend my life looking for stones on the street. If I did do that, I would set myself up as a very exceptional person, perhaps as one person in this world that spends his time, very pleasantly perhaps, looking for stones on the street. And this, whether you believe it or not, brings up the basic principle of Recovery and the basic principle with which you can avoid guilt feelings, or when you have [them], you can turn it into relaxation or into a sense of humor, which is more or less the same.

You see, if I feel exceptional, if I think I should have exceptional vigilance, exceptionally paying attention to things that might harm me, then, of course, I set myself down as an exceptional, singular person, a rare exception, and why should I do that? But if I do, then, of course, I can have no rest. There are so many stones on a street or on the path which I walk, that I would have to spend all my time constantly being busy avoiding mishaps since there is not only a mishap of the kind that I mentioned, stumbling over a stone; there are all kinds of other mishaps. I would, at the same time, constantly have to pay attention to every automobile that passes me, to every streetcar. I would have to exhaust myself not to touch anybody while passing him on the street. You understand my life would be taken up with nothing else but finding a way of avoiding accidents. And if anybody wants to live a life of this kind, that's his business, but I'll call him *an exceptionalist* or *a perfectionist.* At that, I will add that he is very silly.

Now you see in Recovery, we have concentrated our attention and our effort on rooting out the feeling of exceptionality from the patients. We want our patients to be trained to feel and think about themselves as average, not as exceptional. And those of you that haven't seen our system in operation may become skeptical by hearing that that's all that Recovery has to offer. That's, of course, not true. It isn't all that Recovery has to offer. But with all the instruction that we give our patients, with all the endless training that we supply for them, you may take it for granted that underlying all these variegated activities is the principle: Don't try to be exceptional, but be average. And once our patients have learned to be average—and it's very difficult to learn that, very difficult, and I will not tell you why. You have to read in the book that gives practically all the reasons why it is for human beings so difficult to think of themselves as average.

If anybody, it says in the book, should have to believe that he is nothing but average, he might get a fit. But in Recovery, this is what we teach our patients. Now, you will understand when I think of myself as average, then everything that is average, that is done by people on an average, is permissible, and I will not blame myself for doing it. I hope you understand that.

If everything that I should do or want to do is average, then I will immediately know after I stumbled over a stone, that on an average, people stumble over stones. Then I will certainly not blame myself for it, and so it goes.

And after Mary had been trained in Recovery to think of herself as average, she also learned to set up a standard of valuations that contained all average standards, nothing exceptional. It did not contain, for instance, the standard that everybody must almost always make an effort to prevent accidents. Why should you? Do your best, your average best, not to be careless, but only your average best. I will add, your average should be good average. You should live a life as the desirable people in the community appear to live their lives. Whether they do it, I can't tell you.

Now you see the difference between a person that gets easily rattled or scared and between a person that is calm is essentially the philosophy which the persons have. I will add, the philosophy that anybody has is either one that is pessimistic, more or less pessimistic about human nature, or one that is more or less optimistic. And you can't have an optimistic philosophy if you think that you have to follow extreme, exceptional, and singular standards. These singular standards, these exceptional talents, which you may want to follow, are what we usually call *ideals*. Usually, by the way, with patients they are what we call *phony ideals*. But suppose even they are not phony, suppose the ideals are genuine, religious ideals, ethical ideals, aesthetical ideals, and so forth. Then, well, then march towards the ideal. There is no question that you should, no question about it, you should do that.

If you adopt ideals, and be sure you all have adopted the ideals that every good average person has adopted, then march towards the ideal. Don't think that you must reach it. Once you have reached your ideals, then you are divine, at least angelic, saintly. Then you are no longer an average human being. That's not the purpose of life: to reach the ideal. At any rate, I don't think it is. The purpose of life is to come as close to the ideal as you can manage, but remember humans have limitations. I have yet to see a human being that is a saint. I have yet to see a human being that is sinless. The ideal would demand that you are sinless. I have as yet to see a human being that is faultless, and if I saw one, I wouldn't want to associate with him. He is not human. I wouldn't want to associate with him. I wouldn't want any of my children to become faultless. They should have their average faults. That makes them human.

But my patients think different, and what do they think? You see the average person has experiences which he cannot avoid because they are average experiences. Every human person is either subject to them, or may at any time be subject to these experiences. I claim that I am an average human being, but I get headaches too. I forget that I bought a paper already and buy another one of the same kind. I have seen mice in the apartment, and, well, when I was young, I got scared and didn't think of picking up the mouse. But Fanny apparently thought an average person must be without fear. That's nonsense.

An average person must merely control his fear. How can you live in this world—or in any other world it seems to me—without having fear? If you have no fear, this means you have no capacity to feel what is going on. If you have no fear, then I doubt whether you will have loved. I doubt it. You see, that sounds very attractive to be without fear, but that can't be done. If you are without fear, then you are not human. Then you are angelic perhaps and saintly, but I told you what I want you to be: average, human and not saintly.

And I hope you will understand now that the average person has fears, and headaches, and numbness, and develops a palpitation here and a pressure there, but if he feels average, then he takes it for granted that that is coming to him and therefore doesn't work himself up over it. If he feels average, he will not blame himself for having palpitations, not even for having the feeling that he is dying away. He will simply take it for granted that he is an average human being with the average human limitations.

I may tell you, in this respect and in this connection, that the very leaders of humanity have had outrageously distressing nervous troubles. You will admit that Abraham

Lincoln was a leader of humanity, but he suffered precisely from the manic-depressive conditions from which my patients are suffering. And the great Washington was not a very relaxed person. He had all kinds of complaints that we now call *nervous*. And if you go further than those and roam through the literature of every nation, to the art record of every nation, the higher you rise in the scale of human personalities, the more do you encounter people, great men, geniuses, that are racked by nervous symptoms, and some of them by mental symptoms. Some of them, naturally, have landed in state institutions, quite a number of them.

So do you see, these are exceptional people. I don't know whether they felt exceptional. It is hardly likely that Lincoln felt exceptional, even though he was, but apparently he did not feel exceptional. If he had felt exceptional, he wouldn't have had that delightful sense of humor that he had, and he wouldn't have been as humble as he was. He certainly did not feel exceptional. He felt average, and, therefore, he had no nervous symptoms. He had what we call now *the manic-depressive condition* that is not just nervous. Well, but he bore it stoutly. He was not treated for it, and you know where he landed: in Washington, which is a . . . , I don't know what kind of a place it is. I never was there, but it has the White House and the Presidency. Well, that's not bad to land there, although it's better somebody else does it and not I.

Well, do you understand now that this matter of being average, or this matter of averageness, is not merely a phrase. And if anybody wants to look down his nose on Recovery and say, "Look here, they talk trivialities," then I'll agree with him. We talk trivialities, and it is these trivialities which touch on averageness, and it is the principle of averageness that makes you human and healthy. And I will advise you, don't expect that your condition, being as complex as it is—and I don't deny that—requires complex methods to check it and to conquer it. That's not so. The simple method is always the superior procedure.

Thank you.

FEELINGS ARE NOT FACTS

16 Minutes
Recorded Saturday, November 14, 1953

The panel will discuss today the subject of "Feelings Are Not Facts." In a sense, that is nonsense. Feelings are, of course, facts. Feelings can upset you to the point that you shake all over. They can inspire you to a point where you forget yourself. So feelings are, of course, facts. But, for instance, when you state that you feel there is something pressing in the brain, and it feels like a tumor—patients make such statements—although I don't know how a tumor feels. I have never known that a tumor feels at all, or that a person can feel a tumor. A person can only feel pressure. But patients are fond [of saying], "I feel it. How can you then say it is not a fact?" When I tell a patient, "Why, there is no tumor," then this is the common answer: "But I feel it, Doctor."

And many people speak in this manner. They feel something, therefore it is there. That's, of course, blank nonsense. Feelings are very emphatic facts. This means they can shake you. They can inspire you. They can make your heart beat faster. They can have any kind of effect, and therefore they are facts. But in ordinary life when we speak of facts, we mean something else, nothing of the kind that feelings tell you about. We say, "It is ten o'clock," and we say, "It is a fact." Why is that a fact? The reason is that you then can say, "Look at the watch, and you will find out."

What we usually mean by "fact" is something that happens, or something that exists, that somebody else can verify.

And he then can state, "Well, you are right. It is a fact." If you say, "This is a brown table," then anybody can find out whether it is brown or blue, and if he finds it's brown, then he says, "It's a fact that it is brown." Will you understand, therefore, that there are subjective facts that the subject feels, and objective facts that everybody who has eyes, ears, hands, and certain intelligence can verify.

And so the title of that article should read, "Feelings Are Subjective Facts but Not Objective Facts." But that title would take up about two lines in the book, and we don't want that. Therefore, we merely let it read, "Feelings Are Not Facts." But you should supplement in your mind the adjective *objective* and say, "Feelings Are Not Objective Facts."

But patients come along and tell me, "I eat, I drink, I take a tablespoon of food in my mouth, and it doesn't go down. It gets stuck in the esophagus. It gets stuck." Some patients go farther and say, "It gets stuck behind the tube, not in the tube." And you can't say that such a thing is a fact. So, I tell the patients, "That's impossible. No food can ever get behind the tube. It could possibly get stuck within the tube." Then some patients say again, "But, Doctor, I feel it." And they mean, well, that proves it if they feel it.

Patients come to me and tell me they feel that something jumps in the chest. They feel that the heart expands. And then again, I have the greatest trouble making clear to these patients that these are merely subjective feelings and not objective facts. Then these patients again come along with the statement, "But, Doctor, I feel it," again implying that feeling, subjective feeling, enables them to find an objective fact.

Now the implication I hope you will understand—the implication that this has for patients. If a patient says that his feelings, his subjective feelings, are equivalent to objective facts, then he can make a diagnosis. And he can then act on his own diagnosis and, according to his own diagnosis, his heart expands because he feels it. You know if somebody should actually be afflicted with an expanding heart, well, that's an extremely serious, fatal condition. That patient really passes the verdict of death and destruction on him, and if he is to avoid that course, then he must learn the difference between feelings and facts: this means between subjective feelings and objective facts.

A diagnosis must naturally not be based on feelings. It must be based on objective facts that can be diagnosed, for instance, by tests, by examinations, by x-rays, by all kinds of evidence that only the physician can supply and which the physician only can interpret. Only the physician knows what can be seen in an x-ray or in a test tube. But my patients trust their feelings. And once they begin to go on the evidence of feelings, then I try to explain to them again what feelings are, the kind of feelings they speak of.

I know, of course, what the common feelings are. I know what is love, hatred, fear. But look here, somebody says he loves somebody else. Then I'll ask him or her, "What do you love in him?" Then they become flustered. They don't know what the question means. I merely want to tell you these few remarks that I am going to make about love. I merely want to tell you that even in such a simple matter as love, people are not competent to state what it is.

If a mother tells me she loves her daughter, well, I have no doubt that she loves the daughter. Should I, however, ask her, "What attracts you to your daughter?" that wouldn't be a silly question. Not at all. The attraction could be very varied. A mother may love the daughter just because she's a mother and she loves the daughter, I grant you, and that doesn't need any explanation. But if I ask the question, "What attracts you to your daughter?" that may be something else than love. A mother may be attracted to the daughter, for instance, by the desire to take care of her, to guide her. But then if the daughter is already eighteen, or twenty, or twenty-five years of age, and the mother wants still to take care of her, although the daughter is married and has perhaps children, then I'll ask the mother again, "What attracts you to your daughter?" And if she is again flustered by this question, I'll tell her what attracts her to her. It is the desire to possess the daughter, not to give up the possession of her daughter, and that's what we call *possessiveness.*

There is nobody else perhaps in this world that will want to be possessed by this mother, that will tolerate her possessing her. What we call *possessive mothers* are certainly mothers that love their children. They would want to take care of their daughter, not of strangers. But along with this love goes this desire to possess the body and the soul, and every act, and every decision of that daughter. And I have seen mothers who don't let their daughters even boil two eggs. They immediately rush up and say, "Let me do it." You can't tell me that this is love.

And if a father loves his children and constantly teases them so that they really become distracted, or he constantly says *no* when they ask for something, don't tell me that is love. That father may still love the children, but his love is outstripped by something that we call *domination.* He has no respect for the desires of the children. The children have no desire to constantly [be] teased. They have certainly no desire to be constantly treated with *no,* with negativism.

And, in conclusion, let me tell you, let me sum up. Even such familiar feelings as love are of such a complex structure, that your judgement about them is not competent. Anybody who has studied this subject of marital love, and has studied it critically, he can perhaps give you an opinion of whether this love in a certain condition is genuine or intermingled with all kinds of other factors, and, therefore, not genuine, not even approaching the state of purity and singleness.

And if that is true, you can now draw the conclusion that whenever you feel something in your body and then you make a pronouncement, you know what it is, you know that it is a swollen gland that you feel somewhere within the body, you know that the food doesn't pass through the esophagus, you know that the pressure in the brain—this means in your skull—is due to a high blood pressure, and you feel now the blood pressure has risen—right now, mind you—whenever you have the intention to make a statement, my advice is, stop it, first, as a diagnosis, and, second, as the result of a feeling. And feelings of the kind that I mentioned should never be trusted as revealing and representing facts.

Thank you.

FRUSTRATION AND DISAPPOINTMENT

30 Minutes
Recorded Saturday, November 28, 1953

The subject which was to be taken up this afternoon, but as usual they did not mention the subject. As usual, when they gave their examples, they had apparently forgotten that the theme was dealing with something like "Beliefs and Order and Convictions." And I don't remember having heard from the panel members any mention of any of these three words. And I have told you before that this is perfectly in *order.* See, I mention the one word at least.

Well, it's perfectly in order because life is so arranged that no matter what you discuss, if it is a significant topic, no matter which significant topic you discuss, it is connected with all other topics that reside in your brain. And don't let anybody tell you that the brain, or our mind, is complexly arranged. It is very simply arranged.

If the mind thinks of love, then at the same time it thinks of fear and of hatred, and everything in the mind is interconnected. And so, if our patients come here with examples that are significant—and that they are significant is undoubted after what you heard here—then it matters not at all what kind of example they offer. I will only mention one heading, under which all examples that the patients offer can be grouped, and that is the heading of "Frustration and Disappointment."

Everybody has frustrations. Everybody has them practically every five minutes of his day, every day of his life. I count my frustrations at a figure that is much larger than that. I don't have frustrations every five minutes but, I think, every five seconds of my life, all day, every day. You may not believe it, but just watch me talking to a patient and trying to explain something to him, and being thwarted by the sabotage exercised by that patient, and you will believe, and you will be fully convinced. And that is in perfect order that the patients frustrate me all the time that I speak to them. Because, remember, I only see patients that have not improved yet or, at any rate, are not cured yet, that are still suffering. And a suffering patient is not easily convinced, and my business is to convince him. And if I speak to a patient for five minutes, I am frustrated all the five minutes. So, my firm belief is that most of the time I am frustrated all the time. Isn't that lovely?

Now look here, one patient told you—Gertie—that she was to have a vacation of three days, a vacation that was imposed on her because of some inventory changing on the job that she works on. And Frances told you that she was frustrated by the fact that her brother-in-law fell sick again. He had some liver trouble, and that event shook Frances, it seems, to her foundation. Her heart, she said, beat like a drum. Well, whether a drum beats so very painfully I don't know, but it's a good expression. And Bill told you again that he was frustrated. He lost his job, but his heart apparently did not beat fast. He handled the frustration in a masterly fashion. The others handled the frustrations in good fashion.

But I want to tell you today something about your frustrations. When I see my patients, and they oppose me, sabotage me, they make it extremely difficult for me to convince them that they should act on my principles and not on theirs. When I see them, I am frustrated all the time, but I am not disappointed. And will you distinguish between frustration and disappointment? I doubt whether there is any man of conscience and responsibility and integrity who is not frustrated in his daily activity, perhaps again every few minutes or every few seconds. The poor housewife—I know a story about that, well, because my wife is one and has been one for many, many years—meets with frustrations, indeed, perhaps every second, especially if she has children. That's full of frustrating experiences. And then the plumbing goes wrong. That's not the worst thing. But then she tries to get the plumber, and that's really a bad ordeal.

And so it goes, and there is always frustration. But there is no reason why the housewife should become disappointed and disheartened. Do you understand? And I hope you do. Life is a matter of frustrations, of continuous frustrations. Indeed, I grant you that in average life the frustrations are not extreme, not severe. They are average frustrations. But with my patients, you know, everything that they suffer becomes severe. And the question arises whether their frustration or the suffering becomes severe through some incidents, through some chance happenings, or through the action of fate. Or whether the patients make them severe, apart from circumstances and apart from the action of fate. And I will tell you something about that right now.

You remember that Frances had this memorable experience of having her dear brother-in-law—[who], she said, was not so very dear—falling sick. And her heart pounded, well, like a drum, or like a sledgehammer, or whatever people say. And why? Why should the heart have pounded so extravagantly because somebody, a brother-in-law or somebody else, fell sick again? I walk along in life, and it is clear to me and ought to be clear to everybody, that anybody can at any time fall sick or fall sick again. That will make me feel sad, but it will not make my heart develop palpitations. This means it will not throw me into a great commotion. I will have silent grief, steady perhaps, or interrupted sadness. And grief and sadness do not cause palpitations. If a sad event happens in life, then one should become sad and not frightened.

Frances became frightened. Whether she was sad at the same time I can't tell you, but knowing that this brother-in-law was by no means her favorite, and knowing how she felt towards him, then I find it again very natural that she should perhaps not have been sad when something happened to him. She should have had some sympathy for him but no sadness. And there are plenty of brother-in-laws and sister-in-laws and mother-in-laws that are not favorite members in the larger family. And I don't consider it a great fault in character if somebody who has been badgered and dragooned, and perhaps very frequently treated unfairly by any in-law, I don't feel it a fault in character if that in-law is then hated. I wouldn't hate him. I react differently. I will simply keep out of his way without pouring hate on him. But if somebody should hate any other person, in-law or not, because that person has been very unfriendly to the one who now hates him, I would not consider this a verdict on the character or the personality of that hating person. I will not approve of it, but I will say this is an average reaction.

But I will add something else. Average, or not average, you can't direct your feelings. As you sit here, and as millions and billions of people are living on this earth and have lived for endless years, endless centuries, this species of human beings has no control over the quality of the feelings, over the *quality*. Over expression of feelings we have control, but not over the quality. And whether, in a given situation, the quality of hatred enters your heart, or the quality of love or the quality of jealousy, you have no control over that. Feelings come. You can't call them up. You can't summon them forth. They come. And if they are there, you can do something with them. You can, for instance, refuse to act on them. This you can. You can refuse to strike out when you hate somebody. You can refuse to become mushy and give mushy expression to your love if love comes to your heart. You see, feelings, once they have settled themselves in your organism, can be controlled in their expression, in their muscular expression. But you can't direct and redirect them as to their quality, as to whether they have the quality of enthusiasm, of generosity, of love, or the other opposite quality of fear, and hatred, and rage, or whatever it is.

Yet Frances, in former days she told you, used to blame herself when she discovered an ugly feeling in her chest. She was not responsible for that feeling. It came. She didn't ask the feeling to make its appearance. She couldn't. And it will be good for you to know that this is the case with feelings. This is also the case with ugly thoughts that come. You don't ask them to visit you—and an ugly thought is a visitation, indeed. Well, this control of feelings, of the expression of feelings, is a very important issue, and we have discussed that at length for years, and now already for decades.

But what I have started to discuss here is not the control of expression but the control of the feelings themselves. And I hope you will go home today with the knowledge gained from me that feelings cannot [be controlled] as to their quality. Whether this feeling or that feeling or another feeling comes to you, you have no means of preventing or promoting. You have no control over the quality of feelings. And I wish my patients would finally realize that, because untold misery is visited on people in general and on my patients in particular, by their belief, by their silly conviction that they are responsible for whatever feelings enter their organism, enter their consciousness.

Keep it in mind. Hate if you have to hate, this means if the feeling of hatred has possessed you; love, of course, if love is there; be jealous if jealousy obsesses you. Be what you are, but don't express feelings of jealousy, feelings of hatred, feelings of anger. The expression can be prevented. And this alone is the object, or is part of the object, of the training which you receive in Recovery. Recovery, or any other procedure, can never train you how to change the quality of your feelings or how to call upon certain feelings or how to prevent certain feelings from entering your consciousness. So, if this is the case, then don't blame yourself for lacking a feeling, or for possessing another feeling that you don't like to possess.

Bill, our friend Bill, who has made history in Recovery by the dramatic manner in which he recovered—Bill was disappoint[ed] [inaudible]. But he, in a more practical matter, he had lost his job because of retrenchment instituted by the firm. And he went to the employment agency, and, I guess, the routine of an employment agency may be to direct and redirect everybody that comes to them in request of a job. They direct him to a counselor, and to a chief counselor. Well, Bill told you the story. In ordinary parlance, I guess, that is called *to give a person the runaround*. For good purpose; I don't criticize the procedure, but it is a runaround. And Bill should have been irritated by this sheer technical manner of being pushed around, although it was not a pushing. It was an orderly procedure in an orderly plan. But he apparently was not ruffled by being sent to one person and then to another person and then to be subjected to all kinds of tests and paperwork and registrations. He lost a lot of time, and be sure he had to wait endless half hours in his trek from one counselor to the other, but he did not report any feeling of frustration. He gave a very matter-of-point report about what occurred, not what happened to him. He didn't consider that as something happening to him. It occurred.

So Bill has definitely learned how to handle his frustrations in the spirit of self-discipline, in self-control. And self-control, with regard to frustrations, means don't expect what will disappoint you. Now, how can you do that? Don't expect what will disappoint you. If I could word it differently, expect that you will be disappointed. The first statement that I made was, "Don't expect that there will be disappointments, that there will be frustrations." That's good. Then you can walk through life and get a blow here and a kick there, and you will not consider it a frustration. That's what Bill does. It's an excellent rule. But I don't tell my patients to apply it. If they could, I would know nothing better than such a practice.

You will perhaps remember that I tell you something else. Expect disappointments, expect frustrations. That's life—frustrations. If life has no frustration, if life were all happiness and carefree living, then it would be boring. You would be surfeited with a life all smoothness, all proceeding on the same level, no downs, no dips, no frustrations, no dis-appointments. That is boredom. Expect frustrations all over, all the time. And if you expect them, then you will not be dis-appointed. Then you will be frustrated, and that will be no disappointment because you expected it.

And that is the lesson that I want you to imbibe partic-ularly with regard to setbacks. If you expect setbacks, if you have your eye on them, then they will never disappoint you because you expected them. And setbacks will be the ordi-nary frustrations that happen in the entire sphere of life. They happen to the doctor, to me, for instance, whenever I sit in my office, and you know I sit endless hours in my office. They happen to me when I drive a car and somebody cuts in on me, or I cut in on somebody and something happens. That's frustration. They happen to the housewife all day, every day, I guess, and there is no individual that is not half dead that has not a record of countless frustration, discrete frustra-tion[s], almost every minute, every day, all day. And will you now imbibe that lesson?

Expect frustrations all over the span of life, every day, all day, then you will not be disappointed. And if you will not be disappointed, you will be calm and relaxed. And if you are relaxed, you will not be much irritated. And if you are not much irritated, there will be not much frustration. And with-out many frustrations, there will hardly be much disappoint-ment in life. So, you see, this prescription of expecting disappointments, of expecting frustrations, is an excellent maxim that you should accept and embody in your con-sciousness. The maxim might run in the form of a little para-dox that means, "Expect disappointments and you will not be disappointed."

Good night.

LECTURE 16

CONVICTIONS AND THE SETBACK

17 Minutes
Recorded Saturday, November 28, 1953

The theme for this afternoon is "Order, Beliefs and Convictions" (I guess). That's a big bill, and I don't think I will discuss even half of it. But the matter of convictions is very important for patients to think about.

Patients come to me with the conviction that they are doomed. Patients come to me after years of suffering, after years of incapacity, after years of doing nothing more than complaining, clamoring for attention, clamoring for relief, and when I see them, they are full of the philosophy of *I can't.* "I can't do this. I can't do what I ought to do, and I must do what I don't want to do." And these are convictions. If anybody has the conviction, "I can't do what others, what average people can do," that's a very pernicious conviction. Or if somebody has the conviction, "I must stay at home. I can't walk out on the street," that's indeed a pernicious conviction. And so you will realize that the matter of convictions is very relevant to the situation of the nervous and former mental patient.

Now, it will be good for you to know what a conviction does, what service it renders. You see, if I have the conviction that I am a fairly effective sort of a human being, that I have fair judgment, that I have, more particularly, solid and firm convictions, then I have self-confidence. And with self-confidence and self-respect I can go ahead and act with assurance.

88

I know that I have solid and true convictions. Whether I have them or not does not matter. If I merely believe I have them, then I know, or believe [I] know, that whatever was done well by me in the past points to the fact that my convictions must have been good. And so I gain more self-assurance, more self-confidence. You will understand that convictions have the purpose and the office to make me act with assurance, with self-respect, with self-confidence.

And now the patient comes to me, and he has formed the conviction that he cannot do what others can do. And if the patient is a housewife, she neglects the home, neglects the children and her husband. She's afraid that she cannot go out shopping, that she cannot get out of bed in due time to do the chores, and now if she has the solid conviction that she actually cannot do it, then that helps her. It helps her to know that, after all, it is not her fault that she is neglectful of her duties, but it is a stroke of fate. Fate has saddled her with a sickness that incapacitates her.

Do you see that this conviction, if it is solid and believed in thoroughly, this conviction that the patient acts as he or she does because of the pressure of fate, gives her the sense of being right, of doing the correct thing. And that, of course, helps that housewife. It helps that patient. If that patient now constantly moans and complains and sobs in front of the children, in front of the husband, she at least has now the consolation that she is right because fate has stricken her. And if she does not consciously think that she is right, she at least can say to herself, "It is not my fault that I can't do what I ought to do." Again you will realize convictions of this sort offer a great consolation, render a great service to the individual that has them.

And now the patient comes to me and engages my services. And then something remarkable happens. That patient is likely to feel an immediate improvement or a rapid improvement. Many of the patients walk out of my office after the examination, and the very least they carry with them is a sense of hopefulness. The symptoms have not disappeared, but a sense of hopefulness has established itself, and the feeling of hopelessness is gone or it's weakened, and the patient may feel relief for a few days.

In the meantime, the patient has been told that he must expect, and patiently expect, the setback. But when the setback comes, the patient has all forgotten what she has been told, and she becomes scared. And now the symptoms come again, and this time the patient thinks they are worse than ever, and the patient becomes again hopeless and resumes the conviction again that she can't do what she ought to do.

And now we in Recovery have pondered this problem, and we have asked ourselves, "Why does the patient get the setback?" and we could not find the answer. We could only find the answer to the question whether the setback can be kept mild or must be degenerating to a severe condition. And you know I have told you, if you expect the setback, if you are sure or convinced that the setback will come, but you can handle it by not being alarmed about it, then the setback will be mild. Otherwise, it will be severe.

And after a few weeks—or a few days, or a few hours—the patient improves again. He again gets the feeling of hopefulness because he has in the meantime been in touch with so many patients that have had setbacks, and the patients can tell this new patient about how to handle the setback should it come again. And the patient comes to my office, and I tell her, "Well, how do you feel?" She says, "Oh, I don't feel good at all." So, I ask her, "You weren't able to sleep when I saw you first. Have you been sleeping lately?" Then the patient tells me immediately, without giving me a chance to continue and terminate my sentence, "But, Doctor, my sleep is bad. Yesterday I didn't sleep at all." So, I tell the patient, "I didn't ask you about yesterday. I wanted to know whether lately your sleep has improved. I want you to tell me how many poor nights you had the last week." And then the patient says, "Well, I had two poor nights," and she's angry at the fact that she had two poor nights. Mind you, before the patient came to me, she gave me the story that for the past six months she has hardly had a good night at any time. And now in one week, she had only two poor nights. This means five fair nights, or good nights, perhaps.

And so we are confronted with this perennial problem of the patient denying an improvement. The patient hates to tell that he has improved, and the reason you will perhaps now see. The patient, after the first setback, becomes afraid of improving. Once the setback sets in again, the patient knows by now that he or she can do what they ought to do. But they have frightful palpitations and head pressures, so they lie down and don't do anything. But now they have no longer a consolation that fate is against them because they had experienced an improvement. And they know now that, especially in Recovery, improvements are easily obtained, and that scares them. Because if they think that they have improved and now are again in a setback, during this setback, there is an imperative urge on the part of the patient to complain, to moan, not to do the chores, to neglect duties. And now the patient can no longer have the conviction that that is unavoidable, that the patient cannot do what he or she ought to do.

And that's the reason, or one of the reasons, why a patient does not want to think favorably of the improvement. The improvement, if it is followed by a setback, leaves the patient stranded. During the present setback, the patient has lost the conviction and lacks the support that conviction has given her that it's not her fault, but fate's doing.

And you see there is this great problem before us to make the patient accept the conviction that she or he can do what ought to be done. And in order to make the patient accomplish this, we must train him, first, to face the setback, not to get alarmed by it; second, by no means to revert to the ancient hopelessness and the ancient conviction that he can't do what he ought to do.

And this requires training, relentless training. The patients must indeed be trained every day for weeks and preferably for months. All we can say [is] that we have the machinery for the training, but whether patients will be able to take care of it, and whether they will be willing to take advantage of our training facilities, well, unfortunately that must be left to the discretion of the patient. And the patient's discretion does not work as effectively as I wish it would.

Thank you.

A SENSE OF HUMOR INSTEAD
OF SELF-BLAME

27 Minutes
Recorded Saturday, December 12, 1953

Well, the panel members, as usual, gave excellent examples, and it will be instructive to see what they told you.

You remember that Theresa was overjoyed by the fact that now she can enjoy her family and her children and her home. In former years, she said, she could not enjoy her domesticity. She could not enjoy herself as mother and wife, and she blamed herself. And you remember that she used this term *blame*. She blamed herself.

What did she blame herself for? She claimed that she blamed herself in those days about the fatigue which she experienced and about the depression [into] which she went. And you might say, after all, it might be rational to blame oneself, but why blame oneself for fatigue? If I am tired, I sit down and rest, but I don't blame myself for being tired. And on numerous occasions, I don't feel good because I bungle something, or because something happened that made me feel dejected, and then I could say I feel depressed for some time, but it never occurs to me to blame myself for my feelings or for my sensations.

So be sure that if Theresa said she blamed herself for her fatigue and her depression, she does not mean that. She blamed herself, of course, for something else. She blamed herself for the thing that resulted from her fatigue and her depression. Her fatigue and her depression—this means her symptoms—forced her to neglect certain things, to neglect the children, to neglect herself. These symptoms forced her not to cook, not to visit, not to meet the demands of social life and domestic life. In other words, she did not blame herself for her feelings. I hope that nobody does that. She blamed herself for certain actions that she performed and certain other actions which she was forced not to perform, which she was forced to neglect.

And I want you to know that you blame yourself—if you do that—that you blame yourself for actions or inactions but not for feelings and sensations. Don't do that, and you don't.

And you heard Ann telling you a story that she used a deodorant instead of a face cleaner, if I understood her right. Well, she was absent-minded and she made this mistake. And be certain that before she came to Recovery, when that had happened—she told you so—if that had happened, she would have blamed herself no end. She would have felt depressed. She would have felt lost from grace, and she would have concluded there must be something radically wrong with her mind. Today she says, and what did she say? Today she spots the occurrence, the meaning of the occurrence, and she laughs. Well, I don't think that she laughs in the sense of breaking into laughter. She most likely meant that she laughs inside. And if she laughs inside about a situation or about an occurrence, then she has done something for herself in Recovery that is very remarkable.

And I may tell you right here that I have observed Ann for now close to a year. She was sent to me by a psychologist, if I remember correct[ly], who was her advisor, and that was about a year ago. I may safely tell you that in this year, or in these ten or eleven months that I have seen Ann, there was a radical change in her approach to herself and to life in general. And if Ann tells me that today she has reached the stage where, when a very marked mistake happens, an error happens in her daily activities—a mistake that could make her appear ridiculous in the eyes of others, and certainly in her own eyes—if she says that she has learned to laugh out of existence a mistake of this kind, I believe that this is the fact. She has made a remarkable change.

And I would like to know what the change means. I don't know completely, but I'll tell you something about the meaning of the transformation that has taken place in a patient like Ann. You see, before she went through our training, Ann reacted entirely differently. When this happened to her—that she blundered, that she committed some mistake that one doesn't like to commit—she, first of all, certainly didn't speak of that mistake to others, as she has done here. So you may safely say she was ashamed of the mistake. Perhaps, also, she became fearful, fearful about the fact that she is likely to make, and therefore to repeat, mistakes of this kind. So, she developed a sense of shame, and a sense of fear, and quite a number of other things which I will not mention because of the pressure of time.

And today when such a misdeed happens to her, she comes here and speaks about it, so she has definitely thrown off the sense of shame about mistakes. So, what she has gained is another sense, the sense of tolerance towards her mistakes. And that's a beautiful development, to proceed from the sense of shame to the sense of tolerance. Or if you say that Ann blamed herself, then be sure the reverse of blame, of self-blame, is certainly self-toleration. So, the march was actually either from shame or from fear, but the direction was towards toleration, self-toleration.

And you will remember that our patients are implacable enemies of themselves. They fear themselves, this means their impulses. They are ashamed of themselves, this means their impulses or actions or feelings. They indeed hate themselves, or, if I am to use a milder term, they resent themselves, but essentially it is self-hatred. And all these reactions, whether you call them shame, sense of shame, sense of hatred, sense of intolerance, lack of toleration, they are all negative. They are directed against somebody, either against oneself or somebody else. And if you hate somebody, you feel antagonistic against him or towards him. That is a negative feature. You approach people negatively.

The positive feature would be the reverse of what I mentioned. Instead of being ashamed of oneself, that means despise oneself, to have contempt for oneself—which is, of course, a negative attitude—instead of having that, the positive feature is to approve oneself, self-approval instead of self-resentment and self-hatred. And if you are ashamed of yourself, well, the reverse would again be self-approval, or perhaps self-respect. It's a positive attitude, a positive approach.

And if you fear yourself, or if you fear your impulses, it's a negative procedure, and the positive approach would, of course, be fearlessness—not courage—fearlessness, or hopefulness, which is about the reverse of fearfulness.

And so we'll say that in the beginning of her suffering career, before Ann joined Recovery, her approach to life, both to herself and others, was negative. And now she smiles and laughs inwardly, of course. Maybe outwardly, too. I noticed that, for instance, she laughed here on this platform while she told the story. So, she may actually break forth into laughter when she thinks of herself, or talks about herself, which would be a very fine reaction. But even if we say she laughs at herself silently, then this connotes a very remarkable change in a personality. Whatever I told you about sense of shame and fear and self-contempt and self-resentment—all of which I call negative features, but all of them have not only the common connotation of being negative—they have another common meaning.

There is something lacking in a person who resents, who fears, who is ashamed. And the thing that is lacking—provided the fear, the shame and the hatred [are] nothing significant and appl[y] only to such silly mistakes as Ann mentioned, so I will repeat—the sense of shame, of fear, of hatred, of contempt applied to trivialities of life have this in common: that they are utterly out of the range of humor. A person hating trivialities, fearing trivialities, being ashamed of daily trivialities, has, of course, no sense of humor. And my patients, as long as they are suffering from their panics, from their frightful sensations and impulses, and so forth, have, of course, no sense of humor. They take their inner experiences too seriously. And so when Ann said that now she laughs at her previous fears and shames and hatreds, then she means to imply that she has now acquired a sense of humor.

And look here, all you would have to do to get well would really be to acquire a sense of humor. Well, I tell you that, and you agree with me, I know that. But go ahead and do it. How will you do it? So, you will keep in mind that everything that I tell you presupposes that you can't just do it through magic. It would be magic to develop a sense of humor in a few minutes, or in a few days, or even in a few months. It would almost be magic just by wishing to have it, just by making up your mind to change. That can't be done. If you want to acquire a sense of humor, and that is the sovereign means for curing nervous conditions, then you must be trained. And the training must be very severe—not cruel, don't misunderstand me—severe, unrelenting, continuous for some great space of time. And that's what Ann did. She underwent training, assiduous training, almost continuous. She spent so much time here in Recovery listening and helping and working and reading, that now her husband is disgusted with her method of getting well. Well, that's a matter that I will not discuss. Husbands have a right to have an opinion different from mine and Ann's. But it's an indication that Ann has really done something for herself that is remarkable, and I have to continue speaking about Ann. I only told you what she did positively, in a positive direction. In a positive direction, she embraced that feature of inner life that we call *a sense of humor,* and she held to it. But she did something else that, on the face of it, is rather negative. She refused to take seriously certain other things, and you will understand that might be called *a negative feature.* It is not, not by any means. No. She refused to take seriously something that I'll have to explain in a few words.

If somebody is afraid of his palpitations after I have told him that they don't mean anything, that they are merely distress but no danger, if he still continues to be afraid of these sensations or impulses or whatever troubles him, then he takes, as I told you, his symptoms too seriously. But there is something else. If he does take them so seriously, then to him they are extremely important, and he develops a sense of importance with regard to his suffering. And then he works on this sense of importance, and he insists that his suffering should be important to others, to wife, mother, father, brother, and so forth, and to the doctor. And then they come to my office, and I have to tell them, "You are too serious about your sufferings. You are too serious about your symptoms. And that means you have an exaggerated sense of importance about this suffering, and your sense of importance you take too seriously."

I have a sense of importance, and don't tell me that it is not so. And I am sure that I will not undermine your confidence in me if I tell you that I am human. Didn't you know that? I hope you do. And as a human being, be sure I share all your imbecilities and your stupidities, and I'm just as dumb as you are in many things, and everybody is. But I take my smartness and my dumbness not too seriously. But you do. It is a calamity to a patient suffering in the beginning without having been subjected to the Recovery discipline. It's a grave calamity if something happens to that patient [as] what happened to Frank.

He made an error in his calculations, in his book entries. You see, what happened to him was really not a triviality any more. It was something serious. It could have upset all kinds of business routine. I wouldn't call it a triviality. But it was nevertheless routine, important routine. But Frank either told you—I don't remember—or he could have told you how in past days he took mistakes seriously, trivial mistakes. And I do it, and I make these mistakes, too, these mistakes that happen to everybody. And it happens to me, first of all, that I do something silly that I didn't want to do, and the one thing that I wanted to do I forget to do, and then I ask myself, "What's the matter with me?" And my answer is, "Well, nothing is the matter with me. I am average." And that's what average people do. And will you understand that to refuse to take trivialities seriously, to refuse to be worked up over routine mistakes, routine troubles, means, first, to use a sense of humor and, second, which is the same thing, to feel average. As an average person, you can safely make mistakes. Don't do it deliberately, I will advise you, but you can make mistakes without working yourself up over them.

So, do you understand now that having a good sense of humor and feeling average are the same thing? And looking on his troubles with a great sense of importance is the same thing as having no sense of humor. So, this matter of importance is opposed to the matter of averageness, and the sense of humor is opposed, naturally, to the sense of importance. And you know how you have been trained, for those among you who are not senior members of this group are still being trained. And you know how this is done. It is done by emphasizing continually, irretrievably almost, that you must get rid of your *exceptionality*, as I call it—this means your sense of importance.

I told you before that I have an egregious sense of importance just as you have it, but I don't take it seriously. That's all. I have it. It always comes up. I always feel I am the smartest, the finest, the most vital person there is. But I don't believe it. I don't take it seriously. And yet I think of it, and sometimes I lie down and dream, daydream, and then I have all kinds of fantasies [of] how important I will be some day. Well, it would be about time if it should materialize. I am not just getting younger. And then all of a sudden after a minute or two I remind myself, "Well, that's all nonsense. Why should I dream about greatness and glamour and fame and fortune, and so forth?" And then I stop. Then I stop because it appears ridiculous to me. I have applied the sense of humor, and it goes. But then it comes back. And then sometimes I say, "Well, why shouldn't I daydream? It's all right.

It's all right with me." But when I say, "It's all right," I permit it to go on; then I still know it's all nonsense, and I don't take it seriously. I only play with the thought that perhaps fortune will smile on you, and everything will be very grandiose with me in my life, and there will be glamour and glory and all kinds of things that go under the same terms.

But my patients do differently. First, they don't dream of glamour and glory but of disaster. And, second, they don't do as I do. They take their thoughts of disaster seriously before they have improved. So, I hope that you will go home now—after having some refreshments, of course—and will give some thought to what you have heard me say. And if you do, don't expect that from now on you will change, even if you give careful thought to what I have told you and what is only a repetition of what I used to tell you and have told you so many times. Nevertheless, once you make up your mind you want to change, in order to change, you must undergo training, and that takes time. And please don't become disappointed if you make up your mind today to use your sense of humor, and you find out that tomorrow that you have not used it. Well, that's perfectly average and human.

Goodbye.

LECTURE 18

TOTAL VIEW AND PARTIAL VIEW

21 Minutes
Recorded Saturday, December 12, 1953

The subject to be discussed this afternoon is "Total Situation and Partial Situation," or, I guess the thing reads "The Total View and Partial View." And this is a subject that is of the utmost importance to the patient. It is of extreme importance for him to know what is a total and what is a part. It's not just academic. It's not just a theoretical subject. It's an extremely practical subject.

And I will have to tell you something about totals and parts. You see a human being is always a total if he lives in a group. And should he not live in a group, there are many departments of his life that are indissolubly immersed in that thing that we call *total,* even if he does not live in a group.

But you will understand that if somebody lives in a group, then, of course, he must always consider himself as a member of the total. He must take into consideration what the neighbor will say. He must certainly see to it that he thinks of himself as a father or brother or whatever his position is in the family, a son, or if it's a woman, as the mother, and so forth. He cannot act just as a person, but, in every respect he is either a father, a son, a nephew, an employer or an employee. And so whatever he does, he finds himself integrated in a group.

Well, I will not discuss this manner of viewing the group and the total that it forms in relation to the individual.

There are other more subtle relations with regard to the total, relations of which you usually do not think, and of which I always try to remind you. Although perhaps in reminding you of your quality as a member of a total, I don't just use the word *total*. I will later tell you how I express it, as a rule.

Now look here, an animal is somehow perhaps also the member of a total. It has the young, the litter, and the mother must take care of the litter in so and so many species. And so you can say that an animal also belongs to a social group, but the quality of this total element that ties the mother to the young is perhaps very weak compared to the human mother. There are in animals certain instincts, but hardly tender sentiments, especially if the young have grown up.

At any rate, there is hardly a tender consideration for the neighbor and the friend in an animal. Perhaps there is no such thing as a neighbor and a friend. But an animal definitely has a lack of certain total relationships which are very important for human beings. And these total relationships are—and you may be surprised—that thing that we call *time*. Time. That silly thing that you read off from a watch. You see, in that I call now *the element*, and one of the foremost elements, of a total.

But you see here I am sitting, and I am so totally different from what I was twenty, thirty, forty and fifty years—I will not go any further, you know, otherwise I don't know where I'll land. Let me say I certainly was as totally different fifty years ago from what I am now that if anybody should be given a picture of me fifty years ago, he would hardly know that it is I. Yet, I was the same person then that I am now. The same ego. Well, I will not go into details. I will only tell you that humans are tied to their past, and they form one total all the time they live.

Don't think that this is a theoretical view. It is not. And as I am here, should I live on for twenty or thirty years, after thirty years I will be the same individual, somewhat different externally, but my ego will basically be the same. And if you find in me certain features, for instance a certain temperament, a certain responsiveness, a certain impressionability, be sure basically it was there when I was a youngster, and it will be there as long as I will live on retaining my functions. Naturally, if I dilapidate after a certain age, then I will no longer be the same person that I was before. But if I retain my basic mental function, my responsiveness, my impressionability, my so-called temperament, my warmth or chilliness as I may have, if I retain these functions, then in thirty years I will be the same person basically that I am now and the same person that I was then perhaps seventy or eighty years from thirty years hence.

There will be a difference, then, if I live on for another thirty years. There will be a difference of some sixty, seventy or eighty years. I will not quote the precise figure, but I will always be the same person with regard to the future and the past.

And the patient forgets that. The patient forgets that essentially one remains the same person all the time, as long as one does not disintegrate. And the patient forgets that a head pressure today is exactly the same, or more or less the same, as it was thirty years ago, and ten years ago, and five weeks ago. He forgets that. And the patient forgets that conditions don't change appreciably with regard to human feelings, human sufferings, human joys. And he forgets that his present condition is essentially the same as it was ten years ago, or five years ago, or ten weeks ago. And then the patient says, "Well, I have had this head pressure for many years. That's correct, I admit. But today it is worse." Haven't you heard that already? "Today it is the worst."

And the patient knows that for endless months and years he has walked the streets and roamed the city, and during all these days, he had the same fear of collapse, and it did not materialize. He had had a fear of collapse perhaps fifty thousand times during the time that he had his trouble and never collapsed. Nevertheless, he thinks, "Today that's different. Today I feel I am in instant danger." And you see with such statements, the patient definitely cuts off that tie that binds us to our past and creates the total, our totality in time, where we are always the same person basically.

And the patient comes to my office, and I ask him, "How has it been this past week?" Or I may not ask such a precise question and merely ask, "How have you been?" And the patient says, usually, "Oh, it was not so good, and last night it was just terrible." So, I ask him "How is it today?" "Oh, it's terrible. I don't think I can get well. I see I can just improve a little bit, and then I slip back." So, I ask him precise questions. And I tell him, "I haven't seen you for seven days. How was the beginning of the week?" And he says, "Well, I had four good days or fair days, but yesterday it was terrible."

You see, he chops up the time into several separate days. He shouldn't do that. Where is the human individual that lives only one day and another day and another day? Humans don't live such particles of time. They live a lifetime. The individual day doesn't count much. How I am today, that does not matter. The question is, how has my life been? Have I preserved my health? And now I can stand conditions much better physiologically [than] otherwise I would. Have I trained myself in the past of bearing pain patiently or not? You understand, these few items will show you the past counts in general in a human life, or the total time, not one particular hour, or one particular minute, or day. But the patient has his gaze precisely focused on one minute, on one day, one hour, when something has happened that he calls *terrible*. The patient looks at himself as a thing that lives just this hour, that day, and not the totality of a life.

And I'll go on and give you another example, but before giving this example, I want immediately to give you an idea what all of this means in terms which you know already. You see, everybody who has a pain doesn't immediately exclaim, "Oh, that's terrible. Today it's a terrible day." Everybody who has a head pressure—I have them frequently—does not immediately go into tantrums because it is unbearable. The average person bears a pain, but the patient does not want to. You realize already the average person bears a pain, especially a pain that he has had repeatedly in the past, because he is linked to the past and does not particularly consider this day but the total time of his total life. And looking back into his previous life, into this total of his life, he knows that his head pressure has been severe at many times in his history, and it hasn't killed him, and he bore it bravely and patiently, so he bears it again. He is determined to bear it again.

But the patient watches this day, and this minute, and not his past life. He is not, do you see, linked to time, integrated with it, and the present day he looks upon as if it were an isolated part in his life and not linked closely to his total life.

And since the average person insists on this linkage to the past, and he reviews the present experience in the light of his past history, and the patient does not, therefore, we can say the patient considers himself an exception to the rule. Everybody else views the past or the present in the light of the past, but the patient doesn't. He always looks at the present suffering and exclaims, "I can't tolerate that. It's intolerable. I can't bear it. It is unbearable."

And so we come back to the conception of exceptionality. The average person considers himself in the light of his past. The patient is an exception. The patient doesn't look into his past. He could get so much consolation out of looking into the past, but he doesn't. He's an exception, and he indulges in that vice which I, as you know, have called *exceptionality*, particularly the negative or undesirable exceptionality. And the patient that I mentioned who says, "Today is terrible," could, for instance, view the entire week that he has passed when he comes to my office on that day, and tell himself, "Well, I had three good days or fair days and only two, three or four bad days." And if he is a patient who comes to me in the first months of his career as my patient, or in the first or second week, and he had already three good days, that's naturally an excellent result for the first week or the second week. And if he views at least the total week, I don't say the total past, but the total week, he would immediately conclude, "Well, that's fine. I am improving and there is great hope that I will soon get well." But if he views the separate day in which he couldn't sleep and now feels fatigue and ignores the three previous days in which he had an improvement, you will understand his pessimism is due to the fact that he does not do what the average person does: to view the total past, or a large segment of the past, let me say the total week. But he always is in the habit of viewing this particular hour in which he had "this terrible headache," as he calls it, totally forgets that in the previous days, there were either no headaches or the headaches were mild and not terrible.

And you will understand that if the patient could be trained to view things in their totality and not in their isolation, as by hour or day, well, he would serve himself a great favor. He would gain the advantage of increasing his fund of health, and generally you would say the patient ought to make every effort to drop his exceptionality view, which is a particular view, as you now know, and bravely embrace the total view of his linkage to the past, the total view of his total life, and that would help him greatly. But, unfortunately, that patient has developed stubborn habits of viewing life from the viewpoint of exceptionality, which you will now know, and I hope you will remember, means something that is closely linked to that thing that we call *the partial view.*

Thank you.

THE PURPOSE OF LIFE IS
TO MAINTAIN PEACE

24 Minutes
Recorded Saturday, December 19, 1953

You heard the panel, and they told you a story, each of them one story. And it would be impossible to discuss each story separately.

There was the story of Mary. She offered to do a favor for a neighbor, and it was bungled, not by her but by her mother-in-law. And that's what we call *an event, a happening, an occurrence.* In other words, something going on either outside you, as in this particular case, or inside you, as in so many daily, hourly occasions. Indeed, every second, every minute things go on. Things don't stand still, both outside you and inside you. And what is more common than to know and to notice that there are events?

And events are sometimes embarrassing. For instance, if when Mary promised to perform a certain service and had to default on it, that's embarrassing, indeed. And other events are perhaps painful. But all of this is average, the average of events taking place and causing certain effects.

So, events are of no great importance. There are events that are extremely important—catastrophes, emergencies—but how often do they happen? We don't discuss such extraordinary situations. We discuss daily life and nothing else.

What you are likely to bungle is not an emergency. An emergency rolls on. Sometimes you can stop it. But if you can't stop it, that's no bungling. That may happen to anybody. That's an average occurrence, that human beings are unequal to emergencies or to catastrophes. But daily life is something that human beings should be adjusted to. They should be able to deal with it satisfactorily

And the question arises: If things in daily life are common, routine, easy to handle for the average person, why is there so much bungling in this world? And why particularly do my patients bungle their lives so outrageously? Their life is average, daily life, just as well as that of other people. There are very few emergencies and catastrophic events in the lives of my patients. Their life is routine, and why do they bungle it and bungle it almost systematically, almost continuously?

You will understand that there is an issue here, a problem that should be discussed and should be settled if possible. The conclusion that I want you to draw is that events in outer environment, and even in inner environment, are routine in the overwhelming majority of instances. So, adjustment should be routine, too, but you know it is not. And if adjustment is disturbed, it is not disturbed by events. That happens sometimes, but as a routine matter, it's impossible that the events that the average person disposes of with ease should be such a stumbling block to my patients. It is not the events.

It is not true, for instance, that if these fruit juice bottles that Mary bungled—that they were the cause for her commotion. That's nonsense. That's an average mistake, a routine mistake that anybody can incur, and that wouldn't disturb anybody except for a short time.

What is of importance is not the event but the attitude that you take to the event. And I want you to distinguish clearly and energetically between the event that happens in environment, either in outer environment or in inner environment, and the attitude which you take—not the event, but you. The attitude is yours. It is not of the event. And if you bungle, it's due to your attitude, and the attitude can be controlled, can be changed, can be improved. It can be omitted, it can be adopted, it can be manipulated. The event usually cannot. Events happen, and if somebody asks you a favor, that's an event. How can you prevent that? And why should you?

If anybody does something outside you, that's an event. How can you prevent events? How can you change them? They are done by somebody outside you. Or if an event takes place inside you and you have a vomiting spell, a crying reaction, or discomfort of any kind, well, that comes. You have hardly any control over it. The only thing you can do is to take an attitude that will not increase the inner discomfort, will not influence the inner event adversely. All you can do is to take a favorable attitude and not an unfavorable attitude.

And we'll ask ourselves, "What does it mean to call an attitude favorable or unfavorable?" If you want to discuss that, you will have to reach out into some sort of a philosophy, into things that are not just capable of being discussed in simple terms. They must be discussed in somewhat philosophical terms. Yet, I will not introduce technical terms and technical philosophies here. You must instead have at your fingertips two words that are very simple but that are usually not used in the context which I will present.

You see, if I deal with myself and with others, what is my purpose? Well, simply speaking, my purpose in life is to make myself and those people that are close to me—let me say the members of my family, my friends, my neighbors, and so forth, my co-workers—to make them feel good and to make myself feel good. And if you want to express it in another term, then the purpose of life is to avoid as many disturbances as possible. And another way of expressing it is, the purpose of life is to produce as much relaxation to my body and to my mind as possible, and also to the bodies and minds of other people that are close to me.

But all of it really means two things. First, to try to produce relaxation and try to prevent disturbances of relaxation. To produce . . . that thing that is the purpose of life, and to prevent interference with that thing, or disturbance of that thing that we call *the purpose of life*. You see, that's what the physician tries to do with the human body when it is disturbed.

The human body is disturbed. That means there is a disturbance; this means an imbalance of certain things that should balance. For instance, the minerals should balance among themselves. There should not be too many minerals of a certain kind and too few of another kind. They must balance. Then they are in harmony with one another. They do teamwork together, and everything in the body is then relaxed if the ingredients of the body are kept in harmony and in balance.

In the mental sphere, if one idea does not fight with the other, if there is no conflict, if there are not too many conflicts, if fear does not wipe out hope and instead fear cooperates with hope and creates just mild worry—worry being a junction of fear, mild fear and mild hope—if resentment does not wipe out peacefulness, but there is a little resentment and yet a desire for peace, then there is balance. It's not all-out peace, but not all-out resentment either. And when we view the entire body, that entire organism, both body and mind, then we say everything in body and mind should be as much at peace with one another as possible.

And so the real aim in life is peace. Before, we called it *balance* and *harmony,* but it's *peace.* And what disturbs peace is mainly temper, aside from physical disturbance. Somebody may have an organic disease, or somebody else may have been run over. Somebody else may have been shot, and so forth. We don't discuss these disturbances. When we here discuss disturbances, then we mean temper and nothing else. And so we oppose temper to peace.

You remember I told you our purpose is to have peace inside and outside, peace with people and peace with oneself. I would like to be at peace with myself and [others]. That's the purpose of life. And temper produces something that is by no means peace. It removes peace. But what it actually produces is the desire for gaining a victory over an adversary. Temper aims for victory, for beating down somebody, for holding down somebody, for telling somebody off, or telling him outright that "You are wrong."

So, temper is a fight and aims for victory, and in order to gain victory, you must use power, strength. But we call it *power.* So, will you understand that temper uses power and creates a life of power, or desire for power, appreciation of power. And the reverse of power is peace.

And so we come back to our original theme. The purpose of life is to maintain peace, peace between minerals, peace between hormones, peace between the various parts of the nervous system, and so forth, but particularly peace of mind, and peace of action, calm of action.

And if power is the reverse of peace, and temper uses power and craves power, then you understand the two forces that work in life are primarily peace and power. And the patient—and that's the only person that I speak about at present—the patient who cannot introduce or maintain peace in his interior, in his inner environment—and suffers untold agonies because of that—is, of course, not at peace. He comes to me because he wants me to restore his peace. He calls it adjustment, relaxation, ability, but essentially it is peace.

He is at war with himself, and his muscles fight against himself, and his stomach puts up reactions which are directed against the person's peace. And his entire body consists of parts that act against the total. And when parts act against a total, there is no peace. Now the patient should naturally know that his purpose in life is to have peace. And so you would imagine that that patient who has lost peace and wants to restore it again would employ peaceful means in order to restore peace, because you can't restore peace with fighting, with power, certainly not inner peace.

But the patient is a fighter. This means the patient develops temper, and through temper he strives to cure himself or to avert certain unpleasant consequences. He fights and exercises his power, so he can't find peace. And the patient's purpose, particularly, should be directed towards restoring peace. Otherwise, he can't get well. And I have to train the patient and teach him how to restore peace to his organism.

And when I begin to train him, what must I tell him? "You must reduce or eliminate your temper." And that is something that is certainly not easy to perform. And, more than that, temper means I want to gain a victory. This means I want to boost my ego. I want to be strong, powerful. I want to be the victor, and he should be the victim. And that can never bring peace. That can never bring adjustment—even if you win victories over victories, but that is not peace. And there are plenty of people that will irritate after the one victim has been downed, and there will be fighting again.

But look here, what a lure it is to a human being to be victorious, to gain victories. There is glamour in it, glory, and that is closest to one's ego. Everybody either craves glamour and glory, or he gives up because he thinks he can't achieve it. But essentially, especially in our day, in the twentieth century, glory and glamour—aside from fame and fortune—are the things that, at any rate, young people crave and the oldsters these days apparently, too.

At any rate, you will understand that glamour, the glamour of gaining a victory over somebody, is something that is close to the ego. You identify yourself with the glamour if you crave it. And so you understand my job is not just to restore peace. It is to make the patient drop something that is closest to him. And I tell you, I personally have not given up temper yet, and I will never give it up. I can't. That's human nature. And yet I keep peace within myself as much as anybody might want to do or can do.

And how do I do it? Not by giving up temper but by controlling it, holding it down. And then I gain a victory over my temper, and that makes me proud of myself. And so I gain self-control and self-pride, or self-respect let me say. And all of this counteracts against temper, and helps me [in] holding down temper. And the more self-respect I gain, the more is my temper held down. And the more it is held down, the easier it is for me to maintain self-respect and pride. And pride produces something that we call *stimulating tenseness*, and that counteracts the irritating tenseness produced by temper.

And you see, this sovereign means of combating temper is control of temper. You can't knock out temper with control, but you can hold it down and create self-respect and self-confidence. And these produce the stimulating tenseness that wipes out the irritating tenseness produced by temper. And so temper hangs in the air, it lives in a vacuum, if you control it and thereby gain self-respect, and naturally, therefore, self-confidence.

Thank you.

LECTURE 20

LEADERSHIP AND MUSCLES

20 Minutes
Recorded Saturday, December 19, 1953

Today's subject will be "Leadership and Fellowship." Now, it is important to know that leadership is necessary in every walk of life, and everybody has some field, as a rule, where he has to exercise leadership. A father, of course, has to exercise leadership with his children. A mother, just the same. I have to lead my patients. And, for instance, when I speak here now, I have to do something that is quite remarkable. I have to lead my thoughts, otherwise they will become confused. They will jump to conclusions. They will, perhaps, not play a game of teamwork, one thought with the other. I am now going to discuss one theme, and I must see to it that no thought, no concept, gets into this theme that does not fit into it. You see, a simple speech means leadership.

Well, it will be necessary for you to know what it requires to be a leader and to exercise leadership, whether it is the leadership of the doctor with his patients, the father with his children, or a person wielding a theme, for instance, in a conversation, not only in a speech. You must be precise in /your conversations. You must be straight. You must not permit any thought to flow into the conversation that does not belong there. And there are fields of leadership which are commonly known. Let me say, the government leads a state, or a city, or a nation. And there must be leadership in the manner in which the government leads the state or the nation. A business executive leads his employees, and you understand leadership there is all over, and a leader leads many people, as a rule. He may only lead one person, for instance, a father, his only son or only daughter, but usually a leader leads several people or many people. And these many people have diverse and different and individual tastes and dispositions and wishes and cravings. And if you deal with many people with different characteristics, with different trends, they may work against one another. And the leader has to array them in such a group that they work together, that they produce teamwork. The leader has to do that. He has to produce the teamwork. But producing teamwork is not so difficult. Maintaining it, that is much more difficult. Moreover, not disturbing it, that's of great importance.

And a leader has to have certain qualities in order not to disturb the teamwork of those he leads. Of course, a leader must have honesty, integrity, character, perhaps initiative. That's understood. If a leader is dishonest, then he is no leader. But no matter how honest a leader may be, how much integrity he may have, how much ability he may have, that's not the main thing in leadership. The main thing is that the leader does not, must not, confuse the flock that he leads. And he must not irritate them, arouse their tempers. So, a leader must first have a clear conception of what he is pursuing, of the goal he aims at.

Second, he must not have temper. At least he must not display it. If he has no clear conception of what he wants, he will confuse the men who work with him or work under him. And if he has temper, there develops a situation that is very tragic. First, with his temper he will irritate his group. And if the men working under him are irritated continually, frequently, how can they produce teamwork? They become irritable and naturally irritate one another, too. They develop temper because of the leader's irritations.

[Third], a leader must not be inconsistent. He must always go about his business in the same manner as the business requires and in the same manner that he has done before. He must not be inconsistent. He must not contradict himself. He must not be arbitrary and jump from one subject to another, from one plan to another. Otherwise, the people again become confused and irritable.

Well, I am not interested in government, not here at any rate. I am not interested here in business, not even in the relationship of father to son and mother to daughter. I am interested in patients. I am not even, at present, speaking of my leadership that I give my patients. I simply speak of the patient himself. And the patient has to be a leader to himself, and that's very difficult to be. He must not disturb himself, not irritate himself, not confuse himself. See, the patient must naturally not develop temper. The patient leads his muscles. He gives them orders. The muscles he can order to do a certain job. Once they receive an order, muscles carry it out. But the leader, this means the patient, must be a leader to his muscles, and, as I told you, he must not confuse them. He must not irritate them.

But if he has temper, then he becomes confused himself. The patient becomes confused himself, and then he confuses his organs. That does not mean that the organs think and can be confused in their thoughts. I don't mean that. I am not that mystical to assume that muscles think. But the muscles become confused in the following manner: You see, if you say that somebody is confused, that means instead of having one plan, he has two contradictory plans. That's confusion. Then he doesn't know which plan to pursue, which goal to follow. And that's exactly the same with the muscles, except that the muscles have no plans that we know of. But the muscles can get two contradictory orders.

A patient can meet a friend on the street, and he gives his muscles the order to stretch out the arm and shake hands with the friend, and he tells the cheek muscles to go into a smile. And all of a sudden he becomes temperamental, fearful. Then he sends down the order to the muscles not to stretch out the arm, not to smile. That doesn't mean that he actually sends the orders, but suddenly the fear grips him, and then he sends down the order to the muscles. This means the fear sends down the order to be careful, to hold back, to step not too lively, to be on guard. And if the muscles in one minute get the order to smile, this means not to be on guard, and the arms get the order to be stretched out in order to shake hands, this means naturally in a friendly manner, and then immediately they get the contradictory impulses to be on guard and not to stretch out the arm because the brain may have two plans: the one plan being generosity, to deal generously with that man that I meet, and the other plan, to be careful. This means to exercise caution, to be rather a little suspicious than confident. And so the muscles receive two contradictory orders at the same time.

And the muscles do not become confused as people may be confused, but they get two contradictory orders. The one order tells the muscles, "Release now stimulating tenseness." The other order tells the muscles, "Release now irritating tenseness." And that's contradiction, and, in a sense, you can call it *confusion.* The muscles don't know which order to follow. And if muscles get two contradictory orders at the same time, all they can do is to create tenseness or to begin to tremble or to stiffen up or all three together. And then there is no action. And you will understand that the patient can in this manner confuse the muscles, irritate them, throwing them into tenseness and spasms and in tremors. This means making them react like you react in temper: tenseness, stiffness. And that's what the muscles do, and then there is no leadership. The person doesn't exercise guidance, doesn't give guidance. And if this happens, the person notices that the muscles don't do as he wants them to do, so he now becomes more irritated, more suspicious that there may be something wrong with him, and therefore more temperamental. And a vicious cycle develops.

The more the person becomes suspicious and the more temper that he develops, the stiffer become the muscles, the more do they tremble, the tenser they grow. And the more tense they grow, the more temperamental becomes the person, this means the patient. And a vicious cycle is [a]foot.

And then the patient—now I call him *the patient* instead of *the person*—and now the patient is working up his temper. He becomes desperate because he can't get his muscles to do what they should do. And the more temperamental that he becomes, the more irritable he is. And then there are people around him—either his wife or his children or his workers, if he has some. And now, being irritable, he talks in terms of irritation. He blames the wife, and he complains in terms of anger. Now the wife becomes irritated, and she talks back. She asserts her viewpoint against his, so he becomes more irritated. And you understand vicious cycle is piled on other vicious cycles.

And I take it you will understand that your leadership is of the poorest—not because you have symptoms, distressing symptoms, torturing symptoms—but because you don't let the symptoms disappear as you work up your temper. The symptoms become worse, your irritability becomes worse, and now you disturb your home life, so you disturb your body and bodies outside you.

And you will now understand why here in Recovery we emphasize the supreme importance of controlling temper and of you learning how to control temper. The importance derives from the fact that you must establish leadership over your body and over your mind. And I will add what I usually emphasize here if you are to be re-educated here, in terms of regaining leadership over your body, that cannot be done in a short space of time. That requires long-term training, which we supply. And all you have to do is to avail yourself of the training opportunities offered by Recovery. And then you may be assured that you will regain the lost leadership over your body and will finally get well.

Thank you.

PERFECTIONISM VERSUS
HUMAN LIMITATIONS

32 Minutes
Recorded Saturday, January 30, 1954

You heard Vicky, who sat to my right here, telling you about her condition. And let me tell you that this condition—the feeling that somebody is dying away—is about the most agonizing thing that I have ever heard about. And be sure I have heard of a multitude of agonies.

I have heard not quite half a dozen of such patients, so they are very rare. I have never found them described in the literature, so others must not have seen many of them, and maybe too many of my colleagues have never seen a case like this, I am certain. Because you understand if I, with my expanding mass of patients, have only seen a handful of such patients, then be sure others, who have an ordinary amount of patients, most likely have very seldom seen such cases. And many of them have never seen them, I guess.

So, Vicky is suffering from a most frightful condition and has only had some relief the past few days. And there she sits here, and did you notice any sign of suffering in her features? Did you notice any trembling of her voice, any strain in her cheeks or in her total carriage? If this can happen, if a condition of such frightfulness can suddenly disappear without leaving a trace behind, how can such a condition be dangerous? I hope you will ponder this question. And we deal here with a most severe condition.

And Vicky told you that she has always been a perfectionist. Well, I may tell you that what she meant, or might have meant and most likely did mean, was that having been a perfectionist all her young life, well, her fears, her panics must have something to do with her perfectionism. In other words, people who are perfectionists are likely to develop nervous symptoms.

Don't engage in such reasoning. In all likelihood, if you wish to study the subject, if you could study it, you would find that there are very few mothers and wives that are not perfectionists. About husbands, I'm not going to say anything. I am somehow suspicious of husbands. Well, the suspicion is very simply grounded. It's understood that husbands do not have as sensitive feelings as wives have, as women have. There is no question about it. Husbands are blunt in their feelings. This means men, men whether they are married or not. And wives, this means women, are sensitive in their feeling reactions. But be sure there are sensitive people among men. There are blunt people among women. But generally speaking, there is this preponderance of sensitive souls among women. And rather, let me say *blunt*—I wanted to say *robust*. I might have said something worse than that, and I have seen the worst men that meant well and yet were quite brutal, not as husbands, but otherwise, and maybe as husbands, too. I have seen that. At any rate, you will understand, women, being very sensitive, are more likely to be perfectionists than men.

Now, what is wrong with perfectionism? I hope that I have some element of perfectionism in myself. As a matter of fact, what we call *perfectionism* is the desire to do the perfect job, and that's what the Bible tells you. You should do the perfect job, and that's what you call *the ideal*. People who have ideals—what does that mean? Such people strive to do the perfect job, to live a perfect life, to think in perfect truth. And if you wish to call this *perfectionism*—which I don't—then you will realize that the term *perfectionism* has something to do with ideals. And don't look down on perfectionistic people. Don't look down your nose at them. They, perhaps, are somehow oriented [to] what we call *the ideal life*, the ideal action, which is nothing wrong, be sure.

And yet people say—and the textbooks say it—that if you are a perfectionist, you are likely to develop a nervous ailment. I don't believe so, and I don't want you to think so. Anyone of you who has developed a nervous ailment has suffered a happening that happened to you. You didn't manufacture it through your character. And remember, if you call somebody a perfectionist, this means you say he has a perfectionist character. And then you reduce his nervous ailment to his character. And, of course, you have learned this statement and this philosophy from, well, from psychologists and psychiatrists and sociologists, from people who ought to know better.

If you say that your nervous condition is due to your character, then your character must be not so good, certainly not so valuable, not so useful. Then it is harmful and no value if it produces such conditions as Vicky suffers from, this feeling of dying away. What's the use having any character, then, if the character can cause nervous ailments? And don't believe that. Although the statement is made on very high authority, don't believe it.

If you have a cold, that does not flow from your character. You know that, I hope. And if you develop a pimple, that does not follow from your character. If it did, then change your character, if you can. If your character can become your enemy, drop it, if you can. I don't know how to drop a character, but if it could be done, then do it.

That thing that we call *sickness*—of any kind—it does not have to be a severe sickness at all—that thing that we call sickness is given you by fate, not by yourself, not by your character. There simply are a number of people in every group that have weaknesses of this kind and of other kinds. I have yet to see the human being that has no weaknesses. If there were such a human being, well then he would be a hero, maybe a saint, maybe a wizard, but not human.

Human beings have their limitations, both in mind and in body, and the one has his limitations in that part of the body that we call *digestion*. He has been born with a disposition to poor digestion, or he has acquired it through some infection, let me say. That's all fate and not character. Fate had given you an infection, and the infection attacked your digestive system, and now you are saddled with weak digestion. And fate has given you, for instance, a so-called *allergy*, and now you are saddled with weak bronchi, weak sinuses, or any other kind of weakness. And so it goes.

And if you want to say that fate was against you, well, I have no objection, but don't say that your character did it—no matter who is the high authority that makes the statement, and I have heard this statement from people who are considered to be high in the ranks of the profession. So, let's drop this subject of perfectionism as the cause of sickness or ailment.

But I will agree that perfectionism is something that should be tempered, that should be handled in such a manner that it is whittled down. And the reason is not because it flows from a wrong character. The reason is different. Perfectionism means, "I want to be perfect in my functions."

You see, an automobile, if it runs, is perfect. An automobile is perfect if it's a good automobile. If it has one little fault, then it's no good. The pedal will perhaps not work; then the automobile is no good. Even if the entire remnant of the automobile is perfection, if one part of it is poor, then the whole thing is poor.

If you want this perfection in which every part must measure up to the highest standard, then you'll have to become a machine. If you want to be human, you can't have it. Machines are perfect, and if they are not, they are useless, perfectly useless, until they are repaired. But without repair, they are useless.

Human beings have their limitations. Machines may be perfect, but who wants to be a machine? Do you? I doubt it. I want to be human, and as a human being, I have my limitations and my weaknesses. Fortunately, I have very few weaknesses, but I am one of those people that have been born—there is no question about that—that have been born with a weakness. I still have some of it, but I have largely overcome it.

All of a sudden, at the age of fourteen or fifteen—I don't remember correctly; it's quite some time back now—at this tender age, I developed a severe nervous condition. And in those days— as I say, it's a little far back, in the midst of the early 20th century—in those days, people did not immediately run to a psychiatrist. As a matter of fact, there were very few psychiatrists. Specialization had just begun.

And I went to my family physician, to our family physician. And when I came to him, I naturally didn't tell him why I came to him. I told him I had a pain in the chest, which I didn't have. That was not imagination. It was simply a fib. I was afraid to tell him what I suffered from, or ashamed to tell him. And since I told him about a pain in the chest, he examined my chest, and so I was sure he wanted to look for tuberculosis. And when he gave me a prescription, I was sure, well, that was T.B. The poor fellow had given me a new idea, but this idea wouldn't have taken with me if I didn't have a weakness in the nervous system that affected my sensitiveness. I became too sensitive in these days. I watched myself closely. Then I watched the doctor while he wrote the prescription, and I thought his face told me a story. He was worried, I thought. Whether he was, who knows? And so I was sure I had T.B.

Fortunately, in those days, it was not so easy to get a doctor to talk about diagnoses. He merely told me, "Well, you will be well very soon. Just take this medicine." And I went to the druggist and had the prescription filled, and I asked him, "Can you tell me what this prescription says?" And in those days, the druggists were not talkative. So, he told me, "Well, it's a good prescription. You just take it." So I was saved the agony of being given a diagnosis. Because if the druggist had told me, "Well, there is nothing wrong with you. The doctor prescribed something that doesn't mean a sickness," then I would have immediately concluded, as my patients do, "He didn't tell me the truth." Then my imagination would have gone on racing and roaring, and I would certainly have been sure that I had tuberculosis.

Well, you see, I suffered from this condition for years: aside from the fear of tuberculosis, also from palpitations and headaches and flushes and all kinds of things. And finally, it disappeared. Fate was kind to me. And without treatment it disappeared, but I had a weakness. And I still have it, and some of the symptoms are still with me, although they have no duration. They come and go, and if they attain duration, they don't bother me because they are very mild, and that's what we call *a cure*.

Symptoms still come, because everybody has symptoms. Don't let anybody tell you that they have no headaches and no fatigue and no tenseness. That's nonsense. Everybody has symptoms, nervous symptoms if he is human, if he lives and doesn't just vegetate. But if a person, a nervous person, reaches the stage where his symptoms come and go, and then even if they stay on, they are mild, then we call him *a nervous person* who, however, is no longer a nervous patient.

And if you distinguish between the nervous person and the nervous patient, then you will know that both have the same assortment of symptoms—naturally not identically the same. But both have nervous symptoms, the difference being that the one doesn't suffer from them to any great extent because they are mild and fleeting. And the other produces panics and vicious cycles, and, therefore, the symptoms gain in intensity and in duration. And that's the entire difference between a nervous person and a nervous patient. And I will advise you to read that article in my book or in the *Recovery News*—I don't remember—which makes this sharp distinction between nervous persons and nervous patients.

Now, Vicky definitely is a nervous patient. And she feels that she is dying away physically. And Elizabeth told you that she is working with a group of girls, and one girl, being very nosey, asked her, "How much did you make yesterday?" Well, that's a very nosey and presumptuous question, and the girl shouldn't have asked such a question. But once this question is asked, then something is done to a woman as sensitive as women tend to be—and Elizabeth is certainly a sensitive woman.

So her temper is aroused; she told you her temper was aroused or her feelings were hurt. She felt that her feelings were hurt, and then temper arose out of these hurt feelings. And she controlled her temper and didn't show it, and before long, it disappeared. That's all to the good.

But what happened to Elizabeth? Why were her feelings hurt? Well, you will immediately realize a question of this kind means disrespect for the privacy of a person. Nobody has any business spying on me and asking personal questions, and this is a personal question. If they do, then they deny me respect, and they disturb, or try to disturb, my privacy. This is definitely a private affair as to whether anybody does a lot of business or less business, whether they make good money or less good money. That's all private, and privacy should be respected. And this woman showed disrespect for the privacy of Elizabeth. And it's perfectly legitimate, then, to have one's feelings hurt.

Now, if my feelings are hurt—suppose they are badly hurt—then I feel that something in me at this moment dies away, something that is extremely important to my life. Privacy is very important to my life. But more important yet is respect due me from others. And if they don't show me the respect they owe me, then I feel something has—something, perhaps a tiny part of my being—has died away for the moment. I'm pretty sure it will revive again.

You see, I identify myself with the respect people owe me and give me or deny me. That's what I call *my reputation:* the respect that I get from others. And reputation in a community, I mean for one living in a community, is a very vital subject. That is a good part of my life to have a good reputation. And you will understand if somebody asks such an impertinent question, he or she showed disrespect. And if I take it seriously, then I feel something dies away in me, perhaps only for a brief moment, and will then revive.

And Elizabeth, feeling that something in her was on the point of dying away, apparently did not get too scared. She developed temper, but she controlled it, controlled it so it couldn't have been a massive blow that she experienced. She only experienced a little stab, not a blow, and she handled it accordingly. She kept her composure, kept quiet, and there was peace in her body and mind after a short time. And that's what we call *the result*, the excellent result of Recovery training: to be human, to be hurt in one's feelings, to develop temper but to hold it down, control it, and by controlling it, maintaining your peace and relaxation.

Well, I wish that Vicky would do the same. She has done an excellent job in the past few days, and I have noticed an improvement in the past few weeks. But that wasn't enough for her yet, and she waited till she would have a complete or a perfect improvement. Then she was ready to admit it. But I had noticed the improvement several weeks ago, and have noticed it advancing at pace.

And if this is an improvement, as she cannot deny, why doesn't she do something which she might do? But I suppose she doesn't do it too perfectly. Why doesn't she make up her mind now, right now, that this is not the cure yet. This is merely the beginning improvement. And since there is a beginning improvement, why doesn't she know that this trouble will come back? If she made herself think, reflect, on the necessity, on the inevitability of symptoms coming back— and they always come back again until there is a cure—but as long as there is merely an improvement—and be sure this is not a cure yet, this is only an improvement—why doesn't Vicky right now make up her mind she is not out of the woods yet?

If she did, then she would expect a setback, tomorrow or next week, or, let us hope, at a farther distance, let me say next month. And then if she expected it, then she would not be floored. She would not be struck down when the setback arrives. If she keeps calm, expecting the setback to come, then when it comes, it will not scare her. She expected it, and it came, so she's not disappointed. She got her expectations fulfilled.

Well, you laugh, and I understand that you laugh and why you laugh, but this is a fact. Patients have to learn not to believe that an initial improvement is the cure. It is only the improvement. If they think that this is the cure, then they have this famous attitude: "Well, I got it licked." But it isn't licked. But if they think they've got it licked, this means if they think they are cured, and then they go into raptures about being well, and then the next day the thing comes back, then they are struck down. And they become discouraged and demoralized, and they say, "Look here, even Recovery and Dr. Low can't help me." And I know that Vicky has had this philosophy of hopelessness from a long time, and she can avoid that by expecting the setback to come. And the more she expects it, the more calm will she be right now; and she will be calm when the setback comes if she knows, as I have told her and I have told you, that the setback is no danger. And if she expects it calmly, she will not be fearful.

LECTURE 22

THE PATIENT AND THE PHYSICIAN FORM
AN INTIMATE GROUP

24 Minutes
Recorded Saturday, January 30, 1954

We will discuss today the subject of "Total Views and Partial Viewpoints." Now, everybody must have a view for the following reason: As we live our life, we have to perform acts, and an act goes towards a goal. I, for instance, have set myself the goal of treating patients, of rearing a family. These are perhaps the biggest goals that I have set myself. And in order to reach the goals, I have to employ means that will make me attain the goal. And therefore I must have a view. I must view the goals and ask myself continuously, "Are these goals well chosen? Do I really advance in the direction of these goals?" And while I advance towards the goals, I must continuously ask myself, "Do I employ the correct means in advancing towards the goals?"

The means must then be viewed as to whether they are adequate or not, and the goal must constantly be sighted as to whether it still serves my purpose. And you will understand that one must not only view a part of the goals or a part of the means but the total of the goal and the total of the means.

Not only this, I must also view myself as to whether I am capable of reaching the goal and using the means. Somebody else might be capable of doing it and I might not. Then I may have to give up a goal and choose another goal, and, you see, in all of these circumstances one must have a view, and a total view. I must not only view my goals and my means but also myself as to whether these means and goals are within my power, my capacity to handle them.

Now, all of this sounds philosophical, and you have not come here to get a lesson in philosophy. You are patients, or relatives of patients, and what I am speaking of is not the views of anybody in general, but I should speak of your views. And I should ask myself, "How do my patients set up goals, how do they choose the means, and how do they view them?"

You see, a patient, like everybody else, is a person whom we call *a self*. He handles himself. He advances himself if he does. He deals with his own self. And if he advances towards a goal, he advances towards it in a group. Everybody who does not live in the wilds lives in a group. And now the patient has to view himself and his group, and it will be good for you to know what kind of groups there are.

If you walk in the street, you are among a group of people, but you don't know them, or you may not know them, and they are a loose group. They are ten thousand people that hardly belong together. They are simply a mass of humanity, and we call that *a loose group*.

And there are close groups, for instance, the groups of myself and my friends. And there are certain groups that are particularly important, for instance, the family. The family is not a loose group; that's a very close group. But it distinguishes itself from other close groups by being, in addition, an intimate group. In the family, one is not only close but intimate. There, one speaks of things that [one] would not even reveal to friends, to colleagues, to neighbors, all of which are close groups, but they are not intimate groups. And after you know these three varieties of groups, I will call your attention to one par . . . —no smoking—to one particular group which is extremely close and extremely intimate, and that is the group, or ought to be the group, of the patients and their physician.

A patient and his physician are, of course, an intimate group, at any rate with regard to health. And health is the major concern of you. So I and you form an intimate group. And in this group, that has as its characteristics closeness and intimacy, in this group, if it is to be intimate, there must take place one factor without which there can't be intimacy. And that is mutual understanding. Without mutual understanding, there is no intimacy. And mutual understanding means that somebody whom I want to understand and whom I want to understand me, we two—the somebody and I—must have approximately the same views. They must have, in other words, the same outlook, the same approach, not in every respect but in important respects.

They must certainly approach one another with a good measure of respect, with a good measure of devotion, of love, but mainly of respect. And if they are devoted to one another and respect one another, they will do that thing that you call *seeing eye-to-eye*. This means viewing things in more or less the same manner, and there is what we call *an identity of views*.

I may tell you that unfortunately this does not prevail in every intimate group. There are too many families—this means in intimate groups—in which there is strife and discord and lack of mutual understanding. But fortunately there are many families in which the reverse prevails. If there is strife and discord and lack of mutual understanding between physician and patient, then they better part company.

It has been my privilege to establish a very intimate contact between myself and my patients. And you will understand, therefore, that between me and my patients, there is a minimum of friction, a minimum of strife and an optimum, or perhaps even sometimes a maximum, of mutual understanding and mutual respect.

But that can only be accomplished if I succeed in making the patient see eye-to-eye with me on the problems of nervous and mental health. And fortunately I succeed in the overwhelming majority of cases—but not in the beginning. And in the beginning a situation develops where the patient does not see eye-to-eye with me in reference to his health. I tell the patient that his condition entails much suffering but no danger whatever. And if I make this statement, then be certain it is based on solid experience, and you are convinced of the solidity of my experience. And yet, for weeks and weeks, you continue to think and to say that your condition is not beyond danger, that your condition has the element of danger, and that's what we call *making a diagnosis*.

And in an intimate group, there are functions assigned to everybody. For instance, in a family, the mother has her special functions, and the little child has no business to interfere with the functions of the mother. The little child cannot take over the functions of the mother; neither can the father. And the mother should not take over the functions of the child or of the father.

And a similar situation obtains between the patient and the physician. I have my functions, and the patient has his functions. My function is to make the diagnosis and to institute treatment. The diagnosis which I make may take a certain wording, but in the main, it means there is absence of danger. That is the essence of my diagnosis.

But then one day, after I have examined the patient, the patient comes to my office and makes some statement, for instance, the statement, "I had one good day, but today I am again in an awful distress. I don't think," the patient continues, "that your method will help me." You see, with this, the patient makes a diagnosis, although he doesn't use any fancy designation to diagnose his case. But he says, "Your method will not help me." And that is a diagnosis that his condition is in danger of being with the wrong doctor, or being treated by the wrong doctor. That is a diagnosis.

The patient comes to me and tells me, "Well, I came to your meetings, and the cases that were discussed are different from mine." The patient here makes a diagnosis. He knows what the cases mean, how they differ from one another, as if I didn't know. And in all these matters and these manners, the patient sets himself up as a diagnostician. He steps in on my territory. He takes over my function. And the patient does that and pays for it heavily in terms of punishment, self-punishment, in terms of suffering.

You know, if you have consulted a physician and have engaged to be treated by him, and then you feel it's not the right physician, that's agony. You feel that you are lost. You feel that you will not get the help that you are entitled to seek and to get. And then with all this self-diagnosing—of which I have only quoted two examples but which I could multiply by the hundreds—in all these instances in which the patient self-diagnoses, he only inflicts punishment on himself. He would act logically if he then dropped me as his physician and went to somebody else. But, of course, we know he will continue on his course of self-diagnosing, even if he goes to fifteen and twenty successive physicians.

Fortunately, I have developed a method which has certain virtues. But the one particular virtue that it has is that my patients stick to me, no matter how much they inveigh against me, no matter how much they sabotage me and take over my function and self-diagnose. Nevertheless, as you see here in this room, somehow or other my method attracts the patients and keeps them bound to me in spite of the fact that they have their grave doubts as to whether they are with the right doctor.

Now let me, in conclusion, tell you the patient will do well, this means you will do well, if you finally make up your mind radically and thoroughly to stop self-diagnosing. Accept my diagnosis. I have the experience, of course, with thousands of conditions and patients. You have the experience with your own case. That's no experience. That is the experience of one case. And even if you say that you have a very close and intimate knowledge of your case, I grant you, you have. You have the knowledge that I don't have. I don't know whether your heart is now palpitating, whether your stomach is tightening up right now. I don't know that. You know, but do you understand what that means? Do you understand whether that means danger or security? You feel what you feel inside, but you don't know what it means. It is only the diagnosis, made by a competent and experienced man, that gives the meaning to your suffering, and that's, of course, very important. If I [know] what your condition signifies, then I can pick the correct treatment according to my experience, which is seasoned.

And, finally, I will tell you, in this patient-physician relationship—which is close and intimate, as intimate as any relation ever will be—in this situation, the patient must see eye-to-eye with me. But I must also see eye-to-eye with the patient. What it means for the patient to see eye-to-eye with me, I told you. And now I will tell you in a few words the meaning of my seeing eye-to-eye with the patient, but only in matters in which the patient is competent to form an opinion.

And the patient is competent to say that he feels very tired. He is competent to say that now he has an awful pressure in the head. He is competent to say that his memory is poor, and so forth. He is competent to state what he feels.

And I think I have seen eye-to-eye with my patients. I have studied carefully what they suffer from, the various distresses they experience. And in an intimate situation, it is of the utmost importance that one takes the suffering of a partner—and the patient is my partner, although he is the junior partner, don't forget that—in an intimate situation, it is extremely important that the senior partner should show understanding of what the junior partner states, and feels, and experiences.

It is of extreme importance that the senior partner should not be sarcastic, facetious. That he should take the patient's suffering seriously. He should not say, "Oh, you are just imagining." That's such a ridiculous statement. I have never learned how anybody can imagine a head pressure. Either one feels it or one doesn't feel it, but how to imagine it, I don't know. I have tried. I try right now to imagine how a head pressure works, but my images don't come. I know how it works from the reports of patients, but not from my own imagination. And if somebody tells a patient, "Oh, you imagine your headaches," what does he mean by that? He means you manufacture them. He means you haven't had, or you don't have, a headache. You merely imagine it. You merely believe you have one. That's a very ribald [worthless] statement. Who is competent to say that he feels a headache except the one who has it? I, the physician, don't know whether he right now has a headache or not. But if the patient tells me he has a headache, why should I doubt that? The patient doesn't come to me for fun. He comes in a serious endeavor, and, in addition, he even pays a fee, and why he should pay a fee for a fib that he tells me, I don't know.

So will you please, will you please drop this silly suspicion that nervous patients imagine their headaches. That means that they don't have them and merely guess or believe that they have one.

Thank you.

LIFE CONSISTS OF TRIVIALITIES

23 Minutes
Recorded Saturday, February 6, 1954

You remember what Fanny told you. She was asked by the boss to do something, to compile some numbers, some figures, and she did. And then some girls complimented her, and one girl made some slurring remark. The majority of the workers apparently paid her compliments. That's not the point that I want to touch on, although I could bring out the fact that Fanny, years ago, would not have been able to stand up under such a situation. This situation would have been an ordeal for her, this means for her nerves. And today she manages this situation with skill, without getting ruffled, without becoming aroused to fear or anger. So she has really learned how to spot in the manner which our patients are taught to do in Recovery. But, as I said, I will not discuss this aspect of the event that she reported. I will rather tell you that most of you who are my patients have come to me at one time or other and have criticized these panel discussions.

I am part of this panel event, in that I discuss what the panel members say. And I must admit none of these patients have ever criticized my part in the panel discussion. I am grateful to them for that. But they criticize severely what the patients say. They don't say that the patients talk nonsense. They don't criticize the contents, the logical contents, of what the patients say. But they come up to me with the remark, "Well, what the patients at the Saturday panel say are trivialities." And I tell them, "I hope they are. I don't want them to discuss anything but trivialities."

Briefly, I will tell you life consists of trivialities, of very little else. If you find out, if you try to find out what you worry about, it's trivialities. Whether you should, for instance, buy a certain item or not. Whether you should buy it now or wait till the price goes down, you know. Should you spend money on certain unnecessary things, or should you save the money, and so forth. These are trivialities. And if you begin to worry about your children, the children don't do anything but what we call *trivialities*. They don't start political action, be sure not. And let's hope they don't commit crimes. I hope they don't. And it has not yet come to the point where crime has become a triviality, this means an average happening.

But the average person deals with average happenings that are naturally in the nature of trivialities. You eat, you sleep, you walk, you visit, you talk over the phone. That takes up perhaps 90 percent of your waking day, if not 98 percent. Life consists of trivialities mainly. How often does it happen in the average family that the father dies? Well, once in a lifetime, naturally. Or that somebody else dies? Once in a lifetime. It's not a common, average, trivial thing. How often does it happen that somebody in the family gets married, that somebody gets born, and so forth? The big item, well, how often does it happen that the house burns down, and so forth? I could go on indefinitely. Whatever you call a big item happens once in a lifetime, as a rule, and sometimes never.

Even of this I didn't want to speak. I could have mentioned that the critics should consider this matter of life being trivial. It's very important as a total, but its individual events and actions are naturally trivialities. There are only a few persons that must constantly watch out in matters of their responsibilities, who must establish a high record of responsible action, of vigilance, of constant looking out. Well, that's a mayor of a big city, or the mayor of a city, the President of the United States, and a few other people, a general in the army, they, of course, deal with very important items. Their lives are not or should not be filled with trivialities. But the average individual lives a life choked with trivialities. As I set out, about this I didn't want to tell you much either. I only wanted to mention it.

What I wanted to tell you is as follows: These trivialities of everyday life have one peculiarity: that they either are not noticed because they don't interest you, or they cheer you because they please you, or they anger you or scare you. Even the simplest triviality can scare you. If your children are misbehaved, after all, if it's not a high degree of misbehavior, it's a triviality. But it can scare the mother that her darling is so unmannered. It can give her all kinds of misgivings about the future of her son. You see, trivialities crowd the life, but any one of them may arouse your anger, your fear, your disgust, your terror, and so forth. Any one of them. After all, in the life of a mother, the fact that the baby cries is a triviality. The fact that the baby today doesn't eat is a triviality. And a thousand things that the baby does are trivialities. But the mother may work herself up over each and every of these trivialities. And will you understand, the closer is a relation between one individual and the other, the more can the trivialities performed by the one person irritate and frustrate and anger and scare the other person if they are a close unit, like mother and baby, or other such associations.

Now, we are interested here in nervous reactions. Our purpose is to get our patients rid of their nervous symptoms, of their fears, of their obsessions, of their palpitations, fatigue, inability to sleep, and whatever these reactions and symptoms are. Now, you would never have developed your symptoms—or, if you had developed them, they wouldn't have continued with you and taken on duration—if you had not developed the process that I call *processing*. This means working yourself up. And that means to be irritated, to become angry, to become fearful, to become disgusted. If you hadn't developed the habit of getting disgusted so easily, of getting scared in a moment, and of keeping up the scare, and the fear, and the disgust for days, weeks, months and years—if you had not done that, in other words, if you had avoided both outside temper and inner temper (I told you about the inner temper this afternoon)—if you had avoided the outer and inner temper, you would have lost your symptoms in no time. Your symptoms. In no time. Symptoms don't develop duration if people keep calm, if they keep relaxed. And you can't relax if the trivialities of daily life irritate you and scare you and anger you.

Well, I could go on endlessly in this list. I'll rather call it: There is *temper*, and temper creates *tenseness*, and if you develop tenseness, then the tenseness presses against your nerves, and your nerves will develop *symptoms*. Not necessarily mine. I can tolerate tenseness, the tenseness of worry and of anger, very beautifully. And, therefore, the anger disappears soon, and the tenseness disappears soon, and I develop symptoms that last only a second or a few seconds, at the most a number of minutes. But you are so riled by the events, the trivial events of average daily life, that you develop a monstrous temper that lasts for days, for weeks, for months. And then your nerves are put under this heavy pressure of tenseness for months or for weeks, with some of you, for years.

And do you understand now what is the meaning of the trivialities of everyday life? Don't snub them. Don't sneer at them. I want my patients to learn how to deal with trivialities. I want you to learn not to get upset by trivialities, or except for a moment, for a few moments. And I don't know how to treat nervous conditions except by beating down your temper, precisely by making you handle without temper the trivialities of daily life.

And if you wish to be trained in Recovery, then I advise you, be prepared when you come here or when you come to the daily classes, to listen to nothing but to trivialities. Whenever a patient here at the panel mentions big things as examples, after the meeting, I take him aside—if I don't forget to do it—I take him aside and tell him, "Will you kindly go back in your next example to the trivialities of everyday life? We don't want anything else discussed here but trivialities." That means but life. That's life.

If you think that discussing the Republicans and Democrats is life, that's nonsense. Life is to get sore at a fellow who doesn't look at you or a fellow who stares at you, a fellow who talks too much or a fellow who doesn't talk at all. That's life. In addition, it is also to eat a poor meal or a good meal. If you eat a poor meal, then you live up to your anger. If you could eat a good meal, then you are filled with joy. That's life. Utterly trivial.

But there are people, and you know, you read about them in my book till you get nauseated, perhaps, and they are called *intellectuals*. I once have been one of them until I gave up. I didn't give up my intellect but my intellectualism. That's an awful thing that somebody should be an intellectualist. This means he should show his cleverness. He should be insistent that he is right and somebody else wrong in arguments. He should start arguments with everybody, with his closest friends. These intellectualists meet in order to have arguments about politics, about the economy and about private life perhaps, too. Mostly about art, economy, religion, politics—precisely the things that can offend people. That's what they like to discuss, you know. My patients have no business discussing intellectualist subjects. I never do that when I am home. Never. I guess never. Very seldom, at least.

When I am home, then I want to enjoy the trivialities of my family life. That's grand. When anything big happens in my family life, well, that's a sector of our life. That's a small sector of life. And people come to me and tell me, "Well, yesterday or last week or three months ago, something terrible happened, and I couldn't tolerate it. I couldn't get adjusted to it. I'm still awfully excited, and whenever anybody mentions something that reminds me of this event, well, I go all to pieces." I have observed such patients repeatedly, and whether they go to pieces, I don't know. I haven't seen the pieces of them yet, but that's how they talk. They go to pieces.

And when you ask them what happened, well, an uncle died, or perhaps a mother died.

Now, the fact a mother dies is really not a triviality. You will understand. That's a very significant event. But why should anybody go to pieces over that? It was to be expected that anybody will die. Do you understand, these daughters and sons that go to pieces over the death of their mothers do something that they must never do, that they should learn not to do: and that is, they work themselves up. Naturally, there is no going to pieces over a natural event. Everybody naturally expects a mother and a father and everybody to die. And if they die, then you should have the proper response, the proper feeling. And the proper feeling is to think, to have a loving remembrance of your mother. But if you work yourself up and go to pieces, then you think of yourself and not of the mother. Then you think in what danger you are because you are so shaken up. Then you think of yourself.

And if a mother has a sick child, and she yells and cries, "Oh, how can I stand it?" then she thinks of herself and not of the child. The child now needs a calm mother that will do the right thing. And that mother should be sad and not excited. If she really wants to do something about her child, or if the mother dies and she wants to retain a loving, kind remembrance of the mother, then she must not work herself up. If she does, then she thinks of herself and not of the mother.

And that's what our patients do. Something happens that is trivial—that is to be expected to happen, that's an average event—and they go to pieces, as they say. They go to pieces. This means they are always afraid that they can't adjust to the thing. There, again, see they think of themselves and not of the thing that happened. And my patients do that regularly, almost regularly. And what they do essentially is this: A thing that was to be expected, an average happening, whatever it was—whether it was death, or an insult that one was exposed to, or some damage that was inflicted on you—that's all average daily life. That happens right and left. And you consider it a terrific blow to you that you cannot survive, or, at any rate, you cannot live through. Then you declare yourself as very important, and that's what the intellectuals do.

They only talk about themselves, or the pet theories that they have. And that's what the patients do. And, therefore, I say with regard to health, my patients are intellectualists, rank intellectualists. They love to complain, this means to have an argument. The members of the family tell them, "Well, yours is a nervous condition. Why make a fuss about it?" But the patient says, "Well, if you knew how I suffer." They always think of themselves. Always how they suffer. And all of this is called *self-pity*.

And if you want stirring arguments here at this table, try to get them. Here you will not get them. We are not intellectualists. I have fortunately trained my patients to have respect for intellect and therefore not to think that they are intellectuals. They are average people. Their intellect has not been thoroughly trained as, let me say, as a great scientist's intellect. Let them know that they are average people and let them talk about average trivialities. And whoever wants to talk of something else—of stirring events in politics, in art, in literature—let them listen to other panels. Maybe they are held. I don't know. But don't let them listen to my patients. My patients are obliged by me to speak of nothing but trivialities, that means of life as it pulsates, as it lives, as it is close, and not of artificial issues like politics, economy, and other things that are artificial in the mouth of somebody who has no special knowledge in these fields.

Thank you.

TEMPER, TEMPERAMENT
AND SELF-BLAME

17 Minutes
Recorded Saturday, February 6, 1954

The panel will discuss this afternoon the subject of "Temper and Temperament." It is important for patients, and for anybody else, to know what is temperament. It is not temper. You see, when I go around on the street or in a park, or if I am at home, then there are events. Something happens. I am asked a question, and I have to answer. Then perhaps there is rain; the sky is clouded. Perhaps there is a flash of light, a sound of a horn and so forth. These are events. And the question is whether I receive the events, whether I pay attention to them, whether I receive them with my eyes or ears. And if I receive them, then the question is whether they penetrate further into my body and are received there.

And then if I am of the kind that pays attention to a lot of things and receives a lot of events, a lot of impressions, then I am receptive and impressionable. I am not dull. I am alert. And then somebody speaks to me, and he tells me a story of some kind. And the question is, how do I receive this story? Does it stir something within me? Does it perhaps even shake me up? Or if it is an acceptable, a desirable story—the story about an event that is rather a piece of luck, is cheerful—then the question is, will I develop cheer? Will I receive the story with cheer? And if somebody tells me about the death of somebody, will that story stir me? Will it make me sad? If it does, then I am emotionally alert. And, finally, after

I receive the story, after I show that the story which was told me made an impression on me so that I was both receptive and impressionable, then the question is, what will I do in this situation? Will I, for instance, express my grief when I am told that somebody dies? This expression of the grief and, at the same time, the feeling of the grief, that's my response

After I have received an impression, then I return a response. And if I return a response, then I am responsive. And these items that I call *receptive* and *responsive*, if a person is receptive to events and to their meaning and responds to them, then we say he has proper receptivity and proper responsiveness. And the organ within us that receives impressions and responds to them, we call *temperament*. It's not an organ in the sense of the liver, that you can touch and take out and study, and perhaps resect and so forth. But it is an organ. Just like memory is an organ, and consciousness is an organ, so is temperament.

And you have seen plenty of people in your life that are very little receptive, very little responsive, and you say they have no spark. And the spark should come from temperament. You say you can't get a rise out of them, and the rise should come from temperament. And if people are easily and readily impressionable and receptive and responsive, then you say they have physical and mental alertness. They are alive to what goes on around them.

So there are two types of human beings. The one has a lively temperament that does not have to rise to steep heights, but lively it can be. It can be, as I said, receptive and responsive. And the others are dull. This means their temperament is not easily aroused. They are dull, unresponsive and unreceptive, or little responsive and little receptive. This is human nature, and you are born with your temperament. As babies, you can show early receptiveness, early responsiveness, or you may not show it. And the one baby that shows what we now can call *a responsive and a receptive temperament*—well, is alert, lively—that's the desirable baby. And the other that shows little responsiveness and receptiveness, well, may make their parents worry and perhaps with a good reason.

On the other hand, of course, you understand some people may be too receptive, too responsive. They are too restless. That's, of course, not desirable either. And now you will understand that what I spoke so far about is human nature that has not yet been touched by civilization, by culture, and is plainly natural, not yet trained.

And what I spoke [of] was something that refers to babies or little children. Adult persons are not so easily analyzed in this respect. Once a person becomes adult, or adolescent, then his temperament is largely influenced and shaped and modeled by the ideas he develops. With the baby, there are hardly any ideas. And the baby responds from his temperament in perfect accord with nature, as animals would respond. The baby becomes fearful when something scares him, he becomes angry if something resentful happens, and he is filled with joy if he is cheered by mother's smile, or he is permitted to use his arms, his legs, his cooing, and he expresses himself in joy.

Originally, the temperament knows nothing but fear and anger and joy—originally. Then comes the later development. And adult people and adolescent people get the idea that somebody may be wrong. The baby just doesn't know about wrongness. He only knows who hurts him or what hurts him but not what is wrong and who is wrong. If the baby is hurt or hurts himself against the edge of the table, he doesn't say the table is wrong, but he spanks the table because it hurt him. The baby knows nothing but pleasure and pain of a physical nature. He does not know that if somebody strikes him or he strikes himself against something, that that is wrong. It merely hurts, but he has not the moral ideas of wrongness and rightness.

But adult persons have that. And then they begin to judge the events that come to them from the outside and stirs their temperament. And their judgments are, as I mentioned, in the nature of declaring something wrong or right. That would be no calamity. And if you declare a person wrong, well, you may do something against this person. You may strike out against him. You may use sharp words against him. Well, I am not interested in this matter of general behavior. I am interested in the behavior of patients.

The patient is, of course, an adult, and he judges events from the viewpoint of rightness and wrongness. That would be no calamity, but he judges himself from the same viewpoint. And if he says something, he judges whether he said the right thing or the wrong thing. And when he is among people, he is always afraid. The nervous patient, I think, is always afraid that he might do the wrong thing instead of acting correctly. And if the patient thinks he is wrong, or he is likely to be wrong all the time or most of the time, then he condemns himself; he blames himself; he has no use for himself; he has no fair judgment of himself; he's utterly intolerant against himself; he suspects himself; he is disgusted with himself. And if that goes on for years and years, then the nervous system is put under a heavy pressure that sometimes is intolerable. And that's what we call *the patient turning against himself.*

Now if I declare something or somebody wrong, that's no calamity. That will not harm anybody provided you don't become violent. But if I declare somebody wrong and keep this judgment of wrongness, I think that he is wrong all the time, or most of the time, that means I indict his character.

Whenever you are wrong once in a while, well, you might have made a mistake. You might have slipped from some standard for the present. That does not mean that your character is bad. But if you should be always wrong, or wrong most of the time, that can only be due to a faulty character organization. And if you accuse somebody of being wrong or doing the wrong thing or wronging you most of the time or all of the time, then you accuse him of a wrong, a bad character. And you indict his character. And then you must perforce suspect him, be disgusted with him, resent him, and you work up your temper. That's no longer temperament.

Temperament doesn't know the ideas of wrong and right. It only knows whether somebody hurts me or somebody pleases me.

And once you indict the character of somebody, again, that's this somebody's business and not mine. But if you consider yourself always wrong yourself—I don't say somebody else—or you consider yourself wrong most of the time, then you indict your character, and that's bad. That's what we call *the inner temper*. Not temper against anybody outside you, but against yourself, against your own character. If you do that, then you are consistently tense, you can't relax. Nobody can relax if he distrusts his own character, if he is disgusted with his own character. And, again, since character is a continuous way of behavior—you don't have character just today and strip it tomorrow—a character is always with you. Since that is a continuous mode of behavior, if you become disgusted with it, angry at it, ashamed of it, then you will be ashamed and angry and disgusted all the time or most of the time. And if you are ashamed of yourself, angry at yourself, if you hate yourself most of the time, then you create tenseness most of the time, and you have a nervous system that stands tenseness very badly. That nervous system of yours is so easily shaken up by tenseness. And if it is shaken up, it develops symptoms, and you are racked by disturbances of your interior. And you will, I hope, understand that temperament has nothing to do with self-condemnation, self-accusation, self-blame. All of this is temper. And if you distinguish between temper and temperament in this manner, you will do a great service to your nervous system. And it will not continually disturb, or disturb most of the time, both your body and your mind.

Thank you.

LECTURE 25

EXCEPTIONALITY AND CONTROL OF IMPULSES

33 Minutes
Recorded Saturday, February 13, 1954

Will you remember that Theresa, to my right, told you that her child had a temperature, was ill. And she said in former days, on such an occasion, she would have taken the child's temperature every hour if I remember correctly. Well, what's wrong with that? You will remember that Theresa told you also that now she refused to do that. And again I ask, what is wrong with taking the child's temperature every hour? Theresa obviously thought it was wrong, and I agree. But I will ask, why is it wrong?

In itself, to take the temperature of a child every hour—or the temperature of any patient—is useless. Of course, a temperature doesn't go up considerably within an hour and doesn't go down considerably within an hour unless there is something that we call *a crisis of the temperature.* So at best you may say Theresa did something that was useless. But is it wrong? Of course it is, and for the following reason.

If I do something useless, for instance playing cards, which is thoroughly useless, yet it's not useless. It depends how you judge an act whether you can then declare it useless or useful or harmful. Playing cards is useless from the viewpoint of doing something valuable. Playing cards does not add to the value of your life. Even if you win, your life doesn't become more valuable by the couple of dollars you make in a game.

Playing cards, however, can be viewed from another viewpoint, and then you can say, and justly, it gives you relaxation, and that may be of value. With relaxation acquired, you can then go ahead and perform a valuable task and can do it better than you would, perhaps, without the relaxation.

So, you see, there are two standards of judgment. I can, for instance, take a swim, and not even think of the relaxation. As a matter of fact, if I swim for an hour—and I don't do that, I assure you, but should I do it—that would not bring relaxation. That would bring added fatigue. But if I swim an hour, or stay in the water for an hour, it gives me pleasure, perhaps, and most likely it does.

And you see there are two kinds of values in life. Pleasure is of value to me. I like it. I like to have pleasure. I guess everybody likes that. And actions can be governed either by the principle of pleasure—which is nothing wrong—or by the principle of valuation. And I may forego a pleasure because I have to do something that is of value, for instance, to my profession, to my professional activity, which is of value to a patient, which is of value to my wife, my children or my neighbors.

And it will be good for you to keep in mind there are two ways in which an action can be motivated. The one motive is pleasure, and the other motive is valuation. Duty, responsibility, that all falls under the heading of valuation. And pleasure has no value except indirectly when it gives you relaxation that you then make use of for a valuable activity. And by value I don't mean anything extraordinary, nothing sublime, nothing ideal. But it is a valuable act for a housewife to wash dishes. That's a valuable act, but you can't tell me that it always gives pleasure. I think I know better.

On the other hand, you can't tell me that doing something valuable, practicing something that does good to your family, to your friends, to your business activity, that that is always devoid of pleasure. That's not always irksome or painful. Of course, carrying out a duty or responsibility can just as well give pleasure, and perhaps more yet. The pleasure, however, we call *mental.* And mark it: men live their lives with the hope that their life will be pleasurable, but that doesn't mean physical pleasure. It means that, too. There is no objection to it. But men, the average man, wants particularly mental pleasure. And mental pleasure you can only get by that act that holds down physical comfort or physical pleasure. Those acts that give you mental pleasure create a worthwhile life. But that doesn't mean that physical pleasure must be frowned upon. Not at all. But there must be a ratio. Everybody who is worthwhile must have it as a rule to create predominantly mental pleasure but not to cut out physical pleasure at all. That is important, too.

And this is what we call *the primacy of the mental comfort over the physical comfort.* This means the thing that is of prime importance and constitutes the primacy is: the mental pleasure must have the primacy over the physical pleasure, but it must not crowd it out.

Now, Theresa told you she took the temperature of her baby every hour. Did it give her pleasure, or did she do it from duty? If you had asked Theresa years ago why she took the child's temperature every hour, she might have said, "I feel it is my duty to do it." I don't know whether she has said that, but she might have said it. But that's nonsense. There is no duty to overdo. Duty merely calls for an average act that is called for, but not for fifteen such acts. Usually, it doesn't.

So, we now know that Theresa at that time did not act from duty. She only tried to persuade herself that it was her duty to watch the child every minute and the temperature every hour. And we'll rather say, and Theresa will certainly agree with that: she acted from fear, not from duty. She was afraid that she would neglect her duty, or that she could be charged with neglect of duty, if she didn't take the child's temperature every hour. And it's a bad practice in life to act from fear. But Theresa did something there that did not do her any good. What did she precisely do? She carried out an impulse. She carried out the impulse to take the temperature every hour.

Now, that impulse might have done wrong or harm to the child. Theresa did not know for sure that it would not be harmful. For instance, if you take the temperature of a child— of a sick child—every hour, you disturb the child more than necessary. You disturb the child, for instance, that may just want to fall asleep, and you take the temperature. At any rate, there is even a danger of infection if you do something too much. For instance, if you insert the thermometer too often in the mouth, the child may have a chap, especially under fever, and whether you clean the thermometer thoroughly you never know. And you might sometimes not do it because you are in fear and forget certain things. And you will here see that what a patient thinks is his duty—or a person, a nervous person thinks is his duty—is a situation in which the person intends to do good. But if he overdoes, he may do harm. And impulses generated by fears are dangerous because in this manner they may become harmful.

And I want to tell you something about these impulses. You see, outside of us, things happen. For instance, somebody passes by me on the street. That is a happening. But now I must react to this happening. And I react, let me say first, with feelings. For instance, the person that passed by me could have been my friend. And suppose he was, but he didn't greet me. If I am calm, then I will say he didn't greet me because he didn't see me. But if I am not calm, if I am sensitive, if I am tense, then all kinds of thoughts may crowd my brain. And one of them may be, well, this friend of mine passed by me, this means he snubbed me. And now a snub may arouse in me either fear or anger. If he is, for instance, a person that is important to me—my employer or somebody that I want to ask for a favor—and he snubs me, then I become fearful. If he's not my superior, not some important person but just a friend, a neighbor, and he snubs me, then I become angry.

You see, the event on the outside, and let me tell you no matter what it is arouses feelings. Of course you may say that I may be indifferent, but let me tell you there is the feeling of indifference, be sure. An event outside you always creates feelings. And what you call indifference is a weak feeling, but it still is a feeling in actual life. In the books, they call it *indifference*, the state of indifference, but there is none in life. I doubt it.

Now feelings have a tendency to produce impulses. If I feel angry at the man who passed by me without noticing me or without paying attention to me, if I am angry, then I have the impulse to show my anger. I certainly get the impulse, well, when I come home, I'll call up that fellow and ask him, "What's the idea? Why do you act like this?" That's an action dictated by anger. And this will show you: feelings create impulses that produce actions. Our action and our life [are] governed by impulses which flow from feelings and by feelings that take place at the bidding of an event. And I only spoke of events outside us. I could just as well have spoken of events inside us, but that would complicate matters.

Now, I said the impulse flows from a feeling, and you see how important feelings are. That's the first thing that happens after an event. I get that feeling, and that creates the impulse. And now something remarkable happens that I think doesn't happen in animals and not in babies—I think. But I don't know animals very well, and babies nobody knows, so why should I know them? So, I better speak in general terms that once the feeling and the impulse have been aroused in us, something remarkable happens. Now you judge them. (Presumably animals and babies don't do that.) You judge them. And now the judgment determines whether the feeling will be acted on and the impulse will follow suit or not.

And you will see now in life everything depends not on feeling, not on impulse, but on the judgment that either releases the impulse or holds it back. No matter what feelings you have and what impulses you have, that doesn't count in life. They can always be controlled, although patients don't believe that. The patients think they can't control their fear impulses and their anger impulses. But that's nonsense. There is no such a thing in waking life as something uncontrollable—no matter what the papers tell you about somebody killing because he has an irresistible impulse. That's nonsense. And the juries and lawyers and judges should finally stop talking of somebody, being awake, committing an act of irresistibility. That's nonsense. That has never happened with awake people who have not lost their minds completely.

And so the judgment is the main thing in life. And when you come here to Recovery, we teach you primarily how to judge your impulses and your feelings and, therefore, how to hold them down. I told you in the beginning of this meeting that there are two judgments. Also, I didn't use the word *judgment,* if I remember. The one judgment states that something that happens was not initiated by me, so I am not responsible for it. I am not responsible for the fact that it is raining. And I am not responsible for the fact that this man passed by me. That was done by him and not by me. And I am not responsible for the fact that it is dark, and I stumble and fracture my leg. Do you understand that in life it's of the utmost importance to know what I am responsible for and what I am not.

Now, Theresa did something that I would advise her not to repeat, and she will not repeat any longer since she has gone through Recovery training. She did something. This means she had a feeling of fear and released impulses, again dictated by fear, and these impulses might have harmed the child—the impulse of sticking something into the child's mouth every hour. And if Theresa says every hour, it might just as well have been at a little shorter distance, because I know how my patients act, and Theresa might have followed the same pattern. That was a lack of judgment, and it is improved now because Theresa has gone through Recovery training.

Theresa had obviously the idea in mind that she was responsible for the child getting well, and she had to do everything to get the child well. Although, be certain, she had a physician on the job, and he had certainly much better judgment as to what the child needs than the mother has. And be certain the physician didn't tell Theresa to take the temperature every hour. A physician wouldn't do that. If he did, then I'll advise him to surrender his title. But physicians don't do that. Except in very exceptional cases, it might be done.

So Theresa wanted to do too much, and from fear. She discharged a number of impulses that should not have been discharged. At least one-third of them should have been shelved. She overdid. And by this token, she obviously did not follow the physician's instructions. She followed her own instructions, her own impulses, and she put herself above the physician, above the expert. So she thought of herself as being either exceptional or dealing with an exceptional case. I presume she did not feel exceptional in point of medicine. I am sure not. But she felt exceptional in thinking that she dealt with an exceptional case, an exceptional situation, that her child needed entirely different care from what the physician thought was good for it.

You see, there are two other judgments which I didn't mention, but they belong to the same class. An event can be judged as exceptional, and one's self can be judged as exceptional, or both can be judged as average. And I ask myself—and you will ask yourself—why do people want to do the exceptional act, the perfect act? It's impossible. There is no perfection in life. All you can do is the act that, on an average, is considered good. But you can never do the perfect job. Theresa wanted to do the perfect job with her child, and naturally it is impossible. And to take a temperature ten times a day, or twenty times a day as it might have been, is certainly nothing like perfection.

Here in Recovery you learn that your feelings and your impulses and your judgments must be average, or they must be treated from the viewpoint of averageness. And if you ever slip into the sphere of perfection, you are likely to do great harm, as Theresa's instance evidences.

And so what are you going to do about that? I have preached to my patients the importance of being average, of considering their situation average, of wanting nothing but an average job, a job that on average criteria is good. But the patients don't drop their desire for perfection, for exceptionality. And why don't they? The reason is simple. People are vain. You and I are vain. Everybody is vain. Do you know what vanity means? Well, I guess you know, but I shall express it in my words. Vanity means I refuse to be like other people. I insist on being better and finer and smarter than other people. I insist on being superior or singular or excellent, and not just average. And if people want to be average, and they all insist on it, they repugn me. If people want to be exceptional, if people hate to be exceptional, uh, average . . . .

Well, you see, my performance is not so exceptional. Because I am average, and therefore I can mispronounce and misspell and miscalculate, and that's all average. And I am not afraid to do that because I try to be average. I say I *try* to be. It's extremely difficult.

Because inside there are powerful impulses that want to perform on a high level. My impulses are for exceptionality. I dream of being, well, the most superior person. So what do I do then? And there [are] no individual[s]—unless idiots or imbeciles—that don't crave to be exceptional and superior, to do the perfect job, to be above others and not average. There is none. That's what I believe.

But there are people—here in Recovery we try to train them, and we did with good success—there are people who control their vanity, who control their impulses to perfection. And I think I do that. But will you keep in mind there is not an adult individual living that is not vain, extremely vain. Everybody thinks he is the greatest person. He doesn't say so if he's smart. But that's what he feels and thinks and dreams of. And I will give you a slogan which will serve you well: Everybody hopes to be superior and fears to be inferior. That's the picture of human beings.

And you understand, for anybody to want to be average means to give up the hope of being superior. And people don't like that. They have lived—relatively speaking, the one twenty years and the other thirty and the other sixty—and they have spent their lifetime in dreaming to accomplish greatness. It doesn't have to be the greatness of a presidency of the United States, but to accomplish something exceptional in their group at least, not in humanity. And now they should give up this sixty-year habit. That's a big bill to fill. That's a big order.

But here in Recovery you must accept this big order and carry it out. Otherwise, the following thing will happen: You want to be superior. This means you depend on others to either recognize you, to give you credit as being not just average, to give you the honor of constantly catering to you, perhaps do you the favor of constantly flattering you. And if you don't get credit and if you don't get honor and if you don't get flattery, then you become tense because you expect it and you don't get it. And therefore vanity and the striving for perfection is harmful, particularly to the nervous patient. Because since vanity is usually not accomplished, since being vain you don't get people to give you the due credit and flattery and honor, therefore you become tense. Vanity always makes you tense. And if you are a nervous patient, and your vanity makes you tense, the tenseness creates symptoms, and you can't get well. At least you can't get well quickly, in due time.

You will now understand why we stress the matter of averageness. You remember at the beginning I asked the question why Theresa said that she has given up the practice of doing the perfect job. Why she said that in former days, she would have taken the child's temperature every hour, and now she doesn't. And I asked, "What is wrong with taking the temperature every hour?" Now I guess you will understand what is wrong with such an act. It is wrong because it flows from the vanity of wanting to perform at top level. This vanity creates disappointments for you, and therefore tenseness, and therefore symptoms.

And you will understand, don't try to get rid of your vanity. You can never accomplish that. I have not even tried to do it. I simply don't care about it. When it rises, I control it. I hope I do. I hope I do it most of the time, although I'm not so sure about it. And by controlling it, it gradually gets weaker and weaker. Presumably, I have less vanity today than I had a year ago. Presumably, a year ago I had less vanity than I had ten years ago. And go back onto that scale, back to where I was twenty years, and to my teenage period, and be sure I had to whittle down a mountain of vanity to the present state. And there is still a good hill of it left.

Thank you.

FEAR, CHANCE AND WILL

12 Minutes
Recorded Saturday, February 13, 1954

The subject to be discussed today is "Will, Beliefs and Muscles." Now, I will want to tell you something about the will which is, of course, the main subject of discussion all along in Recovery. You see, what people are interested in is neither the will nor the impulse nor beliefs or muscles. That's not what men and women are primarily interested in. Men and women are interested in how their actions are, and particularly how they will be. Life and living means to act, not to discuss will—to act.

Now, there are, however, only two kinds of actions. The one action is prompted by something that happens without your will, and the other kind of action depends on what you want to do. This means your will. And therefore it is very important to know how the will operates.

You see, when I go out on the street and it is raining, I didn't make the rain. The rain has nothing to do with my will. That happens. But there is something else in this matter of the rain. I could have done something about it. I could have provided myself with a raincoat, with an umbrella. I could have listened to the radio and could, perhaps, have known whether it would be raining, and then I could have done something about it. I might have stayed home if I could. You see, this is no longer a happening. This is dependent on whether I exercise my will. To take precautions against the happening means to have the will to be cautious. And that's a will.

A will, as you know—and as the article which the patients will discuss mentions—is something that chooses. I could go out in the rain, and I could stay home, and I have to choose between these two possibilities. So, will is the same thing as choice. And if I choose to go out in the rain, the rain is still happening—although I brave it—but it is a happening. And it doesn't happen to my will, of course not, but by chance. To me it is perfect chance whether now it rains or the sun shines. My will has nothing to do with this situation.

And now we can sum up and say some of our actions are dictated by chance and others by choice. And you will understand, chance and choice are identical with happenings and things that I want. This means intention. The happening happens by accident or by chance. The act of the will goes on by intention. So an act may be either a choice act or a chance act, and we can also call it *an intentional act* or *an accidental act*.

The other day a patient came to me and told me, "I went to the Recovery classes, and I attended two of them, and I don't see how I can continue," she said. And I asked her, "Why? Why can't you continue?" And she said, "I am afraid. I am afraid if other people talk about symptoms. I am afraid to listen. I feel bad when I listen to them."

Now, do you understand that if somebody hears something (for instance, on the street) or sees something (again, on the street) he, for instance, hears somebody yelling, for instance, screaming with pain. That would scare him. That happens. That's not choice; that is chance. It's not intention; it is accident. You understand that. Well, now the patient may become afraid, or the person may become afraid. If he hears somebody screaming with pain on the street or somebody collapsing on the street, the fear that happens to the patient is accident. He didn't want to become afraid. He had no intention. He didn't choose fear. And it will be good for you to know if any of you get [your]selves into a state of fear, that is chance and not choice, accident and not intention.

But I get into fear very frequently. Of course, my fears are not excessive. They are not exaggerated. They are not extreme. But I get into fears. A patient doesn't do well; I fear the consequences. And suppose a patient has an accident while I have him in the hospital. I fear the consequences, and I worry about them. What do I do with that fear? Again, the fear came to me by something that had nothing to do with my will. It was chance, not choice.

But now I have to do something about this event. What I'll do will come from my will. And I'll tell you how I handle my fears. I know immediately—even before the event has happened—I know now that if in three years from now, something will go wrong with a patient, I know now what I am going to do, although the patient perhaps doesn't exist as my patient. He is not my patient now. I don't know him. But I can predict, in general terms, what I'll do. I'll bear the fear and take it for granted that to be fearful is part of life. How can I avoid fear by living? I handle my fear. This means I don't permit my will to get discouraged. And I know that everybody in this life either does bear his fears, or he should. And I know everybody can bear their fears.

I was in the First World War, and I was afraid many times. And anybody who will tell me that he was in battle and was not afraid, well, I have my opinion about that. I will not tell you what kind of an opinion. He claims to be a hero, and I don't know heroes. I only know average people, and average people have the average fear. And I remember that once I had to walk through a wide field, and that field was the aim of the Russian artillery in those days. I had to go through it, and I went through it. But I didn't like it, and I was not heroic. I was not fearless, I assure you, but I went through it. And there have been fathers and mothers of no mean number who, when their house burned and a child was inside, they passed through the fire. They certainly were afraid, but they acted with their will against the fear.

And I ask my patients, "Well, if you are afraid, what of it?" To have fear is perfectly average. Don't work up the fear so that it becomes a panic. But you are a human being, an average human being, and you have an average fear. Originally, it was average. It was not a panic. But I may tell you I have had a panic in my life, too, and I bore it. And plenty of people have gone through panics, and they bore it.

And when you come to me with fears, that's what I tell you. You have fears. Will you wait till they will be taken care of? But at present, have in mind you must want to be average, an average person. And an average person can have fears and go ahead and act his life regardless of the fear.

And that's what you are trained to do in Recovery. In Recovery, we tell you everything that you suffer from—fears, angers, anxieties, pains, pressures—it's all average. And all of these are happenings, accidents, chance events. But now you must exercise something that is not chance but choice, not accident but intention, and that is the will. Have the will to go through your fears and angers and pressures like an average person does or is expected to do. And if you do that, then you will have carried out the main principle of the training which we give here, and, in addition, you will get well.

Thank you.

LECTURE 27

OUTER EXPRESSIONS AND INNER EXPERIENCES

31 Minutes
Recorded Saturday, February 20, 1954

What Frances told you about her experience with her son, I would like to take as the text for my remarks. You'll remember that her youngster thought he didn't like these dirty overalls. Well, he used another term which I don't want to repeat. At my age, I don't use such language, but I was once this youngster's age, and I was certainly not different from him.

Now, you remember that when this youngster made these remarks, Frances, his mother, felt provoked. She felt provoked to the point where she felt like wringing his neck. I am afraid even this wouldn't have helped the situation. Youngsters can get a wringing of the neck dozens and hundreds of times, and they still are youngsters. That has been my experience.

But the point is that when Frances felt like wringing the boy's neck, she was obviously in temper. And what did she do? She practiced the Recovery teaching. And the Recovery teaching is not merely to control temper but to do what is needed in order to control temper. And what is needed for the control of temper is spotting. Spotting. I don't know of any organization that practices spotting systematically. And, as you know, we have developed this system of spotting. People spot their reactions.

And if you remember what I told you about half an hour ago when I made my first little speech, I told you at that time that the average person merely has in the forefront of his consciousness the words he uses and perhaps the meanings that they imply, but only the meanings of his expressions, his outer expressions. And I told you about half an hour ago that the outer expressions are not the same as the inner experiences. And a person may come up to me and tell me a story, perhaps a very simple story.

And just today some such person told me the following story. He told me of a certain professor—the man was a student, perhaps an intern—of a certain professor, he told me, who had apparently wronged him, as he thought. And then he told me the story [of] how the professor did him wrong. After he finished the story, and I half listened—be sure only half—then he broke out into a statement that he meant honestly, I think, and he didn't think there was any objection to such a statement. And I must admit I have heard such statements frequently, and people who make them are not embarrassed at the audacity of their statements. He told me, "Well, I tell you, I went up to this doctor so-and-so, and I gave him a piece of my mind." Mind you, the young intern went up to the professor and gave him a piece of his mind. And then he went on to tell me, "And be sure I told him the truth, and he didn't like it."

Well, that's a statement. So I asked myself, what does this person experience inside? I know what he has expressed outside—again, the outer expression and the inner experience—and I begin to think about this event, and I tell myself in the first place there was an arrogance. A youngster throwing up all kinds of accusations against a respectable man who has made his place in the community while the youngster is just a fledgling who hasn't accomplished anything yet. So that was true arrogance. And be sure if this man told me the story, he certainly didn't think that he was arrogant. Otherwise, he wouldn't have told me the story in the tone of bragging: "I told him the truth, and he had to take it."

Then I begin to think if a youngster tells an experienced, elderly person the truth, then that youngster obvi-

ously thinks he knows the truth. And that's an awfully difficult task, to know the truth. There are many truths that I
struggle with, and I am no longer a youngster, I will assure
you. And I still struggle with endless truths and don't find
them. It's an extremely difficult task to know what is the truth
and what is not.

That youngster wanted to reveal to an experienced,
older person what is the truth. And, mind you, he wanted to
show him the mirror of the professor's character. And he
implied that he had to tell him the truth, this means about his
character. So he seems to think, or experience inside, that he
not only knew the truth, but he also knew what is a character
and particularly what is a bad character. And he implied that
he himself was the judge about character, and his judgment
was that his character was good and the professor's character
was rotten. He had to tell him that.

And all of it will show you that the expression of a man
is very frequently—I think most of the time—unlike the inner
experiences that same man has. Now you will understand if
you want to get from the outer expression of a person, or of
yourself, to the inner experience of that person, or yourself,
you can't just listen to what a person says or what you yourself say. You must travel from the outer expression to the
inner experience, and that's what we call *spotting.* You spot
not the words, not the sentence. These you don't have to spot;
they are given to you. So spotting does not mean what you
say, not even what you think consciously. All of this is in the
foreground of consciousness. And the foreground of consciousness does not have to be spotted. That is revealed to
you either in your conscious thoughts or in your conscious
statements. And anything that is conscious with you, you
don't have to spot. You know it. But that's all you know, and
that's very little.

From the outer expression there leads a way to the
inner experiences, but you must know how to walk this way.
And when you come here, you don't know it. And the indication of what the inner experiences are—and which you will

have to spot—are approximately as follows: There are certain things that are expressed in a certain tone of voice. And if you hear somebody swaggering, "Well, I told that man the truth, and he didn't like it, but I told him," then he does not make this statement with an even intonation, with a low-toned voice. He raises his voice. Then you know already he speaks in temper. That is spotting. He didn't talk about temper. He didn't express it. Plainly, you conclude that he has temper from his tone of voice.

And then there are other ways of spotting. For instance, this man told me, whom he should consider a man of some average judgment, that he threw [down] the gauge [glove], that he challenged a leader of some group in our society, a leader of doctors, of professionals. Now, if he, if a young man tells me that he challenged an older, experienced, recognized man, then I can use my logic. I don't have to listen then to his tone of voice. I use my logic. And if a youngster tries to challenge an old, experienced man, then I know that youngster has an extreme sense of self-importance. If he had a sense of group importance, then he would have known that he has not made a mark in the group yet, while the professor has made a mark. That's a logical way of spotting. And that can frequently reveal to you the meaning of an inner experience, and frequently it does not because it's difficult to rely on logic and to rely on vocal expressions—this means the tone of voice.

But there is something else, and that's what we call *experience*. And experience teaches you, if it is real experience, how to spot your experiences and other people's experiences. And, again, that takes seasoned study and seasoned experience. And here I must stop because I can't tell you how experience is acquired. You know. Experience is acquired through hard labor and through long waiting. And this alone should tell the patient that spotting is not easily obtained. The knowledge of spotting is not easily obtained. However, there are certain clues that I can throw out to you, and the clues—

or the main clue—is as follows, and you will do well to listen closely, as you do, and to absorb what I want to tell you about this clue.

You see, in life there are, as I have told you repeatedly, only two elements, and life is built on the quality that we call *duality*, is built on a [twofold] principle. First of all, in physical life, there is right and left, above, below. It's all dual. There are two directions in life. There are also two sets of feelings. There are, for instance, tender feelings and coarse feelings. There are feelings that go out to other people and feelings that remain inside.

And, above all, there are ways of behavior, and there are, again, two qualities of behavior. You have inside you feelings and impulses, and we leave out the feelings. The main thing is impulses and beliefs. And if you want to act, this means if you want to behave, you display impulses. Everything you do you have to do after an impulse tells you to do it. If you want to sit down, then you have the impulse to sit down. If after you have sat a while the impulse comes to stand up, well, you follow, or don't follow, the impulse. But if you do stand up, you do it because an impulse made you stand up. But if you stand up after the impulse made you do it, then you begin to ask yourself a question or two, and usually two questions.

The one question is before you carry out the impulse. Then you ask yourself, "Should I stand up? Is it right to stand up? Is it proper? Is it wise to stand up? Don't I do any harm to myself or to somebody if I stand up? What will people think of me?" And this is a critical view of what I am going to do, and we will simply call it *the preview* of my action that is to follow. So everybody, after he feels an impulse to do something, engages in an action which we call *taking the preview of what I am going to do.* And then, for instance, he takes then the preview that it is perfectly proper to get up and to stand. Then he has accomplished the act, and now, after the act is accomplished, the average person asks himself, "Was that right?" At first he asks, "Will it be right if I stand up?" Now he says, "Was it right for me to stand up under these circumstances?" And that's what we call *the review*.

So I hope you will keep these two words in mind. Every action is preceded by a preview and succeeded by a review, and both the preview and the review can be wrong or harmful.

And now you must spot what is your view. The view, both preview and review, doesn't present itself to you. You do it instinctively, intuitively, so you don't know what is your preview and your review. So how can you spot it unless you are taught how to do it? And let me tell you the most gruesome mistakes are made because people don't know how to spot their previews and their reviews. People don't know how to spot them. And that's how mistakes occur, and sometimes very grave mistakes. It's good to know how to spot views, whether they are previews or reviews. Well, I almost begin to stammer when I pronounce these two words, but I'll try to keep on the right track and not confound them.

You know, if you want to spot views and impulses, then it will be good for you to revert again to the statement that I made that things in life are arranged on a dual scale, on a scale of duality. And with regards to actions, it is good to know that they are always initiated by an impulse. And now you must know what are impulses.

Impulses are, again, arranged on a dual scale, and everything in life is dual. The dual scale for impulses is very simple. An impulse may either harm you or produce an action that will harm you or will please you, will serve you. On the other hand, there are the same impulses [that] may either harm the group or serve the group. And now one and the same impulse can either harm or serve you, and the same impulse can either harm or serve the group. So you must spot at least two relationships. And if you form the view that an impulse is likely to harm you, then you must control it. But if you form the view that the impulse is not likely to harm you, then you don't have to control it, if you only think of yourself.

But then comes this very embarrassing situation that you can't merely view yourself. You must view the group, too. Otherwise, the group will turn against you, or might turn against you, if they feel you are an offensive sort of a person.

So this is, of course, the main thing to spot. Does your impulse harm the group or serve it? If it is likely to harm the group, then you must control it. If it is likely to serve the group, you may safely release it. And now we have, again, a duality of two qualities: control or release.

Now, my patients, my patients come to me, and they suffer. They suffer, and they want relief. And they develop impulses which they think will give them relief. And there is no objection to it. Why shouldn't they give way to impulses which give them relief? Why should they control them? But there comes, in between these situations, that thing that calls—I talked to you about impulses being likely to harm the group or serve it. And every patient is naturally required, while he craves relief through an impulse, then to ask the question, "But even if I get the relief through releasing my impulse, maybe the impulse will harm the group, and the group will turn against me, and, in the end, it will harm me." The impulse promises relief—this means to serve the individual—but it may threaten danger by harming the group.

And don't think that I have in mind here this matter that we call *aggressiveness*. I don't mean that. And no patient, to my knowledge, has ever turned against the group with a knife or with a gun. I haven't seen it. Maybe there are some. But the patient has turned frequently and almost regularly, while he has been suffering, against the group with his mouth or his tongue. And you may say that a gun is more dangerous than a tongue, but not necessarily so. A tongue may be very offensive and therefore dangerous to the individual himself. It may be dangerous to the group of the family. And if a patient thinks he gets relief by getting his trouble off his chest, this means he wants to talk about the trouble, complain, talk [to] everybody how frightfully he suffers, in the hope that perhaps somebody will give him consolation and relief. But what he says may cause offense and may antagonize the people he talks to and then again rebound to his disadvantage. The impulse that he thought will serve him is a boomerang and harms because the impulse, if expressed, offends those around the patient.

And you will understand now that it takes quite good training, a good intellect, a trained intellect, to know which impulse will not boomerang and which impulse will. The impulse that will not boomerang, you may safely release, but the other must be held back.

And there comes now the tragedy of the patient. His impulses are strong, extremely strong. He has an imperative impulse to walk up to his wife or to her husband, and so forth— I mean the male patient to the wife, the female patient to the husband—and complain. And if the patient did that, that would be an innocent thing, but unfortunately the patient's impulses keep driving him for endless hours and days and weeks. And the patient, if he gives way to one of his strong impulses, then he complains for hours, for days and weeks. And no matter how wise a patient is and how many treasures of wisdom he releases—but the wisdom is poured out indefinitely for endless hours, days and weeks—the one who has to listen to them would have to be an angel not to become provoked and [get] sick and tired of the whole business. And husbands and wives do not hesitate to tell the endless complainer, the constant complainer, that that's what they are, sick and tired. Not only tired, but sick. And I believe them. I have yet to know a person that can tolerate continuous stimulation—or, more so, irritation, but even stimulation—if it is continuous.

Let just a hum go on in your home. That can't do you any harm. But if it goes on for half hours and hours, then it exasperates you. You want to get rid of this hum. And yet the hums don't criticize you, [don't] start an argument with you, but the very fact that there is endless repetition antagonizes everybody.

And will you now understand how difficult it is to practice this matter that I call *previewing impulses* and *reviewing* them. You see, when the patient develops a temper outburst, then after the temper has been released, he actually feels relief, but for one second only, for one second. And the reason being that instantly something tells him to shut off. His temper outburst is immediately condemned by somebody who is present. And, naturally, even my patients don't pull temper tantrums if nobody is present. They always do it with somebody around. And that somebody is certain to either fight back or to ridicule the temperamental outburst or answer with temper or condemn it.

And, therefore, the patient, after relieving the impulse, the temperamental impulse, actually has a brief moment of relief. He got something off his chest. But in the next brief moment, somebody reminds him that now the honeymoon is over. What happens then? Then the patient now is provoked himself. First he provoked the listener. Now he is provoked because he is answered in temper or is condemned or laughed at. And now he had a moment of relief, and he craves that moment back. So the only way to get relief in such a situation is to release another volley of temper, and then he has again relief until the other fellow steps in and the relief is gone.

And if this goes on for hours, as it sometimes does, but if it merely goes on for ten minutes, then the patient and the one around him, both of them are likely to get gradually exhausted by these constantly following sallies and parries. And if the patient isn't exhausted in ten minutes, then be sure he has still vigor to fight on. Then he will continue his temper, and finally he will get exhausted. And if he goes on day after day, then that thing develops which the patient calls *fatigue, exhaustion.* And the exhaustion can continue for days, weeks, months, and years. I have seen year-long exhaustion. And the remedy for this situation is to have a correct preview and a correct reviewing of the experiences.

LECTURE 28

EXCEPTIONALITY AND INNER EXPERIENCE

21 Minutes
Recorded Saturday, February 20, 1954

Well, the panel will discuss today the subject of "Averageness and Exceptionality." I guess you know, especially if you have read the article, that there are two kinds of exceptionality. If somebody brags and is aggressive, then he may like his aggressiveness and his bragging, and he will get stimulation from it. So, while the reaction of bragging and aggressiveness is undesirable on the part of the group, but to him it gives stimulation, and, therefore, to him it is most likely desirable. He likes to brag. He likes to be aggressive.

But my patients hardly brag. Whether they are aggressive, well, many of them are retiring, and some are perhaps aggressive in a sense. But they definitely are given to a conduct of life in which they fear. And if somebody is aggressive, he doesn't fear. He is provocative, challenging, but not fearful, not at the time that he is aggressive, at the time that he is bragging. But my patients, even if at times they are aggressive, nevertheless most of the time they are fearful, and this is the reverse of aggressiveness.

But my patients are too fearful. If they think of a danger, then it is an enormous danger. With my patients, there are no average dangers. Their suffering is maximal, they think. They can't stand it. They can't tolerate it. It is insupportable, they say. And why do they say that? They have for years, or at least for months, they have borne this suffering.

They have not had the experience that their suffering is unbearable because they have borne it for months and many, for years. So why do they say it is unbearable? To my patients, all their symptoms are unbearable.

Of course, I guess you know the reason. They want to convince the members of the family that they are really sick, and not, as the members of the family think, their sickness or their ailment or their suffering is imaginary. They want to convince the members of the family that their suffering is not imaginary, but real. And they have the quaint idea—and it is quaint, and I might call it odd—that if you want to convince somebody, you must lay on heavily. A mere statement, a mere report of suffering would not do. In order to convince somebody, they think you must knock them down. You must overwhelm them with arguments and evidence. And then they exaggerate and give themselves over to the philosophy of exceptionality. And they want everybody to believe that their suffering is entirely different from the usual suffering.

And finally, while they go on constantly exaggerating and "whooping up" their temper, they develop so much tenseness that they actually almost burst. And then perhaps they develop panics and vicious cycles, and increase their suffering to such a pitch that maybe it becomes exceptional. Now, this exceptionality the patient does not like. This he knows is not desirable. This is an undesirable exceptionality. And it will be good for you to know that my patients indulge in a sense of exceptionality with suffering, mainly. And that is undesirable exceptionality. And so you will realize why I distinguish between desirable exceptionality—this means desirable to one who brags and is aggressive, not to the group—and, on the other hand, with undesirable exceptionality.

Now, everybody is, of course, average. Everybody whom one usually meets is naturally far removed from the sphere of exceptionality. Take, for instance, a city like Chicago. Well, there are exceptional people. The mayor is exceptional. There is only one mayor in Chicago. Whether he is exceptional in character, in intellect, in efficiency, well, I don't know. But there is no doubt, as far as position in Chicago is concerned, he occupies an exceptional position, and I would say this is a desirable exceptionality. And any President of the United States, well, may be an average person, but his position is exceptional, and certainly, I think, a desirable form of exceptionality. So if we look for exceptional people, we don't look for people of exceptional character, of exceptional genius. They are very rare, extremely rare. The only thing we know in the line of desirable exceptionality are people who have exceptional positions.

And my patients, for instance, think that I am an exceptional physician. Well, that's very nice, and I appreciate your sentiments, but other people will not agree with you, and there you are. There are plenty of people, there are plenty of people that will deny it, and I am among them. I am inclined to be among them, and maybe not. But I am exceptional in all kinds of other respects. To my children I am the only father, so I am an exception to my children. They know only one father. To my wife, I am the only husband, and so forth. And you see there is a lot of exceptionality in life, but in a small way, in a small circle, in the field of family life. And there are exceptional people, for instance, the owner of a shop who employs two workers. He is exceptional today. Whether that means a lot, that a father is exceptional to his children and to his wife, and he may be the only child so he is exceptional to his parents—well, anybody can have these exceptional traits, and so this exceptionality is average, again. It's no longer exceptional.

Well, my patients have a special kind of exceptionality. They feel that they are exceptionally wise. They don't know that, but I may tell you they feel that. And so when I say something—when I, for instance, tell a patient, "Why, don't be so frustrated when I tell you what I told you"—do you understand what that means? I tell the patient that he shows frustration, and such a patient, after I make this statement, is likely to snap back, "Well, Doctor, I don't feel frustrated." But how does the patient know that? How does he know what goes on within him? If he knows, why does he come to me to tell him? He consults me precisely about the troubles of his inner life. And if I tell him something about his troubles, for instance, that he is too much given to a feeling of frustration, he's likely to say, "No, Doctor, that is not so." Now, look here. If somebody makes such a statement, then I'll say, first of all, he is a trifle too positive, even if it happens outside the circle of patients.

And I have my opinion about patients who make such statements, and my opinion is as follows: If I say yes and the patient says no in a matter in which I am an authority, then the patient's answer is arrogant. That patient thinks he knows more than I do about himself. Now, that's arrogance. Then I am no longer an expert, and he pushes me down from my pedestal of expertness, and that's really arrogant. But mark it: The patient does not know that he acts in arrogance. He doesn't. The patient is honestly convinced that he knows what goes on with him, but it is arrogance. And I want you to realize the following situation: That patient sitting before me is boiling inside, and he is boiling inside because somebody has hurt his feelings. The somebody is I. I teach him. I lecture to him. I give him directions about how to handle his inner life. And, let me tell you, if somebody gives me directions about my inner life, then I resent it. But, of course, if the patient comes to me, he comes for these directions. He wants them, and he should not feel frustrated if I direct him.

And he doesn't know that he is frustrated. That's quite likely. He doesn't observe himself. That's one thing. He may not know it. He may think that to feel frustrated means to burst with tenseness, not merely boil with tenseness. He may have such an assumption. But he definitely does not know that he is arrogant with his statements. This he doesn't know.

So do you understand? The patient has two kinds of knowledge or of consciousness. He is conscious of what he has expressed. He said no, and he thinks the word *no* is not a sign of arrogance. He's right. It doesn't have to be a sign of arrogance. But inside he experiences what I know, and that is resentment.

Now, what is known to the patient is in the forefront of consciousness. What is known to me is in the background of consciousness. And I have had an enormous amount of experience. I can say that, although you may think the statement lacks humility. But I may tell you I have an enormous amount of experience. And then the patient came to consult me, so he must be thinking that I have a great experience.

So I know his experiences. I know what goes on with him because of my experience, but he only knows what he talks about. He only knows his expression. So, will you keep in mind, if somebody is an expert and really has knowledge, he knows the depths, this means the inner experiences. But if somebody expresses something, that may be different from his inner experiences. And then you will realize that the patient then has a knowledge of what is in the forefront of his consciousness, but I have the knowledge of what is in the background of his consciousness. I know his inner experiences, and he only knows his outer expression.

I wish I could get my patients to realize this. And they don't. I strike against this barrier to fruitfulness, and usefulness, and to improvement, whenever I see the majority of my patients. And why can't I convince them that I know their inner experiences, and they only know their outer expressions on the fringes of consciousness. And I'll tell you why: The reason is that the impulse to show exceptionality—to show superiority, to show great knowledge and the skill of doing things—is inborn.

Everybody is born with the sense of exceptionality. The baby thinks he comes first. And if mother doesn't rush to his bed when he yells, then he will yell harder. This means he feels he has claim on mother's time all day, every day. So he is an exceptional person in the family. As a matter of fact, he may be, but he shouldn't have the sense of exceptionality. But nature works in such a manner that everybody is born with a sense of exceptionality. And this sense of exceptionality keeps patients—and people in general, but I am only interested in patients—keeps patients from acknowledging that they don't know their experience. And there are only certain people that know deep experiences, and that's the people that have studied the subject for endless years—so-called experts.

So the patient—being a human being, and having been born by nature, and having grown up as a baby and a young child—comes to me with an inner sense of exceptionality which is his nature. And how am I going to root out his nature? It can't be done. But it can be weakened. It can be pushed down. It can be pushed down to a scale where the patient finally is only feeling exceptional once in a while— occasionally—and not all the time. And that's what I have to do, and that requires training.

If you want to train nature to accommodate yourself to the needs of social contacts, then that training cannot be done in two days, and not in two weeks, and not in two months. Impossible to recast nature in a brief space of time. And now you will understand that training must consume time. But nature has endowed human beings with another quality. Not only with the sense of importance, and not only with the sense of exceptionality, but also with the impulse to impatience.

Everybody is born with impatience. If a baby doesn't get the mother right away to his bed, well, he shows his impatience. Inside he has the philosophy of exceptionality, and outside he expresses his anger, this means his impatience. And so when I want to crowd out or push down the sense of exceptionality in my patients, I must also devise means to make them give up at least a considerable portion of their impatience, of their restlessness, mental and physical restlessness. Impatience is, of course, mainly a mental restlessness.

So you will understand that takes additional time. And the patients don't know that, and they resent being treated what they think is too long a time.

Well, it's a difficult task that we perform here, but I will assure you that we don't tire of handling this task. I wish that the patient would not tire—sticking to the job, and holding fast to the task that he has imposed on himself, and I now impose on him—the task being that of training, persistent training, almost uninterrupted training. And that requires that the patient gives the time to the training courses.

Thank you.

LECTURE 29

FRUSTRATION AND THE NERVOUS PATIENT

22 Minutes
Recorded Saturday, February 27, 1954

I will try to discuss the statement of one of them, and I may have time to discuss some other statement. But the one statement made by Genevieve, it seems to me, is worthwhile discussing.

You remember Genevieve told you that she got her paycheck, and she became rather provoked by the amount of deductions that the check showed. Well, that's certainly nothing exceptional. People get provoked by taxes. They're always likely to say taxes are excessive, and I guess there is some reason for believing so. But it doesn't do much good to discuss it and to work oneself up over this matter. So Genevieve drew the conclusion, and she expressed her conclusion in the following manner. She said, "Isn't it silly to get temperamental over a thing that you can't help anyhow?" And this sounds very rational for somebody to say, "Well, since you can't help the matter, since it is futile to do anything about it, so do nothing, and don't work yourself up and do yourself harm."

Then the government does you harm by collecting taxes from you, and you do harm to yourself by getting temperamental. Why aren't you satisfied to have only one harm done you? Why do you have to add another harm? And that, I guess, is the meaning of Genevieve's statement. And it sounds very rational. To me it has the ring of rationality, and yet it is not. It's not at all silly to be temperamental. It's not at all silly to explode, unless you tell me what you mean by "silliness."

I don't think it's silly for somebody to try to climb the Himalayas, Mount Everest. I wouldn't do it, be sure I wouldn't. Even if I could, I guess I wouldn't. But don't say it is silly. These two gentlemen that climbed Mount Everest had a goal. They set themselves the goal to climb Mount Everest, and if they succeeded, then they were likely to reap tremendous awards. I don't mean in money, although they could do that, too. Not material awards I think of, but tremendous awards, first in glory. Well, I don't think that is silly. I have never tried to hunt glory, but I wouldn't say it's silly if somebody does it.

Second, they could get—just aside from glory—the pleasure of accomplishment even if nobody knew about it, even if it were not publicized. People enjoy the pleasure of accomplishment in the privacy of their homes. They enjoy it with no publicity attending the event. And you see what you call silly is so from your viewpoint, and you may be right. You take the rational viewpoint, but people don't act from rationality as a rule.

You know, if mothers would act merely from rationality, then it's not rational to send a child to college, [when] you have to deny yourself all kinds of benefits. That's not rational. And mothers, you understand, don't act from rationality. They act from the sense, "I want to accomplish something for my child—not even for myself, for my child." You can say this is irrational, but that doesn't mean anything. If somebody sets himself the goal of accomplishing something, the accomplishment may not mean anything to you, but to him it means a lot, or it may mean. And, therefore, it will be good for you to know that there are various goals in life. The ones are rational and the others are not. The others are, for instance, the hunt for glory, the search for adventure, which is not at all rational. People brave death in order to have adventure. So, to them, it is not silly to brave death for the sake of adventure.

But we are not interested in glory and adventure. We are interested in our patients, and I doubt whether there are many mountain climbers among my patients. I don't think so. So let's drop that and consider this mountain-climbing episode merely as an example and nothing else.

But my patients lose their tempers. And Genevieve said that is definitely silly, and it's correct, I think. And there is no glory in losing temper and no adventure. I don't know of any. So why does the patient lose his temper, and goes on losing it, even after fifty and a hundred Genevieves have given him examples how futile and silly it is to explode temperamentally? Why does the patient go on being temperamental? The answer is clear from the examples that I quoted. The patient gets great benefit from the temper. There is no question about it. Not his ailment. His ailment is not benefited by it, but the patient is.

Now, what does that mean? You see, if I go out and buy myself an automobile, supposedly then I say, "Well, I need it." So there is a reason, a rational reason for buying the automobile, because I need it. But that's not the reason why I buy it. In addition to buying the automobile, I spent some amount that has nothing to do with the function of the automobile for which I need it. You see, I need the automobile, if I go about it rationally, for speed and transportation in general—whether speed or not, for transportation, for my practice—so something rational. But then why don't I buy an automobile that is fifteen hundred dollars cheaper? That will bring me to the office, too. It is utterly irrational to spend a thousand or fifteen hundred dollars more than I need. I could get myself a little automobile, and it would cost me so much less than my automobile does cost me that it seems silly to buy the expensive automobile when the inexpensive automobile would serve me just as well. And it seems silly to spend fifty dollars more on a suit of clothes while the cheaper suit would protect me against rain and wind and cold. It would do the thing that the garment is expected to do, so why do I spend more money on these matters?

Well, you know, I must stand up to the demands and philosophy, for one thing, of my daughters. If I had a cheap car, well, my daughters would walk, I guess. And I don't want them to walk too much, you know. And I don't want them always to use public transportation. And my daughters say, "Well, the other girls have good cars. Why shouldn't we have a nice car?" You see, what my daughters are after is to be well thought of by the other girls. That's what we call *vanity*, you know. And my daughters think I should spend hundreds and hundreds, and they would be happy even if I spent thousands and thousands of dollars just for the purpose of vanity. Now let me tell you, vanity is a very important thing for young ladies, very important. There is no question about it. Young ladies could really be dressed in something that others would call rags, but they have vanity, and that must be taken care of, if it can be taken care of.

And so you will now realize there are all kinds of incentives for action. First, reason. Plain reason. That's very weak, as a rule. But there are other incentives. They are not reason. They are the reverse of reason, perhaps, and often, at any rate. They are vanity, glory, adventure. You can live without vanity, be sure. You can live a very good life without vanity, and without adventure, and without glory, and without prestige. But then you deprive yourself of pleasures. And to a young lady, for instance, vanity is expected to net very desirable pleasures. In her eyes, they are very desirable. And they are all pleasures. And when I tell my patient not to be vain, not to hunt for glory, then what have I got in mind? Then I have got in mind that if he hunts for glory and if he indulges in vanity, he will meet with frustrations. Somebody will insult his vanity, and frequently. And somebody will deprive him of his glory or will not give him credit for his glory, for his glamour, for his prestige. And then he will be frustrated. I have no objection to anybody being frustrated. I am frustrated so often. It seems to me every five minutes in my life, maybe seventy-five seconds in my life. I am frustrated so frequently that I can't catch up with my efforts to avoid it. I am left behind all the time.

You see, I can afford to be frustrated. It will not do me any harm because frustration, to me, is a thing that hardly creates any tenseness. Frustration will never do anything to my nerves because I expect it, and, therefore, it doesn't scare me when it comes, and it comes all the time. When I sit in front of a patient, that patient is certain to frustrate me. I expect a certain answer, and when do I get the answer from a patient that I expect? That hardly happens, you know.

I expect the patient to do something, and when does he do what I expect, especially in the beginning? He doesn't. I have so many expectations for the patient's good, but he doesn't please me. He doesn't give me what I expect, in the beginning. Later on, of course, the picture changes. So be certain I am the target for a thousandfold frustrations, I think, almost every day. I expect it. I expect when a patient enters my examining room or consultation room now to spend a certain space of time in frustration, but I expect it, and, in time to come, I have grown to love it. If patients should stop frustrating me, there would be something vital missing in my life. You laugh, and I understand, but it's really not humorous. The patient frustrating me is a challenge to me. It challenges my resources of mind and character. And I am proud of my accomplishment of seeing patients in my office, and most of them frustrate me most of the time, and I control the frustration. I don't let any anger rise out of this frustration, or very little anger. I must say, sometimes I flop. I must admit that.

But very little anger arises out of my frustrations, and very little fear, so very little tenseness. And the little amount of tenseness that comes from my frustrations, being little, is not sufficient to irritate my nerves. And so I don't develop symptoms, merely frustration do I develop. And since I expect it, I am used to it, and it doesn't do any harm to me and does not exercise pressure on my nervous system and does not precipitate symptoms.

But you can't do that. Your nerves are not adjusted to frustration, this means to the tenseness that comes from the frustration. Your nerves have not the resistance that is necessary in order to ward off symptoms when tenseness arises, and therefore you must avoid tenseness and the frustration from which it comes.

And I remember my young days when I had a soaring ambition, this means I was extremely vain. I still have some left, but in those days, it was an excess of vanity, and all you have to do is to be vain. This means you will expect to get credit from others, flattery from others, compliments—let me say, well, all kinds of benefits, this means of glory, reputation, prestige. And who is going to offer you as much glory, and prestige, and recognition, and credit, as you expect? If you expect too much of these items, then you are bound to get your feet stubbed and your feelings bruised. And that creates tenseness, and the tenseness increases the more vain you are and the more your feelings are hurt. And the increased tenseness presses against the nervous system, and your nerves cannot absorb this amount of pressure, this amount of tenseness that you are likely to produce. So do you understand now how important it is to curb temper?

It is not silly to the one who can't stand tenseness. It is something that does something for you. Temper, no doubt, if it only lasts a minute or two, and no longer, gives you relief from tenseness. Temper, I meant to say. Temper, if it only lasts in its initial effect, will give you a certain amount of relief. You told somebody off. But if you continue and continue, then the relief is gone. Then you only work yourself up. So will you understand that even temper is not silly? You know now that adventure is not silly. Ambition is not silly, not even the soaring ambition. The quest of glory is not silly, and the question is not whether anything is silly, but whether anything serves your purpose, and, therefore, you must know what is your purpose, and then you will know what to avoid.

If it is your purpose to get rid of your symptoms, then be sure it's silly to create tenseness. And if it is silly to create tenseness, then be sure it's silly to permit temper to develop. And so you find out that Genevieve was right. She said, "Isn't it silly to get temper?" But she should have added one little remark. And she should have asked, "Is it not silly to develop temper if one is a nervous patient?" Then it is silly.

And to the nervous patient I will give the advice, don't do anything that will develop tenseness—whether it's silly or wise does not matter. Even if you pursue the wisest plan, the cleverest pattern, if it is likely to create tenseness, drop the cleverness and wisdom and maintain nervous health.

Thank you.

LECTURE 30

HELPLESSNESS AND HOPELESSNESS

13 Minutes
Recorded Saturday, February 27, 1954

We will discuss this afternoon the subject of "Helplessness and Hopelessness." That's one of the famous formulations in Recovery, that the patient may be helpless, but he should never be hopeless.

Well you see, I am sometimes helpless, and everybody is helpless in some situations, at some moments, at some periods of his life. And what does helplessness mean? I am, for instance, helpless if I have a fountain pen and it leaks. And I am frustrated, and I feel helpless unless I have another pen available. But if I don't have, I am helpless. I can't write with that pen. And helplessness means, at least in one important respect, the tool which I use doesn't work. And I need to work, and I must have the tool, and must get it working, but it doesn't, and then I am helpless.

And sometimes I employ a human tool. I, for instance, make a telephone call, and the operator doesn't answer, or she answers and then I get a wrong number, and so it goes. At this moment, the telephone operator is my tool. Some other time, I am her tool, and so it goes. And the tools fail me. Then I am helpless with regard to this particular task.

And my patients are confronted with a situation in which very vital tools fail them—for instance, the tool of the heart. That's a tool, the tool that carries on circulation. Or the tool of the stomach, that's a tool to carry on digestion. Or the tool of memory, with which I must remember and recall. And patients come to me and say, "Well, I have frightful palpitations," and if they have frightful palpitations, they can't go about their work as they should, with a free mind, with relaxation. The circulation tool fails them.

And other patients tell me that they have frightful pressure in their heads. And let me tell you that this pressure is caused by the blood vessels in the skull and by muscles around the skull, and these are tools. Blood vessels are the tools for the transportation of blood, and muscles, you know, are organic tools for the purpose of making movement. And the patient says these tools fail him. Well, if my pen fails me, then I know one thing: The pen is damaged, otherwise it would not fail me. It's leaking. Then I know. But my patients have no damage in their nervous system, in their stomach, and the nerves to the heart are not damaged. Those parts of the nervous system that predominate over memory are not damaged. Whatever the patient will tell me—that in point of his functions failing him—I know his tools are good. They are not damaged.

So why do the tools fail him? They are good. And if my fountain pen were good, as usually it is not, I wouldn't complain about the function. It would not fail me. And if the operator on the telephone circuit wouldn't just think of something else except on her job—if she really thought of her job— I guess she's a good tool for making connections over the telephone. But why does she fail? She could do the job. But there is something about a telephone operator and about my patients that makes the good tools fail. The tools are good, but the operator fails. The operator is good, too, for all kinds of purposes. But the operator fails me when I want to get a certain circuit and don't get it. The wires are good. The circuits are good. There must be something wrong with the operator at this moment. And what may be wrong I will not discuss. I don't know operators. I had no chance of meeting any of them, if I remember correctly, and I don't like to talk about things with which I am not familiar.

But I know patients, and I know how they use their tools. They use them in the following manner: They notice that the tool once or twice fails them, but they are told by me that their tools are in good shape. So they shouldn't suspect the tools, but they begin to suspect them. I told them the tools are good, the nerves to the heart are good, the heart is good, the memory is good, the nerves that conduct memory pathways are good. I told them they don't have to worry about their tools, but they begin to worry. They think the tools are damaged. They are no good. They think the tools fail them because they are not working or because they are working with deficit, inefficiently. And if somebody has a tool that works inefficiently, he's likely to get sore at the tool. He feels the tool frustrates him. And I must admit I have frequently gotten sore about my fountain pens, about many of them.

And do you understand what is wrong with tools if they fail, but otherwise they are in good shape? It's the operator, not the tool. If I use an employee, and he is my tool for the purpose of conducting some business, or an assistant, and I constantly suspect him of being unreliable, of being likely to fail precisely when I need him, then I will develop temper. I will use sharp words against this assistant, and then the assistant will become temperamental, and he will be disturbed. Then I have created a disturbed tool, and the tool doesn't work well. And that's what you do with your stomach and your heart and your legs and the head. You have an abiding distrust against your tools. You always expect that your organic tools, the tools which you have in your body and your mind, will not serve you right. And all you have to do in order to disturb a servant, or an assistant, or an employee, is to show him suspicion. Then you create in the employee tenseness, if he is interested in doing his job. You will create tenseness in him. If he is tense, he will become fearful, and with fear, every tool is disturbed in yourself.

And so do you understand the utmost importance is given here in Recovery to temper: fear or anger. And now this will explain to you why we stress temper to the point where it makes you almost feel nauseated to constantly listen to examples that deal with temper. And I have heard it said by so many patients, "Well, when I come to meetings, all they talk about is about temper." I don't understand that. It's like saying when you come to a school, all they do is to teach. What else should they do in a school? Well, unfortunately, they do a few other things in schools. I know that. But don't criticize the schools because they do nothing but teaching. I wish they did nothing else. And don't you dare criticize me because I ask my patients, whenever they bring an example, always to view it from the viewpoint of temper and some- thing else—and self-diagnosing. But if you self-diagnose, you create temper. You create fear and frustration, so it's really all temper.

And if you wish to continue to criticize our panels, well, go ahead and enjoy your pleasure. I hope you will enjoy it heartily, but don't come to me and tell me. I don't enjoy your statements that my panel discussions, the discussions which I have created, are faulty. You know the panel discus- sions only for the past few weeks or months. Well, I have cre- ated them, and I created them fifteen years ago, so don't tell me that they are wrong. I have fifteen years of experience with them, and you—well, too many of you—just the last week of experience, and that is not enough for criticizing. At any rate, if you wish to go on criticizing, go ahead, but come to the panels. Attend them.

Goodbye.

LECTURE 31

INNER RESPONSES AND OUTER REACTIONS

30 Minutes
Recorded Saturday, March 6, 1954

You will remember the statement made by Agnes, by Bill, by Frank. I shall try to discuss those made by Frank. You remember that he said he had some doings with a watch. The watch was to be repaired, and he thought it was delayed. He was waiting for the watch, and it wasn't delivered. And finally he found out that the watch was waiting for him for two weeks already, and he had not tried to fetch it.

And he told you a similar story about the bonds that he was sure and positive had come due, and he had not done [anything] about it. And then he had finally found out that the bonds had not come due, that they were still interest-bearing papers. And, if I remember correctly, he quoted another similar item, well, the contents of which I forgot. Two items of this kind should be sufficient for discussion.

You also remember that when he wound up his example, he exclaimed—rather with some aplomb, which was justified—"I not only had the vanity of knowing better, but I also believed it." That was an excellent statement. I will refer to it later.

You see, Frank displayed in these examples something that can be expressed in two terms. And we need both the terms, and we may also need something interposed between the two terms. And I'll try to explain this duality of terms. In between, something is interposed; that is very important.

I have told you repeatedly that we humans are constructed of two parts, or factors, or elements, whatever you want to call them. One part of ours is born—has been given us at birth, or, naturally, before birth—and the other part is acquired. Nobody in this world, I am certain, has been born with the knowledge to write or read. That must be acquired. Nobody in this world, I am reasonably certain, was born with the sense of courtesy. That must be acquired. That's not nature. That's culture. And nobody has been born, I am reasonabl[y] certain, with honesty. That must be acquired. And these features are acquired through education, but the better word is *training*. Education may be misunderstood to imply nothing more than information. But the real education consists of information, to be certain, but far more important yet, of training, training impulses, holding down feelings, those feelings that should be held down: for instance, the feeling of self-importance, the feeling of anger, hatred, anti-social feelings. And that's what we call *education* or *culture*. Culture means, in other words, to hold down many anti-social impulses that are born with us, that are our nature, and to train them to enter the sphere of culture.

And that part of us that is close to nature, and far removed from culture, we call *the individuality, the individual*. That part of us that is close to culture, and perhaps even enveloped in it, we call *the character*, also personality, but leave that out.

Now, what is born in us is always ready to act, to be released. Fear, for instance, is always ready to be released. Anger. The moment you feel anger, you want to act on it, you want to release it. Indignation, hatred. The moment you feel it, you want to release it. And that's what we call *temper*. Temper, in other words, you will understand now, is born with us. The baby on the first day displays temper galore. He doesn't have to learn how to yell and how to kick. He has it. It was born with him. Control, restraint, is a matter of culture and must be acquired.

Now, if somebody displays hatred or anger or fear what he does is first to develop the anger and the fear and the hatred, inside. He does not immediately display or release it. He has it inside. And so he has—if he feels it—love and pity and compassion and sympathy. He doesn't have to display

189

and to release it. Anybody can feel fear and keep it inside. He can feel love and not talk about it and not even act on it. That thing that is inside—in terms of feelings, impulses, sensations—we call *the response*. Inside, we respond to something outside us or something inside us. Once we release the fear, once we release anger (once like, for instance, Agnes' husband releases his anger that she interfered with his craftsmanship, and, as you know, it was very doubtful), once he releases his anger and expresses it either in words or in gestures, threatening gestures, for instance, flashing eyes, that's no longer a response. That's *a reaction*.

And if you distinguish this manner of response and reaction, then you will perhaps better understand that the responses are nature. The reactions can either express the responses plainly, and they are natural to them. Or they restrain them; then they are cultural. But reactions may express the raw material of responses, and then they are, of course, not very cultured, I assure you. I hope you understand that.

Now, among responses there are again two groups. Inside us we are dual, dualistic. And the one group of responses is by nature not against the group. For instance, there is the response to the water. Somebody passes a body of water or he happens to be near a river or a lake, and he wants to swim. That's an innocent impulse. That's not directed against the group. It may benefit the individual, and usually does, but it is not directed against the group, ordinarily not.

You remember now that I spoke of fear and anger. Fear and anger. The angry and fearful inner responses are, from the outset, against the group. They disturb the peace, the organization, the order of the group as we call it. They are disrupting. But even the baby has already, or may have already, some impulses that are not disturbing the group. At a certain time, he smiles. That's nothing disturbing. That's about how far the baby will go in serving the group. Ordinarily, he is an individualistic creature that thinks of himself and not the group, naturally. Now, if I am to live in a group with my family, with my neighborhood, with my country, my religion, and so forth, then I must decide whether I mean business with my relationship to the group or not. If I mean business, then I will hold down those responses of mine that are disrupting group life. If I don't mean business, well, too many of these responses will break through and turn into reactions. And once you react with a fear response, with a hatred response, something has been disturbed in the group.

Well, that's all ethics, and morals, and religion, and good behavior, and essentially we are not interested whether people behave badly or well, whether they are ethical and moral. We wish they should be, but we are not concerned with this field. We don't try to teach people how to be religious, how to be moral, how to be patriotic. We hope they will be, but that's not our business to teach them. And essentially it's not our business to teach the patient how to be ethical, moral, religious, and so forth. There are excellent institutions that do that job much better than we can do it. But we have to deal with these fields of human activity because the patient cannot get well unless he has character, unless he develops character with regard to his symptoms.

My patients have an excellent character, or, let me say, as good a character as the average person has. And I don't have to urge the patient to change his character or to acquire certain features of character. For instance, in his dealing with customers, he knows how to deal ethically with customers as the average businessman knows. We don't have to teach him any such reactions. But what we have to teach him is to watch his responses and not to let antisocial responses turn into reactions, into outer reactions. Because if that happens, then the patient will develop tenseness because he's now in danger—in danger that somebody will strike back, that somebody will jump at him. I don't refer to criminal behavior. The patient is never likely to become a criminal. He is too ethical for that and perhaps also a trifle too fearful. Let's admit that. He is.

What I refer to is character in everyday life, without great problems, without great problems challenging the character. In little life and in the little sphere of daily life, there it happens that I walk through a door. Well, a very trivial example. I walk through a door. For instance, through the door of a store in which I want to buy something, and behind me is another person. And now the question is, will I do the right thing or the wrong thing? Will I hold the door and let the other person pass behind me, or will I just walk off? A very trivial example. But the way I was born and the way everybody on this earth has been born—I think that everybody has been—the way we are born, the first impulse is to be discourteous. You may not believe this, but it is so. The first impulse is not to hold the door and let anybody pass but to pass through the door and let the fellow take care of himself. And if anybody controls that inner response not to be courteous, then he shows character, this means self-control, in a trifling sphere of everyday life.

But let me again tell you, if you don't control your antisocial responses, inner responses, in these trivialities of everyday life, then you will gradually lose the habit of control. Now, if my patients do that, they strike against something that is very deplorable. I mean if they express their antisocial responses instead of holding them down in these trivialities of everyday life, then they have to pay a penalty.

My patients are naturally very unsure of themselves. They constantly doubt themselves. They constantly depreciate themselves. They are afraid that they are below average, below this common standard. And if they become aware that they have been discourteous, this simple, minute failure to be average—or perhaps measure up to average—may produce a reaction in them that is very common in patients. They may begin to blame themselves, or they may become self-conscious because they think people have noticed their discourtesy, and the patient then thinks, "What will they think of me?" And will you understand that my patients are particularly unfavorably placed because they are self-conscious. And if they make a slip—if they fail to control a response, an inner antisocial response—then they become sensitive to it, or they are likely to be sensitive to it. And what they are sensitive to is the opinion of other people. "What will people think of me if they noticed I have not been courteous?"

I don't say that all my patients are of this kind. There are other patients. The patient that I spoke of, that becomes markedly self-conscious, suffers from fear. His self-consciousness is the type of self-consciousness that is, well, bathed in a stream of fear. There is another self-consciousness. Some of my patients have it, not the majority. I can be self-conscious—and everybody is self-conscious to some extent—I can be self-conscious with the particular coloring of fear, and I can be self-conscious with the particular coloring of anger. I can be self-conscious—this means I feel uncomfortable among certain people because they don't pay attention to me—and I become angry. Now I become tense, and now I become self-conscious in the sense that people notice that I am tense.

My patients particularly have the habit of condemning themselves if they are tense for the following reason: My patients have developed an intense tenseness for years, and if they go among people, they usually feel tense because they feel self-conscious. But having gone through this tenseness for months and years, they feel intensely tense, and they notice it. It oppresses them. It forces itself on their consciousness. They have to be aware of their tenseness. And then they draw the conclusion, this tenseness is so severe that it must show on the outside, on the skin, and therefore people must notice it. And my patients, therefore, if they develop tenseness and the accompanying self-consciousness, have always the fear that others will notice it because it's so obtrusive in its intensity, and it's showing.

And, as I told you, some of my patients react to their responses that express themselves in tenseness, mainly with fear and others mainly with anger. If they respond with fear, then this is punishment in itself: to be in fear. That's plenty of punishment. That's suffering. But if they react with anger, anger is no punishment. Anger has some unpleasant tone, but most of it is pleasant. In anger, I look forward to an opportunity when I'll get even with somebody. And that gives me pleasure, a pleasurable anticipation. Moreover, in anger, I try to convince myself, and I may be convinced that I am right and the other fellow is wrong, so that gives me mental pleasure. And therefore it's so difficult to deal with anger and relatively easy to correct fears. But angers are not easily corrected.

But both angers and fears do harm to the patient. They create or intensify his tenseness. And if his tenseness is intensified, then it creates a heavier pressure than usual against the nervous system and precipitates symptoms. And the symptoms are, of course, a severe penalty for the patient's misdemeanor. And what I call *misdemeanors*—I take it you will understand now—does not refer to the field of delinquency by any means. The patient has fallen [a]foul of common manners, of common courtesies. And if he does that with anger, then somebody will most likely come back at him. And the tenseness inside will be increased, and it will precipitate symptoms. If he reacts with fear, if he's afraid—"What will the people think of me if I don't show courtesy?"—then again he creates tenseness, the tenseness of fear, of scare, perhaps of a panic, and again symptoms appear and he gets his dual penalty. First, fear itself is a penalty—it is intensely unpleasant and disturbing—and then the symptoms are a penalty.

And what are we going to do with this problem in which the patient does not know—before he comes to Recovery and in the beginning of his Recovery career—where he does not know how to hold down his responses, especially his anti-social responses, and how to keep them from being expressed in outer reactions? And in the beginning of Recovery, we were faced with this problem. What are we going to offer our patients in terms of training?

I still remember the days in which this organization was thrown at me by circumstances. The patients wanted to form an organization, and there I was—at the hospital, they wanted to form it, and there I was. I was in charge of the service on the wards, and I didn't feel like stopping the patients. This organization looked good to me, and I encouraged them, but then I didn't know how to train them. I had no experience.

Unfortunately, training is frowned upon in present day disciplines, university disciplines, and I hadn't been trained. I didn't know how to train my patients, I mean train to control impulses, tenseness, responses. I had gotten my home training, of course, school training but not professional training in teaching patients how to hold down their impulses with regards to symptoms. But gradually we plowed along. Perhaps we muddled along and found our method. And you know, most of you know, our method is particularly built on the principle that antisocial responses—with their attendant impulses, sensations, feelings—must not be expressed in outer reactions. And, naturally, if they were expressed in outer reactions, the reactions would be antisocial, too.

Now, this is contrary to modern teaching. And I, when I started my career, I was subjected already to some amount of modern teaching, modern teaching which tells the population that they should not control, but express, their antisocial or their violent feelings. Well, all I can tell you is that we developed the method, and it works. And I am happy to state that although in the beginning I was gravely disturbed by the lack of a method, today, fortunately, we have it.

Goodbye.

LECTURE 32

VANITY IS NOT PRIDE

17 Minutes
Recorded Saturday, March 6, 1954

The panel will discuss this afternoon the article entitled "The Vanity of Knowing Better." You may ask the question why such a subject should be discussed with nervous patients. Nervous patients are known to be suffering from symptoms, and very few people might blame them for being vain. And yet they are, exceedingly so. But before enlarging on this statement, I will try to tell you what is meant by vanity. Vanity is not pride. Pride is something that is very desirable, and vanity is emphatically not desirable.

You see, if I can tell myself that I brought up my children to be straightforward human beings, well-mannered, endowed with various advantages that have been developed—at least, let me say, to a certain point—then I tell myself incidentally that that was done by me, and I am proud of my work. And what I am proud of is of the obstacles, the handicaps, that were in the way of accomplishing this goal of bringing up children. And if it is true that my children are of the kind I described, then I have accomplished something worthwhile. And while I accomplished it, I had to overcome the difficulties, the obstacles, and therefore I proved at least that I was stronger than these obstacles were. And of this strength that I have displayed, I am proud—not precisely of the fact that I was stronger than somebody or something, but the accomplishment against obstacles is the title to pride.

Now, bringing up children is naturally a very important and vital task, and some people, for instance, have no

196

children. They may have no opportunity, or little opportunity, to try their will, their desire for accomplishment, at vital tasks. Then they will have to accomplish something in a less important field.

I'll give you an example that happened to me about two weeks ago if I remember correctly. I had a cold, and that's not a vital affair. That's a rather trivial affair. Ordinarily I dispose of my colds within a day or two, but this time I had a sequel to the cold. The nose felt stopped up for several days, perhaps for a week or two. Well, I don't remember exactly. And one day this obstruction in the nose bothered me a great deal. And then I noticed that I more or less constantly blew my nose, and I became aware and embarrassed by this action. And then I went on nevertheless blowing, and I forgot myself. I tried to stop the action and slipped back into it, and then finally I applied our Recovery method. I applied the method, that you all know, that says if you suffer from a nervous condition or from a mild disturbance like a cold—which is not a disease but merely a disturbance; don't let anybody tell you that a cold is a disease—you know that we say if you suffer from a nervous condition, nervous symptoms, from sensations, obsessions, compulsions, panics, the fear involved tells you that you must do this or that—for instance, that you must blow your nose in a cold. And the Recovery principle is, do what you fear to do, and don't do what you shouldn't do. And what you shouldn't do in such a condition is to coddle your feelings, your impulses, and your sensations. If you feel like blowing the nose when you shouldn't, then don't do what you feel like doing. And so I commanded my muscles not to move, the muscles of the nose—in the nose there are plenty of muscles, I may tell you—and the stoppage of the nose went in no time. I tried that soon thereafter when the stoppage appeared again, and it went in no time, and before long, I was rid of it.

Do you see there was a handicap, an obstacle in my nose. It was an obstacle to my social behavior. When I blew the nose—well, for instance, at home—I disturbed somebody. My dear wife was kind enough not to tell me, but I knew I disturbed her. So there was an obstacle placed in the path of

my good manners, and there and then I decided that I'll eliminate the obstacle, and I accomplished it. Afterwards I felt
proud. And you will understand with these examples that I
offered—or with this last example, at any rate—pride means
strength exercised on inner impulses, sensations, feelings.
Pride means self-control, or pride follows from self-control.

This is entirely different with vanity. If somebody is
vain, this means he thinks he knows better than somebody
else, he is better than somebody else, he wants the attention
of people, he wants to occupy the center of the stage. What
does he accomplish there? What is the obstacle? Anybody can
be loud and, let me say, display poor manners. All it requires
is to have an impulse to do it and follow it through. There is
no obstacle to poor manners if you wish to display them. And
if then you are proud because you have called attention to
yourself, that's not pride. That's vanity. You call it pride, perhaps, but it is vanity.

And you remember I told you that my patients are vain
creatures. They should accomplish something, and they are
trained here to accomplish that thing that we call *health*—
health, or inner balance, inner peace, efficiency. They have to
see to it that their palpitations should not interfere with their
efficiency, their fatigue should not interfere with their going
to work. That would be accomplishment because the impulse
inside not to go to work and to stay in bed in the morning is,
with those patients that suffer from fatigue, very strong. And
should they conquer this impulse, they would show strength.
And the strength of self-control—the strength of character, in
other words—they could be proud of that, legitimately
proud.

What do my patients do instead? I mean, in the beginning, when they have not improved yet. They want attention.
That's what they want. They want the attention of those at
home and of the doctor and of the neighbors, and, therefore,
they constantly complain and speak of their suffering and
force others to listen to them—if they can do it, if they can

force them. And I mention here, just briefly, that in pride, you exercise strength. In vanity, you try to exercise force. In pride, you try to exercise strength over your inner impulses, sensations, feelings. That is self-control. In vanity, you try to attract the attention of others. You try to exercise power over others. You try to push them aside and push you forward. That's the exercise of force, not of strength, and certainly not strength of character.

And that's what my patients do. And when they try to push themselves and obtrude themselves to the attention of others, what is the result? First, the result is negative. They don't accomplish anything. Second, the result is not only negative but very harmful. If they force—want to force—somebody to listen to their running complaints, what do they do? They antagonize the prospective listener. That listener becomes provoked because he is forced to listen against his will. And so there develops a running display of temper on both sides. The patient is repulsed by those on whom he imposes his will, and the patient himself returns replies that are naturally loaded with his own temper, and so he develops symptoms.

And a patient, especially in the beginning of his career when he is not improved yet, all such a patient has to do is to develop a bout of temper, and he will pay for it with symptoms, with suffering, with agony. So the patient doesn't accomplish anything, and, on top of it, he harms himself with his vanity.

Then the patient comes here to Recovery, and he is given his training, and what does he learn? He learns to ignore his sensations by knowing they are distressing but not dangerous. He learns to hold down his feelings because he knows—his feelings and impulses—because he knows that the impulses and the promptings of the feelings can be resisted by using muscles, with simple methods. And once he has learned that, he holds down impulses, sensations and feelings, especially the negative feelings of which I spoke to you already. And then he shows his strength, strength of character, strength of will, because character and will have precisely this function, to hold down impulses.

I may tell you that if children in general today were trained as my patients are trained here, well, the population as a whole would learn to hold down their impulses. And what would follow, I am convinced, would be that there would be a holding down also of those impulses that we call, or that we associate with, delinquency and crime. But that day has not come yet when even our leaders think of educating the entire population to the task of holding down impulses and exercising self-control.

Goodbye.

SURFACE THINKING VERSUS SPOTTING

23 Minutes
Recorded Saturday, March 13, 1954

The three members of our group that sat up here at this table told you the story, in almost identical terms, how they manipulated a situation in which somebody, or something, frustrated them. You remember that Gertie was frustrated by her husband. She wanted, she was eager, to accept an invitation to go to Danville—had accepted it, if I understand the situation correctly—and considered the occasion almost as an emergency, as she said. It appeared to her, in other words, that if she should not go to Danville, some emergency might arrive—within her, of course: a severe reaction in other words.

And there was an obstacle, a very pleasant obstacle. They were invited for the night before, and they had accepted there, too. And they were sure they will not be home at an early hour. So, obviously, it was an occasion that they looked forward to, that was bound to bring them some pleasure, that they wanted to taste till a late hour. And Gertie asked her husband, "Are we going?" And the husband says, "We'll see." That's frustration.

I don't know whether it is clear to you what such an answer means. If somebody asks me, "Will we go here or there; will we do this or that?" and I say, "We'll see," that has a multiplicity of meanings. But one meaning is outstanding among this variety of meanings, and it signifies that I have the power to decide. "We'll see." This means, "I will not give you an answer. You better wait."

You see, it's not so easy to glance through a statement and see the meaning underneath it. It's not easy. I remember the time when I was not very well able to do that. But in the meantime, I had to study what patients tell me. And incidentally, I have also studied what I tell patients. I have studied the meaning underlying my own reactions. And so I could eliminate many statements that are too meaningful. It's better to be a little neutral with statements. It is difficult to dig for the meaning underneath statements and actions. But my patients have given me so much opportunity to study their reactions and their statements, that I think I qualify for something like an expert in this matter.

You know, if a superior comes to me and asks me, "Are we going to do this or something else?" then I will not tell him, "We'll see." And you see here already this "We'll see" covers, underneath its structure, the indication, "You wait till I tell you." And such a statement you don't make to a superior. And if you don't make it to a superior but you make it to your wife, then, obviously, you know the difference. You know where to say the sentence and where not to say it. And so we ask ourselves if Gertie's husband would never say "We'll see" to a superior and says it to the wife, does he know what it means? We say he *makes the distinction.* Since he doesn't make such a statement to the boss, obviously in some way he knows the difference. He knows in the presence of whom to make this statement and in the presence of whom to suppress it. So you should say he knows what he is talking about. But if you say that, then you will say he has found out what meaning is underneath this phrase. And I tell you that is not so. He has not found it out. And nobody has found out these meanings underneath significant statements unless he has made a special study of it. And you know how few people have done that.

I have, for instance, for years—at the time when I was very uncertain about underlying meanings—I have for years scoured the textbooks, the encyclopedias to find some lead towards finding the meanings underneath sentences and underneath reactions. And I may tell you I have found very little in the literature about this subject. But that thing that I call here *finding the meaning underneath statements and underneath actions,* that's precisely what we mean by *spotting*.

Now look here. Gertie's husband knew, in some way, that before the boss he cannot make this statement and before the wife he can. So you may say he knew the meaning underlying the statement, and yet he didn't know it. I know that for sure although I have not asked him.

Now, further, Gertie was told, "We'll see." This means she was told to wait till the husband will finally grant her an interview in the morning, and tell her what she was waiting for. And Gertie felt frustrated. Now, if she felt frustrated, then she knew the meaning of that statement, too. And yet she didn't. That's established beyond doubt. She didn't know what it means that the husband said, "We'll see." And the husband didn't know what it means what he said, and yet both reacted correctly. Both had the same idea. The husband had the idea that such a statement can only be made to a wife; anybody else would not stand for it. And the wife knew, without really knowing, that this statement carried an implication, a meaning underneath it that was insulting or frustrating.

And do you understand there are two types of knowledge? Gertie knew that the statement of the husband was frustrating. The husband knew it would be frustrating if made before a boss. But they could not have expressed this much to you. They couldn't have explained their reaction. They reacted correctly, but they didn't know why they reacted correctly. Had they been asked to explain why they make a distinction between the boss and the wife, and had Gertie been asked to explain why this statement irritated her and frustrated her, she couldn't have given the explanation. I will, however, add that Gertie might have been able to give the explanation because she has had years and years of practice in spotting, in the Recovery type of spotting.

Now let me tell you, there are certain things that people know and they can explain them, and certain things which they know but cannot explain. Gertie knew that she wanted badly to go to Danville. There was no question about it. She had made up her mind to accept the invitation. And she had dwelled on it for days or weeks—I don't know how the situation was, whether it was days or weeks. And finally she had decided that that trip to Danville was something that will thrill her, and she wanted it with all the strength of her wishes. So she could have explained that. But that's all on the surface of thinking. That's all, as we call it, *conscious*. She had thought about the trip consciously and could explain it.

Whatever is conscious is at the surface of thinking. And anybody can understand and, at the same time, explain the surface appearances of the mind, but the surface only. Everything else requires laborious training. If you want to go down to the depths of meanings, both with regard to statements or reactions, you have to make a special study. The study will require you to learn the techniques of spotting. And once we speak of the surface of understanding or of thinking, then I told you already that's all conscious. But it's the surface only that is conscious, not the depth. And if a thing is conscious, then you can express it in ordinary language. You can, therefore, start a conversation about it, and you can explain what is at the surface of your mind. And if you do that, then we say you hold a discourse, or you discourse on things that you find on the surface of your mind. And that's the ordinary conversation that we usually carry on. In conversation, you don't go to the depths unless you have some expert knowledge. And, for instance, a professional man can go to the depths of his subject because he has studied it originally, you could bet on that. And since this is done in conversation, or in discourse, we call that *discursive thinking*, whatever that may mean. The name is *discursive*.

And so we will finally draw a preliminary conclusion and say in order to know a certain condition, you must distinguish between two types of knowledge. The one is the knowledge that can be picked up from the surface of the brain and can then be discussed or discoursed about. And anybody can do that with very many items of knowledge.

But if you want to go down to the depths of things— and for patients it is extremely important to know the depths of their statements and reactions—then discursive thinking will not help you any. The ordinary thinking employed in a discourse is of no avail for the task of probing the depths of your wishes, beliefs, impulses, and whatever there is down underneath in the depths. There, if you want to go there—if you want to dig and dip into the depths of your reactions and your feelings and your impulses and beliefs—you must apply a term of thinking that we call *intuitive.* And many people have good intuition, and they feel what is underneath a statement or underneath a reaction. And that's what Gertie's husband has employed, and Gertie. They had an intuitive sort of knowledge of what this statement, "We'll see," means underneath it, and both have it. And having this intuitive knowledge of what the undersurface of the statement meant, they could apply it where it did no harm and could fail to apply it where it was bound to do harm, for instance, with the boss.

But that's not spotting, just to have an intuitive notion what is right and what is wrong. Gertie had the intuitive feeling of what is meant by a statement, and her husband had also the intuitive feeling, the sense of intuition. That is a very good sense if it is properly used. But then if they are only intuitive, if they only see the depths through intuition, then, again, they can't explain it. They can't. Then the depth is not made conscious yet. And you see with intuition alone, you don't reach that stage of knowledge that tells you clearly why this and that statement has frustrated you and why another statement has failed to frustrate you or the same statement in a different situation has frustrated you, while in the other situation it did not. And if you only have the intuitive feeling of the special meaning of the statement or reaction in a certain situation, then, again, you don't really know. You only feel. You have only a sense of knowing what it means. And if the patient should employ this intuitive meaning of what his feelings, beliefs, impulses signify, that would not help him. That would not be the spotting.

Do you understand now what we mean by spotting? Spotting means not to look at the surface of the thing. That needs no spotting because it needs no explanation.

205

Everybody understands that and can express it discursively. Nor does spotting mean to get at the depths through intuition. That's very good. It's good to have some intuition. But that will not tell you exactly and clearly why you got angry, why you developed temper, why you felt frustrated. You will only feel it, but you will not be able to know it clearly and to explain it lucidly.

Spotting means to look underneath statements and reactions and then know consciously what they mean, not intuitively— consciously, or, as I called it before, *discursively.* And you see, since we have introduced this matter of spotting, our patients have gradually learned or are learning gradually to look into their depths and perhaps into the depths of people around them like husbands, friends, and so forth. But I think this is of no great importance. What is important is that patients are now able to look into themselves and not merely to feel and sense intuitively what is at the base of their reaction but to know it consciously and discursively.

You see, if you know something consciously, then, of course, you can make plans how to remove it if it should be removed, how to suppress it if it should be suppressed, how to express it if it bears expression. And then you can handle life, your own inner life, which is the main sphere of life for action, for planning. And planning must be done with clarity of vision. Otherwise it is poor planning, otherwise it is fumbling. And if you want to plan in such a manner that you don't get misguided, misdirected at a certain angle or tangent, then you must know how to spot the meanings of your reactions and the meanings of what you will do, in terms which, as I told you, we call *conscious thought, discursive thought.* And that is spotting. And don't let anybody tell you that this is something that you can acquire just by wishing to acquire it. And don't let anybody tell you that you can acquire it by just coming to a few lectures of mine or by reading one book of mine once or twice. All of this is insufficient.

And in conclusion, I want to warn you. Don't think that now that I have explained the technique of spotting to you in one respect—and if you remember, you will know that I have explained all kinds of other facets of this spotting on other occasions—don't flatter yourselves that all you have to do is to get this subject explained to you, and then you will understand what spotting means, and you will go ahead and practice it. That is not so. Spotting is so intricate, so complex that it requires continuous training. Continuous. I mean it. And I tell you how continuous it must be and must be done. I have stumbled on this subject of spotting about fifteen years ago. And in the meantime, I have made it a life task to study this subject. And I tell you I have studied it very perseveringly, day after day, I must say hour after hour, in all these fifteen years. And you should think that now I am a master of spotting. But I am not yet. And whether I will ever be, I don't know. I'm still too slow in finding meanings underneath statements and reactions, far too slow to suit me, although you may be certain that I am much faster than anyone is who has not studied and learned the technique.

Thank you.

LECTURE 34

THE DIFFERENCE BETWEEN NERVOUS PERSONS AND NERVOUS PATIENTS

15 Minutes
Recorded Saturday, March 13, 1954

Today's theme will be "Nervous Persons and Nervous Patients." And you may ask the question, "What precisely is the difference between these two designations that we use? What is a nervous person as distinguished from a nervous patient?" Well, I'll try to give you a few clues as to how to distinguish between them.

You see, a nervous person is nervous, and that means that every once in a while his organs don't function as they should. There come at times headaches, and sometimes the headaches come in bouts, not merely gradually rising and then declining, but erupting, exploding. But in an hour, in a day, perhaps, they are gone. And now the nervous system can relax, and the person is no longer harassed by nervous disturbances. He is his average self again, and, if he is, then he can function as an average human being. If he is a father, he can go about his business, and [about] making himself the breadwinner of the family. If she's a mother, she can take care of the home, and life goes on in its steady course once the bout of headache is over.

With nervous patients, that's entirely different. Nervous patients may have bouts of symptoms, but, when they recede, they are still there. The bout is gone but not the symptom. The symptom works now on a lower level. It's no longer acute, no longer explosive, no longer working at a peak level, but it is still there. The fatigue was, during the bout, an exhaustion, and now it falls back to the level of a

208

fatigue. But the fatigue is there practically all day, every day, for weeks, for months, and sometimes for years.

That means the person, although not really sick, is incapacitated and crippled. The nervous person is never crippled, except during the bout, and that is of short duration. So one distinction between the nervous person and the nervous patient is the duration, whether if they have a continuous duration or intermittent and interrupted duration.

With the nervous patient, where the symptoms go on unabated for days, weeks, months, and sometimes for years, there is no letup, no period of peace, I mean no period in which the nervous system can be at rest and at peace. And therefore there is never a proper adjustment.

And if the nervous patient is a wife, well, the husband has to put up with a situation in which, when he comes home in the evening, sometimes there may be a dinner, but frequently there is none. And the children are, naturally, not blessed with the benefit of a mother. They only have a patient around them, a suffering individual.

With the nervous patient—nervous person, pardon me—once the bout is over, the person resumes his or her previous functions, and he is again a father, he is a husband, he is a friend and a neighbor, and in all these capacities, he adjusts. His nervous system is at peace, at rest, in balance. So, with him, the maladjustment is only occasional, and, generally speaking, he is adjusted, except for a few occasions.

And the nervous patient is compelled—he does not like it, but he is compelled—not to take his place in his group. He really eliminates himself from the group to a great extent—from the group, for instance, of the family. If the patient is a mother, she is not a proper mother. Either she suffers all the time and therefore has no smile left for the children, no time left to play with them. She is not a real mother, although she makes her best efforts to be.

And if she is a wife, well, as a wife, she doesn't assume her function. She doesn't take up her place in the family with regard to her husband. And as a neighbor, as a friend, how often is social life utterly disrupted with our nervous patients? The patient knows she should visit the neighbors, more or less regularly or frequently or occasionally. But when there is an engagement, in too many occasions, the patient must cancel it because the fatigue is so heavy that she can hardly move. And the result is that the husband has no social life worth speaking of. The further result is that if the condition goes on indefinitely, the husband becomes socially incapacitated. And since husbands are human—of course, I could have [said] the same [thing] of wives where the husband is a patient, but I have started to speak of husbands, and I'll continue—and as I said, since husbands are human beings, they become disgusted. They feel that they have been robbed of their human and social heritage. They feel that the wife has become a liability, and that creates tenseness, resentment in the husband. And there is an atmosphere of electricity between the couple, and temper supervenes. It's almost inevitable that temper should develop in such a situation.

There are other distinctions between the nervous person and nervous patient, and the most important distinction is that the nervous person knows that today he has an excess of symptoms. Today he is out of function. But he knows that tomorrow, or the day after tomorrow, he will be all right.

The nervous patient reasons differently. Today, he says, I feel exhausted in the morning, and in the afternoon, and perhaps all day. Sometimes there is a letup in the evening. I know that. And then the nervous patient, who at present today is out of function, begins to think of the morning. Then he knows tomorrow he will be out of function again. And next week he will be out of function again, either totally or partially, and next month. And some of the nervous patients think next year, and all their lives, they will be out of function. It's not only the present day that is disturbing, but life is disturbing.

And so there develops hopelessness. There develops a spirit in which the patient gives up, and the patient develops despondency. The despondency, if it deepens, develops a depression. And the depression develops the condition in which the patient can't make up his mind, or her mind. And there is nothing done. There is no decision possible. And where there is no decision, there is no action. And patients finally reach the stage frequently where they simply lie in bed—all day if they can, part of the day if it's possible, but as long as it is possible.

And finally the patient is reduced—fortunately, not in too many cases, but in some cases—he is reduced to a human being that has no life, doesn't show life in his actions because he can't make decisions. And there are other distinctions yet, but I will not quote them today. By now you should have a clear picture of the basic distinctions between nervous patients and nervous persons.

Now, unfortunately, we have drifted into a condition for the past almost hundred years—for the past hundred years, I say, because at that time psychiatry began to sort its material—and since then, we have drifted into a condition in which, unfortunately, the emphasis of the psychiatrists has been placed on the serious cases, on those cases that finally reach the stage, which I described, where the patient becomes totally incapacitated. These are extreme cases, exceptional cases.

But the majority of nervous patients do not subscribe, do not answer this description. The majority of nervous patients get well in a fairly short time. But, unfortunately, textbooks have the habit of describing interesting cases. And naturally, what is interesting is a case that is totally paralyzed or incapacitated. And the textbooks describe these cases mainly. And so gradually the people have reached the con-clusion that nervous patients are generally of the severest kind, and generally, totally or largely incapacitated, which is not true.

And here in Recovery we have finally made it clear to the patients—and sometimes we have made it clear to the world—that even if a patient has reached that final stage that is largely featured in the textbooks, we are not afraid of it. And therefore we go ahead, take care of these patients, restore them to health in a great number of instances. And, as a further consequence, we have therefore adopted the slogan, "There are no hopeless cases among nervous patients, regard-less of the final duration of the condition."

Thank you.

LECTURE 35

FRUSTRATIONS, TRAINING AND HABITS

29 Minutes
Recorded Saturday, March 20, 1954

Well, the panel members discussed situations in which they were frustrated. You remember, Frances was frustrated by the illness of her husband, of course not so much by the husband's illness as by his reaction to it, his refusal to rest. And Theresa was frustrated by the shape and looks of her home. And our other member, Ann, was frustrated by something that happened in the office in which she works.

Well, frustrations mean life. A dead body cannot be frustrated. They mean life, and I doubt whether I ever passed through ten minutes in my adult life in which I did not feel frustrated. So they must mean life, these frustrations.

If there is nothing outside me to frustrate me, be sure there is plenty inside me with which I am disgusted and dissatisfied and over which I am disappointed. And where is the person that is so happily placed that he can spend many ten-minute periods without criticizing him[self], without being dissatisfied with him[self], and disappointed over what he remembers or looks forward to.

Believe me, that's no exaggeration. Life is a continuous frustration. Fortunately, most of the frustration is mild if one is well, if one is reasonably adjusted not only in health but in habit.

Now, what is frustrated is, of course, a desire. I doubt whether anything else will ever be frustrated. I have not given this subject too much attention, and it's quite likely that there are other things that can be frustrated, but I doubt it for the following reason: If you act in any manner, no matter what you do, you must have either wished to act or desired to act or planned to act—that's again wishing. And it's all wishing and desiring that precedes an act. And so I can hardly imagine that anything can occur in life that was not wished or that was wished not to happen, which is again a wish, a desire. And you spend life in a flood of desires, a continual flood, either that things should happen or that certain other things should not happen, either that you should do a certain thing or you desire not to do it.

And some desires stem from the inner centers of the body, mainly or solely, and others are influenced by environment mainly or solely—not solely, hardly, because there must always be a desire added to environment, to the environmental stimulation. And if desires stem mainly from the inside, they are either trivial or significant, important, perhaps even extremely important. And the more desire is important, be certain that they flow either usually, or mainly, or always—I don't know that—from principles, from standards. Some people call them *ideals,* but that's a matter of choice of name. It's all the same. We reserve our discussion to the term *standard of valuation.*

You have the desire, even such a trivial desire as to take a bath; and if you have this desire, be sure—maybe unbeknown to you—there immediately crops up the question in your brain, should I take it now? Should I take it at all? Shouldn't I rather hurry up and do something else that I have to do? Should I stop the bath because it may delay me in another act?

Even in such simple situations as taking a bath or taking a luncheon now or later on, there are always questions. And the question itself is already a frustration. You hesitate; you are in doubt. That is frustration. And how can you always avoid doubt and hesitation in this life of ours?

Well, I think it's plain. Frustrations are ubiquitous. They are always there because wishes and desires are always there. And the one frustration and the one wish stems from standards of valuations and the others from simple impulses, sensations, and so forth, and are not significant.

And I think I will dwell now on this question of simple habits or habits that derive from standards of valuation, this means from will, from character. And if somebody has a character and a steady will, that means that character is always more or less the same, the will always tends more or less in the same direction. And the habits with which the character forms are then just as steady, just as long-range, enduring, lasting as the character is itself. And we speak of *character habits* and *trivial habits*.

You see, if somebody has a character, a well-developed character, then he develops mainly, of course, so-called mental habits, mainly. The other habits don't count for much. And it would be good for you to know what is meant by a mental habit. Of course, the habits of thinking are mental, but they may be trivial. If you just begin to think about the lamp here and the table and an insect that may come to your mind and so forth, of course, the performance may be extremely trivial. But if you begin to think of your mother, well, the mother is a physical being, and you could think of her as a plain woman, a woman that looks in a certain fashion and works in a certain fashion and walks in a certain fashion. But that's not done by the average son or daughter. But [if] you think of your mother, you do it with mental habits.

You have developed the habit of love for the mother, of respect, of the habit of paying her attention, of considering her wherever it is possible—this means, of considering her wishes mainly. And you understand that such matters as consideration, love, are mental. They are not physical. And the habit of loving, of considering, of caring for somebody are naturally mental habits. And mark it: When I speak of patients, we have no quarrel with their average mental habits or, if we have, then it's a private affair. I may have quarreled with the mental habits of anybody who has nothing to do with that thing that we call *mental* or *nervous ailments*.

When we speak of the habits of a nervous or mental patient, then we do not speak of his mental habits. We may speak of his mental capacity but not of his mental habits. The mental patient can still have the habit—and frequently has the habit—of consideration, of courtesy, of love, in other words, mental habits. His mental habits may not be markedly disturbed, and in some patients not at all. But the physical habits and something that is usually called mental—but I don't do that—that thing that we call *emotions* that is in between the physical and the mental sphere. With the patient we are mainly interested with his emotional habits, and they are disturbed greatly. I don't say they are wrong, but disturbed. And the nervous patient suffers mainly—not solely, but mainly—from those emotional habits that we call *temperamental:* fear and anger. And they are, of course, disrupting the peace of life and of relaxation.

Now, look here, how have your habits grown up? Suppose you have the simple habit acquired from childhood of eating three meals a day. You must have acquired that habit. It's a physical habit—some emotion entering into it, but mainly a physical habit. You had to be trained to acquire this habit.

The baby did not know about mealtimes. He certainly did not know about breakfast, lunch and dinner, this means about the threefold habit of sitting down at the table. But our groups either demand or they advise to take three meals a day. And the baby had to be trained to develop a taste for these three meals a day, and sitting with others at the table. And meals do not merely require that the tongue should move and the lips should move and the throat should be active. Meals require a few other things: disciplining of the hands. The hands must not do this or that, and the legs must not do this or something else. They must follow a rule. This means a standard.

You can't, or you should not, jump up from the table and rush into the other room and come back and then rush out again. That's not what we call *mannerly eating.* That conforms to no recognized standard. It violates the standard, the standard of good behavior.

And the baby, or the young child, is trained not just to do with his arms what he pleases. The arms must not, for instance, be pushed into a plate and muss up the vegetables there with the fingers. But babies have all the love possible for doing precisely that. They want to smear the vegetables and the soup—well, the soup they can't smear very well, but the vegetables, well—on the tablecloth. That's what they like. And they want to play with the soup and drip it from the spoon, and, at any rate, they don't care for either spoon or fork or knife. They want to use their fingers.

And do you see the baby has to be trained for these simple things. And I guess you will believe now when I say habits must be acquired through training. And that's, of course, what makes the life of a mother miserable, because training must be done uninterruptedly for months and years, for months—for years, of course, not for months—for years and years. Well, I can't add decades, because let's hope this is not necessary, but endless years.

And I want you to know this does not only hold for the baby but for anybody who has to acquire habits, good habits. Poor habits you can acquire in a second. You can begin to drink in a certain second and then not stop very soon, and then repeat it again and again, and establish a very vicious habit in one second. It has been done. I have seen such cases that did not just develop from non-drinking, over merely social drinking, to pathological drinking, but they started out and immediately became pathological in the habit of drinking. Poor habits can be acquired in a fraction of a second, good habits only in long, protracted training.

And you will understand that I am confronted with this issue; I am always confronted with the issue of duration. I must train my patients, and training requires time. And I emphasize this because of the following reasons: Today we live in an age in which there is little training done, believe me, little. I don't say there is no training done, I wouldn't say that, but little training. You don't really have to be trained how to wash a garment or linen. You buy a washing machine. That takes care of it. Where is the man who has been trained to drive? Well, he was broken in but not trained. And so it goes. We live in an age in which there is very little training done. I naturally don't think of the engineer and the people who have to be apprenticed or trained in colleges, and so forth. There, quite a bit of training is being done, but not in daily life. In the pursuit of daily life, well, what I told you about the washing machine and the automobile can be multiplied by the thousands. But there is very little training.

And when it comes to training the children, you know there are theories afloat today, unfortunately backed by the universities and the schools, that training can be dispensed with. Make it easy for the child. Then he can acquire bad habits very quickly. We know that. Good habits he then hardly has a chance to acquire, except that there are schools and groups which still persist in training. But it's no longer the general trend or, let me say, a very strong modern trend dispenses cheerfully with the need for training. And if I again refer to the machine tools that we have created, then you know naturally a woman does not have to be trained [in] sewing and darning and not even cooking. There are excellent soup cans and vegetable cans, and I agree they are excellent. I am not against them, but they dispense with the notion of training.

Now, this is not a criticism of the age. Maybe it is good to restrict the amount of training, although I don't like it. But that's a personal assumption, a personal opinion. Perhaps I should like it, that's all I can say. But I don't, for some reason. But I deal with patients, and therefore I am, of course, partial to the notion of training. How can a patient get well unless he establishes the habit of control of his impulses, control of his temper, control of his keen desire to make his own diagnosis, control of his desire to constantly check his body and find out the spots that he thinks are decaying or rotting?

If I don't establish new habits in him, then how can he get well? How can he acquire, then, the habits that he needs? And if a patient merely accepts what I tell him and goes ahead and applies the methods which I tell him to practice, if he does that once or twice, then he doesn't establish habit. Everything that is done a few times is no habit yet. And without habits, he will continually fall back into his old ways, and the old ways are not good. His old ways are not good. And so I am partial to the subject of training, not only with patients—in other spheres, too—but mainly with regard to patients.

And just yesterday it happened—and it happens every day, I am sure, when I am with patients—one of my dear ones was told in my office to practice a certain function, to practice the function of lying still in bed until he will sleep. And he was told not to twist and not to turn, not to throw himself about and not to get out of bed and raid the Frigidaire.

And he told me, now, what did he tell me? I, naturally, expected him to tell me, "Well, I'll go ahead and do it." This, patients don't say as a rule. What he told me was, "I will try." Well, you know, if anybody asks me to come to visit him, and I tell him, "I will try," what type of an answer is that? This means I will not visit him. I will merely try.

Will you stop this nonsensical language, "I will try"? Once you tell me you will try, then I know this will not be done, except that maybe you will make one trial and if it doesn't work, you will drop it. That's no training.

If people are trained in the acquisition of habits, then it's understood they must go on training and training with perseverance, with determination, and training without letup. *Trying* means immediately something that the patient doesn't know he has expressed. It means immediately, "I don't know whether I can do it." This means a determination not to put up too much effort.

If I tell you, "I will try to write a letter," then you know the chances are I will only try. I am not sure right now that I will really write the letter. I will only try.

And with mere trying, you will never accomplish any training. And why do my patients do this? They do it because, especially in these days, there is a tendency to establish habits by some temporary design, by some short circuit. Now, let me tell you, there are certain things going on in our life that you perhaps have not noticed or not paid attention to. For instance, if we want to establish in the population the habits of cleanliness—I don't know whether we need to establish it—but we want to do it. Some people want to do it. Then they start a clean-up drive, and the drive runs for a week, and they think in a week they can establish habits. That's nonsense. And all these drives are good for [is] scrapping them. If you want to establish any habit and start a drive for them that lasts a week, well, no habit will be established in a week. That's nonsense.

And you see, our professors and politicians that start similar drives apparently have not sat down to consider what is a habit. If I now eat a meal today and the next two days, or let me say, if I now eat a regular meal or three regular meals today and today only, then I don't establish a habit. If I stop the three-meals rule the next day and two days, and pick it up after a fourth day again, and then drop them again, and pick them up again, that will never establish habits. Then you still continue with your sloppy ways, and sloppy habits are no habits.

And the patient does that. He tries once. Then he has perhaps some difficulty or if it's unpleasant, the process is tiring, so he drops the trying for a couple of days or a couple of weeks. Then perhaps encouraged by me, or by the wife, or by somebody else, he picks up the practice again and drops it again, and that's no establishing of habits.

And so you will remember we want to retrain habits, and that means we want to fill in the time with practice. And don't come to me any longer and tell me you will try to establish habits. If you say that, then I know what is in your mind. You will try, but you will not practice perseveringly.

Thank you.

LECTURE 36

QUICK COMFORT VERSUS
LONG-RANGE RELAXATION

21 Minutes
Recorded Saturday, March 20, 1954

Today's subject will be "The Courage to Make Mistakes." We have spoken about this subject repeatedly for years, and it occurs to me that I never told you what is a mistake. What do we mean by saying somebody made a mistake?

Well, you know all kinds of mistakes. You know the mistake that somebody makes when he misspells a word, when he mispronounces a word, when he uses the wrong grammar, when he, for instance, says, "I met Mrs. Smith, and he told me . . . ." That's, of course, a mistake to say "he" of a lady.

You know all kinds of similar mistakes where somebody miscalculates and says, "Two times two is five." All these mistakes have, naturally, no consequences, and we will not be detained by them. What we are interested in is mistakes of judgment. And for speaking in conversation, you don't need refined judgment that will avoid every mistake. You can certainly make a mistake once in a while, and it will have no consequence, a mistake of the kind that I mentioned. But where judgment is involved, there a mistake may be very costly. If you make a mistake in matters of buying a house, and there is some, let me say, some fault in the mortgage, well, that can have grave consequences.

Now, mistakes that are consequential, that are important, are made in two varieties. And in order to explain that, I'll have to go back a little bit and tell you in what respect, with reference to what, these mistakes can be made. And, as

220

I told you, our life is built on the principle of duality. There are two kinds of feelings, two kinds of impulses, two kinds of beliefs, and the one is a group element, and the other is an individual element.

If I feel good, if I feel happy, that has very little or nothing to do with the group. I can feel happy in the quiet of my home. I can feel happy about my own present condition. That has nothing to do with the group. I can have the impulse now to lie down and take a nap. That has nothing to do with the group. And so it goes with everything. You know, experiences are either private or public. This means referring to the group. And so there is this element of duality in other things.

For instance, if I merely do nothing more than taking a walk, then I have set myself a goal. I want to reach a certain destination, and in order to reach this destination I must employ means. I must decide whether to take the car or whether to take the streetcar or whether to walk or, in some instances, to use the train or the plane and so forth. It would be a bad judgment to try to walk from Chicago to Milwaukee. It's better to take the car. It would be a bad judgment, I think a mistake, to have a flat tire and drive on till finally the wheel goes off, and still trying to drive on. A patient of mine has done that. Well, then the police picked him up. They knew why. He had no judgment. He was a mental patient. Had no judgment.

Will you understand, then, that mistakes of judgment can be made either by way of setting yourself a mistaken goal or by picking mistaken means for the goal that may be good. It would be a bad mistake to want, for instance, to start a high-class business and purchase low-class furnishings and low-class employees. And I think that this example will definitely demonstrate to you that you can make mistakes with regard to choosing the means, but you can also make mistakes with regard to choosing your goal. It might be a very poor judgment and a grave mistake to want to start a high-class business [when] you haven't got the funds for it.

Well, these examples should clarify the issue. And now we will turn to the subject of interest of most, and that is the mistakes made by the patient, not by people who want to start [a] business or drive to Milwaukee, and other such instances and persons. But we will now concentrate on the patient's mistakes.

Now, what is the goal of the patient? He wants to be well, to get well, to regain his health. But what does that mean: health, nervous health? In order to know how to avoid mistakes, you must know what nervous health means. And in order to know that, you will have to know what is a nervous ailment. It's good to repeat that, although I remember I have mentioned it frequently. A nervous ailment is recognized by its symptoms, and these symptoms are all and sundry due to tenseness and, as far as I know, to nothing else if an organic ailment has been ruled out.

If it is a real nervous ailment and not an organic disease, then the symptoms are created or intensified by tenseness and nothing else. And what does tenseness do? Well, as I told you, it creates symptoms. That's correct. But then somebody may ask, "What are symptoms?" We wouldn't go that far. I will only tell you what symptoms do, and what they do is to disturb your peace, to interfere with your relaxation. I speak of nervous symptoms. Other symptoms are likely to do that, too, but do not have to do it. A symptom on the skin, for instance, will not be likely to disturb your peace and relaxation. And since now nervous symptoms are due to lack of relaxation, the thing seems clearly to point to the fact that if you want to get rid of your nervous symptoms, you must establish, or re-establish, relaxation. You can call it peace. You can call it equilibrium. You can call it adjustment, but, essentially, it is relaxation. And if somebody wants to restore relaxation or acquire relaxation, he has to do one thing and that is to banish fear and anger from his system as much as can be done.

Now, my patients want to establish peace and relaxation, and they want to remove the sources of tenseness—this means fear and anger. And so you should say they should go ahead and follow my advice and stop the temper, as I teach them to do it, as I train them to do it. But apparently they have another goal, and for this they employ other means, and that's a very grave mistake. They choose the goal wrong. That's much worse than choosing wrong means.

And what goal do my patients choose? They don't know it, and I have to tell them. There are other goals. If I choose the goal of health, then I choose something that I need. How can you live a peaceful life if you don't have health, that means nervous health. But the patient forgets what he needs, and he goes after what he wants, not just what he needs. What he wants is what everybody wants: some sort of comfort, some sort of pleasure, some sort of something that flatters one, flatters one's ego. But in the main, he wants comfort, because in the years in which he had his symptoms, he craved comfort. This means, again, you may say relaxation, but a different kind of relaxation, that I had in mind before. And that I will explain to you shortly.

The patient wants comfort, but what he needs is the type of relaxation that I mentioned before, and that type is as follows: I can sit down here and be comfortable and have a few disturbances, a twinge here and some little sensation there. And I don't mind it because these sensations and twinges are insignificant with me. And, therefore, relaxation is no problem for me. But I may be in a different position. I may have severe symptoms. And then I would like to get rid of the discomfort, but I would like to do it in a manner that acts quickly because the symptom is very agonizing.

And then the next thing that comes to mind is to get reassurance from somebody that I am all right, that there is no danger, and so the patient begins to question other people. "Are you sure I am not going to die? Are you sure I can get well?"

And then the person that is asked these questions may say, "Yes, I don't see why." But that naturally doesn't reassure the patient because that person that he usually asks is no authority. So the fear of not getting well, the fear of dying, remains, so the patient has to repeat the questions. "But are you absolutely sure that I will not die?" And then the partner gives another reassuring answer, but the patient is not reassured again because the person consulted is no authority. And so patients are impelled, in order to gain comfort, to repeat questions incessantly until the one to whom they are repeated thinks, as they say (I don't say it), "That wife of mine just drives me nuts." That is their language. And from now on that the husband is afraid of the questions of the wife, she can never get assurance from him. He will become impatient in his answers. He will tell her, "Leave me alone. Why don't you stop asking these silly questions?" And if somebody calls the questions of the patient silly, then he certainly doesn't give any assurance.

You see, what the patient wants is quickly restored relaxation. That will not help, and he will only antagonize others. Therefore, he will become more tense because the others become impatient and rebuff him. What the patient needs is another kind of relaxation, the relaxation that works over a long range, not only right now, not a reassurance that may work for a second or a minute. And in order to regain, or gain, this kind of relaxation that works continuously over long periods of time, you must change your predispositions, indeed, your character. And that is, of course, a large order.

I have to change the present character of my patients in order to give them the kind of relaxation they need, and that is long-range enduring relaxation. And if I have, for this purpose, to change their predispositions and their character, well, how can I do it quickly? So the patient, in order to gain the type of relaxation he needs, must be made to wait. This means he must acquire patience, perseverance, the determination to go through with the job for a long period of time, and this he doesn't want. This he needs, but he doesn't want it, in the beginning.

And so we reach the conclusion what a patient wants is the wrong means, and what he needs would be the correct means. And the mistake that the patient makes is now fully clear. His means are wrongly chosen. They are mistakes. Perhaps this goal is wrongly chosen, too.

Now, we have the principle that everybody can safely go ahead and make mistakes. "Have the courage to make mistakes," I tell my patients. That, naturally, refers to every-day life, to the trivialities of the daily round, and not to symptoms. With symptoms, you better stop making mistakes. But in the daily round, you may safely go ahead and make your mistakes, and even with symptoms you will make mistakes. You cannot avoid them, but then learn to avoid them. Symptoms can only be avoided successfully if you change enough [in an] almost complete sense. You must change your predispositions and your character. But if I say "character," I don't mean the character that refers to ethics and morals. In this respect, my patients don't have to change anything. I have yet to see the grossly unethical and the immoral patient. If they are, then either they don't come to me, or they are eliminated from this group.

But otherwise, there is a character in everyday life. It is a deficient character if a person, for instance, does not display his interest for the family, even if he has it inside, but he has to display it. It is a deficiency of character in daily life to be temperamental, to disturb the peace of other people and of oneself. To this section of character, I refer here. As I say, I have to change the character of the patient, and I told you that's a large order and requires time. But we in Recovery are not afraid of large orders. And we have ample time for every patient for the simple reason that we do not need a great number of personnel. And another thing, we don't tax the patient's finances when we make him wait.

Thank you.

LECTURE 37

BALANCED HABITS

26 Minutes
Recorded Saturday, March 27, 1954

Well, I have not frequently listened to such excellent examples as were mentioned today on this platform. I will certainly not be able to do justice to the catalog set up by Frank about his experiences with his faulty memory. That was excellent material, but too rich for discussion. But you remember that Virginia told you of an experience that will bear interpretation.

You remember a girl in the office where she works asked her the kindly question, "Aren't you married yet?" Well, it's a courteous question. There was not a hint of profanity in it or vulgarity, you will agree to that. But it's a vicious question, nevertheless. Well, I don't have to explain that.

But how did Virginia handle this situation? She mentioned something about her response, but I will add something else that she did not mention. And I can safely do that because Virginia, besides being the person she is, the individual concrete person, is also a human being. And while I cannot claim that I know what precisely goes on in Virginia, I know quite something about what goes on in human beings in general. And to my mind if anybody is approached in a rude manner, he responds with two reactions—well, let me say, with two possible reactions. You could perhaps say three possible reactions, but certainly no more. The two possible reactions that I mentioned are either resentment or shame, fear, anxiety. We call it *fear* no matter whether it is the one

226

variety or the other. And be certain that Virginia reacted, either with anger or with fear, for instance, with the fear that she will not find the proper response, the proper answer, or the fear that perhaps such a question may be brought up again.

Why am I so certain that Virginia reacted in either of these two manners? Well, if I want to know people, I observe them, and if I want to know them better, then I study them; and in my occupation it is imperative that, first, I should observe people, and, second, that I should study them. And having done that, and having done that professionally for over thirty years, day after day, with the exception of a few vacations, and with the exception of one day of sickness when I didn't go to my office, I should be qualified as an expert in this field. But that's not enough. I am also a human being that observes himself. And both from observation of others and from self-observation, I know that if a human being is approached in a rude manner, he shows either resentment or fear, but usually resentment, provided he is not an angel. And I, for one, had no opportunity at any time to observe and study angels, so I can't tell you how they respond.

You see, what Virginia did—and this was an accomplishment—was to reduce her resentment to a flicker of a second and immediately gain her composure. She was resentful. There is no question about it. Even Virginia is not an angel, I can assure you. So she did resent the rude approach; this means she was human. But she was more than human. She was a human being trained in Recovery. That's more than human. At least I think so. That's human plus past and present training in spotting. And what Virginia did was that she instantly—the moment she felt resentment—she instantly spotted this resentment as temper. And she went on instantly to spot temper as something that creates tenseness, and tenseness as something that creates symptoms, and she knew she had to dismiss resentment.

Right along this line of spotting, there came another act of spotting by means of which Virginia immediately realized that in order to dispose of resentment, this means of anger,

227

she had to avoid drawing a conclusion that this person was wrong and she right. And once you eliminate the thought of somebody being wrong from your brain, you eliminate inevitably the tenseness. Because the moment you don't accuse either somebody or yourself, if you don't blame somebody or yourself, then you relax and there is no tenseness. And with this simple procedure, you can remove any symptom you wish, provided it is a nervous symptom and not an organic symptom, and provided you know how to do it. This means you have gone through this training through which Virginia has gone. And you will now understand why I said the three examples mentioned here were excellent. I have not frequently listened to an assortment of this kind of excellent examples.

What Virginia did was this: She had developed—by heritage, by heredity—habits of feeling, habits of thinking. She was born as a human being, and human beings inherit it, and have it right at birth, the capacity to resent, the habit of resentment; also the habit of fearing, the habit of being apprehensive. You don't have to learn these habits. And babies don't have to come to Recovery to develop the habits of resenting and fearing. They have it by their habits. And as the babies go on in life, they practice the habit of resenting and fearing, and gradually the habit may gain strength and may rise far above the ordinary level of resentment and fear. These are people that we call *nervous persons.* Nervous persons.

If they then develop vicious cycles and more or less continuous habits of fear and resentment, or either of them working on a high level, then they become nervous patients. The duration and the vicious cycles make a nervous patient out of a nervous person. But mark it: There are very few people living in this world—in this modern world which has endless strain and stress—there are very few people these days, living in a complex society as we do, that are not nervous persons, very few people.

But Virginia was a nervous patient. She has been one of my very severe examples of nervous patients. And now she shows a kind of reaction in which the moment the roots of nervous symptoms begin to rattle, she instantly silences them. She silences them through spotting. And so she has risen to a station in life in which she is no longer a nervous patient, but she is not even a nervous person, and don't ask me what she is. I have no name for her or for such people. But I can express it in a manner that you will understand. She is well-balanced. Balanced. And you may ask what is balanced in her? Well, you can say her actions are balanced, but this will not explain too much. And if you add that her feelings are balanced, and her thoughts are balanced, and add anything you want, that does not give much explanation and interpretation to what I said about balance.

One thing only will explain it, the one thing that we call *habits*. Her habits are balanced. Naturally, that includes habits of thoughts and habits of feelings and habits of impulses, impulsive action, let me say. Everything in our minds and bodies develop habits. And once you speak of habits, that includes all functions and all reactions. People have either good habits or bad habits, and what we call *good* is not what we call *moral* or *ethical.* Not at all. People may be ethical and have exaggerated habits of ethical action. That's not good either. They are then dogmatic, aggressive—ethical, but aggressively ethical, fanatically ethical, and that's an extreme. Not good. What we mean by good habits is what I have mentioned as *balanced.* And good habits are balanced habits.

You will do well to realize that a balance means two things, two entities, that balance, that neither go too high up nor too low down. They balance in approximately an even level, and when they do that, they work together. The one is not too high, the other not too low. Then they would be out of balance, or imbalanced.

And there are two kinds of habits, otherwise they could not balance. I cannot very well imagine that three things will balance easily, three separate things. In my opinion, a balance exists between two things and not with any more. And if there are fifteen or fifteen thousand things that balance, then be sure these fifteen thousand could be arranged in two parts of seven thousand five hundred each that could then be sub-grouped under a higher term: the one containing seven thousand five hundred items that are black, and the other containing seven thousand five hundred items that are all white, and they would balance. And keep in mind, balancing points to two things that must balance. And the two things that are to be brought into balance in human behavior, the two sets of habits—and they are sets, not single habits—the two sets of habits that must balance are the habits that are personal and individual and the habits that are group habits, social habits—the personal habits and the social habits.

Among the personal habits, there is a predominance of the habits that I called *resentment, fear* and whatever is derived from them—anger and fear. They can never balance among themselves. It would have no sense to say an anger is balanced by a fear or a fear by anger. But the total habits of anger and fear—this means the total temperamental habits—can balance with the total group habits. And if they balance in a human being, then there is harmony, inner harmony, inner peace.

But you cannot get group habits—this means habits working in the service of the group welfare—unless you control them. And your fear and anger reactions—this means your temperamental reactions—originally do not want to be controlled. They want to express themselves. In fear, you want to run. In anger, you want to strike out. You want to express your anger in an action, this means in an aggressive action. You want to express your fear in an action, that means in a defensive reaction. And you will now see that the two sets of habits that I mentioned are of two characteristics. The one tends towards forceful expression, and the other tends toward quiet control.

And what Virginia demonstrated here was, she was affronted by a crude remark. And be sure a violent resent-ment grew up in her, and she controlled it. You see, her orig-inal responses with which she was born, the temperamental responses, were controlled by Virginia. And the control was done by *the group principle* as we want to call it now. And once those violent expressions were controlled, then control was in preponderance over expression, over violent expression. And whenever you reach the point where most of your actions are controlled and only part of your actions are easily expressed, then you have balance, and balance of the kind where the one scale in the balance rises perceptibly over the other scale, this means the group scale. The control scale rises perceptibly over the expression and the temperamental scale. Temper is not eliminated. It is not weeded out, otherwise you would weed out your nature. But it is pressed down and control is pushed up, and that is that kind of balance in which the group reactions predominate over the individualistic reactions, and that's the only kind of balance we want in life: the balance in which control predominates over reckless expression.

In technique, you have other kinds of balances. There, two substances may really be even. They may actually correspond to one another in weight, in heaviness, in shape, in all kinds of other qualities, and neither of them preponderates over the other, and we call them *equal*. They are equal in weight, equal in worth, value, and so forth.

In life, we don't want equality. In inner life, nothing should be equal. If you have an equal amount of honesty as you have of dishonesty, that's no balance. Be sure that's no balance. If you have just as much good control as you have temper, that's no balance. You see, in life we don't want equality, a balance that means equality. We want a preponderance of control over life expression. And that's what my patients—among them Virginia—establish and accomplish in Recovery. And I shall add my remark that is most likely well-known to all of you, and you can predict it in practically every [one] of my addresses that I deliver here.

If you want to establish a balance of group habits versus individualistic habits, of control versus expression, of temper versus control—the same thing—then you must establish the habits of controlling, and you can only do that if you learn how to spot temper and other things. And if you want to gain good control and good ability of spotting, then you must turn spotting into a habit, and you can't acquire a habit in two days, not in two weeks. If you acquire it in two years, then you are very lucky. And that's all what Virginia represents: A person that has acquired solid habits of spotting, and therefore is in a good state of balance, and is now capable of taking insults, and flaring up in resentment, and instantly scotch the resentment. And that's an excellent kind of reaction and produces a remarkable amount and quality of balance.

Thank you.

LECTURE 38

STEPPING IN AND TAKING OVER

12 Minutes
Recorded Saturday, March 27, 1954

[The theme] this afternoon is "Stepping In and Taking Over." I take it you know what that means. It means that, for instance, a wife steps in and deals with the husband in a manner as if he constantly needed supervision. She stops him in the morning and asks him, "Did you take the rubbers along?" as if he couldn't know when to take the rubbers along and when not to take [them]. She calls him at the office and asks him whether he is sure to get his luncheon. There are such wives, and so it goes. She steps in and takes over. And the husband may do the same thing with the wife, but I think wives are more capable of supervising the partner—at any rate, more ready to do it.

And the mother may do that with the children. And they constantly remind them to have their gloves on when they leave for school and not to forget to have their luncheon at school.

And then there are employers who don't delegate any authority to anybody else. They think they have to do everything themselves. And if an employer or an executive of an organization does that, then the others—the other executives or the other employees—have the feeling that they don't count, that their judgment is not trusted, that the boss is afraid that they will bungle a job that is assigned to them. And, of course, the same holds true with the mother and her children. The children also have the idea that the mother doesn't trust their judgment, doesn't trust their wakefulness, their attention.

And in every such situation where somebody steps in and takes over, he sows distrust. He hurts the feelings of others for the following reason: Everybody must have some important field in which he is permitted to take care of himself, to live without supervision. And that has been called *the urge to self-determination*. And if that urge to self-determination is thwarted, there results the situation where the person who is thwarted feels a fundamental right is denied him. That fundamental right is to use his own judgment, his own vigilance, his own capabilities. And if this right is denied, then there results what I told you already—distrust, resentment, ill feeling and therefore tenseness.

And here we come to the nervous patient. Tenseness is always a suitable bridge to lead over to the nervous patient. The nervous patient has inner organs. For instance, the heart is employed by the person. Memory is employed by the person. So, you have the parallel between the human body—the human person—and other persons who step in and take over. And the nervous patient does that with his organs.

He has a good heart. He has good lungs, a good abdomen. All these are either organs of his, or aggregates of organs, and they do a good piece of work. I doubt whether the heart has judgment and memory in the sense that we understand it, but it has great capabilities for pushing the blood through the body and for distributing it exactly as it should be done. But if I, the possessor of these organs, should become distrustful of them, then I would step in and take over their job.

And what would happen? The heart would now be interfered with by preoccupation, or by distrust, by suspicion, and that would produce tenseness, and the heart would no longer work smoothly. The heart has developed the habit, or inherited the habit, of working in a certain rhythm, sixty to seventy beats per [minute], and, mark it: This is a habit that has been inherited from ancestry. And if somebody steps in and makes the heart race or slow down too much, then the rhythm—the regular rhythm of heart function is disturbed—and now the heart has to resort to a new habit to which it is not equal. It must now too frequently express the habit of racing, a racing pulse.

Memory has to develop new habits, the habits of remembering under stress, under pressure. This means not to remember well. Thinking becomes interfered with by tenseness, and thoughts don't come so easily. And there is no end to how many organs can be interfered with and frustrated by this super-vigilance of the person, by the intention of the person always to step in and take over. And if this happens, then again, tenseness is created. And thinking, memory, feeling, heart action, breathing, are all disturbed, or may all be disturbed, or some of them may be disturbed.

Well, the patient is told in Recovery to leave the organs alone. They have established good habits, and they know best how to perform their function. As I sit here before you, I must tell you I have no idea how I could make my heart beat more regularly, and I don't know whether it would be a good thing to do. But if I wanted it, I couldn't. Nobody knows how to do that except with some drugs, but you can't keep a person always under drugs.

I don't know how the stomach performs its regular rhythmic movements. The stomach knows how to do it. The stomach has settled habits that work very successfully. And if anybody steps in and upsets the rhythm of the stomach movements, he does a very undesirable job, the job of disturbing a good function and creating symptoms. And, mark it: A symptom is a new habit that the patient has developed through tenseness, just a habit as I have described them. And now the question arises after I tell the patients here, "Stop interfering with your organs; stop watching them with anxiety; stop distrusting them," why does the patient not instantly, or soon, stop bothering his organs? Why does he still continue watching them, making them tense, making them either race or dwindle down to a very low pace? Why does he not stop this activity?

The answer is that the patient has to learn how to do it, and what he has to learn has been described in my book, and you can read it up there. And if you have read it up already, then read it again; and if you have read it already five times, read it a sixth time and a tenth time. It will not do you any harm, and it will do your organs a great deal of good. And what you will read in the book is how to spot your desires and impulses, and particularly you will do well to stop your desire to step into the realm of your organs and to take over.

Thank you.

LECTURE 39

SELF-MANAGEMENT VERSUS THE SETBACK

25 Minutes
Recorded Saturday, April 3, 1954

You remember that Ann told you she had to write a check, and she noticed that she was racing while writing. And when she attempted to write the second check, she made herself slow down. She made herself slow down, which means she had to put pressure on her muscles and force them to slow down.

Well, everybody has done that. Everybody does it every once in a while. And if he does it, well, the resulting act may be very effective, very useful, perhaps very well done. But the act is not done spontaneously. Ordinarily, a simple act like writing a check should be done with spontaneity. And since Ann brought up the subject, perhaps without knowing it, I shall now like to discuss it.

There is a desirable form of action. And if I, for instance, sit myself down at the table in order to take my breakfast, I wouldn't enjoy the breakfast if I had to force myself to eat it. And yet I do it every once in a while precisely in this manner. My appetite sometimes—by the way at very rare moments—lags, and I don't feel like eating. But then I remember that I should eat. Otherwise I would go for endless hours without food. And then I make myself eat. This means I put pressure on myself and force myself to eat. And what forces me?

Well, I will only mention one thing. I think that eating is good for health. And then I remember that my family

237

depends—I mean the welfare of my family depends—to a great extent on my health. And then I remember having heard from kind-hearted patients the admonition, "But, doctor, I hope you keep yourself well. We need you so badly." Well, that always touches my heart, be sure. And I perhaps remember that statement of my patients, and then I eat.

I don't know for sure whether these are the sequences, but they could be. If it is so, if I lack appetite and eat because of the welfare of my family and the welfare of my patients, what do I do precisely? Well, I'll tell you. In such an instance, I eat from duty, the duty that I owe to the welfare of my family and my patients. But the duty again forces me to eat. In either case, it is a force that is practiced on me.

And my patients are always under pressure of a force as long as they are ill. Before they were ill, they ate when it suited them, when they felt like eating. And they didn't eat when it did not suit them, and they did not feel any appetite. So, you see, their actions before they fell sick were guided by what pleased and suited them, this means by their inclination, and the act was produced by the patient's own feelings. And that's what we call *spontaneity*. You act from your own feelings. That's the only element that guides your actions. And if you do that, then you practice what is called *self-management*. Now, if your sense of duty has become so organized within you that you feel that it's part of you—and with the average person, that's what is actually the case—then you feel the duty to eat, and you again act from your own feelings.

But take the case of the young boy or young girl, but let me refer to the young boy. Observe him while he plays with other boys and girls, and what he does springs from his feelings. He does what he likes, what he loves, what fills him with enthusiasm. And he is always spontaneous, at least most of the time, when he plays with other youngsters. And this abandonment that the youngster shows when he is with his own people (this means with other youngsters) and is given to some sort of a play, whether it's a sport or any other play (it may even be horseplay)—but it's his will to do it, and his feeling and his desire. And so he has spontaneity. As a matter of fact, children are the marvels of spontaneity—the average child that has developed in a fairly happy environment.

If spontaneity is at low ebb, then you must force yourself to do things. You don't act from your feelings, from your desires, from your likes, from your will, but from an imposed force—either outside you or inside you. But we will only discuss the forces outside you at present.

And if a patient becomes depressed—and about half of my patients come to me because of depressions—if a patient becomes depressed, that means his spontaneity, his life, desires, his will to do things are depressed. And so their actions are no longer guided and propelled by a will, by a desire, by an inclination of their own. But now they do things with force. They have to force themselves, for instance, because somebody—the mother, father, the doctor—commands them to eat or urges them to eat. Of themselves, they might not eat. At any rate, they might not eat regularly and suitably.

And in the one case where I do something because I want it, because I am inclined to do it, because I love to do it, then my feeling, my inclination manages me. And that has been called *self-management.* And people love to feel, to tell themselves—and perhaps even to tell others—that their case is one of self-management. And if anybody can tell himself, "I just go ahead and do things and nothing interferes with my actions. I start to act out my intention, and there, without hesitation, without friction, without fear, I accomplish it." That's what we call *self-management.*

But if the doctor has to step in—or the mother, father, or the neighbor or a friend—and urge you to do something against your inclination, then you are subjected to foreign management. And you don't act in the spirit of self-management. Then you lose your pride, your self-respect, your self-confidence, and you are filled with self-consciousness, self-distrust. You don't feel that you can depend on your own inner structures.

In the morning, you know you should eat breakfast, but your stomach balks. It doesn't develop the appetite juices. It's depressed. You feel you should go for a walk, but your muscles balk. They do not feel refreshed. They feel clogged up, restrained—tired, you call it, or exhausted But essentially the muscles are tense, and so the muscles are against you. They exercise a force, their force of tenseness against your self-management. And, again, what can you do? Perhaps you will turn to your doctor, and you ask him to help you. But then that's foreign management. Even the doctor represents a foreigner to you compared to your own feelings, your own inclinations. What is closer to the ego but the feelings and inclinations?

And patients come to me and tell me, "I am afraid to be alone. I am afraid to be in crowds. I am afraid to look down from high windows." Well, to be alone is something that the average person does frequently from inclination. They say, "Leave me alone." That means "I am inclined to be alone"— naturally not all the time, not most of the time, but at times. And now the patient becomes afraid of being alone. This means fear draws him away from that ideal of self-management that everybody craves. And the fear now is the force that makes the patient act the way he doesn't want to act and interferes with his self-management. And the patients are taken care of here in Recovery, and you know we have developed techniques which, without great trouble, make the patient[s] resume their self-management.

Our techniques make the patients, if they come here regularly, make the patients relax. And with relaxation, there is no fear, and without fear, self-management is restored, and with it, that precious thing that we call *spontaneity of action.*

Well, the patient has then regained his spontaneity, either fully or to a great extent. If he regains it to a great extent, then we call the condition one of a *good improvement.*

If he regains spontaneity fully, then we call it *a cure.* But whatever it is, whether it is good improvement or final cure, the patient is warned that after he has improved, and even after he is proclaimed cured, there are still setbacks to be expected.

But look here, after the patient has lost his spontaneity and his capacity for self-management, and then regains it, he naturally soars into the heights of bliss, and he lives in the highest heaven of delight. He is now so happy that every thought of foreign management is crowded out from his consciousness. He feels he has gained a resounding victory over the tenseness that robbed him of his self-management and now, of course, everything is bliss and happiness.

And I tell the patient, "No matter how beautiful your life has shaped itself, no matter how happy you feel, don't forget the setback." But the patient is always smarter than I am—and I never felt that I am smart, but he wants to be smarter yet. The patient is extremely smart, and not for his good. And he thinks he feels so happy, so well relaxed, so contented that he will not admit one single negative thought to his consciousness. And so he doesn't want to think of the setback.

I told him he has to think of it, otherwise I will not be responsible for what may happen. But, you see, these are negative thoughts, I grant you. And in the height of his enthusiasm over the regained self-management, he eliminates every trace of a negative thought and refuses to think of the setback. Then the setback appears one nice morning, and the patient is thrown into a bottomless pit of despair. If he had accepted my advice and would have thought of the setback, had it come that nice morning, he would have known it is nothing but a setback. And a setback disappears in minutes—perhaps in half an hour, but usually in minutes, frequently in seconds—if you expect it and don't let it alarm you.

What makes the setback—this messenger of foreign management, this fault that wipes out the newly regained self-management—what makes this setback so formidable is that it alarms you. That's all. You become alarmed, and desperate, and work yourself up. And you get back your headaches, and your fatigue, and your palpitations, and whatever you suffer from. And that scares you more. And the more you are scared, the worse become the symptoms, and the worse the symptoms become, the more you get scared. And there is a regrettable, a tragic, vicious cycle set afoot between the symptom and the alarm, or the scare. And now you have lost paradise. You were in paradise, in the paradise of self-management and spontaneity, and you are tossed back to the purgatory of foreign management and tenseness. And why are you thrown back there? Simply because the patient knows better than I do. And I wish to stress this point here.

You see what the patients told you here, what Ann for instance told you, what Myrtle told you, was of a simple cast. They told you there was a frustrating experience. "I wanted a key, and somebody else took it." That was the one experience. "I wanted to write, and the fingers cramped," and that is naturally frustrating. And that happened to patients like, for instance, Myrtle, who had improved greatly. She had regained self-management to a great extent. Ann had regained it to a vast extent, and now they were thrown back into the lowlands of tenseness and foreign management. They didn't manage themselves anymore, but fear managed them, or compulsion. And what did they do? They expected such setbacks. And by expecting them, they knew how to view them. They viewed them as trivialities, and they knew how to handle them. They handled them without temper, without scare, without vicious cycles. And so they retained their calm, their relaxation. And once you are relaxed, you are spontaneous. There is no spontaneity without relaxation and no relaxation without spontaneity. They form a point-to-point, so-called, correlation.

And so these patients have learned—I mentioned the two; I could have mentioned Paul, likewise—how to maintain their self-management, their spontaneity, their relaxation after it has been disturbed by a setback, by returning symptoms. And how do they do that? The method is very simple, the method which the patients employ themselves. They don't think that they are smart. I hope they don't think I am smart, but I have one quality they should think of. I have experience. There is no doubt in your minds that I have the experience. And if I tell a patient, "Look out for your self-management and your spontaneity, and look out particularly against this thing that disturbs your spontaneity—or is likely to disturb your spontaneity and your self-management—and that is the setback," these patients that sat here on the panel listened to me, accepted what I told them. And they constantly are aware of the possibility of a setback. Expect it, knowing that it can be handled without trouble if you expect it and don't let it break in on you. And they knew to expect the setback means not to get alarmed and to avoid the vicious cycle that brings back lack of spontaneity and foreign management.

Thank you.

THE CASUALTIES OF TEMPER

18 Minutes
Recorded Saturday, April 3, 1954

The panel will discuss this afternoon the subject of "Temper and Temperament." This topic should be familiar to you because we discuss it most often. Well, one cannot speak too often of such an important topic. There would be very little nervous confusion and nervous trouble and very few nervous symptoms, if there were no temper.

Now, it is good to know what temper means. And then let me tell you it means many things, but one thing I wish to discuss today, particularly. Temper is an act—an act. You speak in temper; you distort your features, and all of these are acts. You perhaps move your arms. You flash your eyes. You perhaps blanche or get red in the face. All of these are acts. And an act has this characteristic, that it begins with an intention.

Before you act, you intend to do something. Whether it's done consciously, whether the intention is conscious or intuitive—this means *subconscious,* you can call it—does not matter. There is always a conscious or an intuitive or an instinctive intention. And once the act is performed, then, if it is correctly performed, then you have accomplished your intention. And the examples are common: You want to eat; this means you have the intention to take a meal. And if you take the food, eat it, and consume it, then you have accomplished your intention to eat.

But that's not all there is to intention and accomplishment. There follows one most important phase of the act. After you have eaten, this means after you have accomplished the act, you are satisfied. And you relax if the act was correctly carried out, with the correct means, with the correct speed, with the correct carriage of the body. The means must be correct, and if the intention has been correctly accomplished, you are satisfied. You are stimulated. And so you have accomplished not only the act as such, but you have accomplished something else. You created satisfaction. You created stimulation that was created by you. And therefore the act has been creative, or we call it *constructive*.

Now, there are other acts. One of them is the temperamental act. You become aroused, angry, provoked. Then the question is whether you will accomplish your intention, otherwise the act will not be creative or constructive. And when you begin to mouth your words spoken in temper, how can you ever accomplish your intention? If you begin a temperamental argument, that means you declare somebody being wrong or having done wrong to you. And your intention must be, unless you become violent and strike out, unless you do that, you can't accomplish anything because what you intend to do if you don't use violence—which I take it my patients don't use—what you want to do if you don't use violence, is to convince your partner that he is wrong and to make him mend his ways.

Now, how can you ever accomplish that? That partner, naturally from his viewpoint, is not wrong. He is only wrong from your viewpoint, and how can you make him accept your viewpoint? You yell and bellow and shout at him. That only makes him feel that you are wrong. It does not convince him that he is wrong. So, he comes back with his yelling, his bellowing, his shouting, so that reinforces your conviction that he is wrong. Now, he shouts back and thinks you are wrong. What kind of spectacle!

And that's the average temperamental procedure. You intend to convince somebody that he is wrong, and all you accomplish is to fortify his opinion that you are wrong, so there is no accomplishment. And you know that after a temperamental outburst, there are only casualties, only casualties. You are exhausted, and the other fellow is exhausted. There are casualties, a battlefield strewn with casualties. In most instances, only two casualties; sometimes more, especially if nations become temperamental and start war. Accomplished is usually nothing, but casualties are many. Or in an industry, temper flares up, and there is a fight. Usually the results are casualties—perhaps something else aside from that, but casualties are always the result.

But I am not interested in industry. I am not interested in the life of nations, except as a private person. But as a physician, I am interested in what my patients do. And one thing, for instance, that my patients should do is that during daytime they should feel refreshed or relaxed, and at nighttime they should sleep. Everybody should do that. Why not my patients? But the most common complaint with which my patients come to me is that they don't sleep and feel always fatigued. During the day, they crawl and drag through life. And at night, they twist and turn and throw themselves about in bed and complain they don't sleep.

What do they do then when they feel they can't walk comfortably because of their fatigue? They become angry. This means they develop temper. Some of them develop temper against me. They resent the fact that I don't treat or cure them quickly. They resent the fact that I tell them, "You have to wait. You are undergoing training, and it will take time before you lose your symptoms." But they want quick relief, a quick cure which, of course, cannot be supplied in the overwhelming majority of the instances. So they become sore, as I said, partly against me because I keep them waiting and give them good lessons. They think they want help and not lessons. And partly they become provoked at themselves, and they become disgusted with themselves. And to be provoked or disgusted is exactly the same as developing anger. It's tragic if a person develops anger against himself. It is, of course, unfortunate if a person develops anger against others.

But if people become angry at themselves, this means they declare their selves as fighting against them, as being in the wrong.

Well, what they lose is self-respect and self-confidence. They develop a suspicion against themselves, against their body. They are constantly on edge because they are always afraid that their body will kick up against them. They are, for instance, afraid to accept an invitation, a simple invitation for a card game. Nothing great, nothing magnificent, just a social gathering is planned, and they are invited to it. And instantly they are seized with the fear, well, in the evening they will be so tired that they will not be able to go for this engagement. And they will feel exhausted, and the heart will begin to palpitate. How can you go to a social engagement with a body that feels exhausted and a heart that pounds for hours? And this is caused, let me tell you, mainly by temper, by the fact that you become suspicious of your organs, that you become provoked by your organs. And what is to be done?

I have yet to hear patients tell me that they are angry at themselves. They don't use this language. They seldom say that they are sore at themselves, which would naturally be the same meaning in different expression. What they say is, "I am disgusted with myself." They wouldn't say, "I am angry," not "I am sore," because that would have an absurd ring. Why should anybody be angry at himself? But somehow or other, it has become an accepted form of language to say, "I am disgusted with myself." And so the patients use this phrase, and they don't know that essentially they really say, "I am angry at myself." Why the word *disgusted* is accepted and the word *angry* is not, I cannot tell you. But will you understand that once you get disgusted with yourself, you better perform an act of spotting and realize that saying "I am disgusted with myself" is identical with the phrase "I hate myself" or "I am angry at myself. I have no use for myself. I am all wrong." All of these are more or less identical terms.

But if you use these terms that I mentioned, then you have a chance to feel that you do something absurd, that you state an illogical statement. And it will dawn on you that you do something, you perform an act of anger with which you can never accomplish anything creative or anything constructive. You can only do the destructive thing. There will be, after anger, casualties, as I told you. The one casualty is yourself. You then feel more angry, therefore more tired, more exhausted. And the other casualty is either your heart, your stomach, your bladder. They will become nervous, they will become overwrought, edgy. And they will not do what they should do; this means be relaxed. They will be disturbed.

And I have preached this gospel of relaxation for years. And I have told my patients that they can secure relaxation by abolishing temper. I have taught them how to go about the task of eliminating temper, after years—and it's going to be decades soon. It's going to be two decades that I have done this preaching—I have still to continue this sermon and hope to the Lord that my patients will listen and hear and practice the message.

Thank you.

LECTURE 41

GROUP-IMPORTANCE VERSUS
SELF-IMPORTANCE

30 Minutes
Recorded Saturday, April 10, 1954

I will discuss first the fact that—who was here new? oh, Frances—the fact that Frances, who was sitting here at the right end of this table, was for the first time on the panel. I tried to get her to sit on the panel for a long period of time and for very frequent occasions in which I became rather insistent, but she resisted. And finally she went on the panel.

Well, that's a difficult thing for a patient. A patient, even after the patient has improved to a great extent, as Frances has, nevertheless has not necessarily acquired the art of exposing himself or herself to the public eye. That's a difficult thing not only for patients. But patients have gone through a long extended period in which they have been hiding themselves, not literally, but they have been hiding themselves in the sense of making a secret of their suffering, of which they were ashamed. Perhaps not every patient has done that. But there are very few who did not hide their suffering, their symptoms, and, as they thought of it, their disgrace. And that's what we call *the stigma of nervous and mental ailments.* And Frances was no exception to this rule, and she had perhaps a little more than necessary of this stigma philosophy. And now she was here [at] this table and offered an example on how she reacts now to life and how she did before she joined Recovery. And the story you heard; I don't have to repeat it.

But if you watched Frances as I did—and, of course, I know her better than you do, than most of you do—if you watched her, and if you had watched her with my eyes, you would have noticed that she was tense. She had difficulty delivering her speech, expressing herself. And I am reasonably certain that many of you have not noticed. It's difficult to notice such things. And I will dwell on this point for a little while because it is an important point to discuss before nervous patients.

Too many nervous patients—I don't know how many, and I cannot give you any statistics and no estimate of their number—but too many nervous patients feel or fear that other people notice their distress, which would be no calamity if they simply stopped at this and merely said, "I am afraid people will notice that I don't feel good, that I am distressed, that I am disturbed." There would be no harm knowing that somebody is disturbed. If I form the opinion that somebody that I see on the streets or at some gathering anywhere, that somebody is disturbed or distressed, then I draw a very simple conclusion. I say, presumably, a child is sick at home, or the man has difficulty with his mortgage, or business is not as it should be. Hardly any personal conclusion is being drawn in such a case by anybody. Nobody would draw the conclusion that somebody whom one sees distressed suffers from a nervous symptom, from a panic, from a vicious cycle. Hardly anybody will ever do that with a stranger. One only sees that he is somehow upset, and one interprets this upset as stemming from an average cause, this means business difficulties, family difficulties, or any other kind of such average difficulty. But the patient always thinks—or is inclined always to think—that his cheeks show the tenseness to such an extent that everybody notices it. And everybody then knows that he is a nervous or a former mental patient, which is, of course, stark nonsense.

You people here credit the average person with an extreme degree of penetration of insight. He hasn't got it, and I don't have it either. And I give you the proof. If anybody sees people in his office as I do, and certainly people who are upset and vastly upset, he should certainly be able to draw the conclusion, well, this man suffers from this and that. But I can't do that. With endless years of experience, of a large experience with large numbers of nervous patients, I still have to ask the question of the patient when he first comes for an examination, "What is your complaint?" I don't know it. I can't know his complaint by merely looking at his features. Now you may say, of course, nobody expects me to know the precise complaint that the patient has. These are too detailed experiences.

Well, if you challenge my statement as going too far, then I'll make another statement that you will hardly be likely to challenge: If a patient comes to me with his mother, for instance, or with his sister or with her sister, and they both enter my private office, and I ask them to seat themselves, and then I want to write down names, addresses, the address and the name of the patient, then I have first to ask, "Who is the patient, you or you?" Now does that prove to you that one cannot read the inner experiences of a patient from his face? One cannot read the experience of—that could one tell one who is the patient, who of two persons. You would think that should be easy, should be easy for a man like [me] who has experience. But it's impossible in most instances, except if the patient comes in such distress, in such gloom, that the policeman at the corner could also make the diagnosis. Then I can, too, you know. Then it's easy for me, too. And it would be good if my patients finally get it into their heads that there are no mind readers that can reach from the cheeks to the cortex of the brain. There is no such thing. There are no mind readers. That's all there is to it.

It is true once you tell me one symptom that you suffer from, I will most likely be able to tell you a few others that you suffer from. That's the type of experience that I have. But whether you are the patient or somebody else, if you, or if two of you enter my office, I usually don't know. That should tell you a story.

Well, from Frances I would like to drift over to the case or to the statement made by Betty. And you remember that Betty dealt with a situation in which her nephew was drafted for armed services, and Betty's sister was disturbed. She remembered that when Betty had a similar or the same experience, she was not disturbed. She was calm and made preparation for a farewell party. And Betty, in the course of her narrative, made the statement, "Well, I thought of my son, and I did not think of myself when I did that." That's a fine statement. It reveals a fine spirit. Well, I know that Betty has a very fine spirit, and I will not discuss that. But when Betty makes the statement that she did not think of herself—and I believe that she did not, or did very little of it—that's what I would call a large order, not to think of oneself. Of course Betty did not mean it in this exclusive sense, but nevertheless I assume that she might have meant it, and then I'll discuss the statement, because it's very suitable for discussion. Keep in mind this is an extreme statement, and I cannot imagine any individual on any occasion not to think of himself very forcefully, if for no other reason than for the one that certainly played a role in Betty's example. At least, Betty, in thinking of her son, thought plenty about herself too, or of herself. It was her son. But this is not the point that I wish to make. It was still predominantly thinking of her son and not of herself.

But I may tell you that the self protrudes itself into every situation. And in that situation in which I find myself so frequently every day, and sometimes almost all day, that I am confronted with a patient or with a group of patients, you may think that in my mind there is then practically nothing than the patient's interest, the patient's concerns, and not my self-concern. But that is not so. I have something that we call *self-importance,* the sense of self-importance. And it's important for patients particularly to consider very seriously the action of this feeling of self-importance.

Betty has naturally the feeling of self-importance when she gives a party for her son. Her son was destined to go into the Army and perhaps to fight for his country. And Betty had some grief about the situation but also plenty of pride. And both are the outcome of the feeling of self-importance. But I'll add immediately, Betty's self-importance in this respect was very legitimate and commendable because her self-importance derived from the fact that it was her son who was to go to the Army and perhaps fight for his country. That's an excellent example of the feeling of self-importance, and that's what we call *the legitimate self-importance.*

But when I sit before the patient across the table, then I am afraid in too many instances I have a kind of self-importance that does not compare well to Betty's. For instance, when the patient does not cooperate with me, then I become irritated. And which patient cooperates with me in the beginning of his career? So you see, I am very frequently irritated when I face a patient. I doubt whether a good mother like Betty feels that irritation as frequently as I feel it with patients. And why do I feel irritated? Well, I have a goal; I have ambition—well, not too much of it I can tell you. I spare myself somewhat, but I have ambition. I want the patient to get well, and that's my ambition. It's a good ambition. But I have another ambition that's not so good. I want to be comfortable. That's an ambition. By the way, I don't care very much for physical comfort. If I am fatigued, that doesn't disturb me. If I have a pain, that doesn't disturb me. But I have a hankering for psychological comfort. Call it *mental comfort.*

I have no objection if somebody hurts my skin. I wanted to say "or my face," but leave that out—my skin. Should anybody fall against me and hurt me perceptibly, I would hardly be disturbed by that—hardly. But should anybody attack my sense of importance in any way, I am afraid I would feel mentally uncomfortable. I would then not say what my patients and other people say. I would not say, "He has hurt my feelings." I wouldn't say that. I would say, "I don't like being irritated mentally or psychologically." That's all. I don't like it. I don't say the fellow is wrong by irritating me, but I don't like it. And will you distinguish between the one type of sense of self-importance and the other, and the one type of comfort and the other?

My children frequently come up to me—or sometimes they don't come up to me; they only show what I want to describe—and either tell me or show that I hurt their feelings. And presumably every once in a while I do that. But then I ask myself, "What kind of feelings do they have in mind?" And there are two kinds of feelings. I will stray off the theme, but I will come back again to it.

There are two kinds of feelings that can be classified under two headings. The one is a group feeling. I feel, for instance, for my children. They are a close group, the closest group, the family group. I feel for my wife. I feel for the home and so forth. And that is, of course, a feeling that is very valuable. But mark it: nobody will ever hurt this feeling. Who will hurt my family feeling? Who will ever make a statement that is slurring in connection with my family? The people that I associate with, for instance my patients, their relatives or my friends, are pretty well-bred, too well-bred to ever hurt my feelings with regard to my family or to my country, to my creed, to everything that counts in life. They will hardly ever do that. But there are other feelings, and now we come back to that thing that I mentioned before, feelings for myself. That's an entirely different thing.

Well, you will understand now there are group feelings and individualistic feelings. And if you ever say that somebody has hurt your feelings, be sure what you mean is not the feelings for your family, for your country, your religion; that's all nonsense. Nobody will ever hurt that. If you say that your feelings have been hurt, that means your feelings for yourself, for yourself, for your own importance.

For instance, somebody didn't invite you, and you expected an invitation. Or somebody didn't greet you on your birthday. Or somebody, well, perhaps knocked against your fence, didn't do any harm, but your feelings are hurt. He didn't show respect for your home. But that's not true. It's only that you expected something that you call *respect*. And all of this is the feeling of self-importance that has nothing to do with values. And if your feeling of self-importance is hurt, then you become angry, and you develop temper. And the temper causes tenseness, and tenseness produces symptoms in a nervous patient. It doesn't have to do it in others. The nervous patient is allergic to tenseness, to the tenseness of the kind that derives from temper particularly. And if your individualistic feeling of importance is bruised or hurt, and you become angry, then you develop tenseness, temperamental tenseness, and that produces symptoms.

Betty could have told you that. She didn't have time for doing it, or she didn't think of it, or she was kind enough to leave the occasion for me to tell you about these matters. She could have told you that she has arranged her life—especially after she got well from her nervous irritability—she arranged her life in such a manner that herself counts as with everybody. She is not indifferent to herself and what concerns herself. But she is indifferent, or largely indifferent, to the importance of herself. In point of importance she thinks of her son first and of a few other things second and third, and of herself least, or very little. And so she has achieved something that is remarkable and that we foster here in Recovery: a balance, a balance of feelings, which is the most important balance in life. And I want to tell you briefly what is meant by balance.

Balance in life does not mean what it means on the scales. It does not mean that two things are equal in quantity or quality or intensity. In life there is no equality. At any rate, it wouldn't mean balance. In life there is a different kind of balance. In life it is so arranged, or it should be so arranged, that the group feelings overbalance the individualistic feelings without eliminating them. The individualistic feelings are our nature, and they should not be eliminated because they can't be eliminated. They are our nature, and you can't eliminate nature. But they should be kept under control. This means the group feelings and group entities should have a preponderance over the individualistic entities. The group feelings, in other words, should just overbalance the individual feelings, but the individualistic feelings must remain. You can't eradicate them. You can't throw them out of your body. They remain with you from birth to the grave. There is nothing to be done about nature except to control it. And that's what you learn here. The most important feeling that must be controlled is a feeling, the individualistic feeling of self-importance, and to get it overbalanced by the group feeling of group importance.

And whoever will learn that, will then no longer consider that his palpitations are of such world-wide importance and his headaches are so important that everybody must jump if you have it. And you would finally learn that all your feelings, including your feelings about your symptoms, which are thoroughly individualistic, should be held down. They should be controlled. You should not pamper them, and coddle them, and not constantly think of them as being so dangerous and so overpowering. And that's what we call in Recovery *controlling your self-importance.*

And if you learn it to any extent, as the panel members here have learned it, then you may not yet be cured; it may not be a final cure. But you are then so remarkably improved that you may consider yourself happy about your recovered health without, however, again lapsing back into the feeling of self-importance. And let me tell you, the setbacks to which a nervous patient is liable are mainly caused by the renewed tenseness that comes from a renewed temper, which stems from the renewed importance that you give yourself—again, self-importance. And if you have learned the distinction between self-importance and group importance in relation to tenseness and symptoms, well, then you have indeed learned a great deal this afternoon.

Thank you.

Lecture 42

Interpretations and Conclusions

13 Minutes
Recorded Saturday, April 10, 1954

The panel will discuss today the subject of "Interpretations and Conclusions." You will immediately realize that the patient suffers particularly from these two activities. He interprets his inner life in the wrong channels and makes wild conclusions about what his inner life means. So for the patient it is of the utmost importance to know how to interpret his inner life and what conclusions to reach. And that's what the patient is trained to do in Recovery. In Recovery he has, with regard to his health, to use his physician's interpretations only—with regard to health I say—and the physician's conclusions only. And if he fails to do that, then he makes his own interpretations and his own conclusions at his own risk, and the risk is formidable. The risk means sustained tenseness, endless strains and trains of symptoms, and vicious cycles and panics. And one should think that this risk would be sufficient to make the patient pay the price of nothing more but cooperation.

But patients come to me and tell me—the one for instance tells me, "Today I feel fine." That's a good statement. I certainly have no objection to it. It's a positive statement. And then the patient follows up with the other statement, "Perhaps I feel fine because the weather is so nice." Now why does the patient say that? He has had aches and pains and air hunger and palpitations and fatigue and difficult sleep when the weather was at its best. And now the weather is nice, and he feels good, so he says it's not his physician who helped him and not Recovery, but the weather.

But the patient does not know that if he makes a statement of this kind, that it is a conclusion and an interpretation. But the conclusion is fateful. It is disastrous for his health because if he says the weather helps him, well, there is not always good weather. Some days and some weeks there is very poor weather. Then he makes himself believe that he is doomed to suffer whenever the weather is bad. That means presumably half a year out of every year. And since he has had the experience that in the past on nice days he suffered plenty too, remember what a disastrous conclusion that is. But the patient doesn't know that. He certainly doesn't know that by giving credit to the weather, he wipes me out, out of the picture. He gets an idea [in] his brain that I don't help him, and Recovery doesn't help him. He needs the weather to help him.

Now if the patient should learn how to look at such conclusions and interpretations the way I look at them, he would not make such a statement. He would be able to spot the statement, "Perhaps I feel fine because the weather is fine." He would be able to spot that as a conclusion that is damaging to him. And that's what the patient has to learn, and that he learns when he attends our training courses in which he is taught how to spot his inner experiences with regard to his health. And you will now perhaps understand that spotting, among other things, means look into yourself, watch your statements, your thoughts, your wishes, and don't interpret them in such a manner that they do you harm. Interpret them my way and Recovery's ways; then you are reasonably certain that your conclusions and interpretations will not do you harm.

And a patient came up to me frequently and told me, "Why can't I control my temper?" Well, that patient has been coming to me and to classes for many months and has improved, has improved remarkably with regard to her symptoms. She has learned how to spot them as distressing and not dangerous, and her symptoms are practically gone. But she has two children, lovely children, and she has a violent temper. And the children suffer from the temper. And it's remarkable that they nevertheless are lovely children, well behaved. And if the children suffer from the mother's temper, well, perhaps they can bear it. As witness, they grew up to be very nice specimens of humanity and of womanhood.

But the mother can't bear it. She blames herself for her inability to control her temper, for creating discord in the family, for creating tenseness in the children, and now she comes to me and asks, "Why can't I control my temper?" And I ask her, "How do you know that you can't control it? You asked the question, 'Why can't I control my temper?' This means you state already the fact, the conclusion, that you can't control it. That's a damaging statement. You talk yourself into the belief that you can't, you can't control your temper and perhaps that you can't control a few other things." And once a patient asks such a question, "How is it that I don't understand? How is it that I am confused when I go to the store?" then he has drawn the conclusion already that he doesn't understand and that he is confused.

Now if a woman goes to a grocer and has to buy staples and perhaps other things, and she is depressed—and we know, and I could tell her, and I have told her repeatedly that a depressed patient has, of course, difficulty choosing, this means making a decision. And the depressed patient wants to buy a certain kind of meat but cannot get herself to make the decision, and she wavers between the one variety of meat and the other, and finally she leaves the store and doesn't buy anything. That happens very frequently with depressed patients. But this is a difficulty of deciding, and that means the patient is suffering from a depression from which she has every chance of emerging soon. But once she says she is confused, that's an outrageous statement. She is not confused. She knows very well what is the difference between veal and pork, let me say. She is not at all confused. She has only the difficulty of choosing, the difficulty of deciding. And if she should say, "I have difficulty deciding what I should buy," that would be a perfect statement. But my patients are in the habit of making damaging statements, statements that are damaging to their self-estimate. She has now developed the self-estimate that she is a mental patient, not a nervous patient. And that's a very harmful conclusion.

And these few examples, I take it, will make it clear to you: You must come for training as often as you possibly can. If you are not engaged in a job, then you must come daily if at all possible. And you know, I hope—those of you that come to classes regularly do know—that too many of the patients that come to the classes—I shouldn't say too many—fortunately, many of the patients that come to the classes have this record that is characteristic; it's significant: They hear about Recovery, call me and want an appointment. And I give them an appointment, let me say four, five or six weeks ahead, and they have to wait. In the meantime, they come to the classes as often as they possibly can, and then they bloom out and flower into a good degree of health, and the next thing I hear of them is they call up and cancel the appointment.

Will you try to do the same thing? And the more of you will cancel the appointment, the happier I will be.

Thank you.

LECTURE 43

PANICS, TRIVIALITIES AND FEAR

30 Minutes
Recorded Saturday, May 8, 1954

I shall make some remarks about what Elizabeth said here, [at] this table, while she sat amidst the panel members. You remember that she prefaced her panel example by some such statement which I may not quote correctly, because I don't remember the wording clearly. She said, "I have a trivial example." I am reasonably certain that she said something to this effect. If she did not, then we will assume that she has made this statement. And if she did, then why did she make this statement? Why did she say that? Did she expect that we want our members to present spectacular examples? She did not. But she still has the habit from former days, before she went through her training in Recovery, to think like people think. But not in Recovery. We don't want certain aspects of popular thinking in Recovery. And it's the most astonishing thing, and yet it's common, that people in general think that life—the life of the average individual—is anything but trivialities.

There are very few things in life that are not trivial. I have told you repeatedly, spectacular things happen in the life of an individual very seldom. How often does your house get burned down? I ask patients, "How often do people go bankrupt? How often is a child born to a family?" Or "How often does somebody die in a family?" And so forth. The important items in life count for very little in point of behavior, for very little.

A mother doesn't have to be taught how to grieve over her child. And the average young man and young woman don't have to be coached how to fall in love and how to get married. They do that routinely. Sometimes they may want a consultation over the issues. But usually things roll along in life, especially with regard to the big items. Because they usually happen, and once they are there, you find out you had very little to do with their production and their course. The child didn't die because you did something. It simply died. And people get married not because somebody planned it, but they get married because that's the thing to do, or that's the thing that happens.

Well, that's all right. But be sure that Elizabeth no longer thinks in terms of spectacular life. Whatever romanticist inclination she has had before she joined Recovery, be certain, has by now been replaced largely by a realistic attitude. And what we call *reality* has a certain corner in which a person sometimes dies, and another person gets married, and a house burns down, and a bankruptcy happens. But in the vast expanse of the remainder of reality, what is called *reality* could just as well be called *triviality*. Reality really consists of trivialities, mainly.

But the patient, before he reaches Recovery, doesn't know that. And he doesn't know that his trouble has started as a triviality. Go back into the history of any of my patients, and there are only a few in which something happened to their impulses, to their beliefs, to their sensations out of a clear sky. These are, I wouldn't say rare cases, but they are the minority of the cases, vastly in the minority.

And if that happens, that something befalls the patient, it happens to him as, well, as a very rapid occurrence, a sudden development. If that happens, then in the overwhelming majority of my experience, and be sure in the experience of others, this abrupt onset of a nervous condition passes in a few minutes or in a day. That's the average experience. And so it really was a triviality that scared you. If it passes after a few minutes or after a day, then be sure it was a triviality with regard to consequences and with regard to its essential importance. What happens then?

The patient has had something terrible occurring in his life, but he got over it, and quickly as a rule. And the patient then is reassured. He doesn't know what happened to him, but he is reassured because the next day he feels better, and then he goes on feeling better. And after a few weeks, in most instances, the patient has as much as forgotten the incident. Should anybody remind him of it, should anything remind him of it, he will remember it. But essentially he forgets about it, so it was a triviality.

But after two or three weeks what happens? And that's the typical occurrence. Suppose this thing that has happened to the patient, and I mention an example, that he stood waiting for a street car, and all of a sudden his head felt like ballooning out. That's a terrible experience. The experience itself I will not call a triviality, even if it happens only once. It's far more than a triviality. But what follows was a triviality. It developed that this terrible experience had no consequences for the next two weeks. So essentially, in point of importance, it was a triviality. It was only so spectacular and frightening because of its intensity, but not in point of what it did, in point of consequences. But now it happens that two weeks or three weeks later that same person that stood waiting at the street car and his head produced the sensation of ballooning, three weeks later he stands again at the street car and there the ballooning comes again. That's the remarkable thing that in many patients, the original scary event that produced a frightful nervous reaction repeats itself precisely when the patient is brought into a similar or identical situation. The street car again did it.

And now the patient puts two and two together. Or you can say, in this instance, one and one he puts together, the first experience and then the other experience. And he tells himself, "Well, during the past three weeks I felt good, but now the thing came back. How if it comes back again, if I am now doomed to go through these experiences for good . . . ?" And all you have to do is to engage in such a course of thought, and what you do is that you create inner doubt, distrust of your body, distrust of your constitution, of your disposition. And any distrust that you create within you against somebody else, but more so against yourself, will create tenseness. And as long as this self-distrust is maintained, the tenseness will stay with you. It will endure. It will gain duration. And that's the principal characteristic of the nervous patient: that he is likely to produce what other people don't have to produce, and this is enduring tenseness, because he is enduringly disturbed now by his self-distrust.

Of course during the first three, four, or five days, the distrust may not be enduring yet. But if it crops up again and disappears, crops up again and disappears again, and comes at closer intervals, stays at longer periods, then the patient becomes alarmed and is likely to develop a panic. And the more he is alarmed, the more intense becomes his panic. And the more he is panicky, the more is he alarmed. And the more alarmed, the more panicky. And then comes the vicious cycle between alarm, fear, and panic. And then the panic presents or produces tenseness. And the more tense he becomes, the more the patient becomes afraid. And the more afraid he becomes, the more goes the tenseness. And this patient is now in the grip of a continuous, or more or less continuous, panic. And then the condition, if it is not taken care of soon, develops the habit of producing panics. And that creates unlimited and practically unending suffering. And if it goes on for months and months, then the patient develops a chronic condition, or a long-term condition—which is the same word, or with the same meaning.

And finally he reaches Recovery. After a long trek from physicians to physicians, from hospitals to hospitals, clinics to clinics, finally he arrives here. And when he arrives here, we have to train him. And Elizabeth has this history of having experienced frights, and panics, and vicious cycles, and having been hospitalized, and having visited private physicians. She wasn't the worst offender in this respect. She has not visited dozens of physicians, but a certain number. And when Elizabeth arrived here, what was her condition? Well, she mentioned she had symptoms the moment she worked herself up. When she became angry, her heart palpitate[d], she developed head pressure, and naturally fatigue, which at that time she called exhaustion. Her sleep was poor, and so forth. And why did she develop these symptoms?

All of it can be reduced—all the experiences of a nervous patient can be reduced—to the fact that he develops tenseness. Without tenseness, the patient would relax, normally relax. He would have average relaxation. But with tenseness, relaxation is gone. And if relaxation is gone and tenseness installs itself on an enduring basis, then symptoms appear. The nervous system of a nervous patient is allergic to tenseness. And if you want to lose your symptoms, you must lose your enduring tenseness. Intermittent tenseness can be handled. That doesn't do any harm. But the tenseness, running along for stretches of time, finds that your allergic nervous system cannot endure the tenseness and develops symptoms. And the more symptoms you had in the past, the easier can they now be developed by the tenseness. And, as I said, if you want to get rid of the symptoms, you must get rid of the tenseness, and if you want to get rid of the tenseness, you must learn how to relax. That's the only method that I know by which tenseness can be removed.

But how are you going to relax? Well, you know how you are trained here. But compare tenseness with relaxation. Tenseness cannot be maintained if you don't fear, or if you are not angry. You must neither be fearful nor angry, and there will be no tenseness, as far as humanly possible. So the way to remove the tenseness is essentially to remove fear. Leave out the anger at present—although it shouldn't be left out, but it's too clumsy for discussing two items at the same time. We will only discuss tenseness as created by fear. But then the patient must know how to handle fears.

I will repeat again. You want to get rid of your symptoms, that's your ultimate goal. But in order to get rid of your symptoms, you must get rid of the tenseness. In order to get rid of the tenseness, you must get rid of your fear. Once you do that, you will relax. Without fear, there is relaxation. But how to get rid of fear, well, we'll have to introduce another element.

Fear is a belief. That's the great element that is stressed in Recovery, that we teach you. Fear is a belief. Nobody knows how to remove fear. If I am afraid, I will have to wait till the fear disappears. But the ordinary fear is easily removed from the body. A dog jumps at you, and you get scared. Well, the moment you look around, you see it's only a dog, and you relax. But how do you relax? The dog jumped at you. He made you feel scared. There is no question about it. So, the dog created your scare. And who removed it? The dog didn't remove the scare. But after you look around and see it's a dog, you relax. The fear is gone. Now, who removed the fear? The patient didn't because he didn't know how to do it. Who removed the fear? It's the man who made the patient see through his fear, spot it, to see through his fear. And that's what we do in Recovery. And the patient is told, at that time when that dog jumped at you and you got scared, then you looked around and saw it was a dog, then you relaxed, at that time you carried out two acts of spotting, of looking through reactions.

You got jumped at by the dog, and you formed the belief that there is danger. Then you looked at the dog, and you formed the belief there is no danger. The first belief, that there was danger, made you tense. The second belief, there is no danger, removed the tenseness. It wasn't done by the dog. The dog couldn't have removed the tenseness. The dog removed himself, but not the tenseness. And this simple example will show you what we mean by spotting, and spotting doesn't tell you anything than what everybody knows anyway.

If I tell somebody, "Well, fear is a belief," well, everybody will agree with this, I hope. It is a few other things, too, but essentially it is a belief. But there are many things that people know and don't know. They don't know that they know that. That's important to know, that you don't know that you know something. And sometimes you believe that you do know something, and you don't know. But you think you know. And therefore, in order to make you look through the meaning of disturbing events, you have to be trained to know what you do know, what you do know anyhow. And everybody knows that a fear is a belief. But they don't think in these terms. People don't call fear a belief. They call it a feeling, an emotion, not belief. And they are right. It's a feeling, it's emotion, it's a thought, too. It's sensations, palpitations; everything is in a belief.

But the most important thing there is in the belief, people don't think about. They know it. They know it's a belief in danger, but they don't think about it. Nobody has taught them how to do it. Those psychologists that speak to people about fear always call it "feeling" or "emotion." I doubt whether I ever heard anybody or saw anybody write a sentence in a book that fear is a belief. I doubt it. At any rate, if it has been done, it happened so seldom that I don't remember having read it. And when it came to me once, well, I can't get my patients rid of fears. How can I do that except over years and years of analysis—you know, that's usually the method—then I began to search for some method that is simpler. And it took me time to find out this trivial truth: that, after all, fear is a belief, the belief that there is danger. Now I knew what to do about fear. If it's a belief, well, then I can train the patient to do what I do every few minutes, certainly every few hours.

I accept beliefs, and then I drop them, then I pick them up again. Everybody can do that. I wait for somebody, then it comes to me, well, there he is, so I believe he's coming. Then I look, I see it isn't he, so I drop the belief. And then I begin to think of him, that he may be out of town. Then I get the belief that I am in danger, that I will not find him. Then I begin to think about it and realize, well, he couldn't be out of town because I just saw him this morning or spoke to him over the phone. Now I change the belief that the man is out of town, and I pick up the belief that he is in town. And these are in important situations where I am eager to meet somebody. These are not even trivialities. They may be important situations. And in such important situations, you drop beliefs, you pick them up, you retain them, you don't, or you try to get rid of them. Beliefs can be manipulated.

But fears, I didn't know how to manipulate fears. And I still don't know except if I make the patient change his beliefs. And so I must give him my beliefs, and I must form my beliefs first. And so some day I formed the belief that the patient suffered from beliefs, from the belief of danger, or, in angry temper, from the belief that somebody did him wrong. That's what Elizabeth mentioned, her angry temper, where she formed the belief that somebody wronged her or did wrong.

But look here. It's a simple method. You just tell somebody to drop his belief, and he could do it. It's simple, but he doesn't drop it. He keeps his belief. And if I want the patient to drop beliefs, well, he makes an effort, but they don't work. They certainly don't work immediately. And there was one thing that I forgot about it when I formulated this theory: I forgot the fact that humans develop habits, and that habits are stubborn.

If they have been developed and retained for months and years, like with my patients, then the habits resist being changed. And if it is a habit of thinking in a certain manner, a habitual belief, then the patient particularly is likely to become addicted to the belief. And then how am I going to remove that addiction? We call it *an obsession,* and patients have plenty of obsessions. But that's no problem, and I soon found out it wasn't a problem. Oh, it was a problem, but not an insuperable problem, not a problem impossible of solution.

And the answer to this problem was simply take your time and give training, continuous training, persevering training, and then you overcome the handicap of time. Time can be crowded out by other time. This stale time, this time that got stuck, can be eliminated by waiting, by your spending time till this thing that got stuck will disappear. And in life everything disappears. It may come back, but in life everything moves provided you let the thing go. Then it will gradually go, provided you let it come back, it will come back. And that requires training, and you must learn the technique of not working up an experience. But of this I can't speak.

I wanted only to show you that, first, Elizabeth started from her fear that she spoke of trivialities, and I wanted to tell you there is practically nothing in average life but trivialities. And I wanted to show you that the patient starts out with a thing that could have taken a trivial course if he hadn't worked it up. And then I wanted to go on to tell you that the method with which to deal with all these conditions is again a trivial method. Relax, remove the belief of fear, replace it by a belief that you can put in its place. But you must wait. That's again trivial. And everything that counts in life constitutes a triviality, and don't let these trivialities scare you.

Goodbye.

LECTURE 44

GROUP-MINDEDNESS AND SELF-MINDEDNESS

23 Minutes
Recorded Saturday, May 8, 1954

The panel will discuss this afternoon the subject of "Group-Mindedness and Self-Mindedness." I guess you know that this is a chapter taken from *Mental Health Through Will Training*, and let's hope you have found time to read it. Now, if you speak about a group, as in this phrase, and you oppose it to the self—and you will remember the title is "Group-Mindedness and Self-Mindedness"—so if you oppose the group to the self, what do you mean by that? Or you may ask, what do I mean by that if I make this opposition? And it will be good for you to know that this is very important for the patient to know that the group is largely—and sometimes perhaps totally—opposed to the self of the individual.

As I sit here, I am an individual. Well, that's understood. That's no statement of great wisdom. If I am an individual, then I have to conduct my own individual life. And the patient has conducted his own individual life in such a manner that he got stranded. And here you will already notice the close relation between such items as group and self to the fate of the patient. The patient will do well to learn how not to [get stranded] in life.

And that patient, being an individual, is placed between two forces as every individual is. The one force resides within you. Your impulses, your beliefs, your sensations, your feelings, they all can go on a rampage. And then you are racked by frightful impulses, frightening sensations, beliefs that become compulsions and obsessions. And you will understand now what I mean by saying you are placed between forces, two forces. The one is within you. The one within you I have described. And you know that these implacable forces that we call *sensations, impulses, obsessions, compulsions* have wrecked a good deal of your life.

There is another force outside the patient, or we can say now outside the individual, that has nothing directly to do with his self. That other force is the group. Now, don't think that the group is essentially against you. That's nonsense. It is against you, in one respect, and for you, and inevitably necessary for you, in another respect. But when the person grows up, his first impression in this life is that the group is against him, particularly the group of father and mother, teacher, later perhaps the boss. Everybody grows up as an individual. This means he has impulses, and he wants them carried out. And the group says no, for instance, the group of the parents. And you will understand from this brief statement that it is perfectly legitimate to say, in many respects, the group opposes the self, the individual self.

You see, there is a patient, and in the morning he has to go to the office or to some place where he is required to do some work. But he feels fatigued. The fatigue has nothing to do with the group. That's an inner experience. And when a nervous patient feels fatigued, then he doesn't say, "I am tired." Well, that would be a very trivial statement, and the patient doesn't make trivial statements. The patient complains, and a complaint is very difficult to make about a trivial thing. If the patient complains, then he is prompted to exaggerate. If he doesn't exaggerate, then his complaint is trivial. So, I have yet to see the patients that don't—when they think of their fatigue—that don't express it in terms of exhaustion. Fatigue isn't enough. It is not dramatic enough. It's not impressive enough. And the patient somehow gets himself to believe that he suffers from exhaustion. But I correct him and tell him it's fatigue. He doesn't like that as a rule. And when somebody feels he is fatigued or exhausted, then of course all his impulses are then directed against his going to the office. But going to the office is a duty for a family father, for instance. He must go there because he wants to maintain his family.

And here I want you immediately to grasp the fundamental nature of this contrast, or opposition, between self and group. The self that is fatigued feels he wants relief. He wants relief from his exhaustion. That's his main objective now. When he suffers, he wants to get rid of the suffering. But the group is not interested in your suffering and in my suffering. The group goes its way. It may provide certain institutions—hospitals, and so forth—that will take care of your exhaustion, but essentially the group walks on its way. It doesn't bother about this single individual. If it provides relief, it does that for masses, not for the individual. And so the individual is left out.

And he goes to the doctor, and the poor wretch that falls in[to] my hands is unlucky because from me he can't expect instant relief. I will tell him to wait. You know that. He has to show patience, and the very least thing that the patient wants to show is patience. He wants instant relief or as speedy relief as possible because his suffering is really outrageous. But I, as the representative of the group—and that's what I am with you—have to employ group methods, and I tell you what the group methods are.

Every group requires its members to conform with certain standards. And if you come to me, I am your group leader, and I tell you I don't know how to give instant relief. I can only train you, and training takes time. Of course, I don't have to tell you that I give you instant relief very frequently, too. But I pooh-pooh the value of instant relief. That will never cure you. And I, as the representative of the group, want to effect cures, not merely improvements and relief. And so I, the representative of the group among you, am opposed to you, and you are opposed to me in this respect. Otherwise not. In this respect, that I insist on cure that takes time, and you insist on getting relief that may take no time. And it's good for all of you to know this opposition. And when we go further, then we will see that if I make you wait till you will be cured—in the meantime I give relief, plenty, you know that, but I pooh-pooh it; relief is not the important thing for me—if I then make you wait, what do I ask you to do? I ask you to forego that thing that you want to get. A few minutes ago I called it *relief,* but now I will call it by another name.

Why do you want relief? The reason is that suffering is something that naturally is most unpleasant. It's painful. It's agonizing. Suffering is the reverse of being comfortable. But let me tell you that every individual in this world craves to have a comfortable life. It doesn't have to be physical comfort. There is moral comfort, mental comfort, social comfort. But everybody craves comfort, and suffering abolishes comfort. So what the patient craves is comfort. And the group is not known to supply comfort to the individual. It may, and frequently does, but that's not the calling of the group, not the essential purpose of the group. The group doesn't care much essentially about these matters that you call *comfort.* What it cares for is effort, not comfort. The group requires you to do certain things that the group calls *duty, responsibility,* and *plain accomplishment.* But your impulses ask for comfort. Your sensations trouble you so energetically that they demand that you give them comfort. And that's what we call *the appeal of the muscles,* or *impulses,* or *sensations.* The inner self, as represented by its impulses and so forth, appeals to the individual to supply comfort. But the group wishes you to make effort, not to have comfort. The group is not against comfort, but it's not the business of the group to supply it.

And there is another opposition: comfort, well, versus effort. And I, as the representative of the group, tell the patients to wait. This means they must apply effort. It takes effort to wait if you suffer. It takes effort even to wait for an elevator, even if you don't suffer. To wait for a streetcar, that is effort. It certainly is not comfort, you know that. And what the patient wants—again I go back to the theme—is comfort. But that's not precisely what he needs. It is only what he wants.

The patient and everybody can live along with suffering. He can adjust for it. He can, for instance, show how to tackle his suffering, as we do in Recovery. But I want you to understand there are all kinds of oppositions. Group against—oh, I shouldn't say against—versus the individual, comfort versus effort, wanting versus needing. I didn't mention this word yet. The group wants you to do what you need, not what you want. I will not dwell on that. But the one thing I want you to understand, the group has one goal, and the individual has another goal. The group is not in the way of the individual, but it's not interested in it. If you want to take a swim, the group is not against it, but the group is definitely against it if you want to take a swim while some task waits to be performed. The group wants you to discharge your obligations. But the individual, when he is in trouble, has inclinations, the inclination to get relief. Well, let's be done, let's have done with all these oppositions.

The group sets down rules, and we call them *standards, standards of behavior.* And the standards of behavior that the group sets down are not just in force this afternoon but over long periods of time. And the group tells you you must always think of your work, not only of comfort. And where work collides with comfort, there you must make your choice in the direction of work. Again, you must make effort and not look for comfort. But it's difficult to know what comfort is permissible and what effort is dispensable. And when the patient, for instance, wants some comfort, why shouldn't he get it? And he should get it if it can be provided. But if it interferes with a duty and obligation, for instance, the duty to get well, then I would advise the patient not to look for comfort and rather to make an effort to reach the goal of health.

And you will realize now that there are many opportunities where you don't know. Should I go after my comfort or should I go after my effort? Should I go after my obligation or inclination? After what I want or what I need? And in order to decide that, in many instances you must apply to a person who has excellent judgment, fine training, and solid experience. And that's what we call *the leader.* And in Recovery this whole choice is made easy for you because we have leadership. And the leader can tell you in what situation you may safely go after your comfort, and in what other situation you have to do, not what you want, but what you need, not to look for comfort, but to apply effort. And in order to be advised by the leader, you must have leaders, of course. And in Recovery we have to supply leadership, this means many leaders that will advise you. And that requires training.

And if the leader has to advise the patient that is in his group, then he must train the patient, for instance, how to understand what the leader tells him, how to use our language, the Recovery language, and all of this requires time. It requires time to train the leaders, and it requires time for the leaders to train the people in their group. And in order to take one's time, you must wait, and waiting is an effort. It is against comfort, and we come back to the whole, well, circle of the terms that I explained.

And the only thing that I can tell you, and you have heard me tell you repeatedly, if you want to get well, you must be prepared to wait. There is no task that can be performed on the spot if the task is significant. And where is there a task that is more significant than to restore your health? And then finally to effect a cure and to give you final comfort, not transient comfort. And that requires time, I must add again. And it must require particularly much time because we don't want you always to depend on leadership, but finally you must learn to establish self-leadership. And that's what we call *self-help*.

And now you know that this is our ultimate goal, to make the patients help themselves. I don't have to tell you, I hope, that that again requires time and waiting. And if any one of you doesn't want to spend the time and doesn't want to wait, well, let me merely say I hope you will finally find your rest and peace without waiting, without spending time. But I am afraid that is a very pious wish, and you know pious wishes usually do not materialize.

Thank you.

LECTURE 45

DUALITY IN LIFE AND THE
UNIFYING PRINCIPLE

30 Minutes
Recorded Saturday, May 15, 1954

You remember that Ann, who sat to the right of Phil, spoke of such things as pies which she baked, and brownies, and later she spoke of flour and sugar, of which she perhaps didn't have enough, and whatever connection she spoke of it. And what has that to do with health? Why should people come here and listen to somebody telling them that she baked pies and brownies and used a certain kind of flour? Well, that's no news, indeed not. Now obviously Ann did not mean to mention these ingredients of baking and cooking. What she wanted to mention was something that happens or happened during the cooking and during the baking. And that thing did not happen outside Ann but inside Ann. And the thing that happened was that an impulse arose, an impulse. And Ann had an impulse that expressed frustration. And let me tell you briefly, I don't know anything else in life that can be frustrated except an impulse.

You may say that there are beliefs, and strivings, and ambitions that can be frustrated. But they are all based on an impulse. And you may take it on trust that if something is frustrated, it is always an impulse no matter by what name you call it. So, Ann told you about the life of her impulses. And you remember that she told you that while she was cooking and baking, she was rather stimulated. And all of a sudden her animation faded, and she felt a dismal fatigue, something like an exhaustion. And all of this is nothing unfamiliar. All of this has been discussed here, and in other places, and in all eternity, I guess, and means a great deal. But it's not particularly the topic of Recovery, although it is one of the topics.

But while Ann went on describing her reactions to frustration, and separated her reaction that she expressed before she had joined Recovery, and the reaction which is now hers after she has gone through Recovery training, while she described all these beautiful occurrences—I mean she handled them beautifully—she delivered herself of a statement that I may not have caught completely. And I am not sure whether I quoted truthfully. She said, as far as I know, "How can one be full of pep in one moment and lose ambition the next?" That's, of course, something worth discussing. But I would first ask the question, "Why was Ann amazed at such a thing?" When she asked how can one be something in one moment and something else in the other moment, she expressed amazement. So, this phenomenon of somebody changing suddenly, abruptly, as she had done, was an issue for her. She questioned the possibility of it. She knew it was possible. But in a rhetorical manner, she asked this rhetorical question—I take it that's what it was—and it most likely, nevertheless, expressed amazement.

Well, if I had noticed something of this kind—and I have noticed it perhaps thousands of times in myself—and if I had noticed it in a patient, that would not have amazed me. And I don't think it should amaze anybody. This phenomenon of somebody changing abruptly from one state to the opposite state, from liveliness to dullness, from sympathy to even hatred, from love to hatred, all of this is nothing uncommon. And I mention very, very spectacular contrasts: for instance the change from love to hatred, and that even is not at all uncommon. It's, indeed, I think, frequent. If this is true, then why should one be amazed at that?

Now, nobody would be surprised to see one condition in our inner life suddenly being transformed into its opposite if we knew a great deal about inner conditions. Then we wouldn't be surprised at that. And you will agree that perhaps I have had very intimate contact with that thing that we call *inner experiences*. If I didn't have these intimate contacts with the field of inner experiences, well, then you made a great mistake consulting me. I hope you didn't make a great mistake.

And in our inner world, there is a certain arrangement of forces, particularly impulses. And I told you everything in our inner life is expressed through impulses that become active and create some action. In this interior of ours, there are always contrasts. Whether there is something else there, I can't tell you, but the contrasts abound.

Of course, contrasts are very common in our outer life, too. There is the right arm that contrasts with the left arm. Everything that is above our midline contrasts with everything that is below our midline. And there are two eyes, two ears, two legs. You see the contrasts, what you call *a contrast*, expresses the fact that two things are so different from one another that they contrast with one another. That's what contrast means. I didn't give you a very learned explanation, but I hope you will understand that contrast is based on the duality that characterizes a human body and a human mind. They are always dual. So, from now on, will you do me a favor and don't get insulted or scared if somebody says you may have a dual personality. You'd better ask him, "Do you think you have none?" Whatever he will answer, be sure there is nothing but dual personalities. I didn't say split personalities. That's something else. That is not the commonest thing. But a dual personality, let me tell you, I don't know anything but duality in life. Everything is dual. And the terms that I bring to you, you know have been cast in this terminology of two, everything being arranged in twosomes.

And there [are], for instance, needs and wants. These are contrasts as we view them. They are certainly contrasts if you add the adjectives *objective* and *subjective*. And you know if a need is objective and a want is subjective, then be sure they are contrasts because objective and subjective are contrasting forces or conditions. And if I tell you that impulses must be controlled and certain impulses must not be expressed, then perhaps you will by now realize that control contrasts with expression. If this is not clear to you, then read my book, and it will become clear. And you will just as well realize that, of course, if you use the word *average,* the contrast is exceptionality. And so it goes.

If you step down from the height of your pedestal and go down to simpler terms that are used all over, then you will realize that good is the contrast of bad, tall the contrast of short, man of woman, and so forth. Do I have to go on any further?

There is a human life on this earth, and that is based on contrasts. And a person can, of course, be full of pep, as Ann said, in one moment and devoid of ambition in the next moment. Two contrasting elements have been exchanged, but they were there. Why should you be amazed to see them then following one after another?

But this experience that one, one important and powerful impulse of yours can suddenly be followed by its contrast, by its exact opposite, is startling and frightening if this is so. Then what is the guarantee that after you have grown up to be an honest and upright citizen, what is the guarantee that at a given moment suddenly your honesty and uprightness [are] wiped away and the opposite impulse establishes itself and directs action. So, Ann was right when she was amazed at this possibility.

You see, this brings up this question of character and valuation. There are two characters in human beings and two scales of valuation. Of course, everything is dual, as I told you. And there is a firm character and a wobbly character. Both are characters. There is naturally a good character and a bad character. You see, character is subject to the same principle of having to deal with contrasts. And it is being balanced on contrasts. And the one contrast can be knocked out, and the other contrast rises in height. And that can become dominant and direct your actions. So it is a startling situation.

But I am not here to alarm you. I hate to do that. And when I told you right now that certain startling things may happen in life in the field of character formation and in other fields, well, I will calm your anxieties immediately by telling you that we have created forces that can prevent this sudden exchange of contrasting dispositions. And there are forces which prevent dishonesty [from taking] the place of honesty; weakness, the place of firmness; and everything else that is arranged in these two series. And the average individual with an average training—I mean character training—does not have to be afraid of losing the social character and having established in its stead the antisocial character. But both characters are in your interior and in my interior and in everybody's interior.

And you see in human life, it must be arranged in such a manner that there is leadership. Inside you there must be leadership. And if there is solid leadership inside you, then forget about your duality. Then you are unified. There is one leader. And if you are subject to one leader, if you have established one principle within you as leader, then you don't have to become alarmed about the waywardness of your inner experiences, or of some of them.

And patients come to me and tell me, "Well, I got an awful thought suddenly coming to my brain." It shot through the brain, and remained there. And we call that *an obsession.* And patients have sometimes frightful obsessions. They have the obsession that they want to do harm to their children, to their mother, to anybody, to riders on the streetcar, to strangers. But it is, of course, particularly painful if these impulses are directed against mother or children or both. And I tell these patients, "Don't worry. That impulse is not yours. It's a stranger in your brain." And I am not going to explain that today. I am not going to explain why I tell patients that their impulses—or the impulses of this kind—are not theirs, that they are strangers in the brain. I will only tell you that I could explain it very minutely and directly.

These impulses shot into the brain. They were not admitted. They broke in, and nobody has to be ashamed of a burglar. The burglar wasn't called by you. He came. That is fate. And if an idea shoots in your brain and you can't dislodge it, that is fate. That was not called in, was not summoned forth by your leading principle. Your leading principle—that is, for instance, let me say, the ordinary standard of values—does not recognize this intruder as belonging under its wing. That leading principle hates the intruder. It doesn't accept it. And that can happen to people.

That is not duality. That's an intruder that got into the web of beliefs, impulses, strivings of the individual. And the individual is advised by me to keep calm, not to try to get rid of this intruder, and the intruder will remove itself. That always happens if a patient ignores the obsession. It may take time, but it happens.

Now, I want to tell you all about something that will counteract the statement that I made to you that might have frightened you. I told you our life is built on the principle of two, a twosome, duality. But it's not precisely true. If we were not brought up, if we were not the beneficiaries of training, I don't call it education. By training I don't mean information in logic or in languages or in art or literature. It's good if training is accompanied by education, but training means something else. Training means to make the muscles which carry out your impulses, to make the muscles carry out those impulses only that are in accord with a leading principle. If your leading principle is to adjust to a group, and you mean it, then you will not permit your muscles to carry out a crime. That's out of the question. The impulse will be there, but [you] will not permit it to see the light of the day. And we say then if somebody has really accepted a principle of action, and we merely refer here to the group principle. And let's

hope the group which gave us the principle is not a degener-
ate group. If it is the ordinary group, then don't worry about
the value of the principle.

If you have imbibed and absorbed and digested the
principle of rightful action, whatever that may mean, then
unrightful action is impossible. Impossible. Well, there may
be some exceptional cases where even this is possible, but
ordinarily this is impossible. And so you say that a certain
person has a behavior that is impossible. What do you mean
by that? I guess you understand now. Or this remark that
somebody made, "Impossible. He's an impossible person."
And you will now understand, a person that is admitted to
your circle of friends or to your family is expected to follow
more or less the same principle of action that is dominant in
your family or in your group, whatever the group is.

It may be the group of the state, the group of your
church, the group of your family only, and so forth, or a combination of all these. If he joins your group, then by this token
he has indicated that he wants to join you—this means to
share conversations with you, to share your opinions. And he
has no business coming into such a group if his leading principles are contrasting with those of the group. At any rate, if
he comes to this group in some capacity, let me say, as a salesman, then, of course, he can have contrasting impulses and
principles. But then we advise him not to mention them, not
to mention them. Every group has the right to keep its members what we call *homogeneous*. And nobody has the right to
steal into a group, to infiltrate. You have heard this term these
days plenty. That's infiltration. And that's very reprehensible,
nauseating. Certainly in civic life, there it is nauseating.

And now perhaps you will understand that these two
contrasting impulses, beliefs—I should say these two sets of
contrasting experiences that everybody has within his interior—can become unified by a unifying principle. And so we
get people through training, through upbringing, to develop
habits that conform to one principle solely or mainly, to control the impulses by means of reference to this one dominat-

ing principle. And, therefore, the individual is safe from sudden intrusions of the hostile principle, of the antagonistic principle. But I am not interested in philosophy—although privately I am, I must assure you. But as a physician, I am not interested in philosophy. As a physician, I want to treat patients, and I want to get them well. And I need a philosophy for that, too, but that's not my chief interest.

I know, for instance, that my patients have had that unifying principle that told them which act is possible within the principle and which act is impossible. They knew that. Then their nervous system broke, and they still retained that unifying principle that they had before. For instance, when they remained in business, when they were employees or employers, be certain that they carried out that principle that had guided their civic and business life before. But they lost that principle with regard to their body. They were no longer a unifying leader to the impulses, sensations, beliefs of their own body. And after they broke, they developed wants and desires and strivings that were contrary to this unifying principle they had before they broke. Before they broke, they were humble people. Now they became arrogant. Now, don't hold that against me if I say that my patients became arrogant. They did. They demand too much. They demand too much attention. They demand too much affection. They demand all kinds of things. And you will now understand that the patient has lost his humility that is part of that unifying principle that makes a person know what is possible and what is not possible in action.

And if you will ask me what does the training in Recovery amount to, I will tell you. We here strive to reunify the person with his body and his nervous system. And I will assure you, those that are not unified yet, we have the means of producing this unity that you have lost.

Goodbye.

Lecture 46

Wants and Needs

22 Minutes
Recorded Saturday, May 15, 1954

The panel will discuss today the subject of "Wants and Needs." Wants and needs. I repeat the phrase because it is of extreme importance for patients. Now, everybody has wants, and everybody has needs. But they must be kept apart. The patient must get to know what is a need, and that must be supplied; and what is merely a want, and that may be supplied. It may be legitimate to supply it, but not when it clashes with a need. You know, naturally, that this is so in the physical sphere. There is a need, an absolute need, for air, of course for food and certainly for fluids. And we call them *the necessities of life.* And that a necessity is needed, well, that does not have to be discussed. But, mark it: Water and air and food [are] necessary and important and of greatest value, if you wish, to the individual, not the group. The group doesn't eat food. It doesn't even breathe air. The group has no such needs as I mentioned.

Now, it is a bad thing even in trifles that somebody should think he needs candy. That may have bad consequences—well, addition of weight, for instance. It may injure health. And you will understand that candy is a want, not a need by any scale. And it's not so that people need to talk a lot. They merely want to talk a lot. Well, these examples should be sufficient in order to make you distinguish between want and need.

Now, it may surprise you, but it is a truth, that my system of training patients is mainly based on the distinction between needs, which are objective, and wants, which are purely subjective. I guess I have explained that with the examples that I mentioned. But, of course, I am not much interested with candy and talking only. I am interested in what the patient does. And the patient is eager to express his wants, mainly. He is not so eager to pursue his needs. His need is health, nothing else, aside from what I mentioned, necessities of existence. But his supreme need is health, and you will not deny that. But that's not what he wants. He merely wishes it. He wishes to be well. He wishes, naturally, to get rid of his suffering. And this he can only do if he gets well. But he doesn't want it. Now I made a mistake. He doesn't even want it, he only wishes it. With him, health is not even a want, it's a wish, but you will agree that it is a dire need. And the patient will agree to that, too, but he will work on his wants and wishes and not on his needs. Of course, one understands that the patient suffers acutely, and he wishes and wants to get rid of it. And that is a legitimate wish and a legitimate want. But the way he wants to get rid of it is very harmful.

He is, for instance, seized with palpitations. Naturally, he wants to get rid of them. But what does he do then? He suffers, and what he wants now is help, which is legitimate. But what kind of help does he want? Well, I am here to help him, but he wants help right now. And I'll tell you later that in some respects I can supply it. But, generally speaking, the patient has to wait. Health cannot be secured in five seconds, but the patient wants relief in five seconds and preferably in half a second. Oh, it sounds laughable, I agree with you. And yet the patient can get some relief in a second or two. He can, for instance, at that moment, get attention, and sympathy, and affection. And he can be given the opportunity to talk about his suffering. That gives him some relief. All of this. The attention that is given him supplies a modicum, almost a minimum, of relief. But it's gone in a second. The moment the patient gets relief from the attention he receives, from the fact that the husband listens to the patient's complaint and gives a sympathetic ear to it—which the patient receives very seldom—but should the husband supply that sympathetic ear, the patient would feel better, but only for a second. And then the relief goes, and the palpitations go on, and the headache grows [more severe]. And then the patient thinks he has had relief for half a second. He will go on talking again and demand attention. Maybe he will get another second of relief.

And the patient is now continually on the hunt for this second of relief. And so he doesn't stop hunting for attention. And since he can only get attention (he thinks) when he talks, when he asks for the attention, when he tells the partner how terribly he suffers, then he goes on constantly talking about his suffering, always in the hunt for this second of relief. And so the condition gets worse and worse because the second, the third, the fourth time, the husband becomes tired of the procedure. And he withdraws his attention and his affection. And so the patient is worse than ever. And mark it: If I have now the impulse, or the wish, or desire to ask for help, then I naturally want to get this help immediately, right now, if I suffer severely. And that's what we call the short-range goal. The goal that is now in the patient's mind is meant to bring something on this minute. It's a momentary, short-range goal. But when I tell the patient I am going to get him well, naturally, I don't mean that I'm going to do it this second.

My goal that I set before the patient is not meant to get into action or to be reached this moment. It is meant to be reached in weeks or months. So the goal that I have set for the patient is a long-range goal. But the patient who suffers now is not particularly interested in what is going to happen in five, six, or ten months. He wants relief now and not a minute later. And you will now understand that that's what the patient wants. That's his want, but the goal that I set for him is his need.

So you will understand that the patient, in my opinion, is little interested in what he needs, and all interested in what he wants. And the result is that the patient who constantly hunts for attention, who tries to force those around him to offer the attention, that this patient, with his constant drive for affection, attention and sympathy, alienates those around him. And what he wants to get right now is against him and prevents him from reaching his long-range goal, his need. He himself blocks his path toward reaching the goal that he needs to reach, because he alienates everybody around him. And the poor wretch cannot help it. He is driven by an over-powering impulse to do it, to do that thing that neither brings fulfillment for what he wants, nor for what he needs. And the patient is lost, both with regard to his wants and his needs. He cannot reach any of them. And then he comes to Recovery, those of them that come. And what am I going to do, or what are we going to do with this patient who is not interested in long-range goals? Our remedies are long-range.

I tell the patient, "Well, I can give you relief in seconds, too. I can give you excellent relief." If I tell the patient that his symptoms are distressing but not dangerous, should he really accept what I have told him, he would get relaxation in a second. But he would have to accept it. And some people don't know how to accept. They have an uncanny knowledge of how to not accept, how to reject a notion, but not how to accept it. And there has never been a human being living that—I mean a human, a patient, a human being that is a nervous patient—who would not lose his symptoms instantly, if he actually accepted this dictum that there is no danger, there is only distress. It is true, even with this formula, if the patient gets immediate relief, nevertheless, the suffering may come back in a second, or in two seconds. But then the patient has now something in his own hands that he can apply and get relief another second. He can do that without the help of his wife or husband or brother and sister. He can now use this formula as he previously used this mechanism of constantly complaining and driving the members of the family frantic. He can now get exactly what he wants of the relatives by this simple formula. And there is no harm done. But the patient doesn't want it.

He doesn't want it because he has the idea a human being needs sympathy and attention. That's nonsense. That's not a need. In some respect it is, but not for the patient. That is a want, and the patient constantly confuses the term *need* with the term *want*. And again, what are we going to do? Now this method that I mentioned, this accepting the dictum there is no danger, the patient could use to much better advantage than I described.

Anybody who has really accepted that there is no danger gets relief when he first applies this dictum for a few seconds. Then the symptom comes back. If then the patient goes on undeterred to apply the dictum again, the next time when he relaxes, he will relax for five seconds, for seven seconds. The next time he will relax for two minutes; the next time, for an ever-lengthening interval. And I have seen patients getting well quickly because they applied this dictum with determination. And I gave you another means of getting instant relief, and I will merely mention it and not explain it in detail: the motionless sitting. I will not explain it.

I have again yet to see the person who, if he applies this mechanism of motionless sitting as I want it applied, I have yet to see that patient who doesn't get sustained relief from it for a far longer period than can be measured in seconds. But again, the patient sticks to his wants. And I have offered to him, as I told you now, a formula for fulfilling his needs, the need for health. I have offered him this method of accepting the dictum that there is no danger. I have also offered him the method of motionless sitting, which has an unfailing effect. But the patient sticks to his wanting—not needing—attention, sympathy, affection.

Well, do you understand that here in Recovery we have only one way out of this deplorable situation? We have to wait till the patient will be willing to pursue his needs for health instead of his wanting attention. And while the patient is impatient and refuses to wait patiently, fortunately, I and my organization are very willing to wait. And we make the patient wait. And so, so many of our patients don't mind it. They learn quickly that they have to wait. And once we keep them waiting, and in the meantime indoctrinate them with the idea that nervous symptoms are never dangerous, and that a steadying of the body, by means of motionless sitting, gives instant relief which at first is brief, but then lengthens and lengthens and produces a real sustained relief. And let us hope that our patients, all of them, will finally realize that in Recovery they are offered both fulfillment of their needs and fulfillment of their short-range wants.

Thank you.

LECTURE 47

THE INNER SMILE

28 Minutes
Recorded Saturday, May 22, 1954

You remember that Frances, sitting to the right of where I am now, spoke of her brother-in-law, who wanted to do something that I didn't understand. I think I understood he wanted to "cate" a wall, but I am sure you didn't mean that. *[Frances explains:]* Put on "converwall." That's for tiling. *[Dr. Low continues:]* Oh, now, well, I don't know much better now, but it's all right. At any rate, she had some sort of a difference of opinion—perhaps a little altercation—with her brother-in-law. And she claims that she handled it well, and I agree with her. She handled the situation very well. But I will discuss the manner in which she termed and phrased the statement she made.

She said, "I had no temper on that occasion. More than that, I had no symptoms." Well, I am certain that Frances is competent to state that she had no symptoms. Symptoms she certainly had to notice, especially if she looked for them. And [if] she had them, she would have noticed them. But if she says that she had no temper, that's something else. Whether she knows that, I am not certain.

It's remarkable that anybody should not develop temper when he is provoked, when he is confronted with something that displeases him, that riles him, that irritates him. And I presume that Frances was irritated by whatever her brother-in-law meant to do. Otherwise, she wouldn't have had a story to report here. And so we conclude, Frances developed temper because she was irritated. What she should have said was, "I had no sustained temper." The temper was there merely in a flare, not in a violent effect, and with no aftereffects.

Well, you know, this is something that my patients will do very well to ponder. I doubt whether five minutes pass in my life when I don't develop angry temper, because I have yet to see the five minutes of my busy life when I don't have irritations, either at home from the children or in my office from these other children that I call my patients. And they are my children, be sure. That's how I feel towards them. They feel to me as children towards a father, and I am very happy about it. And there are very few fathers who, being with their children, at a certain age of the children, don't get irritated by them, especially if they are boys. And there are very few fathers who don't get irritated by the children very frequently if the children have not passed the teen age. Now, I can't enlarge on this subject. But be certain that I, confronted with those of my children that are my patients, am irritated very frequently. And I have not exaggerated when I stated that there are no five minutes passing in my office in which I don't have irritations.

Well, patients don't always cooperate. And even if they do cooperate, they don't accept. They cause me trouble in my effort to get them well. So I am frustrated. And frustration is irritation, and irritation causes temper, angry temper. And so when I am in my office, I am practically always in temper. But I hope you haven't noticed it. I hope that I have had the skill to conceal it, this means to stop it the moment it flares. But it always flares. It flares up very frequently.

And what Frances spoke of was the flare phase, that phase of temper that we call *the flaring up*. There, you can immediately hold it down if you watch it, if you spot the flare. But once the flare passes into an expressed temper, into a temper which you cast in the shape of a sentence—once you say, "Stop that! Why do you do that? Don't you know any better?" you don't explode then. But you put your anger into the proper words and, moreover, into the proper intonation. This thing is no longer the flare, the temper flare. This is the temperamental effect, and we call it *the immediate temperamental effect.*

Once you do that, once you pass from the temper flare to the immediate temperamental outburst or effect, then in all likelihood you have now started a chain of reaction. You now will pass into the aftereffect of your temperamental experience. And now you will begin to rave and to argue and to shout. I stop here.

I know that my patients don't strike out, but they shout, they yell, they argue as most people do when they pass into the aftereffect. And if the aftereffect goes on and the argument stops, the aftereffect remains.

And the person that provoked you may no longer be present. The person may have departed, but now comes the inner aftereffect in which you fret, in which you still dwell on this bitter experience that you have, and in which you now rail against the person that provoked you without using words. You rail inside against him, and that may go on for hours. And you may, inside you, have the feeling that this person dealt you a blow, that he gave you a dirty deal. Maybe you think precisely in these terms.

And you will now crave to come back at him on the next occasion when you meet him again, and then you will tell him a piece of your mind. And you'll get everything that you have on your chest off your chest and throw it at him. And this aftereffect, the silent aftereffect that proceeds inside you, may go on for endless periods of time, for hours, for days, and for weeks sometimes. And that's the most dangerous portion of the temperamental cycle. And you will understand now that this temperamental cycle begins with the flare, then passes on to the immediate effect, then to the aftereffect, which first works in your consciousness, or, at any rate in the open, in the form of words spoken, and later gradually sinks down to the level where no words are spoken, but thoughts are formed inside.

Now this thing that we call *the flare,* the flaring up of the temper, is unavoidable where there are irritations—unless you are dull, and, of Frances particularly, I know she is nothing of the kind. And since she is not dull, she experienced that flare-up of the temper. But she has been trained to spot that while it is still flaring and has not developed yet into a spoken immediate effect. And at that time it's easy to spot it as a temper flare and to hold it down; this means to refuse to give it expression. And how do you do that? How are you going to hold down a temper even if it is still in the flare stage?

And Frances has learned that. You saw what she did while she sat here on the platform. When she recounted the story of her encounter with her brother-in-law, she laughed or smiled all through the narrative. Of course you may say it's easy now to laugh and smile at a past temper outburst. But this smiling was precisely the means with which she approached her temper flare.

The temper flared up; she immediately spotted it as something that we call *temper.* And now she knew in a fraction of a second that it is ridiculous to let temper rise and express itself. And this thought that I have in my mind that something is ridiculous we can call *the inner smile.* The inner smile. You don't have to smile at temper or at anything else. But you do smile if you have the thought planted in your brain at this moment that the reaction is ridiculous. And that's what we call *the inner unarticulated, unspoken smile.* The smile is neither expressed—or the laugh—neither expressed in a, let me say, in a joke that is spoken, nor in the features that produce a laugh. But it's simply an inner reaction in which you feel or say to yourself, "That is ridiculous."

So keep the word in mind: that is, the internal smile, to plant at a certain moment the thought in your brain, "That is ridiculous." If you declare something ridiculous—your own reaction—if you declare it as ridiculous, then you don't take it seriously. And there is never an anger that is not taken seriously. Once you have an anger, and you experience it, and you express it, that means, in itself, you are now very serious about the insult that you have suffered. If you don't take a reaction seriously, then it cannot be temper. Temper and not-be-taken-seriously don't go together. So if you begin to say that "My temper, my present temper is ridiculous," you abolish it, you throw it out of your system, if you really mean that it is ridiculous.

You see, not to take things seriously means not to fear them, not to be embarrassed by them, not to get angry at them. You see, all these expressions—fear, anger, worry, and so forth, embarrassment—mean that you take something seriously. And if you want to get rid of it, form the idea—the belief in your brain—that this whole reaction is ridiculous. And that's why patients in Recovery are constantly indoctrinated in the manner of telling them that temper is nothing but infantile, childish, an unreal reaction. And once you spot it as such, then you ridicule it. Then you don't take it seriously. Then it disappears.

And that's the experience that Frances had. She didn't know that for sure. I am fairly certain that she didn't know much of this statement that I made here: that if you don't take a thing seriously—a danger, a worry, an embarrassment—then it disappears. I can state that because I don't remember having spoken of this subject frequently, and maybe I never spoke of it, although I have written about it.

Now this thing that we call *the flare-up of temper* is unavoidable. It is our nature, the moment we feel a provocation, that our temper flares. I said that's our nature. And you can't get rid of your nature. And Frances' example illustrates this situation very clearly, after I told you that there can be no doubt but she experienced the flare. She wasn't aware of it, but there can be no doubt about that. Yet we know she experienced it and acted correctly on it. She immediately spotted it as nothing but temper. And to her that means you don't have to take your reactions seriously. And perhaps she thought precisely of these words and this phrasing, but I doubt it. She simply had learned it. It's now at her fingertips not to take seriously anything that starts as a temper. And once I have learned that reaction, or a knowledge—to the extent that it is now at my fingertips—I do it mechanically without any thought entering into the performance. And I do it intuitively without thinking about what I do. And that's the stage which Frances has reached. That's a very desirable state. It's almost an ideal state.

Once you have this ridiculing reaction—this means this inner smile—at your fingertips, then you can apply it any time and every time. And once you reach that stage, there is no danger of you developing symptoms. And you remember that Frances, who knows the Recovery philosophy as well as anybody would know it—maybe I should except myself, but I have caught myself falling short of this knowledge, too— Frances, who has acquired this highly desirable knowledge, doesn't even have to spot anymore. I am sure she will substantiate this statement of mine. And if I should describe to you what kind of a temper Frances used to have, well, you would not believe it.

For weeks in the beginning, when I began to take care of her—I don't know how many weeks; I'm afraid it was only one or two weeks; let me say, for weeks, without specifying the number—she was in a continuous panic, not only in fear, not only in temper, in irritation, but in a continuous panic. It was not the panic of the type where you strike out and rush and run and yell and throw hysterics, not that type. But she could never relax. She was always apprehensive. And that went on for years, for years, not for months. Finally she came to me.

I couldn't have helped her if I had seen her in my office only, because if I treat a case of continuous panic, or call it *a continuous apprehension,* in the office alone, I have to wait and work slowly. In the office, I can't work fast. It takes time till the patient really gets proper instruction from me in the office. It takes months and months till I can convey to the patient as much instruction as I have, for instance, deposited in my book. And the patient is then still in the panic and doesn't get relief, so he drops out. A patient like Frances, treated in the office only, would have dropped out after a week or two. That's always been the picture of a patient who constantly suffers and is treated in the office only.

But Frances did something that all of you, I hope, have done. First of all, she studied immediately my literature. And there she got so much instruction that she could get at home, she didn't have to wait till I would have time to give it to her. And she improved rapidly. And then she came to these classes. In the classes, it's not necessary for the patient to get much instruction, although they get it, and you know you get it. In the classes, it's sufficient for the patient to see that somebody who had a similar suffering got well or improved, because he gave up the fear of collapse or any idea of danger. Then he felt secure. And he could feel secure because he now saw, or Frances now saw, that there was hope for her. Previous to coming to classes, she didn't know that there was anybody in this world that suffered the same condition. Now she knew there are others, and they get well.

Previous to coming to classes, she was hopeless. She felt hopeless. She was in utmost despair. Now when she saw that she was not the only one in the world that had such a condition, and that other patients, whom she saw here and who told her what I am telling you—that other patients actually get cured of this continuous apprehensiveness and panic—now she breathed freely. She discarded her fear, or part of her fear. She knew then that she was no longer doomed forever, and that there was a good chance for her to do what the other patients had done to get well.

But getting well does not mean to lose one's nature. Frances had been in continuous fear before I have seen her, and before she came to Recovery, and continuously irritated by herself and by others, for instance, by her children. Be sure, children are irritating, little children particularly. And so she was in a continuous anger, too, particularly anger about herself, disgust with herself, this inner temper. And, of course, she could not throw that out of her system. She could only change it, control it, hold it down, and make it a very mild reaction. But the flare she could never get rid of. That is definitely nature, and nature you can't throw out of your organization. But you will now understand that what Frances told you was this: She lost that part of temper that is expressed in words or in actions, the immediate temperamental effect. And she lost that part, that other part of temper that may be expressed in words or buried inside, but working on there—the aftereffect. The flare remains and will remain for all her life. But she has learned how to spot it and not to take it seriously. This means she counteracts the temper flare with the inner smile.

And I hope you will understand this situation now, and that you will do what Frances does. And that does not merely require that you go home now and make up your mind, "I'll be another Frances." That will not help you. What it means is that you must practice and learn how to do it. And both practice and learning, real learning, require time. And will you please see to it that you don't get discouraged because you have to wait. At the end of the waiting period, there is the great reward, the prize. And will you please wait till you get the same reward and the same prize that Frances got.

Thank you.

EXPECTATIONS AND DISAPPOINTMENTS

24 Minutes
Recorded Saturday, May 22, 1954

The panel will discuss today the subject of "Expectations and Disappointments." Well, I forgot the subject, but I expect such happenings, so I am not disappointed. That's good for you to know that one can forget, that one can blunder, that one can do things one wouldn't like to do. One may even be ashamed of them, and one does not have to be disappointed. These are human limitations, and average human limitations.

Now, this subject of expectations and disappointments is of the utmost importance for patients. In point of suffering, the patient creates his own suffering by being disappointed too frequently and [for] too long, too long a period. The patient is, of course, disappointed that he got into trouble. He is disappointed that the treatment takes too long. Naturally, it's always too long for a sufferer. He is disappointed by what the doctor tells him. He expected something else, something more reassuring perhaps. He expected perhaps a different mode of treatment. And there is no end to the disappointments that the patient experiences from his nervous trouble and from moves around and about this trouble from his doctor, from the other patients, from the members of the family. The way they handle him is disappointing to him. And the net result is that he becomes more tense the more he is disappointed, because disappointment—discouragement, dissatisfaction, which all mean the same thing—creates tenseness.

The other day I saw a lady whom I'll describe only in general terms. The most general term in the description is that she is a patient. But I am not going to tell you what kind of a patient she is, what kind of symptoms she has. Another generality is that she is a quite intelligent person. And the third generality is that she cooperates well.

Now, I have seen her in my office the second time, at first during the initial examination, and the second time during a subsequent visit to my office. And I will add that prior to coming for the initial appointment, for the initial examination, she had to wait. And while she was waiting several weeks to receive her appointment, she came patiently, almost religiously, to the Recovery meetings that are held here in this hall. So she certainly cooperated. More than that, she has learned a great deal about nervous conditions and how they can be handled, before I saw her.

And when I saw her the other day in my office, she made the following statement. Some few days before the visit to my office, she attended a panel meeting here in this hall, and during this meeting one of the patients made the statement, "Well, I have been coming to these meetings," the patient said, "for seven months, and I have not improved yet." Well, that's a statement that some patients make, and I guess it is correct. Some patients have to wait till they learn how to accept. Even if they cooperate and come regularly to meetings, listen to me and to the panel leaders, nevertheless, they may not accept what they are offered, although they give good cooperation. And I want you to know the difference between giving cooperation and accepting.

And so there are patients who cooperate but do not accept what they are offered in point of instructions. And then they have to wait. They can't get well if they don't accept my opinions and if they cling to their own opinions. And when my patient, whom I discuss now, heard this statement that somebody had [been] coming to Recovery for seven months and had not had improvement, my patient tells me, "At that time, at that moment, I felt a heat crossing through my body, and everything shook and trembled, and I sweated and palpitated." And she catalogued a whole number of symptoms she got. She got them immediately, the moment she heard that statement. So I told her, "Well, you got a scare then." She denied that. She said, "I was not scared." So I told her, "Well, perhaps we can find a common meeting ground if I change the word *scare* into the word *fear*. And you conceived a fear." And she said, "I was not afraid." I was patient with this lady, and I told her, "Let's change the meeting ground again, and I'll tell you that you were startled." She didn't accept that either. So finally I told her, "My stock of expression is almost running out. I can't go indefinitely changing my ground and bringing forth new words, new meanings, new terms." And I told her, "Now, I don't want to be contradicted anymore. I'll tell you what I know about your interior life. And I tell you definitely you were disappointed." She said, "No." So I turned to her and said, "I don't want you to contradict me any longer. And I'll tell you you were disappointed, but you didn't know it. And you were afraid, but you didn't know it." She naturally gave me the current reply that patients make, "Don't I know what I feel?" So I told her, "Yes, you do know what you feel. But you don't know what you think about your feelings, what you believe about them. Your beliefs you don't know. And I tell you, you believed at that moment that that was disappointing, disheartening, discouraging."

And then I went on explaining and told her, "Naturally you were disappointed because you expected something else. You expected that no patient in Recovery should have to wait seven months before she gets an improvement, and since this patient didn't even have an improvement after seven months, so she was most likely slated to have to wait longer yet. And that disappointed you. Your expectation was that you should get well or get an improvement quickly." Moreover, she had improved beautifully. That patient had improved beautifully.

And then I began to explain to her, "You knew that you trembled"—well, everybody feels that, of course—"that your heart palpitated, that you sweated, that you felt a heat wave through your body. All these things you knew. They didn't have to be spotted. If you know a thing, you don't have to spot the thing. But you did not know that you were afraid."— Well, what does that mean? I'll tell you later.—"And you did not know that the fear had come through a sudden startle. And you did not know that if somebody becomes afraid, that he has in his brain the belief that there is danger. And you did not know that you expected not to be in danger, no longer to be in danger, because you had begun to improve nicely. And therefore you did not know that you were disappointed in your expectation. You expected no longer to be in danger. And then the remark of this patient that joined the discussion on the panel gave you the idea that your expectation was disappointed. And you didn't know all these terms although they were developed in exactly in the order that I mentioned." And then I told her certain things that were meant to show her that that's how people are. They know the surface phenomena of their experience but not what underlies in the depths, underlies these phenomena.

And I want to tell you in a few brief remarks what this whole situation means. You know the situation, for instance, in which somebody standing, strap-hanging in the car, in the streetcar, and somebody else stands near him, equally clutching the strap. And all of a sudden there is a jolt. The streetcar comes to a sudden halt, and your neighbor begins to sway and falls. And in the fall, he steps on your toe. You know that happens. Or he may step on your toe without even falling. What happens now? You get sore, you become provoked, you are into anger. And that happens very frequently that somebody steps on his toes. And he becomes angry, and he has no reason for getting angry. If he does get angry, then certain beliefs form in his brain. But he doesn't have to know that. There is no earthly reason why anybody should become angry at somebody falling against him because that person did it accidentally. He didn't do it intentionally. And how can you become provoked over an accident that happens to you?

So if this person whose toe was stepped on had been able to spot, as I want my patients to learn how to spot inner events, he could have drawn the conclusion, first, "I have pain here in my toe, but it was caused by accident. But I got angry immediately. This means I formed the belief in my brain that it was that man's fault." And if it is his fault, you formed another conclusion: that he did step on your toe by intention. You can't get provoked against anybody unless you assume that he did what he did to you by intention. And without knowing, you formed the idea in your brain that this man struck you by intention. But you didn't know that you formed this idea. It is underneath the surface of your thinking, that thought that there was intention involved. And that had to be spotted if you wanted to get rid of the provocation, this means, of your anger. If you want to get rid of your anger, then be clear on this point. You have already, without knowing it, formed the idea that somebody did you wrong by intention. And if you spot that, and you know that you formed a silly belief in your brain, that that fellow who was thrown at you by the jolt that everybody experienced, that he [had] the intention to step on your toe, then you can begin to laugh at it and give up this idea of intention.

And my dear patients, of course, constantly create beliefs in their brains that they don't know of, that they are not aware of, and these beliefs are very harmful. And patients come to me and tell me, "Well, yesterday I got something shooting into my brain. It felt like an electric current. I never had that before. How is it that I get this symptom now?" And when the patient says that, then he shows me that he is disappointed by this symptom, and that he didn't expect that a new symptom should arise in the pattern of his ailment. But the patient didn't know that when he made the statement, "How is it that there is a new symptom?" that he felt disappointment and that he did not expect getting new symptoms.

And new symptoms are naturally very common in nervous conditions. And the patient should have known that because when, years ago—in the case that I have in mind right now—[he] had come to me after years of suffering, and when I saw him at that time, he had already a record of some fifty to sixty or to seventy symptoms that he had had in various successions. He had first a batch of five or six symptoms, later another symptom came, later another; so he had ample experience that nervous conditions create new symptoms. We know that, and you know that. He had forgotten that. And when he made this statement, "I never had this symptom before. How is it that I get it?" he didn't know that he was disappointed. This means that he had had the expectation that he should not get new symptoms.

And everyone of you have had the experience that you improved, and then you got your setback. And when this setback comes, I have told you so frequently, you must always think before the setback comes that this is possible, very likely that you will run into a setback. And if you think that you are in for setbacks, if it comes, you will not get alarmed.

And now the setback is there. And the patient, who has heard me speak about the setback and about the necessity of not getting alarmed, and who knows that if he does not get alarmed about the setback, the setback will disappear very soon and will be very mild, the patient then comes to me and tells me, "Well, I have had a setback all week, and it doesn't go." So I tell him, "Well, you didn't expect it. You didn't think of it." And he admits that. "And then after the setback was there, you have now been in a constant alarm, a constant worry about the setback." And the patient usually says, "I didn't worry about it. I just tell you that I have the setback." That patient would be a hero if he didn't worry about the first setback that he had after an improvement. And you know, I have yet to see heroes among my patients. If I see one, I will not trust my eyes. I will say, "There must be something wrong with my vision."

And here again you have an example in this matter of the setback that the patient has worried for fully seven days before he came to me. And when I told him, "You shouldn't have worried about the setback," he said, "I didn't worry."

Well, the worry was deep inside, the belief that the setback will now stay with him, that he is now doomed to suffer again as he had suffered, but the belief is not conscious. It is inside, in the depths of his experiences. And he came here to Recovery and to my office, where he was trained to look into the depth of his inner experiences. And he was given the techniques how to do it, and he didn't. And so when the setback came, he could not spot his worry, his belief in danger.

And all I can tell you in conclusion is that you must finally learn—and most of you do learn it—that you know only the surface of your experiences in things in which you have no practice, in which you have no special knowledge. And about how the brain works inside, you have no special knowledge about that. And, in other words, you must know in matters of nervous symptoms, in matters, in other words, in which you have no special knowledge, you must know one thing that will save you, and that is you must know that you don't know, that you only know the surface. And I will give you a final advice. If you come to me and report to me about symptoms, and I tell you, "Well, if the symptoms still persist, then you have done certain things," may I beg you not to tell me, "No, I didn't do them."

Goodbye.

Lecture 49

Frustrations and Self-Distrust

25 Minutes
Recorded Saturday, September 25, 1954

Well, you heard the panel members conducting a conversation or a discussion, and what did they discuss? When you listened to them, you cannot have escaped the impression that they again and again spoke of temper, of having failed to control their temper before they went to Recovery, and now controlling it after they spot it. And I guess those of you that have come here for a long period of time could trace this subject of temper to every panel discussion that you ever heard.

I add that the patients also speak of spotting and of averageness. And that's what I want them to do. And many of you—not precisely of you patients here but of many patients—have complained to me that after all, when they come to Recovery, all they hear is about temper and controlling temper. I usually then tell them, "Well, that's precisely what I want you to hear every time you come to Recovery. And I want you to think of temper control each time you are awake for even a minute." In that minute, the subject of temper control must be of paramount importance to you. Without temper control, you will never be able to cure your nervous symptoms, except perhaps after years and years. But you will not be able to control them within a reasonable period of time. And after I have spoken to you about temper perhaps five hundred or a thousand times—remember, I have given these talks for seventeen years each Saturday and each

Tuesday, so I am entitled to speak about thousands of times—after I have spoken to you about temper thousands of times (naturally not to all of you but to those that have been present in various years) I want to add another talk about temper today—the best theme that I can choose if I want to help you.

Just reflect what life consists of. Well, life consists of one series of experiences which we call *pleasant,* or *satisfactory* or *agreeable,* or whatever you want to call them, or *harmless,* and another series which is called by the name of *frustration.* While I am sitting here, I look around, and while my eye sweeps the room, I see all other eyes turned on me. Well, that's pleasant, a pleasant experience. But sometimes I look through the room, and I notice that somebody has great trouble keeping his eyes open. That's a frustration for a speaker, to notice even one person not being able to keep awake while the speaker speaks. And again I may mention this thing that happens so frequently, that one expects somebody, not only an elevator operator, but a guest at home, and they are late, and you have to wait. That's frustration. And Anne told you that Gertrude got in touch with her and wanted her to pinch-hit for her as a panel speaker, and Anne became frustrated. She had just served as a panel speaker, and now somebody comes along and wants her to serve again. That's frustration.

And Fanny told you approximately the same story. She got two invitations [at] short intervals for the same task, sitting on the panel, and she felt frustrated. And so it goes. And one lies on the couch and wants to read, but there is a fly flying around; well you are frustrated. And on some evenings you can't fall asleep, and you are frustrated. And there is no end to frustrations.

But the worst frustrations come from the inside, not from elevator operators and from flies pirouetting around you—that's not the main variety of frustrations—inside forces that are against you. You have an important job to perform, for instance, to make an important visit to important people. They are important to you. And all of a sudden your heart begins to beat like a sledgehammer, and you can't go. The frustration is on the inside. Your heart is a nervous heart, and it frustrates you at a moment when you have an important task before you. That's frustration, indeed. And while you are sitting and talking or playing cards, all of a sudden you feel an electric current rushing through you. That's frustration. You become so panicky that you can't continue the game or the visit. That's frustration, and that makes you panicky as a rule.

There is worse frustration yet, far more tormenting: the frustrations that proceed from your viewpoints, *viewpoints* from your opinions, particularly from the viewpoint about yourself. All of you have formed disastrous viewpoints. Eleanor mentioned that she knocked over presumably a valueless object, over the counter in some place. And you will remember that she spoke that she was now acutely aware of the fact that now she may act with what she called her *passion for self-distrust*. Well, she has learned the lesson very well. Why should anybody distrust himself? And let me immediately tell you that if you do distrust yourself—especially if you have cultivated a habit of self-distrust for years or decades, as so many of my patients have—I doubt whether there is any more distressing pain, mental pain. Self-distrust will make you do things that are calamitous.

If you have a distrust of your heart, then you would constantly be worrying about the heart and will make the heart more nervous all the time, as long as you worry about the heart. The palpitations will grow worse, the air hunger will increase and will be more frequent, and there comes that famous pain over the left chest that has certain characteristics that are never encountered with real heart diseases. But my patients develop that famous pain because they have an abiding distrust of their heart and constantly think about it, constantly are preoccupied with it. And you know they are not preoccupied with their happiness over their heart. They are preoccupied with the threat, the dismal threat, with which they conceive of their heart.

So, if you have any of these harmful, dreadful viewpoints about yourself, you only make the trouble that you have worse and worse. You develop a vicious cycle. And while in the beginning, before you develop the self-distrust, the heart has a good chance of finally giving up this nervous excitement, now you are unable to stop your nervous reaction. At least for months and months and years and years, until you—somebody—makes you drop your self-distrust that creates self-consciousness and therefore preoccupation and constant badgering of your nervous system.

And my patients develop conditions that distrust not only their body but their mind. And again, when Eleanor paid her bill for herself and her mother—although the mother had slipped her the money and [it] shouldn't have been mentioned, I guess—well, after she did that, she forgot the change, if I understood her right. The ordinary individual would say, "Well, I am forgetful. My teachers have been forgetful; my pupils have been forgetful; I am forgetful." It's an average feature in life. It's not even a frustration. It may be, but it's a common occurrence, as common as cleaning the nose. The nose needs cleaning. That's no frustration; [it's] a common occurrence, and you do it. That's the same with forgetting. But my patients, should at any time this dreadful thing happen to them, that they forgot something—which is an average occurrence with everybody—but they have a sustained suspicion of every function of theirs, therefore of memory, too. And they blame themselves and fear their future and get grisly ideas about a possible brain tumor or a mental collapse. And, be sure, most of you, if not all of you, have gone that far in self-distrust. I would say all of you, but I may be gracious and deduct two or three percent. Not more.

And how is this self-distrust to be combatted? Well, the patients told you. I don't know whether you heard them tell you. I did. Maybe you didn't hear it, because they didn't repeat the word too frequently. But if I remember, they did repeat it, and the word is *averageness.*

You remember that I have told you frequently that there are two attitudes that everybody assumes without knowing it: the attitude "I am a singular individual," everybody has that, I included—although I have tried to teach you to give up this idea, but I haven't given it up yet. Well, how long can I wait yet? I'm not a youngster. I'll have to wait till my last day. That's nature, human nature, that one feels proud and vain. Human nature consists, among other features, of pride and vanity. I should say vanity and pride, more vanity than pride. And I, as a vain creature that everybody is, detect many indications during every day, sometimes during every hour, maybe sometimes minute by minute, that I actually believe or wish or crave to be singular, superior, to be at the top, to be the center of the stage, that I am very important. But naturally everybody is important in some sphere of life. And a mother is important to her children, the children important to the mother, and patients important to the doctor, and the doctor important to the patients. This is realistic importance. It's natural. The other is not realistic. It's imaginary. Everybody imagines that he is the most important person. Be sure I have found it in me.

Now, this human nature you can never get rid of. It will always be with you, just as anger will always be with you, fear will always be with you. You can't get rid of it. But you can control it so that it doesn't do any harm, and it remains in the background and doesn't push to the foreground. And what you are trained here to do is to control your human nature, not to throw it out, to eradicate it. That's impossible. And if you tell me of a man that I have never seen, and you don't know either, then I'll tell you, although you don't know him and I don't know him and we don't know a bit about how he responds, he is vain and thinks he is the most important person in this world. Everybody is. That's all right. But if you have this sense of importance, of self-importance, then you will be frustrated right and left. Then you multiply the frustrations, because you will meet a friend and he doesn't think that you are the most important person, and he will treat you as an average person. Then you are frustrated. And he will make a remark which will indicate that he thinks not too highly of you. He thinks you are average.

You know, it happens to me very frequently that a patient or a nurse or some neighbor explains to me a medical problem that I certainly know. If she knows it, then I know it, too. By explaining it to me she, without knowing it, but still deliberately—I mean intuitively deliberately—tells me that I am not so important. She knows as much as I do. Anybody who tells me something that I ought to know anyhow, tells me, "Well, you are just average, as I am. You know only what I know." And if you haven't learned to analyze these words and sentences that you have heard, then you are suddenly struck by something, and you don't know what you are struck by. Therefore, you must learn how to spot what people say to you and what you think, especially what you think about your body and your mind, your personal views (that are, as a rule, to the point of ninety-eight percent) which are always based in the stream of self-distrust.

And Eleanor was right in saying that you and I have a passion for self-distrust. Because we always feel very important, and then people come along and treat us like average people, and we hate to be treated like average people. And so there is always frustration. Aside from the fact there are other frustrations, of course, but the main stream of frustration flows from your sense of self-importance, which invites everybody to frustrate you because they treat you as average and not as important.

And I hope you understand that, that in Recovery we must discuss these items and must discuss them again and again till they sink into your brain and finally travel to the muscles and you have them at your fingertips. That's what the expression means. You must have it at your muscles, at the fingertips. And once you have acquired the knowledge of our principles of spotting, of averageness, of temper control—this means muscle control, as you know—then you will not feel frustrated as frequently as you still do. And if you don't feel frustrated in an undesirable frequency, then you don't create much tenseness inside. Remember, whenever you are frustrated and resent it, you then become tense. And if you reduce your amount of tenseness working within you, there will be no pressure on the nerves. And there is no chance for nerves to arise for any length of time if you are relaxed. For brief minutes and seconds they can arise in everybody. So it seems it would be very desirable and very profitable for all of you to avoid precisely these pitfalls of adjustments that we discuss here.

And you remember I started out speaking about temper, and I didn't tell you anything about it. I didn't mention temper, just fortuitously. It was not deliberately done. But nevertheless, I spoke of nothing else but temper. Well, if you are frustrated and you react violently to it, or severely, that's temper. So when I spoke of frustration, incidentally, I meant temper. Why I didn't mention [it], I can't tell you. It is the imperfection of the human soul, of the human mind that is at fault, not I. I say not I in order to demonstrate to you that I think I keep my passion for self-distrust under reasonable control. Therefore, I say it is the fault of human imperfection, but not particularly of I, of me in other words. Keep that in mind. Stop blaming yourself for your averageness, for your average human imperfection, for human limitations. And if you stop blaming yourself, you will, incidentally, naturally whittle down that thing that you now call, that I ask you to call *the passion for self-distrust.*

Thank you.

PRACTICING BETWEEN SYMPTOMS

14 Minutes
Recorded Saturday, September 25, 1954

The panel will discuss today the article on "Muscles and Mental Health." We have discussed this subject of muscles endless times. And whenever I have to discuss it again, because it is the theme of this afternoon, I find there is again another angle to the subject that I can find. And in the future there will be new angles to the subject whenever I will have to speak about it again. That's what life is: inexhaustible in meaning.

Well, the muscles are used for curing patients and for explaining nervous conditions. As far as I know, they are used here only. Nowhere else. And you know what results we obtain by placing this emphasis on these poor, misunderstood, and rather looked-down-upon muscles. And yet muscles have an extremely dignified position in the scheme of the human body. Remember: What are people proud of? You will be shocked to hear me say they are proud of the function of their brain and of their muscles, and nothing else.

People, if they are somehow reasonable, sensible, are certainly not proud of their stomach or of their kidneys. But ask a first-class baseball player, and he will soon tell you what his particular distinction is: muscle coordination. I think I am not wrong. He has pushed the excellence of his muscular performance to a peak, and he is very proud of it. And if you ask a violin player, he will tell you his fingers move with such a precision, with such a smoothness, with such a delicacy, well, that he can justly be proud of it. And think of the dancer, of the actor. He is proud that he can express human emotions to an exquisite degree, through the muscles of his cheeks, the muscles of his throat, the voice, through the muscles of his arms and his gestures. That's what he is proud of. So muscles should not be treated with contempt. They take a high position in the inventory of human skills. A painter is proud of the skill of his fingers; this means his muscles. And so forth.

Now, my patients are asked to use their muscles primarily for the control of sensations, and more so yet, perhaps, for the control of obsessions and compulsions. They are, of course, also asked to use their brain in refusing to believe, and in spotting. But leave that out for today

Well, if somebody is afraid of walking alone on the streets, then he can perhaps stay out of the street for days, weeks, and months. And the panics don't come if he stays at home. So if I ask him to practice with his muscles, well, he stays home, and sometimes he ventures out perhaps one or two blocks. If he does that once a week or twice a week, how much practicing does he do for two blocks twice? That's no practicing. That's very little. And even people who have nothing more than violent palpitations and a fatigue that feels like an exhaustion, they don't practice much, only when the palpitations are there, and only when the fatigue reaches the stage of exhaustion.

And therefore my patients will have to learn to practice in between the times when they have their symptoms. There is a vast opportunity for everybody to practice controlling muscles, quite aside from the symptoms. I control my muscles consciously, well, perhaps a hundred times a day. For instance, years ago I had developed the habit of eating fast. Then one day it occurred to me that I could train my patients to control their muscles while eating fast. They should slow down in their eating. Then they would learn how to control their muscles in some field, not just with their symptoms. If they did that, they would have an opportunity to practice about three half-hours or three [quarter-hours] a day, depending on how long they sit at the table. But most of my patients are constantly picking something from the plate, and they have hardly pushed it in the mouth, they pick again and push it in the mouth. And eating is a race with them, an unfortunate race.

And most of my patients talk too fast. And since they talk a large part of the hours during the day—most of the people do that—they have an excellent opportunity to practice controlling muscles. But, mark it: You will not do it unless you think of it—you think of doing it—unless you are determined to do your utmost to practice muscle control. And I have noticed when I started slowing down—on my gait on eating and speaking, on walking, too, the gait—I relaxed immediately. All I had to do is consciously to hold down the movements of my fingers towards the spoon and plate and towards the mouth and make them move slowly. The body relaxed. And so with speaking, and with walking, and even with standing.

Now how can you stand fast, rapidly, with speed? You can. Just wait for an elevator, and the elevator doesn't come. What do you do then? All kinds of impulses are aroused, impulses of anger. You want to walk, to walk out on the elevator. And if you keep standing and keep standing—and remember that this is a childish piece of behavior, that you think the elevator operator must always be ready for you particularly. He has, of course, other customers and other floors to go to. Remember that this is a sign of exceptionality. You don't consider yourself an average person that naturally has to wait his turn. You consider yourself, without knowing it, an exceptional person that should be served immediately. Everybody feels exceptional. And if you practice standing at the elevator and waiting patiently, not impatiently—waiting patiently—and if you consciously think of controlling your impulses to become impatient, then you relax. You relax physically because standing patiently makes the impulses quiet down. And mentally, you relax mentally because you gain mental comfort from the knowledge that you have controlled, and that you have successfully controlled.

My patients are particularly fast, quick, rushing, when they are on the toilet and are to evacuate. That can't be fast enough. And when it doesn't come, they get up and say, "I am constipated." That's nonsense. They are not constipated, but they don't practice sitting on the toilet seat patiently. They rush, or they want the bowels to rush.

And if you do what I told you now to do, if you slow down in every function that I mentioned, well, then you develop healthy habits of controlling muscles in general—not with regard [to] symptoms, but that will then help you to control symptoms because you have developed habits of being the boss with regard to your symptoms. And if you have the symptoms that I mentioned, then you are by no means the boss over the muscles. The muscles are your boss, and you are their slave.

And I have not stressed this subject as a rule. There isn't always an opportunity to speak on one particular subject. There are thousands of subjects that one can speak of. But when I was told that today there was to be a discussion, a panel discussion about muscles and mental health, I thought, well, there is the opportunity to crowd all the speed reactions into one discourse and tell my patients that they should slow down in all the functions that I mentioned.

Thank you.

LECTURE 51

COOPERATING WITH THE PHYSICIAN

30 Minutes

Recorded Saturday, September 26, 1953

When I listened to the panel, my thoughts went to the one patient that was just speaking, and I reviewed in my mind the history of the reaction which the patient offered. Well, since I dealt with three patients, it would be difficult to recount here what I thought about each one of them. I'd rather concentrate on what Lloyd said here. Well, he said quite a few things, and even if I concentrate on him and limit my remarks to his story, it would be impossible to do it justice in the space of twenty or twenty-five minutes. So, I shall concentrate on one sentence he mentioned and presume that this will be a fit topic for discussion.

You remember he told you that he had an itch that almost drove him frantic. And while he was on the train, he either decided or casually did pick up a paper and read. And, as he put it, he wanted to concentrate on reading and apparently had the idea if he concentrated, he will relax. It's remarkable how patients get these ideas which are correct, and I wonder how they pick up correct ideas of this kind. I guess Lloyd is not the dumbest here, rather, among the top smart ones.

Look here. Ordinarily it is hardly likely that anybody would say, "If I want to relax, I will concentrate." My idea is that concentration is rather the reverse of relaxation. I relax when I float along on what I think or what somebody tells me, without concentrating too hard on the meaning of what he says. And yet Lloyd was right, and you will better ponder the lesson which his remarks have offered you.

I saw just yesterday a young boy in my office. The mother told me, or had told me, that the boy was difficult or impossible to control. And when she told me the story, there was no doubt the boy had a streak of something in him that made him act in the sense of irresponsibility. All of a sudden he would, for instance, walk off—the twelve-year "shrimp"—and come home at ten or eleven o'clock at night. And he didn't walk off at nine o'clock at night but rather at two o'clock in the afternoon or so. He would stay out with some friends, riding on his bicycle for miles, or then perhaps come back after the ten, twelve or fifteen hours without bothering to telephone his parents, who are very desirable people.

The parents told me some other items which rather testified to some sort of a sense of irresponsibility in this boy. When I had him before me, I did what I usually do with patients in general and youngsters in particular. I told this boy, "When you come into this office, you have to behave." That's all. And I told him, "You behave through your muscles. And while you sit in this chair, will you please keep seated and don't shove your weight around the chair. Don't jump, don't wiggle. Keep your arms to your body." And children understand these orders very plainly, while, if I [had] told him, "You have a complex" of any kind, well, he certainly would not have understood. But when I tell a boy to sit down and keep the arms to the body, and stop wiggling your fingers, and don't throw the head from right to left, it's simple. And he stops and does it, if he cooperates. And there are very few boys that will not cooperate instantly with somebody that means status or prestige or authority to them. And a doctor still means authority to most youngsters. They are even afraid of him, so they respect him. That's the only kind of respect they have left these days, I guess: fear. And the boy, who understood my wording, sat and ceased moving.

And now I tell you what happened to this boy, who didn't know that that's what's happening to him. He stopped his movements, and therefore he relaxed. Therefore he relaxed. With boys, the restlessness expresses itself mainly in muscular movements, not in racing of thoughts. You, you patients who have restless movements or restless muscular behavior cannot just merely sit down quietly and then have everything be remedied. Your restlessness is still in the region of thoughts, and that must be corrected in adult people, too. But with youngsters, there isn't much thought. Their thought can be expressed in about two words, three I would say.

What they want is fun and more fun. So, it's four words, pardon me. Fun and more fun. And there is hardly any occasion for confusion of thought if all somebody wants is fun. So, with a boy, it's perfectly sufficient to make him relax by stopping his muscular movements. Well, the boy was relaxed—there was no question about it—for a minute or two. Then he became restless again and moved, wiggled, shoved himself from one edge of the chair to the other, till I told him, "Stop now, that's enough." And he stopped and relaxed. Do you see here, that boy shifted his attention. He did not concentrate it—I mean, before I took him to task. And it will be good to know that attention can either be scattered or concentrated. And you know very well that there are too many among you that are restless and could stop the scattering of their impulses and their attention through concentrating the muscles on just doing nothing.

But that's not our problem with adult people. With adult people, the problem is entirely different, although the muscular component is active there, too. While I am sitting here before you, I concentrate on what I am going to tell you. And what I am going to tell you, you will, of course, notice later. But at present, I want you to know that what I am speaking before you is usually called by the word *theme*. I pursue a theme. And while I speak to you about the theme that I have selected, I will perhaps use several thousand words, several hundred sentences, and all kinds of notions, ideas and suggestions. That is a multiplicity of mental concepts. And all these multiple notions and ideas and thoughts which I will present to you, and have presented partly

318

already, form a theme, one single theme. Now, you understand if you have to produce, let me say, several thousand words and several dozens or hundreds, perhaps, single ideas, there can easily take place a scattering and a wandering off of some ideas, some sentences, some words. But I must avoid that. I must go on with my theme. By the way, I must not permit any strange theme to crowd into my exposition. The theme must be single, it must proceed in a straight line. It must not wander off into other channels. That means I must concentrate my attention now on the theme, not on the single words and notions that I produce. Well, I guess I do that.

But while I talk to you, I spy somebody here or there, and that somebody may, for instance, irritate me for some reason. That somebody may, without irritating me, remind me of something that I should have done and forgot. That certainly is nothing far-fetched. And the moment such a thing happens, the moment it happens that somebody in the audience irritates me or reminds me of something that does not reflect favorably on my sense of duty, my attention will be forcibly deviated into these channels, and I will be diverted from the theme.

And that is what happens to my patients. You will be surprised to hear that what I spoke of so far was to picture to you how a patient acts. And what he does is this. There are two themes in his life: the theme, "I cannot get well," and the theme, "I can get well because my doctor told me so." The one is a theme of defeatism and the other the theme of cooperation, full cooperation. I ask the patient who delivers himself unto my care to abandon the thought of defeatism and to accept the thought of courage, cooperation. What the patient is to do, is to give up his theme and to accept mine. And that requires acceptance, which the patient hardly offers without resistance. It has been my experience in thousands of instances that extremely few patients accept thoroughly and consistently what the doctor offers them if the condition is one of a nervous ailment. Well, the patient is to accept what I offer him, and what I offer him is a theme, the theme of accepting and cooperating with what I tell him and what I ask him to do. If the patient directed his view, his eyesight, his mental eyesight, on my theme exclusively or almost exclusively, he would be well within a short time, within a surprisingly short time.

But the patient is diverted from the theme, just as I am sometimes diverted from my theme when I speak here. He is diverted from something that is very distressing, by his symptoms. Even the best patient, the patient with the finest intentions to cooperate, is put to it very hard to offer and to practice cooperation if all of a sudden a palpitation occurs, a massive palpitation, a severe head pressure, an almost exhaustive fatigue. And you know what I told you: The patient is then confronted with the body language, and the body knows how to speak far more effectively than I will ever learn. My language pales away if the body begins to speak. And that frightful palpitation that the patient is seized with, or an exhaustion that we call *fatigue* but he calls *exhaustion*, speaks such an insistent language that, of course, the patient is then diverted from the theme that I offered him. And he returns to the defeatist theme that he has practiced before he saw me.

And he now concentrates on defeatism. And the trouble is when he becomes defeatist, then he establishes a vicious cycle and creates a quantity, an abnormal quantity, of tenseness. And the tenseness keeps the heart racing, and the palpitations get worse. And the worse the palpitations get, the worse becomes his panic. The worse the panic, the worse the palpitations. And, as a result, the patient no longer thinks of my theme but exclusively of his theme; this means of the theme that the body speaks to him.

And I told you that this body language has only one word, a one-word vocabulary. It always talks of danger, always of insecurity. And you see when I gave my patient my diagnosis, it was couched in the language of security. I told the patient, "All you are suffering from is nerves." That means there is a great deal of torture, suffering, distress, but no danger. And therefore the patient had to keep apart these two themes: danger on the one hand, security on the other. I preached the theme of security, and the patient accepted the theme of danger, or returned to the theme of danger.

And what is to be done? The patient is in the throes of suffering, and I am in a quandary. I have to get the patient out of his suffering. I have to give him relief, relief as soon as possible. But the patient listens to his body language, to the theme that the body language throws out. Now, if so, the body language is opposed to what I tell the patient. So the body language is my opponent, not the patient, and I am stymied. I don't know how to counter this threat of the body language, how to convince the patient's body that it uses a wrong language, the language of danger. And seventeen years ago, when I realized the futility of my single-handed fighting symptoms and their body language, I finally decided to turn to my patients and ask them for help.

You see, if one is confronted with an overpowering enemy, one cannot expect to conquer him single-handed. Then you need allies. Then you need others to help you. And if I am to deal successfully with the body language of the patient, I have to ally myself with those to which the body language listens. You see, when the patient is left to himself, the body language is very convincing. It tells the patient, "Well, Dr. Low can make mistakes, too. And your condition is not just nerves. He is mistaken." And then, "You didn't tell him the whole story." You know. And then, "The doctor doesn't know how much you suffer. He doesn't suffer," and so on. The body language is a formidable antagonist, and single-handed I could never, never deal with it successfully.

But let the patient come here among other patients and see that this patient and that patient, who have suffered frightfully in the past, whose body language did not give [them] a minute of rest, whose body language continually distracted [them] from the doctor's theme to the body's theme—let him come into this group and see the many patients that in former days failed to concentrate on what I told them, and they concentrated on what their body told them. Let them come here. And when then the body language tells him, "Well, Doctor Low doesn't suffer; he [doesn't] know how much you suffer," but there is somebody in this corner—and somebody in this corner in that group—that definitely suffered and knew how he suffered. And he got cured. And you will understand, without my going into many details, this job of sidetracking the theme of the body language and of instituting consistently and irrevocably my theme—the theme of the doctor who treats you—can only be done if the doctor succeeds in securing the assistance of his other patients. This means only in a group like this, where patients have been trained in the techniques of self-help and mutual aid.

Now, don't let me be too literal. I have been a well-known psychiatrist—far better known than I am now, by the way, because I have more or less retreated. I have been a very well-known psychiatrist, both locally and nationally, twenty years ago, certainly eighteen years ago. And in those days, I think I treated patients successfully, although I had no allies. But when later I looked up my records, I found that the number of patients that I succeeded in treating successfully was distressingly small. Only a small portion of the many patients that I saw could I treat without enlisting the help of the patients, which I later did. I hope you will draw the moral from this story.

I have too many patients that get tired coming to this group, naturally, after a certain decent period of time that they have attended the group. Let me warn you: Don't do that. Stick to the group as much and as long as you can. The body language is your worst enemy, and it is a vicious sort of enemy. And don't trust too much your capacity to concentrate your attention, as you should, on the doctor's theme exclusively. If you don't make it a point to cooperate with this group for a long period of time, your attention will not remain concentrated on the theme that it should concentrate on.

Thank you.

LECTURE 52

SPOTTING DEEPLY-SEATED HABITS

28 Minutes

Recorded Saturday, November 21, 1953

I must apologize for being late today. But I must also tell you that, having been late, I was unable to listen to the panel in its totality, and I will talk to you about the few remarks that I happened to pick up.

Agnes told you that before Recovery, if the thing that happened to her—and which I don't know—if that thing had happened to her at that time, she would have been provoked and would have been sarcastic. Well, what is wrong in being sarcastic? somebody may ask. I will tell you later what is wrong with that.

And Ray told you that he was depressed some day and was out of sorts, in a low mood. And again he told you the story that before Recovery he would have developed all kinds of symptoms, tenseness, palpitations, and so forth. Now, both told you that now that they have been trained in Recovery, they spotted their reactions. And I would like to know what they spotted and how they do their spotting. I have noticed that it is very difficult to explain to my patients what precisely is spotting.

You see, you do not spot the fact that you are depressed. It is plain and almost visible. All you have to do is to look in the mirror, and you will see you are depressed. But you don't have to look into the mirror. You can feel the depression. And what you feel, and what you see, and what you can hear and touch, you don't have to spot. You spot, for instance, some person in a crowd. This means that you have not seen the person. You don't know that the person is there.

Will you understand, once for all, spotting must only be done about the thing that you don't see, don't hear, don't feel—this means about the thing that you don't know. I know a lady who does the following things: She enters an elevator, and the sign reads "No Smoking" or "Smoking Prohibited by City Ordinance." But she pulls out a cigarette and lights it. It's not that she merely enters the elevator smoking, but she lights a cigarette. She lights the cigarette. When you tell her— and a lady who is a very close friend of hers told me that she, if she is with her in the elevator, tells her and calls her attention to the fact—that there is no smoking in an elevator, she immediately puts out the cigarette. The fact that this lady throws the cigarette to the ground shows that she apparently forgot. She didn't light the cigarette deliberately.

And there are people who are visited by somebody, and they take the center of the stage. They do all the talking. And should you, after the visit is over, call their attention to the fact that they did not just act as a host, that they were rather rude, they didn't give anybody a chance, then they are flabbergasted. They didn't know that they were rude. But you will add immediately, So they did not spot. And I tell patients: Spot your talking, spot your walking and spot your eating. And I add: You talk too fast, too violently or vehemently. You walk too fast; you eat too fast. And any speed thrown onto an action is bad for the nerves. The fast speaking, the fast talking, the fast walking gives you tenseness. And that's unfortunate for your nerves because the tenseness produces or precipitates symptoms. And if I hear the person talking fast, and if I see the person walking fast or eating fast, then one asks oneself, why doesn't the person herself notice it?

Well, the answer is, we do not notice things that have become strongly habitual. A deep-seated habit becomes, not unconscious, but little conscious. It is done spontaneously, and it is not reflected on. And fast walking, fast talking and fast eating has become a deeply-rooted habit that one does not reflect on. So one does not know, or one is not aware of the fact, that one does things with too much speed.

If then I tell the patient, "Reduce your speed," then, at that moment, the patient may immediately begin to speak slowly. But in a minute, he forgets the admonition and rolls off a rapid lecture and becomes tense again and precipitates his symptoms, or may precipitate them. A minute after I have given him the admonition, he has forgotten that he has a habit for speed, and he rolls on at a violent tempo. While I told him about his speeding, it became conscious to him. Then he didn't have to spot it. A minute later, when he again resumed his speed, he was no longer conscious of speeding. Then he was required to spot the speed. And what I want particularly to mention here is this fact: that patients must learn the distinction between things that are known to them and things that are not known to them, particularly between symptoms or temperamental reactions or other unfortunate reactions—unfortunate for the nervous system—that they perform but do not know they perform. These actions must be spotted.

Now, for instance, you may say that if a person has temper, he ought to be able to know that now he is in temper. But that is not so with certain temperamental reactions that are rooted, deeply-rooted habits. Then you are not conscious of them. When you walk on the street, you are not conscious of your walking. You don't have to be. But you are certainly not conscious of the speedy walking.

And you will understand now that, for instance, people may have developed a deeply-rooted habit of being sarcastic, and sarcasm is, of course, stinging. It is a very disturbing habit. It is disturbing to the people at whom the sarcasm is directed. If somebody comes up to me and immediately makes a sharp joke, I don't like that. I don't want to be treated sharply. And since sarcasm is a deeply-rooted habit, the person is not aware that he is sarcastic. He is only aware that he makes a joke. He thinks he is very smart.

And there are fathers and mothers and friends who constantly endeavor to release a joke. And if a father is perpetually joking, then he jokes about the remarks of his wife and, what is worse yet, at anything that the children may say. And that is fatal for the development of children. Children, of course, want to be taken seriously, at least as seriously as one can take a person, an ordinary person. Children are extremely sensitive to not being taken seriously. They feel that they are not respected, and therefore not loved. And a child wants to be loved. And there are so many fathers that are driven to make jokes almost indefinitely. And that has become a deep-rooted habit. The father is not aware of the fact that constant joking means never to take a person seriously. And that's a deep insult to the soul of a child, particularly. And sometimes I deal with a father of this kind, and he comes to me and tells me that the son cannot be handled, that the son is refractive to order, to admonitions, to advice, that the son has developed a violent temper. And he has developed symptoms, and he brings the child to me because of the symptoms.

And then I delve into the subject of how the father treats the child. And usually the father will tell me, "Well, I think I am a good father, or the ordinary father. I always think of my family. I save my money in order to give the children a solid education." And so he thinks, there is the evidence that he is a father as he should be, a well-meaning father, a considerate father, a father who loves his children. And before long I have a conference with the mother, and I ask her about the relation between father and son. And too often do I get the story that the father is a very good, kind father. He never spanks the children. As a matter of fact, he goes out of his way to read to the children, to go out with them, to play with them. Well, that's the story of a desirable father.

Then I sometimes ask the mother, "Does this particular child enjoy playing with the father or having a story read to him by the father?" And gradually I direct the conversation down to the story and how it is told. How does the father play with the children? And then I throw in a remark telling the lady, "Your husband, while he was in my office, talked freely. And I noticed he is fond of telling jokes. And he is fond of laughing and of picking up a remark of mine and turning it into a joke. Does he do that with the children, too?" And now the mother remembers. Well, that father is in the habit of making jokes on any occasion, on every occasion, with everybody.

And I remember a case where I once wanted to have an intern on my service. And there came about three or four people applying for the position. And they were all good, and it was difficult to choose from among them. But the fourth intern, the fourth man who applied for the position, joked to me. I made a statement, and he returned a jocular statement. Then I knew he had no respect for me. He treated me disrespectfully. He came for a position, not for a friendly conversation with me. If this man had spotted his joking—that must only be applied once in a while and in the proper place—he would have known that if he comes applying for a position, this is not the place to become familiar with me. I am the one who is to give him a position, and, if he immediately becomes familiar with me, I don't want him on my service. He has no respect for the man he speaks to and no consideration for the nature of the situation that he acts in. And so I had eliminated one already. He certainly didn't get the job.

You see here, if people don't learn the proper method of spotting, they can do great harm to their children. They can lose jobs. And with patients, if they don't spot, there we deal with a situation that has nothing to do with joking, as you may think, with sarcasm. You may say the patient is not sarcastic with his suffering. He doesn't joke about his symptoms, I grant you. The patient's situation is the reverse of the person who is sarcastic or jocular. You understand that the habit, the deeply-rooted habit of joking is one in which a person refuses to take seriously things that may have to be taken seriously. For instance, a child has to be taken seriously by the father.

The patient does something else. When he has a symptom, he loses all capacity for joking. He becomes too serious. He takes his symptoms so seriously that they scare the wits out of him. And in a scare, naturally, one doesn't joke. And it will be good for you to know that spotting applies particularly to such elements, but to many others, of course, as joking on the one hand, sarcasm that Agnes mentioned, and taking things too seriously on the other hand. The patient, far from being inclined to make jokes about his symptoms, is scared by them and takes them too seriously.

And if a patient says, "I read in the paper that somebody died, and I got awfully scared," then he takes things too seriously. And what does he take seriously? Not that somebody died, because he may not have known him or he may not have been close to him. He takes too seriously something that is very common to all my patients, as long as they have not improved sufficiently. He is already afraid that, having read about somebody having died, this will upset him. He is not upset yet, perhaps.

He even takes too seriously things that have only remotely a contact with his symptoms. That patient may be afraid of his palpitations, but reading that somebody has died is certainly nothing dangerous. It doesn't have to upset him. It may make him feel sad, but it doesn't have to upset him to the point where he becomes scared. Sadness is not fear, and if somebody dies, one should feel sad and not scared. But that patient takes his palpitations so seriously that he is automatically already afraid of anything that might remind him of his palpitations, of dying. Not anything that will really harm him, that will really be likely to upset him, but something that merely reminds him of his trouble.

Now that's, of course, the acme of taking things seriously. That patient has to be trained to spot his lack of humor. He is too easily scared, first by things that go on within, second by things that he reads or hears or sees that have some remote resemblance to his symptoms but actually have no real relation to them. And I will on this occasion remind you that if somebody has a symptom—let me say fatigue or palpitations or sleeplessness—and constantly worries about it, constantly is afraid of the damage that symptom might do, what he must spot is that he makes a diagnosis. But he doesn't know that he makes a diagnosis. He simply says, "I am scared. It scares me no end. I am constantly on edge." Everybody knows what these terms mean. Apparently they don't have to be spotted. But if a patient says that he is constantly on edge—that means that he constantly worries, that he is constantly afraid of something—then he has made a diagnosis. He has made the diagnosis that the thing of which he is constantly afraid is serious and dangerous. And to make of one's condition the diagnosis of being something serious and dangerous means to make the diagnosis of a serious ailment. And that's, of course, a diagnosis. Now the patient made innocent statements, and he did not know that they contained a diagnosis.

And once you learn these simple few facts that I told you, then you first know what spotting means. It means to look for something that has become a deeply-seated habit and therefore is not conscious to you. The meaning of it is not conscious to you, and therefore you must spot it. It doesn't present itself to you plainly and visibly. It must be spotted.

Now, every patient in the beginning makes the statement that he can't stand his symptoms any longer, that they are frightening, that he is constantly in terror. And the question is, does he spot these statements as meaning that he considers the underlying condition as being very severe, serious and dangerous? If he does so, then he has made the diagnosis of a serious and dangerous condition. But he is not aware of having made a diagnosis. And this must be spotted.

Well, that's enough for today, and thank you.

LECTURE 53

MUSCLES, PREOCCUPATION
AND ROUTINE

27 Minutes
Recorded Saturday, April 17, 1954

I will make a few remarks about the statements made by Elizabeth. You remember she was to fetch an item from the stock, some toy if I remember correctly. And that was an item the location of which she did not know, and she was in a quandary. And when she said she used her muscles, well, it's a very good expression. I like it. It's my language. But what did she do with the muscles?

Well, she said she went up to another experienced saleslady, and this lady told her where to find the item. And you remember that afterwards, Elizabeth stated that in former days, before she had training in Recovery, she wouldn't have been able to use her muscles. She wouldn't have been able to ask for information. Her voice would have stuck in the throat, her tongue would have tightened, and she would not have been able to ask for information. And I want you to know what that means in terms of dynamics—not merely in terms of telling a story, but in terms of describing the forces which [on] certain occasions make the muscles stiffen up and [on] certain occasions make them relax.

Before I continue, I will again remind you that practically all your behavior—and certainly all behavior with which you act on the outside, on other people or on other objects—all your behavior is carried on by muscles. And that should be such a simple truth that it is surprising that we had to come to pronounce it. But nobody knew that, apparently, although all one has to do is to mention it, and everybody then knows it is the simplest truth.

If you sit with somebody in a room and do nothing much but sitting, then you exercise a function. You initiate behavior. That is very important. Not the sitting, but you sit with another person in the same room, and you don't talk. That's very significant behavior. Your sitting and not talking may, for instance, arouse the anger of this person, and perhaps it often does. Or it may make this person tense because he doesn't know what to do about it. Should he talk to you? Should he not? Should he maintain a sitting position or should he walk out? And the poor fellow usually doesn't know what to do if he doesn't want to be rude. And you see this simple matter of not moving muscles is a very significant act of behavior.

Then remember the occasion when you walked on the street and somebody passed by you that you knew, and you later find out that you didn't look at him. The looking is done with the muscles of the lids and the muscles that move the eyes. Your muscles didn't behave right, and that person was perhaps insulted because he thought you cut him on the street. And all of this is done with the muscles.

I don't mean this common behavior that everybody knows to be associated with muscles: let me say, being violent. Naturally, your violence is expressed with muscles, but don't forget the muscles of the eyes and the muscles that make you sit or get up. And they may be very dynamic. They may produce an extremely dangerous behavior, socially dangerous.

And there is the handshake, and you shake hands with somebody. That may be extremely important. You may win a friend. Or you fail to shake hands, and that may be extremely important. You may lose a friend. Or you may lose a job because your boss thinks you are not courteous enough, and the courtesy is expressed with muscles. How else? Speech muscles, at the least. And if you use your speech muscles in the wrong places, at the wrong times, with regard to wrong persons, then you are in trouble. All the trouble and all the benefits that [are] caused by behavior ultimately [go] back to the muscles. If you want to express friendship, then your eye muscles must move in such a manner that your eyes show friendliness. If you want to talk to somebody and influence him, your voice must just be attuned to the import of the situation. And if you are tense, this means if your speech muscles become tense and your tonal muscles in the throat, then you bungle the job. Your behavior is poor because your muscles are tense.

And there is no end to the examples that could be quoted, and I will merely sum up by saying, everybody speaks of the brain as governing behavior. That's all nonsense. The brain plays quite some part in behavior, but not the principal part; the principal part is played by the muscles. The brain influences the muscles, there is no doubt. But the muscles can influence the brain much more. Much more. Just speak to somebody and your voice cracks or suddenly falls down to a lower pitch. That's done by the muscles of the vocal cords, by the tongue, by the interior of the mouth, and so forth. That's all muscles. And then after you have bungled the situation through your muscles, you experience self-blame. The muscles have produced self-blame in the brain. Criticism, shame, all these feelings have been produced by the bungling of the muscles. If the muscles hadn't bungled, you would at that moment not feel ashamed of yourself, not blame yourself. Do you understand that the muscles influence the brain at least as much as the brain influences the muscles? In my opinion, much more, particularly with patients.

And I will tell you something about what Elizabeth meant to tell you. But fortunately she didn't tell all, so I can come back to her statement and supplement what she said. She asked somebody for help. Well, I do that, I think, every day; I think several times a day. And there are very few people that don't do that endless times, every hour, maybe every five minutes. And why was it so difficult for Elizabeth to ask a question? It still is difficult for her at times, although she has made a remarkable improvement.

Well, to ask a question is what we call *routine,* routine for everybody. It may come up any time. The need for asking a question may come up any time. And if [this] comes up, average people discharge of this need by simply asking the question, and that's what we call *routine.* And if I look upon my life, my daily life, or the entire span of my life, then I know whenever a thing becomes routine with me, I have no difficulty whatever carrying it out. And so it is with everybody. And if a thing has become routine, then it's not fatiguing, it is not straining. You have done it so frequently that you don't think about it anymore. You do it unthinkingly.

Let me say washing in the morning: You don't now think, Now, I'll open the faucet, now I'll put the right hand under this jet of water, now I'll pick up the soap. Nobody does that. You just go ahead and do the thing unthinkingly. And you see that's why we have the routine activities, and that's the great benefit of the routine activities. We don't have to think. If you always had to think consciously about whatever you do, you would have to pay attention to every step. Your attention would be strained. Your attention would become fatigued. And then you would be under strain and under fatigue.

That's precisely what happens to our patients if they don't improve. Every little item is thought about consciously, and that is fatiguing. And why do people think about things consciously, turning the full floodlight of attention on the object they are dealing with and therefore fatiguing their attention if they do it too long, if they use it too long. And my patients are constantly in attention, as long as they suffer acutely. And that's what makes them fatigued: not work, not the work of the muscles, but the straining of the attention.

Now, my attention is also strained on many occasions. For instance, something happens in my family that appears to me as a threat of some kind. Then I think of it. I think of it again. I try to efface it, but it comes back. I try to divert my mind, but the moment I am relaxed again, there is the thought about my family, about that thing that has happened or threatens to happen, and my attention is always on this one thing. And should it be interrupted and diverted, it would revert back to the thing all day and perhaps for several days. And during these days I don't feel ambitious. The muscles are limp, appetite is poor, because of this constant straining of the attention, which makes the attention fatigued and therefore the muscles limp. That's what attention does. And we call that *preoccupation*.

Ordinarily, I go along in life and will sometimes think of myself, and then at other times of my neighbor, then of my children, then of my wife, then of the streetcar that passes by, of the sky that is clouded, and so my attention will wander. And occasionally then I see a patient and talk to him. Now I think of the patient. Then I see the janitor who comes in with something. My attention is constantly wandering from one situation to the other until I steady my attention. For instance, I want to study something. Then I sit down, and attention is then concentrated. But in the example which I mentioned where there is apparently a threat to the welfare of my family, one occasion constantly occupies my attention, and that's what we call *preoccupation*. I am preoccupied with one item, and the moment I pay attention to another item, before long, instantly my attention is again reverted back to the preoccupying item, and, as I say, I am then preoccupied. And what am I preoccupied with?

There are two things that can make you preoccupied: either happiness or unhappiness. That's all. Security or insecurity. Danger or no danger. If you are preoccupied with a happy event, you know, there is a wedding in the family, or you think of a promotion that is due you or you did an excellent job somehow, then have your attention dwell on this item and be preoccupied with your joy and happiness. That will never harm you any. But if the object of your preoccupation is unhappiness, fear, insecurity, then see to it that you don't have your attention constantly riveted on this item. And that's what my patients do, precisely that's what they do. They are constantly preoccupied with danger.

Now, you remember I told you something about the routine. I do my routine as I do things in general. It proceeds without straining of the attention. I hardly pay attention to the job that I do. It has become my second nature, and so it goes with most people. That means that I don't think that my routine has any element of danger. I don't fear the routine. But that's precisely what my patients do. They fear the routine.

Since their muscles are tense, since the muscles of the eyes are tense, the muscles of speech, the muscles of the arms, and so forth, they indeed don't carry out their routine as it should be carried out. Even if they wash the dishes, they feel it wasn't done with spirit, it was clumsy, stiff—not that they remember they did the dishes at times, at least, with spirit. If it was only done with the spirit of wanting to get through with it, well, that's a spirit, too. But today they simply don't do the washing dishes so that it pleases them, so that it is a routine act.

Everything is a problem. While holding a dish in the hand, the patient is afraid he may drop it, and that bungles the job. Because if you are afraid of dropping dishes frequently, all the time, then you will drop some of them. The hands become trembly; then you will drop some or one or more. And since that happens to the patient again and again that his tenseness makes him clumsy and therefore things happen that shouldn't happen— breakages or failure of any other kind—he develops an abiding mistrust of his body, of his muscles. And he is afraid that if he carries a cup from one room to the other, he will spill or drop. He is afraid that if he begins to talk, which is routine—talking to somebody in the overwhelming majority of cases is routine—if he begins to chat with the neighbor, he is instantly afraid that he may use the [wrong] word, that he may forget what he wanted to say. And all around things are no longer routine, and whenever things are no longer routine, we call that, we call that *a problem.* Things become problems.

The simple act of looking at somebody, looking somebody in the eye becomes a problem. The act of talking becomes a problem, and everything else. Of course, the act of getting up in the morning, the act of getting to sleep, to relax in bed, all of these become problems, and when ordinarily they are routine. And there are endless nervous patients that can't write anything in public. They can't deposit anything in the bank, if they have to make out a slip. A perfectly routine action becomes a problem. And so my patients are what has been called *problematic existences.* They exist by problems. And now if I am confronted with a problem—for instance the problem that I mentioned, there is in my mind the idea that something threatens my family; that's of course a problem; that's not routine; let's hope it is not routine; that's a problem—then, of course, my attention is constantly directed toward this problem. Then I am preoccupied with fear, not with joy, not with happiness. And the patient is that all the time until he improves. And the existence is not only problematical but miserable, the utmost misery.

And how are you going to overcome this matter of the problematic existence, of an existence to which everything has become problematic? Everything is an issue and a problem, and therefore everything—whatever you do—engages your attention. And your attention is bound to be fatigued all the time. Now, perhaps, you understand what nervous fatigue is. It's the fatigue of attention. You can't relax. This means attention cannot relax.

And in former days, I didn't know this problem anyhow. Seventeen years ago, when I was already a professor known all over the country, I didn't know that such a problem existed. Fortunately, it was thrown into my lap, and fortunately it stuck there. You know, so many things are thrown in my lap, and they drop off the lap. But this fortunately stuck. And I had to study and to make a very serious study of the conditions of my patients, and there I still remember the day I dropped on this problem, the problem of the problem, the problem of the problematic existence of the patient. And I thought, How are you going to explain this to the patient? And I didn't know how to do it.

And then before long these panel discussions developed. And the panel discussions are of such a nature that they bring up simple examples—the simple example of Elizabeth, that she couldn't find an item and asked somebody to tell her where it is. What more simple item can there be in life? And if one gets such simple items, then, of course, the problem has an intense light thrown on it. But in former days I was a big professional, and when I sat [at] the table and the patient opposite me, I was the official. Well, and the patient was— well, what is a patient, anyhow? You know. That was about the situation until here in this group the patient became the supreme object of my work, not only my smartness but the patient's suffering. When I was the official opposite the patient, then I had to, well, I had to show smartness, cleverness, knowledge. I had to impress the patient with my professional art.

Today I can afford to sit here in this group and to listen to Elizabeth telling me that she had lost something, or that she didn't know something and somebody else told her where it is. In former days, when I was the official, well, I would have immediately thought that, well, why should I bother about such drivel, you know, everyday life, sheer routine. Today, that's what I want. I want to learn where the difficulties of my patients reside. And they reside precisely in those things that people call drivel, daily drivel. And you will now understand: The difficulties arise from the fact that to the patient these simple things are not drivel. Daily they are, hourly, every minute they crop up, but no drivel. And to the doctor they shouldn't be drivel either, because they are the daily life of the patient which takes in quite a space of his life. And ever since I have learned that, I have made up my mind I'll talk to the patients [about] whatever they bring up, and I'll use my language. And even if it sounds highfalutin, well, with the examples they offer me, I can easily explain this language that may sound highfalutin, but is a language that I have noticed my patients lap up with great relish and with great benefit.

And keep in mind when you come to Recovery what you have to learn is finally to develop such a skill in ridding your muscles of tenseness that the muscles again regain their agility, their relaxation, and then do things as routine and no longer as a problem.

Thank you.

LECTURE 54

SYMPTOMS INTERFERE WITH PLANS

9 Minutes
Recorded Saturday, January 23, 1954

The theme is . . . . Now I forgot. What was it? Oh, yes, "The Passion for Self-Distrust." That's a remarkable theme. And I had it in mind, when I read the title this morning, that it is remarkable that when I arrived here, apparently I became worked up and forgot the title after I mentioned it.

You see, both you and I are human beings, and a human being lives in the future. Don't let anybody tell you that a human being lives in the past. If he does, then he needs treatment. He better not. He should live in the future. And this living in the future we call *planning,* looking ahead. But the correct expression, the desirable expression, is *planning.*

When I came here today, I planned it. If I had not planned being here, I wouldn't have been here. I wouldn't be here. If I take a seat here, I planned it. I made sure, or I was sure, that the chair will carry my weight. I was sure that it is not a broken chair, in other words. For some reason, I felt sure. Maybe I was mistaken, but I felt sure that in this place they have only chairs that are not broken, and you can safely sit down on them. All of this is planning.

And in the morning when I get up, I dress according to a plan. Sometimes I pick this suit, sometimes the other, sometimes this tie, and so on—everything planned. And if I sit down to eat, then I plan first to eat perhaps a soup. And I plan to pick a certain spoon, not a teaspoon but a soup spoon, and so forth. Everything is planned in this life, unless it is done in coma or in a state of unconsciousness. But even in states of unconsciousness, there is a lot of planning.

But if you plan, then you plan something that can be expressed in terms of seeking a goal or reaching a goal. You plan to reach a goal, to accomplish reaching it. And that's what you call *accomplishing*, to set out for a goal and reach it. That's the only kind of accomplishment, I think, we know in life. This accomplishing is done by the human being. Everything else happens to him. But this is done, this seeking for goals and reaching goals.

And if I want to reach goals, I have to employ means for reaching them. The means lead to the goals. And, for instance, when I came here, I had to employ means this afternoon. I had to employ an automobile. It could have been some other means of conveyance, but it was an automobile. And when I get into my automobile, I either have trust or distrust. I either remember and cannot shake off the thought that yesterday the car didn't start. It so happened yesterday. It's true. And I was annoyed, and I lost time, and I wasn't sure whether I'll get the car going. Then if I think that this condition may happen now anytime, then I am distrustful of the means that I employ, what I am about to employ. And so I become self-conscious. And it will be good for you to know that self-consciousness has a great deal to do with the goals you set yourself and the means you employ towards reaching them. But more than that, I will not tell you. You'll find a great [deal of] material on this subject in my book, and I will advise you to read that book. Not only to buy it but to read it, too—as a matter of fact, to study it, not only to read it.

And what has this to do with patients? Now, you see a patient lives and plans and tries to accomplish his plans. He, for instance, wants to visit a friend. That's planning. He wants to take his children for a walk. That's planning. He wants to read to his children—or he or she—and all of a sudden the heart begins to palpitate, or a terrible fatigue settles on the man's or woman's body, or there comes a pounding headache, and so forth.

You see, the man planned something. He planned some action. He wanted to reach his goal and perhaps would have used the proper means for reaching his goal, the goal of playing with his children or taking a walk or visiting. But something interfered and that is the palpitation, the fatigue, the pounding headache. That doesn't happen with ordinary people. Ordinary people, if they want to do something, the question is whether they can do it. There is no question that the heart will suddenly palpitate or some other part of his body will interfere with his planning and reaching his goal. That's what we call *nervously sound* or *healthy individuals.* They are not interfered with, with the task of reaching their goals, by sensations and symptoms.

So, will you understand that the patient, the nervous patient, is an individual that can plan, and reach his goals, and choose his means exactly like anybody else. He's not mentally disturbed; he's only nervously handicapped. But when he plans and when he sets out to accomplish what he plans, then his own body may interfere at any time, in any intensity. And that's what makes the patient's, the nervous patient's, life such an ordeal, almost a nightmare. And I think it is a nightmare for most patients.

And you see, you must, in order to reach your goals in ordinary life and to employ the proper means, you must eliminate the disturbances of your own body. And that requires training.

And I only wanted to set the problem before you without going into any deeper discussion. I want to tell you that the purpose of this organization is not to teach the patient how to be smart and clever and efficient. Not at all. The patient is clever, as clever as people are. He is efficient, as efficient as average people are, and perhaps more—or less. I don't know. But the patient must be rid of the handicap of his symptoms—this means of his own body and his own mind interfering with his choice of goals and the choice of means.

Thank you.

Lecture 55

There Is No Hopeless Case
(Part 1)

29 Minutes
Recorded 1953

I will present to you a patient tonight, a man who was in the middle thirties when I saw him the first time. That was in 1944, so that's now nine years. Since it was in April of 1944, it's going to be ten years. Well, I present this case because he had, after an initial improvement during the first few years, then slipped back. And lately there was no progress—one of the few patients that perform in this manner, but we have a few such patients.

The man is here tonight. Well, he gave the story at that time that about five years, six years, before I examined him, he suddenly felt that a heat wave or waves—he was not very positive about the nature of the wave—suddenly began to swing in his head. And it felt as if this wave moved the skull from the inside.

Well, I guess you will realize that is a very scary situation. I don't think that I would take such a sensation lightly, but this man did not get scared. For some reason he thought his blood pressure might be high. The reason I don't know because he didn't tell me at that time or later that he thought he had a high blood pressure. On examination, he did not have any. And I want you now to realize that there a man experienced a sensation suddenly that certainly is expected to be frightening, and he did not get scared. I think you would, and I do conclude that this man [didn't have] much fear. He was rather fearless, not easily frightened.

Then why did he become a nervous patient? There is no nervousness without fear. If you want to call it *fear,* you may do so. If you want to call it *terror,* you may do so, or in its milder degree, *worry* and *preoccupation.* But here we deal with a man who had a sensation that I would consider as most frightening, and he did not experience any scare.

Well, these waves continued. They came only for a second or so and then disappeared very rapidly. But then they came back every few minutes. And in the evening they stopped, and that was all. He was not scared. And the waves stayed away for several months, well, because he was not scared. And you better take this lesson from a case of this kind.

There is no nervous symptom without fear. But after a patient has developed fear and cultivated it for years, then, of course, it's not so easy to get rid of it because there is now a determined habit of fearing. That goes just as well for anger, but we don't discuss anger tonight. We may revert to it later.

Well, the waves continued on that particular day, but for months they stayed away. And you understand now that this was only possible if the fear was gone or was not there from the beginning, which is better. But after four months, the waves returned and disappeared again. But the next time they returned after a shorter period, after two or three months. He did not give me an accurate record, because when he came to me, he had already gone through six years of trouble and didn't remember the details very well. Patients have a notoriously short memory for their suffering, fortunately.

Well, the next time, the waves came back, perhaps after a month, and the next time after three weeks and then stayed a little longer. And then the interval between the spells became shorter, but the spell longer. And finally, after this situation had prevailed for about two years, the waves remained for good and were there all day, every day. And in the meantime, he developed other symptoms called the common variety of sensations: palpitations, headaches, numbness and so forth, you know, tremors. In addition, he developed one symptom that was not so common: When he talked to people, he had to sway from side to side. That doesn't mean that he had to, but he had developed a symptom that came to the fore when he talked to somebody, when he was engaged in some sort of conversation. But we will not be detained by these common and perhaps commonplace symptoms although they are very distressing. But we know them from all kinds of conditions. But gradually he developed bizarre sensations, not common sensations, but let me call them *eccentric, bizarre sensations.*

When he walked on the street, he felt that the head was tightening up. The heart began to pump violently. That's nothing bizarre. That's still common symptoms. But when now, after two years, these symptoms of palpitations and tightening up of the head came up, then he felt his body was beginning to shrink. And because the body shrank and the head felt light—a condition that many patients have, and quite a number of you know about it because you have it; they call it "light-headedness"—so he felt he had lost his point of gravity, and he was afraid he was going to keel over. And that means sudden death, as he conceived it. Now he became afraid. And that obsession—that when he was on the street he might keel over anytime—well, gripped him, and it became a sustained obsession. And again and again he felt that his head suddenly ballooned out. Well, I tell you, I wouldn't like to have such sensations.

And then he felt at various times all kinds of other symptoms that are not the commonest variety. All of a sudden his upper lip began to jump. Well, that's not so common by any means. Steam, he felt, hissing through his ears. And then something shot through his head, and then pulled the head to the right. All of a sudden, he noticed once that his eyelids closed and opened of their own. He didn't want the reaction. He didn't make them close and open. They opened and they closed spontaneously. And that's, of course, a very distressing symptom, and not at all common.

As I told you, he improved during the first year, kept up for the next following years a fair degree of improvement, sometimes for a day and sometimes for a week. Once he had a good improvement for a month. And each time the condition came back.

As I say, I want to present you tonight with a patient that has not been successful in losing his symptoms. And I may reword this statement by saying I have not been successful in giving him permanent relief. One of my failures. But I will tell you immediately, and I want this gentleman to hear what I say, I will, at the end of my presentation, map out a plan for speeding up his recovery. And he will listen to it, and we will discuss it some of these days privately.

Now, what happened to him if you wish to explain it? Well, he had symptoms for endless years. First, for about four years—six years, indeed, but the first two years were mild—for four years before I saw him. And then for almost ten years, if we include the period, this short period of improvement, and it was about ten years thereafter till today. And I saw him last week, and he is by no means relieved.

A condition of this kind we can aptly call one in which the symptoms held the patient in their grip. And that means that he is suffering from the tyranny of symptoms. Keep that term in mind: *the tyranny of symptoms.* And the more frightening the symptoms become, the more do they suggest danger—the danger of collapse, the danger of keeling over, the danger that the head, which is ballooning out, might go on ballooning out. And what will happen? That's the suggestions that the patient receives from the symptoms. That means they scare him, and his imagination becomes active and summons forth visions of dreadful danger. And that's what we call *the terror of suggestions.* So, he suffered, if we want to express it in fancy terms, from the tyranny of sensations and from the terror of suggestions. But it's good to keep these phrases in mind.

Now, a patient of this kind, having symptoms more or less continually for years and years, does something to his nerves, but no damage. Nerves are never damaged no matter how you abuse them, except if they are injured by a violent force, by an explosion, by a stabbing wound, by a bullet or by pressure of some sort. But nerves are never damaged by nervous symptoms; this means by nervous tenseness. Never! Let nobody tell you that there is an incurable nervous ailment. If they tell you, don't listen. If you have to listen, forget. If you can't forget, then reject your belief or recast it.

Now, when nerves are subjected to continuous tenseness, and the continuous tenseness is naturally generated where there are continuous preoccupations, worries—and particularly so if the worry and the preoccupation and the fear are in the form of terror. And this man has lived in terror when he went on the streets; otherwise, not so much.

And he has never withdrawn. He has never developed that famous condition that you call by a fancy name, *agoraphobia*. That's, of course, all these phobias. Well, these names are good for the textbook, but not for people who want to learn something. I may tell you I have learned a lot from textbooks, and now I am endeavoring very seriously and earnestly to forget what I have learned from the textbooks. And I can't forget. That's unfortunate.

Now, I want to tell you something about this matter of nerves being made something. I'll tell you soon what they are being made by tenseness. If anybody has a symptom—for instance, I have symptoms frequently. A headache, oh, that's quite common with me. I have other symptoms: palpitations—that happens to me, not frequently, but not infrequently either. Of course, I have sweats, be sure, and backaches, and pullings somewhere, and pushings somewhere else, and fatigue and poor nights. I have them. Well, I see a doubting smile on your faces, but I have them. Everybody has nervous symptoms. You know I have told you. Everybody who has life in him—some people haven't—but if he has life in him, he worries and frets and is preoccupied and looks anxiously into the future and blames himself for the past. And he can't avoid symptoms if he does that for any length of time. And that's what we call *a nervous person.*

The difference is that nervous patients develop panics, not merely symptoms. And the panics keep the symptoms going, therefore continually create new tenseness, and new tenseness, and give the nerves no rest.

When I have a symptom, it disappears after a second or a minute or after five minutes, and a headache sometimes after half a day. And a depression may sometimes last a full day with me—sometimes, usually only half an hour. When I get up in the morning, and apparently I had some bad dreams which I don't remember, then I am a little bit out of sorts for a half an hour or so, maybe only for ten minutes. But then my nerves get rest again after the depression lifts. And all a nerve needs to recover from pressure is rest, even for a second. Then it recovers. And if you then resume your worrying and fretting and preoccupation, then, of course, it is again put under tension until it resumes symptoms. It creates symptoms again.

Now, if a nerve is constantly badgered by your worries, by your fears and preoccupations, in the beginning it will take the nerve perhaps two, three or four or five minutes or ten minutes before it develops a palpitation, or any other symptom—before it develops a fatigue. The symptom comes after a certain period of time in the beginning. But as you constantly pile tenseness on this nervous system—the next week, the next month, and so forth—you may have developed such a sensitiveness, such an irritability of that particular part of the nervous system that now the palpitations, the fatigue, and so forth, can be released much more quickly. The moment you begin to worry, there is the palpitation. In the beginning, it took an interval before it came on.

And finally the patient comes to the point where he develops the so-called *trigger symptoms.* All you have to do is to think of your heart and then it palpitates—the trigger symptoms. And finally you reach a stage after years where you don't have to think of anything, but the symptom goes on like a wound-up clock, day after day, year after year. And that's what, more or less, happened to this patient.

He developed what we call *the sustained handicap.* And he developed this because he became fearful. You remember in the beginning he was one of those rare individuals that apparently were not likely to develop terror, scare, fear. And now, of course, due to years of suffering, he would be a hero if he didn't develop what I described as, first, the trigger symptoms and, finally, the continuous sustained condition of symptomatic existence.

So, you understand if one wants to cure a patient of this kind, one must first steady his nerves. And there are simple methods of doing that which I will discuss later. But second, there is something else. And you remember I told you that this patient, like every other patient, first suffered from his nerves—the nerves as they come from the brain or are in the brain, the physical nerves. And they develop symptoms when they are put under tenseness. But they will never be put under tenseness unless the brain becomes disturbed—not physically disturbed; nothing dangerous—disturbed by, well, you know, by fear ideas, by danger ideas. And if the brain is to conceive fear ideas, they must come to the brain. Seldom will the brain develop these fear ideas out of thin air. They must come.

There must come to the brain impressions of danger. The brain must get the impression that there is a situation that connotes danger. But the brain, confronted with an impression of this kind, must accept the impression. It can reject it. Anybody can, with his brain, refuse to believe. A suggestion comes from the outside or from the inside. And you can refuse to believe, if it is a suggestion of danger, and you can reject it. For instance, if you know that your doctor has told you there is nothing dangerous in this matter, in this situation—you only get the suggestion of a danger, but in reality there is no danger—then you should be able to reject the idea. Well, you know, I am not so optimistic as to believe that you are always able to reject suggestions. It takes more than mere willingness to do that.

Well, you remember now that I told you that the nerves—in the beginning, prior to being pelted with volleys of tenseness by you, at that time, before they are put under

severe pressure—have a resistance. They resist the swift production of symptoms. And gradually their resistance is worn
down, and then they are in the grip of tenseness and under
the tyranny of symptoms. That's similar with suggestions.

As I sit here, I am suggestible to some extent or in some
situations. And in some other situations I resist suggestions. I
am easily suggestible, perhaps, through sympathy with suffering, let me say. And somebody can fool me. Don't jump to
conclusions. Patients will not fool me. But somebody else,
some fellow who disguises himself as a blind beggar, well, I
am not going to investigate whether he is really blind and
whether he needs begging. I just toss him a coin. And maybe
that is suggestibility. But in other respects, I am very little
suggestible. And a salesman that comes and wants to convince me that I need a pile of insurance has no luck with me.
I am simply not suggestible to this matter of safety, I should
buy safety in the form of insurance. Sometimes I have done
that, but there is a limit.

[Continued in Lecture 56.]

Lecture 56

There Is No Hopeless Case
(Part 2)

28 Minutes [Continued from Lecture 55]
Recorded 1953

Now, if I am not suggestible, or little suggestible, that means I have immunity to suggestions. And if I have a far-going immunity to suggestions—or immunity from suggestions, if you want to call it—then certain ideas can't get in my brain, at any rate not massively, not in numbers. And with me, I guess, it is particularly the idea of danger to which I am thoroughly immune, within reason, naturally, within reason.

And the patient can only be cured if he learns to reduce or decrease tenseness. This means if he learns to build back the resistance of his nerves, nerve resistance; and second, if he learns to restore immunity to suggestions, immunity to the suggestion of danger. I hope that's understood. And as far as I am concerned, this is the basis on which rests my system of treating you. I restore the resistance of your nerves and restore the immunity to danger ideas.

And I tried this with this particular patient, and succeeded some. But essentially I failed. Now, if a patient of this kind is to be cured, if, in other words, his nerve resistance is to be built up and his suggestive immunity is to be built up—by the way, this is not such a good term as you might think it is—it should rather mean doctrinal immunity, but I don't like the term—if this immunity has to be restored, well then the patient must cooperate and cooperate hard.

Now, it's a remarkable thing that this patient has cooperated. And yet I was not successful. And you will know from previous discussions there was something else wrong with him. He cooperated, this means he came to the office whenever I wanted him to come. I may tell you that he has attended these classes very faithfully for years and years. If I am not mistaken, he has stayed away only for a very short period in these ten years. So in point of cooperation there can be no criticism.

So, what was wrong? And I think you know: There was no acceptance. He cooperated, but didn't listen to me, didn't accept what I told him. And he has not accepted yet the simple statement that nerves can never produce any danger. He has not accepted it. To this day, when he walks on the street and gets this keeling-over sensation, he becomes scared and remains scared and insists it might happen that he keels over and collapses. He has not been able to accept the idea that there is never any danger in nerves. And you must admit it's a very surprising thing that a man who has had the sensation of keeling over hundreds and hundreds and maybe thousands of times—I don't know whether it's hundreds or thousands—if he has had this sensation of keeling over for hundreds of times and he did not collapse, why doesn't he believe me? Why doesn't he believe, finally believe, that the condition is not dangerous?

Well, you know, a patient has always an alibi. He says, "Well, it didn't happen yet, but it will, or may," you know. Well, there is, of course, no argument with such a rationalization or such a reasoning. Well, we must cure a patient like this, and no matter how long his suffering has lasted, he can be cured. And you know our motto: *There are no hopeless cases.* You have heard me say that repeatedly, no hopeless cases. But, of course, a patient can give up. Then you can't do anything. But this man cooperates. So he has not accepted what I told him, but he cooperates, so he has not given up. And if he has not given up, why should we give him up? So, there are no hopeless cases. But there are difficult cases, and he is one of them.

Well, you know that here in Recovery we don't believe in complex theories, as some of my colleagues do. Here we deal with simple means. Our teaching is very simple, constantly centering around one thing: danger and no danger; danger and security. The patient always speaks the language of danger, and I always preach the language of security, until finally the patient and I become a unit, and we both preach the subject of security. Then the patient is cured. Very simple, yes, but not easy. Simple. That's all it is.

I tell a patient of this kind, first, to practice extremely simple means. And when I looked up my record of years back, ten years ago, there I found I had told him to do something very simple. You know of it, of course—I mean you who have been here more than once or twice know of it. I told him that thing that my colleagues laugh about but is very efficient, very effective. But they laugh about it because they are used to handling complex explanations. But the body is not complex. That's nonsense. The body is very simply built. And so if anybody wants to formulate a theory that is meant to cure a patient—this means to cure his body, his nerves—the explanation should be simple, too. And when I realized that my complex explanations and complex theories, which I had twenty years ago borrowed from a textbook, which borrowed it from another textbook, and so forth, I discarded them because they didn't work. I noticed that I didn't get results until finally I got in touch with you people and began to learn some things from people and not from textbooks.

And there I learned the body is built according to a simple pattern, and a treating theory should be equally simple. And when I found out—which the textbook did not tell me—that nerves, after all, develop symptoms because they are under tenseness, so I set about to find a simple means of removing tenseness. And it occurred to me that I am less tense when I sit than when I stand. You try it out, and you will find out. In sitting, I am less tense than standing. And if I manage to lie down, then I am less tense yet.

So, I investigated my sitting function, and I found there are two kinds of sitting. You can sit down and wiggle your hands and fingers, and look here and there, and turn around and twist around and can shuffle your feet. That's not resting. That's sitting, but not resting. But there is one sovereign way of resting, and that is where not a particle of the body is permitted to move. If you sit, as I sit now, my eyes are focused at one point. My lids move very scantily. The legs are kept in perfect calm, immobility, and so are the arms. And every finger of mine is now not permitted to make the slightest movement. The best thing under such conditions would, of course, be not to talk, but you are nevertheless, under such practices, permitted to talk slowly. Unfortunately, the slow speaking is an ordeal for a patient. The patient always rushes along on his language, his phrases.

And so I told this man, practice motionless sitting. And several times later, I mean several weeks later, on various occasions, then several months later, I asked him, "Well, did you practice motionless sitting?" He almost invariably told me, "Well, I forgot." Well, how anybody can forget something that is so important—if his doctor tells him, "This is something that will remove tenseness from your nerves," that should be important enough. So that's nonsense. He did not forget. He simply wasn't interested. In this respect, he did not cooperate presumably because he thought, "Well, is that going to help me? I have such a complex condition, and I should remove it with simple practices?" He couldn't believe that. He didn't tell me that, but that's my explanation for the fact that he claims he forgot. That's nonsense, of course.

I don't remember whether I criticized him for it, whether I bawled him out. Maybe I did. Sometimes I do that, as you know. But I have it on record that he did that. Now, he may have forgotten it. Well, he did not cooperate. I told you before that he cooperated, but he didn't. He only cooperated in externals. He came when I asked him to come. He even listens, be sure he listens. He is serious about the condition. He is certainly serious. He is not facetious about it. He doesn't play with his condition. But somehow or other, patients, as you already know, sabotage. They sabotage me, and naturally that means they sabotage their own purpose, the purpose of getting well. But human beings are saboteurs. They sabotage every [inaudible] of their purposes. They sabotage their religion, their patriotism, their citizenship—naturally only in a slight degree, nothing that borders on treachery and so forth. But generally speaking, we are all sinners—don't think that I exempt myself—not hard sinners, but sinners we are. And the patient is.

Well, these mechanical modes of practicing didn't suit him. And you may be sure that I gave him that slogan that all of you know: *If you fear to do a thing, go ahead and do it.* That's the only way of convincing oneself that there is nothing to fear about. But when he was scared on the street because he might have keeled over, he immediately stopped, sat down or went into a house, instead of walking on fearlessly. Since he knew that nervous symptoms can never be dangerous, you can never fall, slip, from nervous symptoms. You can never collapse. Then naturally I told him to disregard your discomfort and walk on. Do what you fear to do. Or do what you hate to do.

Well, plenty of patients, I mean the overwhelming majority of my patients, cooperate in this manner, too. Not only in the mechanics of coming to meetings and coming to my office, as this patient did. They also cooperate with my commands, with my directives, for instance, with *do what you fear to do, motionless sitting,* and, you know, many other formulas that I will not repeat today. Some other time you will hear about it.

The only thing I want you to realize tonight, that I now spoke to you of the mechanical technique of removing tenseness or pressure from the nerves. And then the question comes, what is the patient to do with this other element that produces tenseness and maintains it: the suggestions in his brain, the suggestion of danger? How is he going to restore his immunity, his suggestive immunity? Well, this term, if I remember correctly, used today for the first time, will come up in other presentations and will be explained more minutely. But today, just take it home with you. It's this term of *suggestive immunity* and resistance of the nerves, or *nerve resistance.*

Well, look here, there is perhaps no animal that ever rejects a suggestion. I don't know. But if there are animals that do that—I don't mean domestic animals; domestic animals can be trained to do all kinds of things—but animals in the wild presumably never reject a suggestion. If they see a victim, then they pounce on it and devour it. I doubt whether they ever begin to think, Is that good? If the suggestion comes to me that I should jump at this animal—should I control it—well, animals don't do that, you know. They give way to their suggestions the moment they come up in the brain.

What does that mean? Controlling suggestions, rejecting them, is not natural. That's cultural. Only under human culture do you learn how to control impulses. And suggestions generate impulses. Once you accept a suggestion, you act on it. And the problem is that of nature versus culture.

If I bawl you out, I do that due to my nature. If I control the outburst, then I am cultured. And my patients must control the impulses, must control their suggestions which fire off impulses. And they must become immune, largely immune to fear and temperamental impulses. You know we distinguish [between] the fearful temper and the angry temper. They must be controlled. And so I claim that I teach you, or train you, how to act as cultured individuals.

Well, that sounds easy, but gardeners know something about how to control. They don't have to control weeds. They grow. They act. I said *control;* I shouldn't have said that. They don't have to help weeds to grow. They grow of themselves. But with flowers, it's different. They must be cultivated. And in order to cultivate flowers, weeds must be controlled. Now

I came to the point: The flowers must be cultivated, and so it is with a human being.

Culture, this means control of impulses, must be cultivated, and nature must be held down. And that's what you must do. If you run away because you have a palpitation, that's natural, natural giving away to impulses. But if you brave this sensation and don't run away, and stay and brave, and keep calm in spite of a frightening impression or a frightening sensation, then you show culture. And that cures you. And so, as I told you, I make you cultured individuals when I train you how to control your impulses. And you know, that's what we call, in another field, *poise*.

Poise means controlling impulses, not frightening impulses, but, for instance, controlling restlessness. It's called by other names, *relaxation*, and so forth. Well, do you understand? Flowers must be cultivated, and weeds must be held down. They must not be permitted to grow. They must be weeded out. That's your symptoms, your sensations. And how are you going to cultivate control?

Well, you are born without control. You are born in a condition where you give way to impulses right and left without restraint. Look at the baby, how [it] kicks about. No restraint. Look at the boy. Look at the teenagers. Well, then, there is nothing more to be said about the modern teenager, at any rate. I wouldn't discuss that. That's too difficult a subject, and strikes home painfully.

Well, you will understand now, in this particular patient we have to cultivate the flower of life, and that is control. But how are we going to cultivate it? Well, he came to these meetings very faithfully, but he didn't accept. And for some time we didn't know what to do with these refractory patients, the patients that are somehow refractive to successful treatment. Today, in the past few months, we are no longer afraid of them. And this man will also be subjected to our new method, and I tell you what this new method is.

There are certain soils in which flowers can't grow. Weeds can grow in every soil. But you can seed that soil and reseed it and seed it again and put in all kinds of ingredients, vitamins and so forth. I don't know what the gardeners use. They use all kinds of stuff. I only pay for it. But that's all I do—I know—about it. But they constantly stir up the soil, and that may be called *the continuous seeding*. And that's the method that we have recently introduced here, and the results are astonishing.

I have now on record at least four patients whom I was unable to make well for months and months, and years and years. And when they developed a setback, it was a frightful thing to get them to control. They became so discouraged that I didn't know what to do with them. But since you know that my patients have a habit of sticking to me, I finally get through with them, but with some it takes too much time.

Well, briefly, in the past couple of months, we have introduced a method in which anybody who has slumped, distressingly and persistently and apparently irrevocably, is now enabled to attend classes every day. We have now the system. It's established. And in the past four months that this system was established, well, we had remarkable results from it, results that I couldn't obtain in my office. And here it is obtained in most refractive cases. And this patient that I discussed today is one of these refractive cases, and I immediately thought that he should attend these classes every afternoon. But unfortunately he works, so there I am stymied again.

Precisely with a view to this patient and a few others, we are therefore going to introduce night classes, too. And it seems to me that with this, our organization is reaching its climax of efficiency. Well, from now on, in other words, there will be no excuse for anybody not to improve quickly or in a decent length of time. A lot, of course, we don't know. I have experienced so much sabotage on the part of patients that even with the finest and most exquisite methods of therapy, patients may still contrive to produce a sabotage that will kill all our methods. Let us hope this patient will not.

Thank you.

LECTURE 57

THE FEAR OF LIFE EBBING AWAY
(PART 1)

29 Minutes
Recorded 1953

I will present to you tonight a patient who, when I saw her the first time, was in [her] early thirties. At that time, it was in 1947, she had come to Chicago to consult me. She came from a southern state. And her story was approximately as follows: Seven years prior to her consulting me, one afternoon she walked on the street with her sister, I think, and her brother-in-law, and then they entered a restaurant. And when she was inside the restaurant, all of a sudden she developed a spell. And the spell was in the nature of a sensation of dying. She felt she was dying.

Well, you understand, sensations are what they are, one sensation being of the same order as the other, one sensation being treatable like the other. But there is still a difference in the various sensations as to whether they scare you a trifle or whether they scare you very severely. And let me tell you, this is a sensation that I have encountered very seldom among patients: the feeling that now you are dying away, not that you collapse. That happens very often, the sensation of being about to collapse. But the sensation of now dying away gradually is entirely different from the one I mentioned, the sensation of threatening collapse.

Well, when the patient tried to describe how it feels to be dying away, she could not perform. It's an indescribable sensation. And no patient that I have seen suffering from this condition—and it is a very rare condition, and I happen to have had a few patients of this kind—no patient has been able to describe in detail what he feels. For instance, when you ask them, "Can't you catch your breath?" they say, "That was not it." Later they develop various other symptoms. This patient, like the others, during the first spell, for instance, did not have any palpitations, no air hunger, no pain.

Well, before long, the patient developed other symptoms. And before long the heart felt like swelling. And that's a frightful thing to feel. And when the heart began to feel like swelling up, the patient suddenly felt that the heart was swelling and crowding out the lungs, and she couldn't breathe. She developed air hunger. It's a symptom. The heart didn't swell, I assure you, and it didn't crowd back the lungs, but the patient had the sensation.

And on many occasions, patients come to me and tell me, "Well, that patient that you discussed last night in the class, well, he's entirely different from what I am, and I would gladly trade with him." Well, I usually tell these patients this is not a trading post, and if it was a matter of trading, I would just ask the other patient to consider your symptoms, and he would certainly say, "I would be glad to trade with him." Do you understand, here in this class there are only one kind of patients, and they can be treated with the same method. The type of patient that I deal with does not have to be specified. It's simply the nervous patient.

Your nervous systems have developed the tendency to release frightening symptoms. It doesn't have to be the symptom that this lady has. There are thousands of symptoms, and fortunately I have not seen a patient that has had thousands of symptoms. Nature has arranged it so that out of the thousand possible symptoms every patient develops only a few. In the beginning when the patient develops the first symptom, it is usually one only. But the patient works himself up and multiplies the one symptom into many.

Before long, she began to describe the same symptom that she could not describe. And one description she gave it was the swelling of the heart and the crowding out of the lungs. Another definition that she gave it—and I have found that in the other patients, too—was that the body is draining out. Can you imagine such a dreadful sensation, the body draining away? I heard that from the other patients, too, from the other patients that have this symptom. And, naturally, now the patient began to work herself up. And when a patient works himself up or works herself up, there comes a spate of symptoms that would not have come if the patient had known how to avoid the working-up process. But that was seven years before she saw me, and how could she learn to avoid working herself up?

I am certain that I am, to this day, the only one who has developed a thorough system of training the patient how to avoid working herself up. And fourteen years ago—this means seven years before she consulted me—even I didn't know much about temper and about the working-up process. At that time, I was just in the beginning of my career of a class teacher, just in the beginning. And at the time, I had still a great deal to learn, and, of course, I will always have to learn a great deal.

And as it went on, she developed the symptom, a common symptom—but in her case nothing was common—the symptom of choking sensations. And now symptoms came and came and came: palpitations, air hunger, pain in the chest, sweating and so forth. The unfortunate thing is that the patient became now, naturally, afraid of actually dying, not only of having the sensation of dying away, but actually dying. And while she had been able to sleep all this time, all of a sudden it came to her that if she falls asleep and dies, who can prevent that, and how can anybody be called in aid? And so when she had an attack like this, like, let me say, choking or the heart attacks during the night, she was afraid to fall asleep. And so she stayed up till she was exhausted and fell asleep anyhow.

Let me tell you in reply to those patients that claim theirs is a much severer case than that of their neighbor—the patient's neighbor I mean here—let me tell you that this case that I described today is undoubtedly, in my opinion—who after all should know something about these things— undoubtedly the severest type of case that I have ever seen.

So, will you please not compete for severity of the case. You have no chance with this patient.

Well, these are the symptoms. I could add plenty of others, but they would be of no interest. She felt so miserable, so hopeless, so desperate when she had such a symptom that no matter what was the time of the day—this means of the night, mainly—she rushed to the phone and tried to get hold of anybody who she thought could help her. She tried to get a doctor, and if she could get him, well the thing was done, but if not, she tried to get hold of anybody so as not to be alone, at least.

In addition, aside from the actual acute attack, she visited, prior to seeing me—this means in the course of seven years—numerous clinics outside her community and her state, and in her state, too, and one hundred eleven private physicians. That's a record. One hundred eleven different private physicians. That's the highest count I ever encountered, although my patients are famous for not sticking to one and the same physician, except to me.

Well, let me tell you, it so happened that at that time, in 1947, we had some publicity. I don't remember what it was. Some magazine sent a reporter to Chicago and had Recovery written up. I think it was in some magazine called *Your Life.* And this lady read the article. So she thought she will try the hundred and twelfth physician. And she came to Chicago. If I remember correctly, she came unannounced. I don't think she wrote me before, asking for an appointment. Most likely that is correct because she was always in a rush, always in a panic.

Within a few weeks, she had already some improvement—had had it never before—and within a few months, the improvement proceeded but never to any impressive extent. The spells were still there. In a case like this, I am very happy if I get fairly good results in a year or two, fairly good results. However, in 1948, there was quite a considerable improvement.

I have here a note that in February 1948—I have several such notes—she came to my office and told me, "Last night I felt the heart swelling. But I spotted it as being not dangerous, and it stopped. The swelling stopped." Well, if I get such a result even once in a patient like this, I am happy. After she told me that, I said, "Well listen, you certainly did well." Whereupon she said, "But I am afraid it wasn't the right kind of spell." Well, she spoiled it for me, but I was not discouraged. I knew she was right, and it was the right kind of spell. But, of course, if you have read my book, you will know a patient will never acknowledge that she has a fair improvement. Even if she says, "I have improved," and at the same time knocks the table, nevertheless, she will retract. Should it not happen, then it would be a rare exception, and I don't remember having met this rare exception.

A patient will not acknowledge, or will try not to acknowledge, a mere improvement. They call it a mere improvement, and logically so. And patients have told me that, "Why in the past I have had plenty of brief improvement, but when then the condition came back, I felt much worse." And that's what the patients are afraid of. They will not settle for any less than a complete recovery. This they will recognize as a good result.

And I have here a note that about a month later, March 1948, the patient said that the night before, she had a choking spell, and the throat and the neck felt paralyzed. The throat then filled up with mucus. (That might have happened, although it was no doubt filling up, but it might have developed mucus.) And she felt that the mucus [would] certainly obstruct the passage of the throat, and, of course, she became panicky. Then she told me, "In former days I used to jump out of bed and keep myself awake, because I was afraid I might fall asleep with that spell, and I might die from suffocation." And then she added, "Last night I made myself stay in bed and fell asleep." Well, that was an excellent improvement. So, again, I told her, "Well, that's excellent. That was real spotting, as I like it." And then she says, "But will I be able to do it again?" That's what I have to contend with, [with] you. You see, she would not admit that it was a real improvement. Well, at any rate, I may tell you that before long she pulled herself together and got herself a job. And that was a heroic decision. And to this day she has held the job continuously, except when once in awhile she has gone to the hospital for a checkup. And I had no objection to that.

Well, this patient is still in Chicago, and she is a key member of the Recovery organization. She is not completely well, but she controls her symptoms to the point where she can handle herself in any kind of an average situation with great merit.

Now, look here, how did she improve to this extent that I have outlined to you? If I had seen her fourteen years ago—and, I must add, if fourteen years ago I had solid experience already with my present method, which I did not have at that time yet—then it would be a simple condition. She had a frightful symptom, but she would have been indoctrinated in the law of Recovery, which means she would have known that no matter how frightful a symptom is, it's never dangerous, provided I examine the patient and tell him or her, with my experience, that this is a nervous condition. And you know, I have the faculty of making my patients accept my diagnosis. If I had seen her at that time, then it was at least likely that she would not have developed what she did develop, and what all of you have developed: the thing that I call *processing*. She would not have processed her symptoms. And I want you to know, those of you who don't know yet, what is meant by this term *processing symptoms.*

Well you know, for instance, what is processing meat. You have meat, which is a raw material, and then you cook it and dress it and bone it, and whatever you do with it, in, let me say, in the stockyard, and then the meat looks different. It has a different taste. It is dressed up. It has changed. Usually it is then fit for consumption. This means it is adjusted to its use, to the use that people will make of it. But the point is that by processing, you change a raw material into a manufactured material. I guess we will agree on that. And it's good for you to know that that's what a patient does.

From nature he gets raw material: a symptom. Now he begins to process it, if he hasn't gone through Recovery training. And the processing, you know, is done in a very simple and in a very conventional manner. Everybody processes certain other things, not just symptoms alone. You become angry at somebody. And you can process that into a bitter anger, for instance, into a paroxysmal anger, into an anger where you [want] just to kill that person that has angered you. But nature has not endowed you originally with that kind of anger. Your anger originally was a traditional anger, rather middle-ground reaction.

And if you begin to worry, that's a natural reaction. Anybody can worry and has to worry about a thousand things. And if you ask me, then I'll tell you, and very truthfully, that I doubt whether ten minutes have ever passed in my adult life in which I have not worried. I doubt whether there is any adult individual that can live ten minutes [at] a stretch without worrying. But if I begin to worry, for instance, about a patient—and that, of course, happens very often to me—then the question is, will I let the worry where it stands by dint of its nature, or will I work it up and process it? Will I process it into an anxiety, into a state of despondency, into a state of great apprehensiveness? Will I develop the feeling of being trapped and hopeless? And that's what we call *processing*. You work yourself up either about a feeling that has arisen, the feeling of fear or anger, or about a symptom.

I have two teenage daughters, and there I can easily observe another type of processing, not of fear and anger, but of love. Our teenagers these days, you know, peddle in love very joyfully, enthusiastically, and I can easily observe how love is processed. All you have to do is to receive a letter from a boyfriend, and put it under your pillow, and then shed tears, and in the morning you wake up and see the pillow all bathed in tears, and then you feel very sorry for yourself. And love is then processed, the great feeling of love.

[Continued in Lecture 58.]

364

LECTURE 58

THE FEAR OF LIFE EBBING AWAY
(PART 2)

27 Minutes [Continued from Lecture 57]
Recorded 1953

Well, I am not interested in the processing of love. But I am very vitally interested that my patients should learn not to process symptoms. And the symptom is processed invariably and unfortunately when the patient begins to make his own diagnosis.

Now, there are two types of diagnoses. Don't misunderstand me. I don't mean to say that there are only two diagnoses in this world. But there are only two types of diagnoses. Either the doctor, after examining you, tells you there is something wrong with you, or he tells you there is nothing wrong with you. The one is called *the verdict of security,* and the other is *the verdict of insecurity.* And we come back, by a devious route, to our old standby: security and insecurity. Let me tell you that it's always good to come back to this pair of contrasts. Because life is nothing more than that, either security or insecurity, or a combination of both in various degrees.

Now, I want to assure you that if my patients make a diagnosis, they don't diagnose security. I guess you know that. They diagnose a case of grave danger. And you will understand now, if somebody makes the diagnosis of "I am in danger," that he will certainly process his symptoms. But in order to understand that, you will have to know how a symptom can be processed, this means developed further towards expansion, towards aggravation, towards developing and perpetuating itself for endless periods, perhaps.

One thing you must know about nerves—and that will make you understand this matter of processing—nerves are the one tissue in the body that is exceedingly sensitive to tenseness. Let me assure you that your hair, your nails, are not at all sensitive to tenseness; the skin, the bones, very little, maybe not at all either, except insofar as they have nerves. But nerves are sensitive particularly to tenseness. And if you want to irritate a nerve, and if you want to do harm to a nerve—not bodily harm—if you want to upset a nerve, all you have to do is to develop tenseness. And if you develop a certain type of tenseness due to worry or anger in sufficient amounts, then the nervous system may or may not resist the tenseness. Then we say the nervous system has resistance.

And there are people whose nervous system is so resistant that they seldom develop nervous symptoms. They are rare. Most people develop nervous symptoms. But I would say that perhaps the majority of human beings have a tolerable resistance to tenseness. This means their nerves can become affected by the tenseness, but they resist the development of symptoms. They don't just develop symptoms.

And my patients belong to a group of people whose nerves develop symptoms easily if they are put under pressure of tenseness. And I hope you will keep that in mind. Whether your symptoms will stay with you a few minutes or a few weeks or months depends on whether you put your nervous system under too much pressure of tenseness, and, on the other hand, on whether your nervous system is constitutionally not very resistant from the start, from the outset. Both factors come together in my patients.

But no matter what your constitution is, I have told you—you who have been here frequently have heard it—constitutional weakness can be strengthened, strengthened to the point where the weakness disappears. Plenty of people are constitutionally weak in their muscles. Well, with exercise, they can remove, or at least diminish, this constitutional deficiency. And I have proof here in Recovery—I hope you know that—that a patient of the kind, for instance, I have described here, arrives for consultation with a nervous system that is always deprived of all its resistance, and after a certain time I restore the resistance or strengthen it or revive it. Let me tell you that this excuse that "I have had weak nerves all my life" does not count a thing in point of curability. Every nervous condition can be cured, regardless of its duration—by the way, also regardless of its intensity.

Now if you put your nervous system under too much pressure from tenseness, the original symptom will multiply, and you will get more symptoms and more symptoms. And it's not only the number of symptoms that will increase, but the intensity of symptoms. And you understand what that means in point of increasing suffering.

Now, how did this patient learn to control her tenseness? You will understand, controlling the tenseness means controlling the symptom. And there is no other way of controlling symptoms except through control of tenseness. When she had this first symptom of life dying away, what happened? What was the next step? Originally, this was a sensation. Well, any sensations in the body come and go, and I have never known of any sensation that didn't conform to this rule: that it comes and goes.

I may tell you here that last week I had a series of the sharpest sensations, and how sharp it was I can only describe in the following manner. Those of you that had appointments on that day know that I wasn't in the office—the first time in my life that I have, through sickness, stopped working for a day. Well, that's a good record. But on that day, in the morning, I suddenly got a symptom that I had before already, in which I could not stand. When I stood up, I had to lie down. When I lay down, I had to get up. When I sat down, I had to lie down. I couldn't sit, stand, lie on any side, anywhere, and constantly got up, lie down, sit down, got up, in about this sequence.

Well, after a short while the thing subsided, and I decided to go to the office, against my better judgment. And while I was driving to the office, there in the car it started again, but somehow or other I got downtown. While I walked to the office from the parking place, there it was again, and finally I arrived at the office. Don't ask me how, because I don't remember. And then I got busy in the office, and there it came again. And finally I decided I had to go home. Why, I don't know, because at home I couldn't do much either. And my dear wife, of course, immediately summoned a friend of mine to examine me. And he examined me, and, of course, I could have told him what would be the result. He couldn't find anything. Well, I hadn't found anything either. But he was smart enough, when he looked at my face, he told me later, not to say, "There is nothing the matter with you," as you have been told by doctors who examined you.

This symptom, that I know very well because it is a nervous symptom that I will not mention because you don't have to know everything—it's good to eat of the tree of knowledge, but one shouldn't overeat. Well, this symptom has a capacity to attack one particular nerve. Well, I can tell you the name: the vagus nerve. I don't know whether you know what that is. And this nerve has the capacity to control the actions of the entire stomach and intestines and heart and lungs. And so when this nerve gets busy, as it got in my case, you first have a terrible cramp in the abdomen, and it feels as hard like a board, and second, you can hardly breathe. And, well, I don't know about this thing that I am going to tell you, but Mrs. Low told me, "You look ghastly." Now, my wife wouldn't tell me that and wouldn't use such an expression if it weren't so. And all day in perspiration and choking for air, gasping for air—it's no pleasure, I can tell you.

And that evening when I went to bed again, it was very difficult to [lie] in bed, and I had again to jump up, although it was better, and so forth. And there it came to me. What do I tell my patients? I thought. I tell them, "Brave the symptoms," and above all I told them, "Don't adopt the philosophy of 'I can't.'" You always can unless the condition is known to be an incurable disease. And I knew that my condition was nervous. And so I reminded myself what I tell my patients. And I tell them the first thing, "If you have any painful sensation, any distressing sensation, don't do anything about it. For instance, don't jump out of bed. Lie motionless." And there it was.

I couldn't sit. I couldn't stand. I couldn't lie in bed. But there I made myself lie in bed, and in a few minutes the thing stopped, but came back. So I made myself lie again, and it came back. It would stop, but came back. Then I began to experiment with this thing. And when it came back, instead of lying down, I got up and held on to the chair and stood, and I could stand. I made the discovery: Before that, I couldn't lie, I couldn't sit, and I couldn't stand, and now I could stand, and the pain went. And the breathing got easier. And then I was smart enough not to stand too long and went back to bed. And now I made up my mind, of course, it will be just lying on the back and waiting [to see] what will happen. And before long I fell asleep. And in the morning I woke up, and there was nothing left of the whole—you know, like the other day somebody told me—of the whole shebang, a good expression perhaps.

And you see, I was fooled by this symptom, because it is a real nerve that puts up this condition, and I thought it was an organic condition. And now I know these real neuritis[es] and neuralgias can be treated in the same way with the same system that I have worked out for you, and finally used for myself. And do you understand now what it means to process? I processed my symptom. I assumed from the start that since this was an organic nervous symptom—organic, physical—therefore I couldn't do anything about it. You would think that I should have been smarter than that, but I found out I was not. And it means I developed the philosophy that I can't help myself. And that's what this patient did that I described to you today. And that's what any patient will do unless they come to Recovery and learn how to deal with symptoms and tenseness.

And the patient that I described today did the same thing that I did last week: She developed a philosophy of "I can't." And she made the diagnosis that this is an intractable and perhaps an incurable condition. And once you call your condition a condition that can't be helped—this means that it is either untreatable or incurable—well, then you naturally develop a scare, alarm; you become hopeless, and you work up tenseness. And the moment you work up tenseness— especially day after day, twenty-four hours a day, if you are awake twenty-four hours, or as long as you are awake, you can work up your tenseness—then the nerves, your nervous systems, are put under the pressure of continuous tenseness. And naturally they will develop a wealth of symptoms. And the symptoms will become worse and worse because their intensity increases. And the cure is, of course, to cut out the tenseness. And those of you that are regular customers here know that to cut out tenseness means don't make a disastrous diagnosis. Don't diagnose insecurity, incurability, untreatability. Diagnose as I have done. Accept as I have done.

When you consulted me, I told you, "Yours is a nervous condition." Otherwise I wouldn't accept you as my patient. If I gave you the diagnosis of a nervous condition, then accept it. And don't do as even this patient did, this patient who offered the finest cooperation. Nevertheless, you remember, she had the nerve to tell me, "But it wasn't the right kind of a spell." You see, she diagnosed the spell as a different kind from what I diagnosed. She said, "This spell was weaker. It was a different spell." And she meant to say, "Well, a weaker spell I can perhaps handle, but my strong spells that may come on [the] next night, how can I handle them?" You see this is a subtle kind of self-diagnosing. This patient didn't change my diagnosis. She didn't say, "Oh, Dr. Low is wrong." But she made a certain diagnosis for herself.

Now, those of you that have what they call severer symptoms than others have, will naturally agree with me that it's best to get rid of the tenseness. But every once in a while a patient comes to me and says, "Well, I don't develop new symptoms, and I don't feel the tenseness. I have always one symptom." With this they want to contradict my diagnosis that her symptom, or his symptom, is nervous, too. And of course it will be very desirable that patients should endeavor to accept my diagnosis blindly, whether they understand it or not. Arguments are cheap and easy to develop, but they will not help you.

Why don't you [do] what my patients have done when I was in private practice. If I saw a patient and made the diagnosis of a pneumonia, that patient didn't come back and ask, "But, Doctor, how can it be a pneumonia? Look here, I breathe with ease." Well, that poor patient doesn't know that there are pneumonias where you breathe with ease. And so many patients could have told me, as my patients now do, "How could that be a fracture of the clavicle, you know, if I don't feel pain?" Naturally, the patient doesn't know that there are fractures of the clavicle where one doesn't feel pain. Can I tell a patient every slight deviation and variation of symptoms?

And, look, it's such a needless waste of my time and your money to come to my office and start an argument with me. When I was in general practice, when I told a patient he has a pneumonia, the patient didn't say a word. He took it for granted he had a pneumonia. And if I told him he had a fracture of the clavicle, I didn't have to demonstrate a fracture to him. He believed it.

And this patient that I described today developed this tendency to believe me almost 100 percent, as my patients in general practice did, but not just fully 100 percent, as you have noticed with the examples that I gave you. She still tried to deny her improvement, but she did it in such a gentle manner that I nevertheless credit her with a cooperation of ninety-nine percent, and that's a good rating.

Thank you. Goodnight.

THE FEAR OF HEART DISEASE
(PART 1)

29 Minutes
Recorded 1953

Well, tonight I am going to present to you a patient, a lady patient in [her] late thirties. She was examined by me eight years ago. And I will tell you immediately that she was a very loyal patient, did her best to get well and got well pretty soon and is doing well today.

The thing started in the following manner. Four years before I saw her, this means in 1941, she was downtown in the Loop and had to make a telephone call and went into a phone booth. And after she entered, she experienced a sudden palpitation, and it came and went, and came back and went again. And she rushed to the family physician who examined her and then made a remark which he should have avoided. He said, "It might be a heart condition, but I don't know for certain." Well, as I said, that remark could just as well have been left unvoiced. At any rate, the patient became scared, and she thought now of the heart condition. And she went to a heart specialist. He examined her and assured her that he couldn't find anything wrong with her heart. He subjected her to tests, especially to an electrocardiogram, and it was negative. And thereafter she was good, for three weeks.

And this is a common story for so many patients, that they get a scare and develop symptoms. And too many of them are then good, especially after they are reassured by a physician. But they are good for two or three weeks. And then if something happens again and scares them and they develop the same symptom or similar symptoms then they become discouraged. And they may become one of those patients whose condition runs for years and years, and nobody can convince them that it is merely a nervous condition. They are certain that the condition is heart damage. Or if they have a headache and it continues for years, then they are certain it is damage to the brain, and so forth.

Well, after three weeks in which she felt good, she had something to have done on her teeth, and she went to the dentist. And while she was sitting in the dentist's chair, all of a sudden she got again something, some symptom of the heart, or in the heart, and got scared. And the symptom that she got was a so-called skipped beat. Well, whatever that means. I guess you have heard about that. And with the skipped beat, she got immediately palpitations again. And now she had it practically all day, every day, and it stayed with her.

And gradually she developed other symptoms: air hunger, symptoms that patients associate with the heart, chest pain, fluttering. She felt a so-called fluttering of the heart. And then she developed certain symptoms that scared her particularly. She developed a pulse in the legs. She felt the pulse there particularly at night when she lay in bed. And then she felt a pulse in the skull, especially behind the ear. And now she drew a conclusion.

She was first convinced that her heart was damaged because she had the palpitations and the skipped beats, and the air hunger, and the chest pain. But now she drew the conclusion—and that's, as you know, [what] we call *a diagnosis*— she self-diagnosed the condition as one that now began to spread because she felt something in the legs and behind the ear. And before long, she developed all kinds of other symptoms that were somehow related to her, not so much to her heart but to her experience with the heart. She developed, for instance, fatigue.

Now, I have hardly any patient that doesn't develop practically all these symptoms: palpitations, and fatigue, and air hunger and chest pains. These are the common symptoms of practically the majority of my patients. And since her second panic had developed in the dentist's chair, she hated to think of dentists, to read of dentists, and naturally to go to the dentist. And she had to neglect her teeth, which she certainly disliked to do, for a solid four years before she came to me. Gradually, she developed other symptoms, the common symptoms that are so familiar to practically all of you, headaches and dizziness. Now she was afraid the condition spread to the brain. And all of this is, of course, the traditional self-diagnosing of patients.

As time went on, she became afraid of anything that had something to do with the heart. And she reasoned, perhaps more or less sensibly, that since she had a heart condition, she could not walk up stairs. And so, since she had a second-floor apartment, the family had to move and find another apartment, and that was during the war years. And you can imagine that it was not easy a sacrifice for the family to contemplate, but they had to do it. And she feared stooping and she feared lifting or pushing something and, finally, she feared plain walking. And she developed the fear, at any rate, of walking alone on the street because what happens if she collapsed? At least somebody should be with her, and she should not be picked up by strangers that might call the police and cause quite a few complications.

And in further development, she was afraid of stepping into a car. She was not afraid riding in a car, but stepping into it, lifting a leg with this damaged heart, as she thought. She could not ride the suburban train, and she lived in a suburb, because the suburban train—even if somebody lifted her into it—she could not use, because the suburban train had few stops. And the stretches that the suburban train traveled from one station to the other [were] too long. And if something happened on the train, how could she get to the doctor immediately? And I guess you realize that patient became a cripple, a cripple if there ever was any.

Naturally, she developed, in consequence of the condition, poor sleep, poor appetite, constant fatigue, and the fatigue reminded her of the heart again because, of course, with a damaged heart, you easily become exhausted. I don't know why, but that's what she thought. And fatigue meant exhaustion to her. It happened, naturally, in consequences of this "crippledom," that she lost interest in anything.

A patient suffering as much as she did naturally turns inside and becomes constantly, forever preoccupied with her inner trouble, with her own suffering. And there is no time left to think of somebody else or of something else. And this massive preoccupation with oneself means that all the interests of the person is centered on herself. And many of you—if not all of you—know that from personal experience, that while you suffered, you had either no or very little interest in anything or in anybody except yourself. That's understood.

But the lady had three children, and she noticed that she had very weak interests for the children. Many of you have experienced that. And then when this dawned on her, when she noticed her decreased interests, she feared that she had lost her sense of values, her sense of responsibility. And so she feared that she is, perhaps, losing her mental health, her mind. And then she noticed, in further succession, that it was extremely difficult for her to make a decision, to make up her mind to do anything. And then she couldn't read. She couldn't concentrate. And all of this suggested to her that her mind was going, or maybe was gone already. And I don't have to emphasize that this is one of the very severe cases. Well, not any severer than the average patient that I see, but severe enough.

Now, on top of all of this, she finally developed, shortly before she consulted me—this means in the fourth year of her ordeal—certain compulsions. For instance, when she was on the street—with somebody, naturally, always accompanying her, because she couldn't walk alone on the street—when she was on the street, suddenly she got the impulse to strike a passerby that she didn't know. And when she got such ideas, she was thoroughly convinced that her mind was slipping, of course. On other days, she walked on the street and felt the impulse to yell right in the open street. She went into a house and perhaps had to go to a consultant who wanted again to check on her heart, and if the consultant lived on a high floor, she felt the impulse to jump out of the window. She had all kinds of sensations, aside from the palpitations and so forth. She had a pressure in the throat, a dryness in the mouth, dimness of vision. But I will not be delayed with these common symptoms.

Well, this severe case had one great feature. She cooperated. If I told her something, she did it. And when I told her to come to these classes, there was no flicker of a doubt, and she came. She hated to come. She didn't want to be seen by people. She had withdrawn from every conceivable social contact. But somehow or other she cooperated with me, and she came. And the very first night when she attended a class, I happened, just by chance—it was certainly not premeditated—but I happened to present a case here similar to hers. And in those days, the old-timers will remember, I didn't present cases. I interviewed the patients, and it was quite effective.

Well, after this first attendance at the meeting, she felt a remarkable improvement. She had first seen that there were other patients that had not only a similar condition, but a condition of similar severity, of similar intensity. And here the patients in the interview indicated plainly and expressed it very forcefully that they had improved greatly in spite of this apparently hopeless condition. And this patient improved very quickly, but merely improved. She couldn't get well quickly. As I told you, today she is well, and she has been well for about five years, and continues well.

And the question is, how did she get well? In order to discuss that, I will tell you that when I first saw her, she made a statement that I will quote here. She said, "I get the palpitations and the skipped beats when I just think of them." Well, this is a very well-known complaint of patients. And you know from the book that you have read that this is called *the trigger symptom*. All the patient has to do is to think of palpitations, and there they come; to think of chest pain, and there it comes; to think of the skipped beat, and it is there. And when the patient makes such a statement, and it's not merely a report, it is also a complaint. And what the patient complains about is that she gets these symptoms shooting into the chest in a fraction of a second, and she says, "What can I do about it? How can I help it?" The implication is that she is trapped by the symptoms. They come with such sudden velocity that it is impossible, she thinks, that she should do anything about it. She couldn't. That's what she said. But you know patients are fond of thinking in this manner. They are fond of thinking that they cannot help themselves.

And you know, when you come here, I tell you the reverse. I show you how to help yourself. But before we go any further, I will want to expatiate on this matter of the patient thinking he is helpless. Because when he thinks he is helpless, then he certainly adds the other thought that he is hopeless. And once a person thinks he or she is hopeless, then that paralyzes them. Then they say, "What's the use striving and trying? My life is gone." This means, "My social life is gone, my life of mental and nervous health is gone." And the patient, drawing this conclusion, will not do anything for himself, because he says, "It's hopeless. What's the use [of] trying?"

Now, you know, if a patient is to do anything, if a person is to do anything, what happens is this: First, the patient wants to do the thing. This wanting means an impulse is discharged from the brain, through the nerves, down to the muscles. And when the muscles get that impulse, well, they have to act. And they do act. And if a patient sends down to his muscles the impulse to walk, the legs will walk. There is no question about it. Muscles obey impulses that come from the brain.

But I want you to realize a thing that I have told you repeatedly, but you may have forgotten: There are two kinds of impulses, and, therefore, two kinds of wills, two kinds of beliefs, two kinds of everything. The two kinds of impulses are, either you can do a thing; you sent down an impulse and you know you can do it, or you sent down an impulse, but you sent it down in such a manner—which I will describe later—that the impulse hardly reaches the muscles. Or it is so weak that even if it reaches the muscles, it's no impulse for getting the muscles to do something. And that patient who does that has the philosophy of hopelessness. Everything with him is weak because he doesn't care to exert power, strength. And if he sends down weak impulses to the muscles and then the muscles will of course not move, then he becomes ever more convinced that he is half paralyzed, so he doesn't care even sending down impulses, and he stays in bed in the morning, perhaps all day.

Now the one person who sends down strong impulses to the muscles feels secure. And the more his muscles obey the impulses, the more does he feel secure. The other person, being hopeless, naturally feels insecure. And so you will understand that there are two kinds of impulses. The one flows from the belief that I can do things—this means I am a person who can act with security. And the other person sends down impulses from a belief that I am insecure—that my condition is that of helplessness and hopelessness. He will naturally send down to the muscles weak impulses. And then he says, "I have no initiative. I have no impetus. I can't make up my mind. I am afraid I am losing my mind." You understand that this is the philosophy of insecurity that sends down impulses of weakness to the muscles.

Now, this patient had acquired this philosophy, and you know that you had it in times past. And she sent down weak impulses to the muscles and there was naturally little initiative, little decision, little promptness, and precision. And the result was that the patient naturally lost her self-trust, self-confidence, her courage. But there is something else to be discussed. If a patient acquires the philosophy of hopelessness and helplessness and then comes to my classes and hears another patient who had a similar condition and got well, the thing that happens to that new patient is that he or she walks out of this room and has now more hope and more courage. That happened to this patient, and it helped her for a day or two. I don't remember exactly, but for a short time. And on the third day, or on the second day, the weakness came back. The philosophy of hopelessness and helplessness reinstated itself again. Of course, it can't be otherwise.

Remember that that patient has been ill for four years before she came to me. During this time, in these four years, the patient had established habits in her muscles and in her nerves and in her brain: the habits of hopelessness. And the muscles have become used, in four years of experience, to be[ing] weak and flabby, psychologically speaking, not physically. There is never a physical change, any sign of deterioration or damage from nerves even if you develop deleterious nervous habits for ten years, twenty years, thirty years.

I have seen one patient who came to me the first time after forty years of daily nervous sufferings, particularly palpitations.

[Continued in Lecture 60.]

LECTURE 60

THE FEAR OF HEART DISEASE
(PART 2)

26 Minutes [Continued from Lecture 59]
Recorded 1953

Now this man, who had suffered for forty years every day, as he stated—and while this statement might have been somewhat exaggerated, it was not far from the truth; that man was credible and his story plausible—now this man stayed with me yet some ten years till he drifted away. And I don't know what happened to him, but for solid fifty years, he had severe nervous trouble. And there was not the slightest evidence, on examination, that there was any damage to the nervous system. In those days, I didn't have Recovery, and I was unable to give much benefit to a patient like this.

In the meantime, I have seen patients who had suffered from frightful obsessions and compulsions and panics for thirty years. And there was no trouble here with this group to effect nice improvements. One of them I consider cured. It took me about eight years to get him cured. He is over sixty years now, and he got married last year. Do you need any better proof that he is improved?

Now, let's continue. How did this patient get well? I told you her habits were established, and they had gained momentum and vigor. And at best you could only expect that this patient could be cured after months and months. But there she suffered a setback on the second day or third day after the initial improvement. And in such cases I know my course, but I remember days and years before when I didn't know my course well. I had to learn from you, from my patients. And today I know something.

My patients suffer—all of them, no matter what their condition is—they suffer from one thing, and that is from tenseness. Without tenseness, there would be no nervous symptoms. If you could get rid of your tenseness, you would relax. Your body would relax. Your brain would relax. And with a relaxed brain, there can be no nervous symptom. But the relaxation must be a real relaxation. It must be thorough, not just something that you call, "Oh, I feel better." That's no relaxation. It must be a real relaxation. And in order to learn how to relax thoroughly, that takes time.

Now, if a patient is tense every day, practically all day for four years, something happens to his brain. No damage, but something happens there, and to his nerves outside the brain, and to the muscles. And the thing that happens is this: The nerves and the muscles outside the brain lose their resistance, I mean the resistance to tenseness. Now, I am always tense. I hope I am. That means I am alert. I am awake. I am not asleep. When I sleep, I am perfectly relaxed. I shouldn't say that; Mrs. Low is here. She knows that I toss and twist in my sleep, but I don't know, so I am relaxed. The body is not so relaxed, but that doesn't matter. When I get up in the morning, I feel refreshed, so my relaxation during sleep must have been quite good. But during the day, I am tense.

Well, if I sit at the one side of the table and the patient at the other side, naturally, how can I be relaxed? There is lots of doubt in my brain. The doubt—especially if I see the patient for the first time or for the first few times—will I get the patient to cooperate? I don't know, so I have doubt, and doubt means tenseness. No relaxation with doubt, and no doubt with relaxation. But when I am tense, I don't develop symptoms. I am just tense. I worry, for instance. I doubt. I question myself whether I have done the right thing or whether I am doing the right thing, but I don't develop symptoms. And, briefly, that means my nerves—even if they are subject constantly, or more or less constantly, to tenseness—

are resistant to developing symptoms. And that's what we call *resisting nerves* or *resisting muscles.*

And if I want to cure a patient, I have to see to it that I make the patient develop better resistance in his nerve-muscle mechanism. Nerves and muscles go together. I must get the patient to be able to undergo severe tenseness all day, perhaps, but not develop symptoms—then the patient is cured—or to develop only minor symptoms, which is the same thing, reminders perhaps of symptoms. In order to do that, I must do something with the brain of the patient.

How does one become tense? I told you a patient sits opposite me in my office, and what happens to me when I am confronted with a patient? Well, the thing that happens to me is that somebody in outer environment, whom I call my patient, gives me an impression. And that impression is picked up by something in my brain that I call *imagination*—not yet thinking—imagination. And I look at this patient and I see something in his eye that shouldn't be there. Whatever it is, I'm not going to tell you. And then I notice that something is missing in the face that should be there. That thing that is in the eye and that thing that is missing in the cheeks gives me the impression that the patient isn't interested, that I haven't gotten hold of him, that I have no grip on him. I have not impressed him. Now he gives me the impression that I am going to fail with him. He will be a failure. I don't know that. I only guess it. And the organ in our brain that does the guessing is imagination. You will understand if you say he imagines. That means he guesses. He doesn't know. And, briefly, let me repeat: You get an impression from the outside. That impression is picked up by the imagination, and the imagination now begins to guess, "What does that mean?" In my case, it guesses in a certain situation that I will not have much luck with this patient. That is guessing, but we can call it by another name which is much more important.

I say then the impression from the outside suggested to me that I will have no results with this patient. It suggested it to my imagination, and everything of this kind is guessing and imagining. And there are, again, two kinds of imaginations that a person can have. If I think, this means if I imagine, that I can help the patient, then I feel secure as a doctor. Then I feel that I will have results. That gives me security. And if I feel that I have no chance with this patient, then I feel insecure as a physician. I feel insecure with regard to my work, my vocation. And just as I told you that there are two kinds of impulses, two kinds of reactions, two kinds of beliefs, and so forth; there are two kinds of imaginations: The imagination, or *the suggestion* we can call it now, the suggestion of security and the suggestion of insecurity.

And now you will understand that my patients don't know of any suggestion of security. They embrace the philosophy of insecurity. And the impressions that they notice on the outside give them the suggestion of insecurity mainly and sometimes solely.

With this particular patient that I have presented to you today, well, she had developed such a sense of insecurity that all she had to do [was] to somehow catch an indication, a little indication that she [was] going to have palpitations, and instantly she got them. What does that mean? She was highly suggestible in her imagination to the idea of insecurity, and her nervous and muscular system had become highly irresistive, had lost, practically, its resistance to tenseness.

And now you will understand if I want to cure a patient, I have to get him rid of, first, the easy suggestibility, which I will now call *the trigger suggestibility*. I hope you understand that. The suggestion lodges itself in the brain—and naturally always the suggestion of insecurity—with trigger velocity. So, the patient has a trigger suggestibility and a vastly lowered resistance in the nerves and muscles, and I have to change that.

Well, the particular patient that I am speaking of tonight I said cooperated. Well, if she really cooperated, as I happened to imagine at that time, then it would have been a simple task to get her well. I would have told her, "Scratch all your imaginations and suggestions of insecurity, and you will not fear. I tell you, after due examination of your case, that your condition is nervous. This means there is no danger, no insecurity. So after I told you that, and you are a cooperative patient, why don't you drop all your suggestions of insecurity?"

Well, that sounds very simple, but it is not. It is not simple for the following reason: A patient must not merely listen and understand what I tell him, and not merely cooperate, but he must do much more than that. He must accept what I tell him. And acceptance in ordinary life is not difficult.

If a candidate comes along and tells me he will give us a fine government, well, I may as well accept his statement and give him my vote. But, you see, then I don't risk much. I don't risk much. I have to vote for somebody. And the two candidates that are offered me are not so vastly different as to personality and philosophy, and so voting is really not a great difficulty, a great decision. You can make your choice with pretty good ease. Or if I want to buy an overcoat, and it seems to me it's a little more expensive, and I consider buying perhaps another overcoat that is less expensive, the decision there does not deal with vital issues. And I can make one decision quickly.

But when it is a question of somebody asking me to drop habits of thought, habits of muscular action that I have had for four years every day, all day almost, well, I try to drop them, but is it easy? Is it as easy as making a decision to buy a topcoat? Of course it is not. And the reason why it is not easy is as follows: You know I have dropped many habits, and so have you. But if you asked me how many bad habits I have dropped, well, I will not answer. I know too many that I still have. I once dropped smoking for several months, but I picked it up again. Well, I will not go beyond this statement. I will not tell you all the other habits that I have and that I didn't drop. And mark it: My patients not only accumulate years of habits, but they accumulate years of bad habits, harmful habits. And it is notorious. And someday I'll tell you why it is so that harmful habits and bad habits are very difficult to drop.

You just try to get a drinker to drop the bad habit of drinking. If he has been a fairly heavy drinker for four years, well, try and make him drop it. You can talk yourself hoarse and give him the best arguments of how drinking harms him and not drinking would instantly restore his health. He'll listen to you, he will cooperate with you in many ways, but he will not accept what you tell him. And accepting means something that is not easily effective, especially not with bad habits.

You see, the patient has developed a lessened resistance and a high suggestibility. And what does that mean? If your nerves and muscles are shaky and you try, for instance, to drive a car, all you have to do then—if you are very suggestible and your nerves are not resistant to tenseness—all that you have to do is then to get the idea into your head, "Well, maybe I will not be able to put my foot down quickly on the pedal." Once you have this idea in your head, something happens to your muscles. If you say, "Maybe I will not be able to put my foot correctly on the pedal," the nerves and muscles don't understand this language. Muscles and nerves understand only one language, and that is, "I cannot put down the foot on the pedal." You can paralyze the muscles with this simple statement.

The muscles now become tense, and if they are tense, they will most likely not promptly reach the pedal. And so your fear that you may not reach the pedal—if you are, first, highly suggestible, second, your nerves have little resistance—your fear of not reaching the pedal promptly with your foot may really create a condition where you will not do it promptly. I'll give you another example. If you want to bring a glass of water from one room to the other, and you say, "Maybe I will spill. Oh, I hope I will not spill," the muscles don't know this language. But they understand that you are afraid of spilling, that you think you will spill, or may spill, and the muscles become tight. The fear idea makes them tight, and then you will spill. And so it happens with symptoms.

After the nervous system has become thoroughly devoid of resistance, or poor in resistance, all you have to have in your mind is the suggestion that you will get palpitations, and you get them. This can only be avoided if a patient is just as convinced of security as he was for four years convinced of insecurity.

Now, our patient had a total conviction that she can't be helped. She was totally addicted to the idea of insecurity. And now if you give her a little bit of a sense of security, that will not overcome this total sense of insecurity. For such a patient, just to improve a little bit does not mean much. In the beginning it means something, but should it go on for another year and another year with a mild degree of improvement, that doesn't count. Because this moderate sense of security that you give her with a mild improvement can never overcome the total sense of insecurity that she has felt for four years. So, I must give this patient a total sense of security. There should be nothing in her brain but the suggestion of security. And you will understand that this requires time. And while there are a few patients that are cured quickly, or relatively quickly, all the others, the vast majority, have to undergo what we call here *apprenticeship*. And apprenticeship requires time.

And apprenticeship requires something else: The patient must constantly be trained. This means whenever he makes a mistake in his reactions—whenever, for instance, he self-diagnoses, whenever he develops severe temper—he must be corrected. There must be either somebody, or a group of somebodies, to supervise him, to teach him, to train him, to correct his reactions, and that takes time.

And fortunately we have here an organization where we can take our time. We can take our time because in an organization like this, there is either very little expense or no expense, if you only come to the organization and not to my private office, too. And so we have established a system where we are no longer afraid of the high suggestibility of the brain and the low resistance of nerves and muscles to tenseness. We can relieve the patient of these handicaps because, as I have told you, we can afford to take our time without taxing the patient's finances too much. And, therefore, our patients, although they have to wait, of course, can afford to wait.

And if they wait, we get results, as we have gotten them with this patient that I have presented here, who, after four years of daily agonies, got well in the course of about one to two years. At the end of one year, she could have considered herself pretty much recovered, but after two years she was recovered, and today she is an excellent specimen of humanity.

Thank you.

LECTURE 61

THE OBSESSION OF BEING
CONTAMINATED (PART 1)

25 Minutes
Recorded 1953

I shall present to you a case tonight, the case of a young lady who, when I examined her in 1950, was nineteen years of age. She was a college student, and she told me the following story.

At fourteen years of age, her father asked her one day to put on perfume, and she did. And then the father said, "Well, that's too strong." On that same evening she went to a school dance, and there she had the feeling that the boys and girls looked at her. Well, perhaps they looked at her. Why shouldn't they? They looked perhaps at all kinds of other people. But she felt that they looked especially at her, watched her, and she became self-conscious. It seemed, even to her, that she heard them saying, "That's too strong," the remark that her father had made. That was at the age of fourteen years—and I saw her at the age of nineteen—in other words, five years before I examined her. And ever since, she feared that she had a body odor and that people noticed it. She felt unclean.

And gradually she developed a habit of taking showers endlessly, several times a day, whenever she thought she smelled her body odor. Before she went out, she had always to take a shower. When she went visiting people, after about half an hour she could not continue the visit, and had to make arrangements to quit, to take leave of the people, and to go home and to take a shower. When she went on a date, it was the same story. After a short time, she felt she had to go home to get the shower. And you can understand that her social life gradually faded away.

She drew away from people physically. This means when she went among people in a crowd or in the streetcar, or anywhere where there were a group of people, she felt the urge to draw away from them, and whenever she could, she walked away. She was always afraid that people might smell her body odor and notice it, of course. She had to change her clothes several times a day because she always felt the smell through the clothes. She told me, "Well, of course, our cleaning bills are horrendous." I can imagine.

One day she told me that she sweats all day, every day, and has been sweating like this for four years. When I heard that, I asked her a simple question. I asked her, "How many handkerchiefs do you use per day?" Thereupon she said, "One or two a day." You will understand that that can't be so. If a person sweats all day, even if she only sweats in the hands, two handkerchiefs will not fill the bill for such a situation. And yet that patient didn't tell me a lie. But I caught her on a contradiction, not a lie. She didn't know that that was a contradiction, and I take it for granted she only used one or two handkerchiefs. I will tell you what this contradiction means after we get a few other contradictions to discuss.

She told me on the same day, if I remember correctly, that she feared she had an odor in her breath, in other words, that she had halitosis. It did not just fit in exactly with the picture that she had given me of her condition. For some reason it doesn't fit in there. So, I asked her, "What do you do about that?" And she said, "Nothing. What could I do?" Now, that's definitely a contradiction. If somebody has, or fears he has an odor in his breath, then he will do something about it. He will chew gum or eat Life Savers—I guess that's what you call them—and you will understand that was again a contradiction.

Then she told me on some other day, "If I have a cold, I don't smell anything," which is correct. If I have a cold, I don't smell much either. Then she continued, "If I have a cold and don't smell anything, then I am relaxed with people. I don't look for an odor." That was again a contradiction. She naturally knew that a cold does not remove an odor except for herself. Her own nose doesn't smell, but the noses of other people smell whether that patient had an odor or not. I guess you will agree with me. Moreover, remember what she said. "If I have a cold and don't smell my odor, I don't look for the odor," she said. Well, apparently she knew that she constantly looked for the odor. And now I'll tell you what these contradictions mean.

You know, if somebody has an obsession—and what I told you about this girl was, of course, an obsession—the obsession may be genuine and may be spurious, let me say, not so genuine. And I have seen patients with genuine obsessions, but then they acted correctly on the obsession. This patient didn't. And if you remember a week or two weeks ago, I spoke to you about an obsession of jealousy. And at that time I called your attention to the fact that there were contradictions in the picture. And let me tell you here, I have seldom seen a real, genuine obsession in patients. Usually there is something phoney about them, because there are contradictions. But I have seen some genuine obsessions in patients.

Now, an obsession should be, naturally, a belief, like everything is. Every fear, every anger, and so forth, are beliefs. But when we speak of an obsession, we don't mean merely a belief, but a strong conviction, an addiction to a belief. And that means a belief without doubt, and that is rare. Doubt has a tendency to creep into every brain except where there is a belief that is definitely foolproof. Then it may eliminate their doubt almost to a maximum. Well, this patient obviously had an obsession which was not one hundred percent an obsession. I will return to this subject later on.

But you will remember and understand a case which I shall briefly outline without describing a concrete case. I will merely outline it as an example. And that is the case of a patient who thinks or believes or fears that his heart is damaged and that he will collapse. He may collapse any time.

Such patients all of a sudden are seized by a panic because they get palpitations or air hunger. And when they are seized by a panic, they naturally fear or believe or are obsessed by the thought that now they are going to collapse. So, they want help immediately. And what do they do? They rush to the door, open it frantically, dash down into the street, run to the streetcar or to the bus and finally reach the doctor's office.

And in one particular case I remember that the doctor had an office on the third floor of his own home. That patient, hardly had she reached the house in which the doctor had his office, up she rushed the two flights of stairs, and dashed into the reception room, and then walked over with fast steps to the desk where the receptionist was sitting. And what did she do? She began chatting with the receptionist. And finally when the doctor called her in, she walked in with slow steps, not panting for breath. She hadn't panted for breath the moment she arrived at the doctor's reception room. And then she told the doctor how she suffered and asked him to examine her heart immediately. She was afraid she was collapsing. She was still afraid, but, in the meantime, she had already held a conversation, had sat down and had remained seated until the doctor called her. Do you understand that this is contradictory?

If somebody really thinks that he has a damaged heart and then feels he is going to die now, he will never rush for the streetcar. He will never dash up two flights of stairs. Even if he thinks he has a damaged heart, he will lie down and not move. The most he will do, he will go to the telephone and call up the doctor, but he will not rush to the doctor. And this example will perhaps show you what is meant by contradiction. This means the action of the patient contradicts the panic or the belief that he is going to die immediately.

A patient, who has an obsession of this kind and acts in contradiction to it, dimly notices the contradiction. The particular patient that I mentioned, who feels his heart is damaged and he is going to collapse, and then rushes to the doctor—this means endangers his heart—well, when he leaves the doctor, he begins to think and then asks himself (and patients have told me that) "How could I have rushed up to the doctor if I really had a damaged heart? I couldn't have walked. I certainly couldn't have run." With a damaged heart, you can't do that. And a patient of this kind becomes ashamed of himself. He feels there is something wrong about him and about his fears. And when he becomes ashamed of himself, he works himself up to a pitch of tenseness, and the tenseness revives his symptoms. And then he gets again palpitations, air hunger, and headaches, and whatever he may get, fatigue, of course, exhaustion.

Now he knows that it is his fault, at least partly, that he suffers. He knows that part of his suffering, if not all of it, is caused by himself. His nervous condition is self-inflicted. That is brought to him on such occasions. Whether it is true or not doesn't matter, but he feels guilty about his own behavior, and there develops a vicious cycle. The more guilty he feels, the worse become his symptoms because he produces tenseness. And the worse his symptoms become, the more guilty he feels. And it's an awful thing if a person goes along in life, first, with agonies of suffering, and second, with the feeling of guilt. The feeling of guilt robs a person—if it is continuous—it robs a person of his self-respect. And a person without self-respect has no self-confidence, and without self-confidence, you have no self-assurance, and you fear doing anything without self-assurance. And that person, that patient, reaches a stage in which he is actually afraid of his shadow. And he is incapacitated, crippled to an extent that is frightening to him and to others when they live with him.

Well, let's return to that patient. And in the course of time she developed, aside from the obsessions, compulsions. Very many patients with obsessions add compulsions to the picture of incapacity. For instance, when she visited anybody or when she came to her own home and she went to the bathroom, she had to count the towels in the bathroom. Usually, you know, there are hand towels and other towels. She had to count them. After that, she had to go into the kitchen and count there the dishes, and you know what a job that is. If one has to count dishes, there may be dozens of them in every kitchen. She had to count the lights in every room. When she walked on the street, she had to count the windows on the houses, and there are, you know, there may be fifty houses in a block where she walks, or two or three blocks. When she was downtown, she could, of course, hardly count the windows in a skyscraper, but the stories of the skyscrapers she had to count. And should it happen that while she counted, somebody or something distracted her attention and she stopped counting, she had to start over all again.

And the real ordeal was when she was sitting at the window of her own home or at anybody's home or in an office building downtown that looked on the street, she had to count the cars, the automobiles, as they passed by. And naturally some move very fast, some slowly, so you can miscount. You lose track of your count. Then she had to start again for about half an hour. And when she then in the meantime missed the count, she had to start all over again and count a stretch of time for the cars. Well, I don't have to tell you that this is very agonizing, very distressing, and life is actually ruined if a person has both obsessions and compulsions of this kind.

Well, let me tell you, today we have 1953. That is about three years after the patient was first seen by me. She was nineteen years at that time, now she is twenty-two years, and in the meantime she got married and has a baby. Well, that should tell you that she obviously improved beautifully. And when I saw her the last time, that was about a year ago, she definitely had improved to the point where she was quite comfortable. I can't say that she was completely cured, but she was definitely comfortable. And if a person like this had the courage to accept the offer of a young man and start a family, she must have felt comfortable.

At the time when I saw her first, she naturally never thought of accepting the proposal of a young man. She [kept] out of their way. She had to move away from everybody. If she had gone out with a date, she would have to rush out after half an hour and take a shower, and she can't very well do that in a restaurant, I guess. If she then got married and has a baby—and when I saw her she was very happy over her pregnancy and later over her baby—she must have been very comfortable at that time.

[Continued in Lecture 62.]

LECTURE 62

THE OBSESSION OF BEING
CONTAMINATED (PART 2)

23 Minutes [Continued from Lecture 61]
Recorded 1953

And we ask ourselves, "How did she get well?" Well, of course, I told you repeatedly, if you remember, I have never been able to cure an obsession or a full-blown compulsion if the patient did not come to this group regularly.

Well, she came, but that didn't save her. If she had just come to this group of Recovery, Incorporated, and had attended this Tuesday evening class, that would have helped her, but hardly to the extent that I told you she was helped. She did something entirely different as you all do—but some of the men and women that come here don't do it, some few—she took part in the social activities of Recovery. Even this is not absolutely certain to effect a cure, but she did something else that many of you do. Whether all of you do it, I don't know.

When she went out on a social enterprise with Recovery members, she talked to them about her trouble. She immediately told them, "Well, I don't know whether you know—maybe you do or maybe you don't—I have had frightful obsessions." And in the beginning when she talked to them, she didn't say, "I have had obsessions." She told them, "I have, I am having, frightful obsessions."

Now look here, if somebody has an obsession, then the one thing you can tell of him or her, he will not talk about it. In this particular case of this young lady, she couldn't talk of it at home.

The parents didn't know about her obsession. I don't understand, and I asked the mother how is this possible that she didn't know, because she noticed that the girl constantly changed her garments. They had to buy dozens of garments in a space of time where the average lady will only buy perhaps half a dozen garments. They had a horrendous cleaning bill, as the patient told me. And so one would expect that the mother would have known, would have noticed something, and yet she didn't say anything. For a solid five years, the parents were in ignorance of the condition. And I asked the mother, "How is it that you didn't notice and you didn't give any thought to the fact that you got such a gigantic cleaning bill, that your daughter spent so much money on new clothes?" "Well," the mother said, "Let me confess. I noticed it, and I noticed how tense my daughter was, but I feared asking her."

We'll see what the fear is. After, finally, the girl told the parents that she had to go to a psychiatrist, the father said, "That's not so. You don't have to go. In my family, there has never been such a case." Mind you, the father told the daughter, "And if you pull yourself together, you will be all right. And I don't want you to go to a nerve specialist." He didn't call it a psychiatrist. He wouldn't let the word pass over his lips. So, you realize why the parents didn't notice anything. They didn't want to notice anything. That was a family in which the stigma of mental and nervous ailments had taken possession to an extent that the parents were obsessed with the stigma. And with them, it was a genuine obsession. They acted on it correctly. They didn't want to know anything about their daughter's condition.

If a girl lives in a home like this, then she certainly has no incentive to talk to father and mother. Father and mother were not confidants to her; they were remote from her, especially with regard to her nervous ailment. So, she was alone in her family, and essentially she lived in isolation, in mental isolation. A patient like this is utterly lonely. She cannot share her experiences with anybody. She cannot consult anybody. She cannot request help of her social acquaintances, and certainly not of her relatives, if she lives in a family of this kind. You understand that the father expressed contempt for her nervous ailment. The mother didn't say anything.

What did she do when she spoke to our members in this group? Well, she declared herself independent of the opinion of her father and her mother. She discarded the statements and the meaning of the statements of her parents. And with this, she declared herself independent, and she formed her own opinion. And her own opinion was the opinion of Recovery, this means my opinion. And my opinion is certainly not of the kind that declares that a nervous symptom is disgraceful, is contemptible. I take it you understand that this is, of course, the beginning of a cure if a patient, a nervous patient, by frankly speaking of his symptoms here in Recovery—he doesn't have to do that on the outside—accustoms himself to the idea that there is no stigma attached to his ailment.

And all of this she did, and every patient does, through the models. And she learned quickly how to cure herself the Recovery way. And, of course, if she took part in Recovery activities, as she did, she soon learned the philosophy of Recovery. And she knew that symptoms are conquered through the muscles. And I don't have to tell you what that means. And she demonstrated how this can be done.

She did all kinds of things with her muscles in order to do away with symptoms. For instance, the maid in her parents' home had a body odor. The patient told me immediately when she mentioned the fact that her mother admits that, too. So, she had a body odor, and when my patient told me that she had one, she did not formulate another obsession that somebody else has a body odor. And so my patient pleaded with the mother to dismiss the maid. And she told me, "If our maid has dresses of a certain color or cut or pattern, I can't wear anything similar." Well, you know, suppose this maid had some sort of dresses in three different colors, so our patient could never wear anything in these colors. And how many colors are there, after all? So, her range of garments was very restricted.

Then she went on and said, "The other day, the maid wore a navy blue dress." And so, if she had not improved, she could then not have worn a navy blue garment. But she said, "Then I went to the ladies' dress store in the neighborhood and bought a garment of the same color. It needed some fitting, but I took it home and wore it all afternoon and evening and didn't care whether it fitted or not." She said, "I did that for practicing." And I asked her, "What did you practice with?" And she immediately said, "With my muscles." And I asked her, "What is the meaning of this muscular action?" And she was well versed in Recovery lore, and she promptly told me, "Well, you told us, 'Do what you fear to do,' and you have to do it, naturally, through your muscles." And since she feared, she had feared, wearing a dress the color that the maid wore, she instantly went to the store, bought a dress of this kind and wore it. Well, that's excellent Recovery practice.

One day she came to my office at the time when she was improving neatly, and she told me she went out with a boy who had dated her—now she accepted dates—and she felt the odor. And she felt the imperative urge to run away from the boy, to excuse herself and to go home, take a shower, and change garments. But she didn't. She stuck it out, spent the whole evening with the boy, and she felt fine. You understand that was done through the muscles.

She told me on the same day that lately she had adopted the practice of wearing the same dress on two successive days. Of course, she had never done that. She changed dresses several times a day. And she did that sheerly for practice, for nothing else. Well, I don't remember too often having had such a cooperative patient. Of course, she never moved away from people any more. And she said, "Well, I must say I even move closer to them." I told her not to overdo.

But you know that in Recovery I tell you that it is not just sufficient to move your muscles. You must also spot. And one day she came to me and told me, "Well, today I felt dirty again," on a certain occasion. And she says, "I immediately reminded myself that if I have dirt on my fingers or somewhere on the body, well, that's average." Well, that's going a little bit too far, I guess, to say that dirt is average. But she said, "Well, if I have a *little* dirt on my fingers," and I must admit that should be average. I have noticed that in myself, too. And then she goes on and says, "After that, I just looked at my arm, and I saw it had, it really had, average cleanliness."

Now, you understand, if anybody spots that what troubles him or her is an average thing, then she spots immediately and incidentally that thing that we want all our patients to spot. And that is that she has an exceptional standard, an exceptionally high standard. This means she is perfectionist, and we don't want perfectionism. But in order to get rid of it, the patient has to spot the particular reaction as meaning exceptionalism. And here again you have the evidence that this patient certainly had grasped the fundamentals of the Recovery teaching and practiced it with magnificent skill.

On the streetcar, she told me, some day she again felt the odor. And now she says, "I spotted it, and got rid of it immediately." And I asked her, "How did you spot it?" And she says, "I refused to believe that the odor was real. I knew then it was nothing but a sensation, and sensations are distressing but not dangerous." She quoted my book. But not only did she quote it, she practiced it exquisitely.

And I told you she is well now, although for about a year, I think, I have not seen her. But as my patients are, if she had some trouble, I would hear from her, and I would see her. Unfortunately, I cannot, as I usually do, keep in touch with her family because the family is still convinced that I didn't do anything for this patient, that she just outgrew a foolish notion. They called it "foolishness." So, I naturally don't think of getting in touch with the parents. I could have gotten in touch with the patient, but she got married, and I don't know her new address. Otherwise, I would have gotten in touch with her.

Well, I feel impelled, while I now close the discussion, to add a melancholy remark. I told you that it has become a stated conviction among my colleagues that severe obsessions and severe compulsions are incurable. And my colleagues have resorted to the device, which I deplore very severely, of having patients who have such an obsession or a compulsion—or certainly if they have the combination of obsessions and compulsions—to have them undergo a brain operation. You understand now that that means they are partially crippled. Many or most of these patients then are forced to live a vegetative existence after the operation. True, they may lose their obsessions and compulsions if certain pathways in the brain are cut. But then they are likely to lose a most valuable part of their minds, namely, initiative. And recently a fine brain surgeon accused the men who recommend this brain operation for this condition, he accused them by saying, "Well, a nervous patient, if he is subjected to this brain operation for his obsessions or depressions or compulsions, loses his character as a nervous patient, but he assumes the character of an idiot." So, he expressed that state of affairs very concretely and in a very telling language.

I don't go that far, but I must voice a very sad thought. Here in this organization we cure obsessions and compulsions and the milder forms of depression without any operative or any other severe treatment in the overwhelming majority of our cases. And uncounted thousands of patients that could be cured with this technique that we have adopted are denied the benefit of our method because, unfortunately, my colleagues have not shown interest in our techniques, although the techniques have been available to them for seventeen solid years. And, of course, it is a very melancholy thought with me and with you that thousands and ten thousands of patients should have been deprived of the opportunity to be relieved of untold suffering and to be subjected instead to a mutilating treatment which, far from helping substantially, is likely to increase their incapacity and their loss of function. I felt impelled to tell you this, but I can go no further.

Good night.

THE OBSESSIVE FEAR OF DIRT
AND GERMS (PART 1)

30 Minutes
Recorded 1953

The patient whom I will present today was examined by me November 1944. That means nine years ago. At that time, he was fifty-three years of age. I mention here an item that is somewhat related to one feature of his case that I will mention later on. I shall mention the fact that he was of Greek extraction, and when I saw him, he had been in this country for about thirty years and had not acquired anything that you might call an understandable English. You will see later why I mentioned this fact.

Now this man, at the age of twenty-six years—that is, twenty-seven years before I saw him—in 1917 it was, he conceived a fear of tuberculosis. It had developed gradually, but in 1917, he became thoroughly conscious of this fear. And people have the idea that if they have tuberculosis—or the fear of tuberculosis, I mean—they must not touch objects because germs may be all over. It is not so, but people develop this idea. And in consequence, he developed an obsession that we call *the fear of dirt and germs,* both dirt and germs. And he was afraid to touch anything.

He was afraid to touch the table, to touch knives and forks, and any utensil which he had to hold in the hands. He was afraid of touching his own clothes, and, naturally, should he touch anybody else's clothes, he would be afraid that he might have contracted an infection.

But he was not afraid of touching everything. I asked him, when he told me about his fears, I asked him, "Are you afraid of cleaning your rectum after elimination?" And he says, "No." Now, you will understand, that is a contradiction. If anybody is afraid of germs and dirt, he should certainly be afraid of the excreta from the rectum. He had no fear of that.

He was a barber by trade, and a barber must touch, or cannot avoid touching, the hair of his customers. At any rate, they may easily fall on his fingers. Even if he arranges not to touch them with his fingers, be sure he can hardly avoid having them fall on him. But he was not afraid of touching the hair of his customers. I have told you already what these contradictions mean, and I'll revert to that soon.

You will understand that this is an obsession, and obsessions are so many: the obsession that one cannot be alone on the street, that one cannot be alone at home—all kinds of obsessions—the obsession of counting. An obsession is simply a fear, a severe fear, a fear that interferes with your actions and forbids certain actions.

Now, you would presumably think that an obsession—this means an extreme fear of doing certain things—means that the patient is forced to avoid certain actions. Now, he was forced to avoid touching the table or touching his clothes, touching perhaps anything except the two things that I mentioned. If that is so, then you can conclude that this man had lost that capacity that everybody should have, the capacity to choose what to fear, what not to fear, to choose—about annoyances, dangers—as to whether they are trivial or significant. He could no longer choose as we do.

I will enlarge on this subject, and I will remind you that whatever I do in life suggests something to me. If I eat—plain eating—if I eat, the food suggests to me either that it is very tasty or that it is not very tasty. And then, according to the suggestion that I get from an object outside me, I can make a choice. And I will say, "Now, the smell of this food is not attractive to me, and I'd rather pick another kind of food." Or I can say, "This table looks really dirty, and I will not touch it," but then I see another table or another part of this table, and I say, "That doesn't look dirty, and I will touch it." But a patient of the kind that I mentioned had no choice left. He is under a prohibition to touch the table no matter whether it looks clean or dirty. A person of this kind is then restricted in his liberty of choosing between which suggestions to accept, which people to associate with and which objects to manipulate.

Then that person has lost his will. He has no will with regard to his obsessions. He can no longer choose. He may be able to choose in other ways, in other respects, in other fields of life, but not with regard to that obsession. A person like this can, for instance, not make a social choice. I can choose whether I want to visit somebody or whether I don't want to. But he had no choice. When he touched the table, then he had to go to the bathroom and wash. Now, if he visited somebody, the chances were he would now touch a table, then a chair, then a dish, then a person would brush against him and would touch his hand. And on each of these occasions, he would have to run to the bathroom. And how can he do that as often as he would have to do, if he is invited in[to] somebody's home?

You will, therefore, now also understand that with a compulsion or obsession of this sort, a person is restricted in his social choices. That means he is a cripple with regard to social life. And, of course, many of you have noticed that, at the time when you were acutely suffering, your social life was a shambles.

Now, it is always good to know what a term means when you use it. And what does *will* mean—or *choice*, which is the same as *will*? The best way to explain a term is to show what it does not mean. This means to quote the opposite of this term. And the opposite of will, or free choice, is fate.

If fate does something, if fate, for instance, brings a hailstorm—which is, of course, brought by fate—if fate produces a flood, an airplane crash, which may not always be fate but could be fate, if fate does something, then your will avails you nothing. You can't fight against fate. You can't prevent fate from exerting itself. You can't stop fate. I guess you will agree with me. We will later see the limitations of this statement, but at present I wish you would oppose will—that means free choice—to fate, which you can't choose. It comes. It grips you. It comes upon you, that thing that we call *fate*.

Now, look here, that patient had the obsession to touch things, and I explained to you what kind of a handicap that is. But I also told you he was not afraid in two items which I mentioned. He was not afraid to touch his rectum, to clean his rectum, and he was not afraid to manipulate his customers. So, do you understand he was in the grip of fate, but he broke up fate in these two items. That's remarkable. How can anybody thwart fate? How can he prevent fate from working, working its destiny? And you remember that I called that *a contradiction*. That man contradicted himself. And if he was able to touch his rectum and to touch the hair of his customers, be sure he should have been able to do everything else, to touch everything else. And that means he was not under the pressure of fate but under the influence of his will. Certain things he willed, he wanted or permitted himself to touch, and certain other things he did not permit himself to touch. And that man sensed that. I know that because the moment I told him that, he did not contradict me.

And other patients contradict me if I call their attention to the fact that they act in such a manner that they choose between this item that they permit themselves to touch, and between the other item which they refrain from touching. And too many patients notice their reactions which are contradictory. And then it dawns on them that if they touch the one series of items, they could also touch the other series, and they become bewildered. And they ask themselves, "How is it that I only cannot touch certain items, but others I can?" And they reach the conclusion, without knowing it consciously but sensing it intuitively, that if they can touch one series of objects and cannot touch another series, the selection of what to touch and what not to touch is made by their will.

And when patients reach this conclusion, they realize that all the misery of their life is not due to fate, but to their will.

And then they accuse themselves, they blame themselves that they don't use their will as they could. And if they develop this guilt feeling, they condemn themselves. And now they have two sources from which they derive untold misery and tenseness. They derive the tenseness from their actual suffering, from their obsession as it works in daily life, and second—a far greater source of tenseness—from their knowledge that they could stop it and fail to do that. In other words, they derive the greater portion of tenseness from their guilt feelings, from their self-condemnation. And I will go on to tell you what other symptoms the patient developed.

One day, all of a sudden, it struck him that when he looked in the mirror in his room, his face, his features, looked ghastly. They did not. He was not a paragon of masculine beauty when I met him. But that was some twenty-five years before I met him, and, well, I can't say how he looked at that time, but presumably again he was not what you would call a Valentino, you know, by no means. But when he looked in the mirror on that day, he thought his features looked ghastly. And ever since, he could not look into a mirror. Now, do you understand what that means?

If he wanted to go visiting somebody, well, there are very few people that don't hang a mirror in some of their rooms, or in most of their rooms. And he had to restrict his social life again because of this obsession. And when he came home, he had immediately to grab a sheet and cover up the mirror. But, in the morning, he had to shave, and even though he was a barber, he couldn't completely avoid the mirror. And he had to shave at home because when he went to his shop, well, there are plenty of mirrors in a barber shop. He couldn't avoid them there. And again we must say that man was certainly a miserable sort of a person.

And then some years later—about two or three years later, if I remember—he had another experience. He went into some place where they sold Christmas Seals, and the

Christmas Seals have to deal with tuberculosis, the thing that he was so frightfully scared by. And so he got scared when he went into this shop that sold the Christmas Seals. And, as it happens frequently with Christmas Seals, as far as I know, they have a tendency to be traced in red. Or a red color, if I remember correctly, is very frequently the main ingredient of the color of a Christmas Seal, or some ingredient. And henceforth, he was afraid of the color red. That sounds very simple. After all, can't you avoid the color red? You can't. You will see an apple that frequently is red. A tomato, be sure, you will see that is red. And you know, especially women, there are very few women that don't wear red dresses once in a while at least, and very frequently perhaps. And the red lights in traffic—there is no end to where a person can encounter the color red.

And you will now realize that every new obsession that this person developed restricted his life to a very narrow fragment. He mentioned as particularly painful to him because— of this fear of the red color—that now he couldn't eat red cabbage. He loved it. Well, but that was one of the minor troubles with him.

And about three or four years after that, he suddenly conceived a very odd idea. I don't remember having heard it from any other patient. Mind you, in my experience, maybe I had a similar case, and I don't just remember the case. And I might have to look up my records in order to hunt it. He became afraid of shadows. Shadows. Not of his shadow alone, of shadows. Now, you understand, how can you ever escape the sight of a shadow? There is either the sun out, and that throws shadows, or you are in a room with lights, and you will find shadows. All you have to do is to raise your hand, and you see your shadow, not only your hand, in a lighted room. And from that moment on, he could practically go nowhere except in dread fear, because he saw shadows.

Then as he went on, he developed all kinds of other minor obsessions, and I was able to observe them while I was treating him. And I want you to remember that I began to treat him twenty-seven years after he had begun to have these obsessions. And during these twenty-seven years, he had not been well for one single day.

He tried to get treatment. Well, you know, I can't repeat all the time what a poor record I have had with cases of this kind, with obsessions and compulsions, until I started my group. And I have told you repeatedly that the profession in general declares such obsessions and compulsions as hopeless. And the profession says they must be operated [on], they must be subjected to a brain operation that they call *lobotomy*. And you know how we treat these patients here, elegantly.

But in those days, twenty-seven years ago, or twenty years ago, or eighteen years ago, there was no method with which we could treat these obsessions and compulsions. There was no method. At that day they didn't even have this operation yet. And my groups in Recovery were not in existence at that time. And so this poor person had not a chance at all to get cured. Not for one single day was he ever cured in these twenty-seven years. And while I treated him here, he improved. He dropped the fear of the shadow. He dropped the fear of the red color. He touched objects bravely—trembling, but bravely. The touching he didn't give up so soon.

And while I treated him, he developed new obsessions. But while I treated him, and while he came to this group, and while he frequented the family groups and kept in close touch with the other patients who could give him ample encouragement and support—while he did all of this, it was simple to take care of his newly developing obsessions. He developed these obsessions in a very simple manner. He read a health column, and there he got an obsession. All he had to do is to read a health column or some magazine article about health, or to listen to these societies that try to prevent disease and promote—well, I don't want to say disease, but they promote nervous ailments.

And so one day he read in the health column about swellings in the throat. Well, all a patient of this kind has to read is "swellings in the throat," and he will do something with the swellings in himself. And henceforth, he became afraid to swallow food. He felt immediately a lump in the throat. Nervous patients can find that very easily. They can develop spasms and they feel then that they represent a lump, which means a swelling. And this patient developed the fear then of swallowing food. And consuming one simple meal in those days might have cost him hours. But then he came to my office, and I talked to him about it. And well, I don't know whether I had good results with him. I can't tell you. But the next day I saw him, and I asked him, "Well, do you still have the fear of swallowing food?" He said, "No, no." But I was a little bit befuddled about his answer because I noticed he had left my office and he wasn't visibly improved. And if a patient improves while I talk to him, well, I notice it, and I had not noticed it with him.

So I inquired, and on inquiry, he told me, "Well, you know I went to the family meeting, and Gertie was there,"— well, that was one patient—"and I told her about my fear of swallowing, and, well, I got so much encouragement from her," he said, "that I went home and ate a hearty meal that evening." Well, I didn't feel the best about that, because Gertie had cured him and I hadn't, you know. But, naturally, it pleased me no end that my patients actually practiced a magnificent habit, a magnificent art of self-help and mutual aid. And Gertie really had cured him of this obsession.

Well, and [one] day he got notice that a friend of his was operated on for a cancer of the throat, and after the patient had heard this news item, he went home and immediately he found a pimple on his lip, and the throat felt sore. He thought he had caught the cancer.

[Continued in Lecture 64.]

THE OBSESSIVE FEAR OF DIRT
AND GERMS (PART 2)

30 Minutes [Continued from Lecture 63]
Recorded 1953

Well, you see, obviously that man was extremely suggestible, as suggestible as you are. And one day he came to the office and told me of another obsession. All of a sudden he became conscious of hands, and particularly of his own hand when he moved it.

Now, don't think that this is a strange idea. It is strange compared to a normal idea, but it is not so strange among patients. I have seen patients who suddenly become conscious of any part of their body. A patient becomes conscious of his eyes, another conscious of his voice, and so forth. And you may think, after all, why make fuss about such a consciousness? And what of it if somebody is conscious of his eyes, of his breath—I had a patient of this kind—or, as with this patient, with the hand, hand consciousness?

Now, you know the patients—and many of you have answered to this description—the patients who become heart conscious. Well, that's simply understood. That's simply explained. These patients usually develop palpitations, and then they know that's developed by the heart, and they become heart conscious. You might ask, what of it if the heart palpitates? They are nervous palpitations and harmless. With a nervous patient, the heart is not damaged and never in danger, no matter how many years the palpitations have lasted. But the trouble is here not the heart, but the consciousness.

And I want you to know that we cannot be conscious of too many things at one time.

And if I speak to somebody, and I want to engage his attention, and I want to be convincing—should I speak to somebody, for instance, as a physician—if I speak to a patient, then I want to concentrate on what I tell the patient. If I do not concentrate on what I tell him, I may slip and say something that I should not say. So, will you understand that in too many pursuits of life, it is of the utmost importance to be able to concentrate on somebody, or on some task. But you cannot concentrate thoroughly if you are conscious of something that has nothing to do with the business in hand. And if I should speak to a patient and try to be convincing, try to put over a point, and at the same time I would have to think of my eyes—to be conscious of the fact that I had to consider the eyes—my attention would be concentrated on the eyes. To the extent that I am now conscious of the eyes, I could not concentrate on what I was telling the patient.

Now, if this goes on for any length of time, even only for ten minutes, then I become worried. And I tell myself, what if that persists, if I will now, from now on, be all the time conscious of my eyes or of my hands? And the more I become alarmed about this consciousness, the worse becomes the consciousness, and the worse the consciousness of the hand, the more alarmed I become, and there is a vicious cycle. And then the fact of being conscious of the hand, or eyes, or breath, and so forth, is a frightful handicap. You can't concentrate on anything else.

If this type of consciousness that I describe, if that increases and increases, it absorbs all your attention, as an obsession does. And so you will understand that this matter of becoming conscious of the hand is not merely an oddity in a symptom, it is a very severe handicap.

Now, with this handicap that he developed, or with this obsession that he developed, I was definitely able to cure him in that sitting in which he mentioned it. And he was cured before he ever had a chance to consult Gertie, you know. Well, this man, who at that time was fifty-three years of age and is now sixty-two, sixty-two years of age, this man got cured pretty soon. I mean in a case that had gone on for twenty-seven years before I saw him. And if I tell you that according to my record, by 1947 he was practically cured—this means three years after I started treating with him—I would say that's an excellent record.

But in the meantime, every once in a while he developed a fear reaction and a more or less trifling obsession. And the obsessions that he developed were then so mild that he didn't come to my office for years and had the girls take care of him, the girls in the family meetings. And they did a wonderful job. He used to come here to these classes in the first two years, if I remember correctly. And then he concentrated on the family gatherings, and for some reason he favored the girls, not the men, in the family gatherings. And I saw him very infrequently. Once in a while he came to my office and told me again about some trouble that he still had and mentioned either one of his former obsessions or a new obsession. But there was no trouble to get him to shake off the obsession. And then I heard, either from him or from somebody else, that he was doing very well. Then about half a year ago I had final proof that he really did well. He got married half a year ago, at the age of sixty-two, which is no calamity. That's not such a high age. Well, I qualify as his partner in this age.

He got married, and that's definitely a proof that he is as well as a person of this kind will want to be after twenty-seven years of sickness without treatment, and then several years yet under treatment when he was not well yet. He got married, and when we had our recent anniversary party in November, there he came with his wife, who impressed me as a very nice person. And I took occasion to question the wife, took occasion to take her aside and question her, and she definitely gave me a report that indicated that he was doing very well.

Now, mark it: There was a person that for twenty-seven years had not only one frightful obsession, but three more of them that were just as frightful, which means that this man definitely had no social life. He had no practice, let me say, of approaching a woman, of having or enjoying a woman's companionship. He had no practice in social conduct and social amenities. And for such a man to become married really requires a tremendous amount of courage even if he didn't have obsessions. So, he had regained a great amount of courage. And again I mention he was definitely cured even if he had some difficulties yet every once in a while. And the question is, how was he cured? What method was employed in curing him?

You may say, "Well, he came to classes, and there he got all kinds of explanations, and that cured him." And you know, that's the common method that is employed these days for curing nervous patients, to explain things to them. Well, before I had these classes, I did such an amount of explaining that I talked myself hoarse almost with every patient. And the results were very poor. And while a patient has to get explanations, and while you know that I give very abundant explanations, nevertheless, let me tell you, in a condition of this kind, explanations will never produce a sizeable improvement, and certainly not an improvement of the kind that this patient secured for himself. That's out of the question. And I know that because in former days, I tried very faithfully to give the patient as much explanation as I could give and never had the desired results.

Well, in addition, you will remember that I told you that this man was of foreign extraction. I mentioned that he was of Greek nationality, and he had a history which was unfavorable for his acclimating himself in the United States. He somehow came to the United States and was thrown into a Greek social setting only. And he told me that he hardly ever had a chance to talk English, except with his customers, and they were mostly Greeks themselves. With his English-speaking customers he kept quiet as a rule because of his language difficulties. So, do you understand, it is hardly to be assumed that this man was helped by explanations. To this day, he has not sufficient knowledge of the English language to make his speech really understandable. It is very indistinct, and it requires effort to listen to him.

And I remember an Italian woman of about sixty-two, who came to consult me, and I could not get a history from her because she did not speak English. Fortunately, she had a younger sister who had attained a fair command of the English language, and an interview was arranged at which that sister was to serve as an interpreter. The sister knew about my classes, and I told her, "Well, I shall be glad to enroll the patient in the classes, but she will not understand." It was then arranged that this English-speaking sister came to the classes with the Italian-speaking patient. The understanding was that the gist of my address was to be explained to the patient after class, at home. And everything seemed happily arranged, except that soon thereafter, the sister had to move to another town. From there on, the patient continued on her own. She was a regular listener at these Tuesday classes and at the Saturday panels and, of course, at the family meetings. Before long, she lost her delusions, and to this very day I don't know how she got cured.

I have a chance to see her every once in a while at meetings, and she still speaks Italian mainly and very little English. But she is cured. She had delusions of persecution, and her cure was effected without hospital treatment. And some Italian members of this class, who got acquainted with the family, told me how she got cured.

When she was at Recovery meetings, nobody perhaps understood her, but, nevertheless, everybody listened to her. And she felt she had sympathy, support. She felt here she belonged. Now, I don't recommend even the Recovery techniques for people who don't understand the language. I don't do that. But there was a case where the language handicap did not count. And that woman is still well, has thrown off a florid mental disease that had developed into ideas of persecution, which are a very dangerous mental ailment. And she got well. Nobody knows why. It's the so-called group that did it, certainly not I. I couldn't communicate with her.

Well, it's not explanations that cure a patient, although they help cure him, but alone they wouldn't do it. And now let me tell you—and that's nothing new to you—what cures a patient are a few other things, but mainly training. Training, not information, not explanations. They merely contribute to the cure, but they can never do it alone. But training alone can do it. And this patient was trained, and he was trained, as you know, to use his muscles. And you who have read the book, and you who have undergone the training yourself, know that this is the real means for curing a patient.

And this patient was eager to cooperate. He had developed a love for the groups, a love particularly for the family groups where all the girls catered to him. Not only that he was attracted to them, but they were attracted to him. I don't mean physically. They were attracted, they were attracted by the challenge that that patient offered. He offered the challenge to the members of the family group of treating him in spite of his language handicap. And they made him listen to their discussions, although they were pretty certain he didn't understand everything. And that was a challenge to them. And they made every effort to cater to him, and, of course, that helped.

In the process, he learned a bit of English, and then it was easier to handle him. And he was taught by me and by the members of the family group—and I am not engaging in a contest with the groups. I don't want to compete with them whether they did most of the work, or I did it. Nobody will ever know. But the patient was cured by this method, by the technique of muscle training.

And he was told in a simple manner, both by me and by the members of the group, that when he refused or feared to touch a table or a chair or a garment, he did that not because he actually was afraid that he was going to be killed. He did it for an entirely different reason. And any of my patients who have an obsession—for instance the obsession of crossing the street alone—are not afraid that they will collapse if they do cross the street. And he was no longer afraid, as he perhaps was in the beginning, of contracting a disease if he touched the table. That's not correct. But in the beginning he had this fear of tuberculosis, in the beginning.

And when he touched the table, what developed? He immediately felt an unpleasant emptiness in his stomach. That was his symptom. And whenever again he touched something, there was the emptiness in the stomach. He couldn't describe it exactly, but he said it was terrible. Well, that is a description, too. And what he became afraid [of] then was mainly this feeling of the emptiness in the stomach. And don't believe a patient that he is afraid of anything else, except in the beginning. In the beginning, patients may actually be afraid of an infection, or of anything of this sort. But gradually they develop sensations, unpleasant sensations, the sensations of palpitations, of emptiness of the stomach, of light-headedness and so forth. In him, it was mainly this emptiness of the stomach. And what he was afraid of in these twenty-seven years was sensations. And in twenty-seven years, the sensations became so severe that they were really frightful. They were worked up.

And now he was taught: What you are afraid of is not infections but your sensations. And while infections are dangerous—naturally infections could be dangerous—sensations, he learned, are never dangerous, and you can experiment with them. Sensations are merely distressing and not dangerous.

And so I got him, or the girls in the family meetings got him—I don't know; I guess we shared the honors—we got him to try. And he was a very obedient person, and he went home and tried to touch the table that for twenty-seven years had not been touched, or he had tried not to touch it. And then he noticed when he touched the table with courage, with assurance, there was no emptiness in the stomach. That's correct. He went about it with determination, with courage; this means with relaxation.

Anytime you are determined and courageous, you relax. Tenseness means fear. Courage means absence of fear. So, you don't get tense if you have courage; at least for a couple of minutes you don't get tense. And in these couple of minutes, the symptom disappears because every nervous symptom will disappear if you avoid tenseness, if you relax. And you will understand, once this patient was won over to the group—whether he understood completely what we told him or not, this does not matter—once he was won over to the group, and the girls in the family meetings catered to him and made him feel at home, this matter of being made to feel at home is already relaxation.

If you can be made to feel at home somewhere, then you are relaxed. And this is one of the secrets why we have such notable success with our patients. We make them feel at home. But that's not enough. That's enough for convincing them that they can lose their symptoms. But, look here: We have here a patient who has had these symptoms for twenty-seven years, every day. These symptoms have become stubborn. The tissues of the body had developed habits for twenty-seven years, for instance to produce this empty feeling in the stomach that frightened him no end. Now, if the stomach had developed a habit for twenty-seven years to tighten up and to produce this feeling of emptiness, be sure it couldn't lose this habit in a day or two. Tissues don't work that way. The habit was now deeply rooted. And it takes time to throw off such a habit completely.

And will you distinguish between the one thing that we call *making the patient begin to feel at home* and then to begin practice. And then, even on the first attempt, you can make him lose his symptoms. But the tissues have still their habits of contracting and producing symptoms then. And, therefore, he could be made to practice bravely, but then the symptom came back and came back and back. And in order to train a patient of this kind, it is not only sufficient to give him explanations. We know that. Neither is it sufficient just to arrange him in a group where he feels at home, nor is it sufficient to make him practice with courage. All of this is not enough. There is another thing.

The patient must be prevented [from giving] up, and patients are easily induced to give up, to say, "Well, this doesn't help me either, even Recovery doesn't help me, even Dr.

Low can't cure me." And you know I meant to him something more than just an ordinary authority. He had formed a very deep attachment to me, as you have done. We must see in our techniques to prevent the patient [from becoming] lastingly discouraged and then finally to give up and not to come any more.

And that is the supreme accomplishment of this group. It keeps the patients, and the patients cling to it because they feel at home. And no matter how much the symptoms come back, we see to it that our patients should not get discouraged to the point where they again change doctors. And you know that this is the mark, the chief mark, of our success.

And that's how he was cured. First by the techniques that I mentioned, and you remember what I mentioned: muscles, muscle training, encouraging [him] to go ahead and gain courage to practice with his muscles, and then joining the group, especially the family meetings. I should add, today we have also the one technique of reading my book. At that time, I didn't have this book, although I had other books, but they were much more difficult to read.

But the sovereign means of finally accomplishing the cure is, aside from all the techniques that I mentioned, our capacity for making the patient come and come and come till the final victory is won. And since the patient can gain the final victory only after months and months of weary practice—and since, in the meantime, the patient gets again the empty feeling in the stomach and all kinds of symptoms otherwise—it is necessary, you will understand now, to devise a method that will keep the patient coming no matter how long it will take to gain the final victory. And that was done with this patient and was done very successfully in spite of the handicaps which I indicated, particularly the language handicap.

Thank you.

EXPECT THE SETBACK AND SPOT
EXTREMES (PART 1)

30 Minutes
Recorded Tuesday, February 23, 1954

Well, I will introduce a little change tonight. I will not discuss a case, the case of a patient. Instead, I [would] rather discuss a problem, and particularly a problem related to spotting. It is of the utmost importance that you learn how to spot. And in recent weeks, I made up my mind I'll have to produce a few records on the subject of spotting, and I have done some of it, and I will continue. And today, the occasion is again for one of these discussions of spotting.

The other day, a patient, who is very cooperative, told me a very simple sentence. It was a very innocent sounding statement. And she says, "In the past three days, I have been in a slump." And this came from a patient who had done remarkably well. We discussed that, and I made some statement—I don't remember exactly what kind of statement it was—and the lady said, "No, that is not so." And then I remember that I immediately thereafter, or somewhat shortly anyhow, on one occasion I told her, "Well, you are discouraged," and she said, "No. And I wish to assure you, Doctor, I am thoroughly sold on you and Recovery."

So she wished to assure me that it was not so. And her first statement, in response to my telling her that she is discouraged, was, "No." And the second statement, where she said, "I wish to assure you that I am thoroughly sold on Recovery and you"—this means, "I wish to assure you that I do everything you want me to do"—was essentially again a no, a negation of my statement that she is discouraged. She meant to say, "Why, to the extent that I am loyal to you, how can you say that I am discouraged? I will never be discouraged as long as you are my doctor." Well, that's a very good statement, and I like perhaps to hear such statements and expressions of sentiments. But is it correct?

And then the lady went on in this line until I stopped her and asked her, "How do you know that you are not discouraged?" And the lady tells me, "Well, don't I know what I feel?" So, I ventured to assure her, just as she had assured me, that she doesn't know how she feels. And the lady was, of course, astonished to hear that she doesn't know how she felt. And I could have told her—and in the course of the conversation I did on some occasion—that she doesn't know what she thinks and nobody does unless he knows how to spot. And this I want to discuss today: that people don't know what they feel and don't know what they think. And yet they do know in a sense, but not when the feeling and thinking reaches down to the depths. Then they don't know.

And the patient went on, and I'll tell you soon what I am driving at. When I asked her, "How do you know that you are not discouraged?" she said, "Well, I think of you all the time. How can I be discouraged?" And then she went on, "In the past few weeks I just walk[ed] on air. Well, could that be discouragement?" she asked. And then, "I always felt happy until the past three days, so how could I have been discouraged?" So, there I had a chance to step in and said, "But I speak of the past three days." She said before the past three days she was happy and walked on air and always thought of me. Well, I have no objection to all these manifestations of kind sentiments. But do they prove anything? Do they prove that in the past three days she was not discouraged?

Do you perhaps already get a glimpse of the fact that people don't know what they think or what they feel if things are deep-seated? And you will understand, be sure, if somebody is happy, he knows that he is happy. But that's not the depth of feelings, and I will show you what is at the bottom of such feelings.

You see, happiness means many things. And therefore you will soon find out that unhappiness also means many things. But the patient merely uses the word *happiness*. Now, if somebody feels happy, this means he's confident, you know. He experiences a certain thrill, the thrill that he can do with his body whatever anybody else can do with his body, the thrill of being able now to plan, and there you can carry out your plan. And you don't have to drive yourself. You don't have to do it with effort. You can do it spontaneously, this means with ease, just as I, for instance, walk on the street or board a streetcar or go into a restaurant. I don't have to force myself. But sometimes I have to force myself. Sometimes my mood is low, and then I don't feel like doing things. And if I want to visit somebody, I have to force myself. And if I want to go into a restaurant, I have to force myself. Not that it is a great inconvenience. I have only to apply a little force. But compared to other days, this little force makes the difference between confidence and lowered confidence.

So, you will understand, happiness consists, for instance, in the fact that when I now walk on the street, I step out lively. I don't watch myself, whether I am giving the impression of tenseness to other people, and whether perhaps my shoulder really does register tenseness, or my cheeks. Happiness means, for one thing, I step out lively, and I don't think of myself. This means I don't think critically of myself. I think of one thing only: that now I am happy. I am not self-conscious. I don't think, "What, will people notice that I am happy?" In happiness you don't ask that because you are relaxed. You only ask what people will notice if you are unhappy, if you are self-conscious, if you are tense. Then the opinion of people counts. But not when you are happy. Because then, even if the people notice that you are happy, that's not a matter that counts against you. That will only be to your credit. That's what you think, at any rate.

And happiness means something else. Not only self-confidence and the thrill of now being able to manage one's self with ease and with comfort and with relaxation. It also means that now I think of pleasant things only. And when I am happy, then I don't want to talk about the past days of misery. Most people don't. They want to forget because the present experience is so precious and priceless that nothing must be permitted to disturb it. Even memories must not be pessimistic, negative. Everything must be optimistic and positive. So, positive thoughts only are admitted to consciousness when you are happy. But it must be happiness, not mere satisfaction. And if the patient says he walks on air, and now he really feels proud of himself, and now he really lives—before, he has only existed, he has only lived a mechanical existence in which he pushed himself through life, but he didn't walk on air, of course—when the patient has this experience, then he says, "Now I live. I no longer do the thing that I did before." This means, "I no longer merely exist." And the patient—and the person, every person—is now interested in not letting this happy state be disturbed by negative thoughts, by critical thoughts. He only wants to think of the happiness.

And then he does something that I don't want him to do. He does not think ahead of the setback that is bound to come in the beginning of his career as my patient. I have yet to see the patient who convincingly avoided setbacks. I have seen a few patients that had no setbacks, very few, as long as I observed them. But then they dropped out, and I don't know what may have happened to them. Most likely they got a setback and thought, "Well, Dr. Low didn't help me either, so I [will] go to somebody else." And I don't know whether this thing exists, a patient who doesn't get setbacks. It may exist, but I haven't seen them convincingly.

And if the patient drifts toward a setback, as every patient apparently does—in the beginning at any rate—what happens? He has been so happy for two months, let me say. He walked on air, he felt the thrill of self-management, and so forth, and didn't want to think of anything negative, so he refused to think of the setback. And then, thinking only of positive things, only of pleasant things, he didn't think of the future that might be unpleasant. And therefore he was not prepared for the setback. Since he didn't expect the setback, when it came, it struck him unprepared and scared him, or scared her. In this case, it was a lady. And for three days she was in the dumps, or she had slumped, as she called it. And I explained the matter to her and told her, "Do you now understand that you did not expect the setback, and that when it came, it scared you?" Then she admitted that happened. So, do you understand now that that's what I had in mind when I said, "You have become discouraged?" And she had to admit that means discouragement.

But look here. I had to explain to her everything that I explained to you in order to make her see that this slump of hers was due to discouragement. She could perhaps have noticed that she felt discouraged. I noticed it immediately, for some reason. But she didn't know. But what did she know? She knew that previous to the three days, she had been happy. But now, when she had slumped, she was not yet unhappy. You see, happiness to her meant the mood rises high. Now, in the first three days, the mood hasn't risen deep. It just began to slump. And she could, this little slump of the mood, not properly call *unhappiness.* It was only the cessation of the happiness, just as if a honeymoon ends. The happiness is over, but that doesn't mean you drift into unhappiness. But it's no longer happiness. It's just a trifle lowering of the happiness curve. But if she should wait longer—I mean the patient should wait longer—then the slump might slump deeper and deeper. And then she would call it unhappiness.

You see, the patients know only two terms, and not only the patients. Everybody else is likely to think in two terms only: I feel good or bad, high or low, happy or unhappy. The intermediate degrees are many. For instance, between happiness and unhappiness, there is the term *tenseness.* Tenseness is not, certainly not, happy, but it's not unhappy either. I can be tense without being unhappy. Then there is the term *disappointment.* You understand, disappointment, well, it's certainly not happiness, but it's not unhappiness either. It's somewhere in between these two terms. And then *discouragement*. In other words, there are various gradations that lead from the top term, *happiness*, to the bottom term, *unhappiness*. And the patient calls all these gradations by one name, happy or unhappy, especially if they become extreme. And now I told this patient she is discouraged. Why didn't she admit that? Why did she deal with the terms *happy* and *unhappy* only? And there comes a point that I want you to consider.

I can easily tell somebody, "Well, I don't feel good. I feel uncomfortable." That doesn't say anything about me. Certainly it doesn't criticize me. Nobody can blame me for feeling not good, for feeling uncomfortable, for feeling uneasy. And people can easily express themselves in these terms. And why can they? You will immediately realize it when I contrast the term[s] uneasy, uncomfortable, tense, with discouragement. If I say, "I am discouraged," that's an entirely different situation. Then I say my character has slumped. A good character should have courage. Although on an average everybody is discouraged, people are likely to deny that they are discouraged. They want to give the picture that they are courageous, that they have spirit, character, personality. And there is no character with discouragement, except if the discouragement lasts only a short time.

But this goes on for three days, and the patient is afraid that it might now go on for weeks and months, as it did before. Then, without knowing it, the patient senses that if somebody tells him, "Oh, you are discouraged," he should deny it. If somebody should tell him, if I should tell a person, "I think you are not so happy today," most likely that person will immediately agree without any hesitation, because there is no connection between happiness and spirit—between unhappiness, I mean—and spirit, character, personality. Anybody can be unhappy. If a mother loses her child and she keeps on being [un]happy for endless weeks and months, nobody will say she has a weak character. But if a mother gets discouraged most of the time, or a long time, because of the difficulties that the babies offer, then we say there is something wrong with her spirit as a mother.

And I hope you will understand: Inside we have two kinds of feelings and sensations. The ones are, like happiness and unhappiness, innocent from the viewpoint of valuation, from the viewpoint of character and spirit. Now, you see, if I am happy, that's a private affair. The group doesn't lose with it, doesn't gain, it's just private. If I jump in the water and swim and feel happy about it, that's a perfectly private affair. Nobody is harmed by my happiness, and most likely nobody benefited. But if I am discouraged, I may do a great deal of harm. Should I be discouraged and show the discouragement, my patients would notice it, and it would do them harm. They would, perhaps, lose confidence in me, you know. That would be certainly harmful to the patients.

And now you go a little further. If an employer becomes discouraged, that may do something to his business. It may do something to his sales force. He may infect them with his discouragement, and then sales may drop off. That would be a harm to the business. And then go further, and say an officer in the army becomes discouraged, let me say, in battle. Then be sure it will [redound] to the detriment of the troops, and so forth. And I hope you realize the difference between showing a degree of happiness or unhappiness, or showing a degree of courage and discouragement. Discouragement can be harmful to members of the group. Happiness, that's a private affair, has nothing to do with the group, not necessarily.

And do you understand that my patients, and ordinary persons that don't have the experience that I naturally ought to have, cannot make these distinctions. I have never been able to make these distinctions promptly, in a fraction of a second, and that means spotting. It must be done quickly. I have never been able to do that as far as I remember in former days, until I got down to observing these matters that we call *spotting* and leaving things unspotted. And the patients have to learn that.

This patient didn't learn it because, although she cooperated very beautifully, she permitted herself to become too happy. And in this bliss of happiness, she was afraid to shake the illusion or the condition of happiness. So she refused to think of anything negative, and didn't think, and didn't foresee and expect the setback that is unavoidable.

And you see now why I insist that my patients always keep in mind: to get cured takes time, and it takes a long time. And during this time, you are bound to suffer setbacks, especially in the beginning, because your nerves have not acquired resistance yet. And if you go along for two, three, four, five weeks without any mishap, that doesn't mean that you have escaped the possibilities of setbacks. They will come yet. If you expect them, then you are safe. When the setback comes, it doesn't strike you suddenly, and therefore you are not taken by surprise, and you don't get scared. You expected it. And you expected it with the knowledge that I gave you, that if you do expect it, you will not get scared. And therefore the setback will not be worked up, and it will remain mild.

If you, however, permit yourself to get scared at a setback, then be sure you will work it up. You will now become desperate or discouraged. It does not have to be desperate. You see what gradations there are between the two terms *happiness* and *unhappiness.* I can't mention them all.

Well, if the patient permits himself not to expect the setback, then he drops—and precipitously, suddenly—from the height of happiness to the depths of despair, or at least of discouragement. And that's a frightful slump, or jump. And that has a close relation to that thing that has been called *the condition of defeat after victory.* I have mentioned that to you already on repeated occasions, but there are plenty of people here who have not heard me discuss that phenomenon of defeat after victory.

It is claimed—I don't know on what authority, and I will merely repeat it because it is an instructive statement—it is claimed that when the Germans invaded Holland and

Belgium and Northern France in 1940—yes, 1940—they adopted a policy. I don't know whether it's correct, but I just quote this statement for what it may be worth—they adopted a policy of letting the British and French and Belgians and Dutch gain a little victory here and a little victory there. And usually, it is claimed, they let the Westerners, the Allies, pick up a few little advantages in this spot and that spot. And the Allies naturally magnified this situation and said they had scored a big victory for two days. And then on the third day, the Germans immediately swooped down on the Allies and routed them. During the two days that the Allies were successful, naturally, they gained courage. They breathed freely. They became happy. They thought now the tide has turned. And when then two days later the German aircraft and German Panzers stormed against them, and they suffered a frightful defeat, there was this plunge from happiness down to the bottom of unhappiness. And that is demoralizing. And the Allies are supposed, according to this account, in those days, to have concluded, "Well, the Germans are invincible," so discouraged are they supposed to have been in those days.

Well, whether it's true or not, I don't know, but it's an instructive parallel. That's what happens to the patient. If he whoops up his enthusiasm about his little victory, initial victory, and then the setback sets in, this means the defeat, then he becomes demoralized, and he says, "Well, even Recovery can't help." You see.

Now, do you understand that if you don't expect the setback, you will be struck by this phenomenon that we call *defeat after victory,* and that is discouraging and demoralizing. And the remedy is, of course, to think of the setback, to have it in mind, to know that the present happiness is not of duration.

And happiness is no good for human beings anyhow. One shouldn't strive . . . . It's an evil. Believe me. I mean what I say. Why not just be satisfied? You see, there are the gradations. Inside happiness there are such milder conditions as gratification, satisfaction.

[*Continued in Lecture 66.*]

LECTURE 66

EXPECT THE SETBACK AND SPOT EXTREMES (PART 2)

26 Minutes [Continued from Lecture 65]
Recorded Tuesday, February 23, 1954

And I don't see why patients cannot think in terms of, for instance, a better spirit. Why must it be a high spirit, you know? A better self-management. Why must it be a thorough self-management? But I have preached to the patient whatever I could in terms of making him climb down a little bit from the highest rungs of the happiness ladder. But my voice is one in the wilderness, and the patients don't hear it. And we understand that. You know, while the patient is happy, as he calls it—although it shouldn't be a happiness, it should only be a feeling of a better spirit—but while he is in this condition that he calls happy, he really is, let me say, a changed person.

You see, that patient, in the morning, has experiences that are unfamiliar to him or have been unfamiliar to him for quite some time. All of a sudden, he jumps out of bed and feels fine. Now, he hasn't done that for months and years, perhaps. For months or years, this matter of getting up in the morning was a matter of something dragging. He didn't jump out of bed but crept down along the board, the sideboard. And then usually, after he had made a few movements with his limbs, he crawled back under the covers, and then stayed there in the covers fretting and self-accusing and self-critical. And he suffered mortification because he knew he had defaulted on his duty. His duty is, of course, to get up

427

rather promptly and go to work, but he couldn't do it. And now all of a sudden he has this exhilarating, almost intoxicating, experience that there in one whoop he jumps out of bed. And that is, indeed, something that may fill a victim of a depression with happiness. Nevertheless, he shouldn't. He should steer clear of this feeling of happiness, and I will tell you later why.

And then that patient, for instance, after he has jumped out of bed, slips into his garments with alacrity. There is no trouble. He doesn't have to drive himself. He doesn't have to stop at every move and say, "Well, I feel so dead, I can't slip into my pajamas or slip out of them. It's hardly possible, and I'll better go back to bed," you know. I know the performance of patients in the morning and in the evening and in midday, and that's what they do.

And now, all of a sudden, he goes ahead and washes himself, and there he feels the pleasure of the water. The one feels the pleasure of the hot water, the other of the cold water, and the combination of it. But the point is that he now feels pleasure, and he hasn't felt any pleasure for months or for years. And see, all of these are naturally overwhelming experiences.

And then this patient may then go to his office, and there he steps out freely with vigorous paces. And he hasn't experienced this vigor for months or for years. And you will understand he is really happy. But he shouldn't do that. He should stay away from happiness. It's enough if I can say I enjoy things. Why must I be happy over things? But if you are happy, and this is intoxication—happiness is an extreme of a positive feeling, and then you become intoxicated as this patient becomes, intoxicated with joy, and it's a toxic joy, not a good joy—and once you experience this feeling of intoxication, you want to continue it, to perpetuate it. You want to experience it tomorrow again. And, as I told you, you don't want to think of things negative.

But nobody can stay on a pinnacle for any length of time. There is always a dropping if you reach up too high.

And you see, happiness is an extreme, and unhappiness is the other extreme, and in between are those things that we call *better spirit* or *worse spirit, feeling out of sort, simple average satisfaction* or *dissatisfaction, average discouragement* or *encouragement*. And once you deal with average feelings, then you experience something that is very important. Once you experience an average discouragement, for instance, then you know everybody experiences that. There is nothing to make [a] fuss over, being discouraged. I personally am discouraged so frequently, so many times every day, that I am used to it.

It's perfectly average for me to see a patient the second time, and that patient is impatient, as patients are. They should be called impatients and not patients, you know. The second time that I see a patient, then the third time, and the fourth time, and, with some patients, the fifteenth time, they are unhappy, impatient. They say, "I am not well yet." So, I usually tell them, "Well, I know that, and I don't expect it any better. That's excellent that by this time you at least have improvement." He wants to be well immediately. The patient wants to. He is impatient.

That patient has not learned what he perhaps knew before he got sick, and what I naturally know and average people know: Discouragements and disappointments are the common thing in life. But you see, but after a defeat follows a victory; then the discouragement may gain or fall down to the lowest depths. And that's what is the patient's situation. And I have to teach the patient that discouragements, dissatisfactions are average reactions, just as encouragement and satisfaction are average reactions, if they keep this side of the extremes of happiness and unhappiness, if they occupy the middle lines between these extremes. If they do, then I expect discouragement.

I don't expect that this plain little thing of satisfaction will go on forever. I know from experience that it is constantly disturbed. But if I keep it in the middle line of experience, in the middle part of experience, it's only a moderate satisfaction. And even if this moderate satisfaction is disturbed, I don't fall down to the depths of reactions. I hope you understand that. And the moment I teach the patient constantly to think in terms of middle-ground reactions, of average reactions, whatever he will feel then, if it is average, he can never fall down to the depths of everything, because he never rises to the height of anything

And if I ask the patient to remember that setbacks cannot be avoided, then I make him think of the setback. He thinks of something negative. And then he can never rise to the height of happiness. Therefore, he can never fall to the depths of unhappiness. And you will understand now why here in Recovery we stress the concept of averageness. You will now understand that, from this viewpoint, that averageness is wedged in between two contrast pairs of opposites. And try your best never to reach the opposite, either above or below the average middle.

It is bad to be an extremist, but the patient is always an extremist. And the trouble is he doesn't know how to spot it. He doesn't know that he moves at extremes. For instance, the patient has hardly ever told me—well, either this patient or other patients—hardly ever told me that they have a little twinge of pain somewhere. Patients never have twinges. They have all these explosions and hammer blows, pressures that press on them like tons. See, they always move at the extremes of experience. And when the patients come to me, their pain, their pressures, their numbnesses are of course unbearable. They are never plain pressures that everybody may experience. It's always something that is extreme. And if it is extreme, or if they think it is extreme, then they fear it, and they develop an unusual amount of tenseness. And the tenseness then makes the pressure worse. And when the pressure gets worse, the tenseness gets worse. Then symptoms accumulate, become more intense, last longer because the pressure of tenseness works on them.

But the patient still goes on telling me, "I have not been able to sleep for three months in succession. I didn't sleep a wink," he says. He doesn't say, "I slept a little bit, I agree or admit." He says, "No, I didn't sleep," and then he adds, "and, Doctor, I tell you I know I didn't sleep." And I asked him, "How do you know?" Then he says, "I had the watch near me and I looked at the watch and I know I didn't sleep. I always saw the watch." See, the patient, of course, doesn't know that this is an extremist view, that he always looked at the watch. That's all ridiculous. How can anybody, sleeping or waking, always look at one spot? It's impossible. If he did it, he would instantly, after two or three seconds about, but certainly after two or three minutes, fall asleep. That's all you have to do, to look at one spot, and then you will fall asleep. And you see, the patient tells me such balderdash.

It's notorious that mostly the sensitive people develop nervous reactions, and the sensitive people are not dumb by any means. They are certainly not dull. One wouldn't believe that such a group of nervous patients as I see, who are highly sensitized and have done a lot of thinking about themselves and others—although their thinking, it was mainly fear thinking, but nevertheless it was thinking—they were not dull. They have done a lot of reading, a lot of listening. They tried to study, they read books, and although they read the most god-awful books (I grant you from my viewpoint; from your viewpoint, they may have been good), nevertheless, they read and thought and tried to study. And they are not a dull lot by any means. They are far more sensitive than the average population is. And I tell you that's what you are, far more sensitive. And yet you believe every gibberish that somebody offers you or yourself offer yourself. And you believe—and all of you are likely to have such beliefs—that you can look a total night at a watch. Such nonsense. You would naturally be prevented from doing it because you immediately fell asleep if you do it for a short time. So, you understand, the patient doesn't even know how to spot this statement, "I always looked at the watch."

And I must train him that this "always" means a terrible exaggeration, a moving at the extremes, you know, and leaving out the middle ground. And whenever somebody moves at the extremes of life, at the extremes of experience, then he is always likely to topple down from the extreme to the contrast extreme, to the opposite extreme. And my patients always do that. When my patients finally learn that sleep is no problem, and all you have to do is not to fear sleep, then you will fall asleep. And when you look at the watch, then precisely that's what you do. You don't think of sleep, but you think of the watch. Then you fall asleep, you see. You look at the watch, naturally, not with fear. Nobody fears a watch. But if you think that you will not sleep, then that's a fear idea. That keeps you awake, of course. But it keeps you awake only for a certain period of time, and then you fall asleep. And you wake up and you don't know that you have slept because it was only a short sleep, and so forth. Read up my chapter on sleep in the book.

Now, do you understand now what one type of spotting consists of? It consists of looking at yourself and knowing when you reach to the height or the depth of extremes. And keep away from them. Walk in the middle life and think in average terms. In average terms, the average pain is bearable. It is not unbearable. In average terms, nobody has ever failed to sleep for three months [at] a stretch. That's all nonsense. In average speech, if a leg feels numb, then it's numb, but it doesn't feel like a piece of wood. That's what the patients tell me. In average speech, if somebody has a streak of blood in the sputum and notice it, they don't say, "The blood came from my throat almost like in a stream." People don't say that on average, but patients tell me that, and so forth.

And in average life, if I tell a patient that his pain is due to nerves, then the patient, or the person in average life, doesn't jump at me and say, "How can you say that? I feel the pounding of the tumor." In average life, a person, if he hears something from an expert, especially if he has consulted the expert, doesn't have the audacity to start an argument with an expert. But my patients do almost nothing else but argue with me—almost, not entirely. Sometimes they stop arguing for a second, or a minute, but that's really a great benefit that I seldom experience when the patients are in my office, I mean in the beginning of their career.

So, will you understand that spotting means primarily to avoid extremes, to avoid extremes above and below. And the patient who told me that she was not discouraged, although I told her she was discouraged—she only said she was unhappy. She should have said discouraged. That's in the middle line between the extremes. Unhappiness, as she conceived of it, was down in the bottom. Happiness was up at the top. And patients don't speak of discouragement. They don't speak, let me say, of dissatisfaction. They immediately jump to the one extreme, happiness, and the other extreme, unhappiness. They are always unhappy as far as they suffer. Once they get an improvement, they are always happy. And both are extremes, and they should spot them. We don't want the extremes.

And, as I told you, it's a great satisfaction to be satisfied. One doesn't have to be happy. To be in good spirits, why must they be high spirits? And it's not so bad to be dissatisfied. But the patient being dissatisfied immediately says, "I am the unhappiest person, the unluckiest person, why must everything happen to me?" Haven't you heard that? "Everything," the patient speaks in terms of "everything," this means an extreme. The patient says, "I never feel good," which is nonsense. There are minutes at least when he feels good. But he has the idea things are either always or never. Do you understand these are all extremes?

A patient told me today—that happens very seldom, and this patient surprised me—"I had just a little minute of improvement." Heavens. I improved when I heard that, you know. I don't remember having heard such a statement from a patient in years, I think. This patient, mind you, acknowledged and appreciated a thing that has no extreme value. A minute of improvement doesn't mean anything. And that's cooperation, not always to have the eye on the extreme, to be well quickly. That's an extreme. Can't be accomplished. But to improve gradually, first for a second, then for five seconds, then a minute. The second and five seconds this patient didn't notice. Nobody would. But when it reached the point that she called a minute, she noticed it, and came to me and told me. And I appreciated that very much, that there is a patient who walks in the middle ground of life and keeps away from extremes. She didn't think that you can appreciate health only if you are completely cured. She thought a little improvement, that just a modicum of improvement, is something to be appreciated. And, of course, it's something to be appreciated because it ushers in the improvement, the good improvement, and the final cure. But that's rare among patients.

Instead, patients tell me, "Oh, I slumped again." And if I ask them, "Why, what happened to you?"—especially if I tell them, "Well, you didn't think of the setback," then they immediately say, "No." Then a patient is likely to say, "But something happened to me that got me floored." And I ask him, "What is this something?" And the patient says, "Well, I got notice to vacate my store, and where will I get a new store now? It's so difficult. And where will I find the money? I didn't make much in my business in the past few years because of my illness." And so something happens, and the patient feels paralyzed. But this is so average that there are business reverses and business cycles, and [for] people today, particularly, to get notices, eviction notices. What is more average than this, you know? At any rate, it's quite average.

So, if the patient slips, why does he say it's environment that is against him? Everybody, as I tell the patient, everybody is in for setbacks. So, he begins to blame environment. Environment is against him, against his health. The landlord who sent him a notice, be sure, didn't know anything about his poor health. He didn't aim with the notice of eviction against his health. Environment didn't aim at him. It just happened, as it happens now to so many people, that they get eviction notices. But this patient now happened to have a setback at the same time, and then he says the setback is the result of the eviction.

What does that mean? It means he blames himself but doesn't want to admit it, and therefore blames the environment. That is very convenient for him to put the blame on environment. But he feels guilty, especially after I tell him, "Well, you didn't expect the setback." I really blamed him. And after he hears that, that I say it is his fault—not that he got the setback; to get the setback is nobody's fault—but not to handle it after I warn a patient, "Don't expect to be cured already. Expect the setback." And if he doesn't, and I mention the fact that he didn't expect the setback, then naturally that means to him he is blamed for not expecting the setback. And this is what I did. I did blame him. Now he pushes the blame on environment, and patients always they do that, or very frequently. I think always. So, they exaggerate their own weakness and the strength, the striking power of environment. But that's all nonsense. The patient thinks that environment has a maximum striking power, and the individual, the patient, has a minimal resistance. But that's nonsense. That's again thinking in extremes.

And will you now finally understand: A good deal of spotting is, you must spot your reactions with the knowledge that they must not become extreme but must remain in the middle ground of average experience. And once you learn that—and I'll teach you other modes of spotting, and I have told you other modes—once you learn what I told you today, and what I told you in the past, and what I will tell you in the future, well, you can rest assured that you will not only get well, but you will keep well.

Thank you.

LECTURE 67

ROUTINE VERSUS EMERGENCY

30 Minutes
Recorded Tuesday, May 4, 1954

I shall again present to you a number of cases, instead of the customary presentation of one single case. I have heard comments of patients who seem to be delighted to have this form of presentation. So for the present, we will continue. And today I will present to you three cases, briefly. The advantage of this method is that in the presentation of each of the three cases, one can leave out incidentals and concentrate on the essential points, on the important points that one encounters in cases of this sort.

Now, I will present to you a lady who is now forty years of age. I have seen her the first time about two months ago. And her main complaint is, and was, and still is, the fear that she will hurt herself. Well, of course, that's a common fear, and essentially nobody is free from it. I don't enjoy hurting myself and none of you, I presume, does that. And people fear injuries, but they don't go around fearing it all the time.

This lady has developed, for the past five years, the fear of injuring herself or of falling sick. And I must admit I would rather injure myself than live in the fear of injuries. I have told patients I would rather die of cancer than live in fear of cancer. I certainly would, and so it goes. And I am not at all in favor of trying to prevent cancer by causing people to dread it. These people live in continuous fear of cancer, and I, for one, think that's an awful method of trying to prevent cancer. That's all I can tell you. However, this does not go for cancer only. It goes just as well for the attempt to prevent any suffering by creating the fear of the suffering. I will tell everybody: rather die of a disease than live in fear of it.

Well, this woman, for instance, was likely to get into a panic—not only into fear—into a veritable panic if her husband or anybody bumped against her—accident[ally] of course—or if she bumped into anybody or into anything. She could not read the papers because the papers are likely to report on somebody dying or falling sick. If she saw anything on her skin—a little discoloration, something that she considered a swelling—then she again went into a panic, if in the preceding few minutes she hadn't been in one. Otherwise the panic simply continued.

When she had the suspicion that there is a little pimple on her skin, or a swelling, or some change that she has noticed but nobody else—because I have, in response to her requests, inspected the skin of her arms, of her chest, and all kinds of other parts of the body, and I could never find anything but what the ordinary skin of a person shows; and on this occasion, she would do what she does to her husband every day, and very frequently during the day: She would ask interminable questions. "Are you sure you don't see anything? Don't you see this pimple? Don't you see this swelling?" And these questions would be repeated.

And since I don't keep my patients in the office for an hour or so, as you know, I guess, she had to clear the office before long. And it was a running routine with her. I expected it each time when she left my office, that after about a minute, there was a knock at the door, and there the person was. And she asked again, "Are you sure you didn't see anything on my skin, and are you sure that isn't a swelling?" Well, I pushed her out of the door. I think it was done gently, but she denies it. And, of course, I would certainly not use any pressure because she would get a pimple on the skin then, and I would be responsible for this pimple that she saw and I couldn't see. And she did the same thing with her husband, naturally much more frequently.

And if, finally, I managed to push her (as I say, gently) through the door, and she resisted—less gently, by the way— if finally I succeeded in getting her out of my office, there came the second step in this game of coming back. She no longer knocked at the door. But five or ten minutes later, there the telephone rang—and although my telephone rings very frequently—but if it was about five minutes after she left, then I knew pretty certain that was she. And she called, and she asked again the question, "Are you sure it wasn't a pimple?" And I told her, "Yes" and hung up. There came a second ring and a third ring, but I don't remember a fourth at any time.

Well, you know if somebody reacts like this, then be sure it's a terrific force that drives him or her to act in this manner. This woman knew that it was unmannerly to proceed with this procedure, coming back through the door and pushing through the door, ringing the telephone, and again and again. She is a well-mannered lady, and when she acts like this, then be certain she is driven by an ungodly and mighty force. And while I have to discipline her and hold her down, be certain I don't relish doing it because I know how much she suffers.

Well, when she couldn't ask questions of her husband or of me, of her brother, and so forth, when she was alone and inspected [the] skin of [her] hands, for instance, or of the face in the mirror, and she had nobody to ask a question, she was alone at home, then she could sit for two and three hours and look and look and inspect her skin and keep on inspecting, as I said, for hours. And she knew that that was an obsession; she didn't fool herself. And again this element aggravated her suffering to a pitch of intensity. And this woman undoubtedly suffered exceedingly and still suffers excruciatingly. She has improved to some extent, to a very slight extent. After five years of almost continuous panic, be certain I don't expect a speedy improvement.

Now, this woman could have, of course, spotted her condition. And I want you to learn something about spotting. She could have spotted the situation as one in which she set herself up as an exception to all the rules we know of human life. The average rule of human life is to distinguish between a condition that is serious, perhaps an emergency, and a condition that is routine. And this contrast between routine and emergency is very important for spotting.

Everybody has the right—although he does not have to exercise the right—but everybody can be pardoned for developing a panic if he is faced with a real emergency. Let me say, a mother may develop a panic if something happens to the child. We understand that. But then a baby that injures herself is an emergency to a mother. We understand that. But even then mothers don't develop panics so easily, even if the baby hurts himself, except if they see that there is something very serious that happened.

Now, nothing serious ever happens to patients, to my patients, from the fact that they have symptoms, because they are nervous symptoms and therefore distressing but not dangerous. And nervous patients particularly are known among nerve specialists as individuals that develop organic, dangerous ailments far less than the remaining population. It's something remarkable that we don't know how to explain. But with the hundreds and hundreds and many hundreds of patients that I see in a brief space of time—you know, I see almost five hundred new patients every year; that's a tremendous number—and very seldom have I had an occasion to advise a patient of mine to have himself hospitalized for an organic ailment or having an operation done on him. Operations are relative rarities among nervous patients. And you now in the general population they are common experiences. And, at any rate, organic sicknesses are rarities, or relative rarities, among nervous patients. I tell you that because it is a fact, not with the idea of encouraging you, because those of you that fear that they have an organic ailment cannot be encouraged, I have found. They go on fearing and fearing. Why? Nobody knows, except that my patients, as a rule, tone down their fears, and the fear gets thinner and thinner year after year. But they keep up the fears too long to suit me and to suit themselves, naturally.

So you see, this patient should have spotted this condition of hers as dealing with pimples, with swellings, with discolorations, that, by the way, nobody ever saw but she [herself]. But even if they were there, they were routine affairs. It's routine for everybody to have a little discoloration after they hurt themselves. It's routine to have a pimple once in a while, to have a little swelling that the patient finds but not the doctor. Even if there was a little swelling, that comes and goes. And with her, she observed them at a second time, and five minutes later she didn't observe them, or two hours later she didn't. So she should have known that everything that bothered her was routine. And what did she do? She made an emergency of everything. And mark here: This patient had, first, a tendency to make an emergency out of routine, but that's what all my patients do. That's nothing new. And if that alone was the item that I wanted to discuss with you, it would be a silly undertaking to tell you anything about such a condition because all of you have had it.

You had symptoms, and you made a mountain out of them, and they were nothing but a molehill. And the mountain is the emergency and the molehill is the routine disturbance. And I look around, and when I find—well, I can't look at everybody who has presented this condition because it would take too much time—but everybody here has had to go through this situation for months or for years, the situation that is characterized by what I described in this presentation. What you have, what you suffer from are trifles, just symptoms, nervous symptoms. They are never dangerous. Hence they can never be in the nature of an emergency. But you see in your condition nothing but emergencies. Will you keep that in mind that that's not what I wanted to discuss because that's too common for being discussed among nervous patients. You have had the experience, all of you, and what I wanted to discuss is something else.

My patients mistake trivialities for very important things, or routine for emergencies. But they don't do that for five years in succession, every day, all day, and that's what this patient did. And when she declared the emergency permanent—that's what she did, a permanent emergency, that's how she looked on her life—then she did something that the average patient doesn't always do, and indeed very seldom. And that is unnatural. It's unnatural to think of something in life as permanent. That's utterly unnatural.

And what we call unnatural is this: In nature things hardly change. At any rate, we don't see changes where there is no life in nature. That's what I should say. A tree changes, a flower changes. But where there is no life, there is no change. Naturally, life means change. And a stone can remain exactly in the same form, in the same size, in the same density, in the same color, and so forth, for millions of years. No change. And that's what we call *no life.* The main criterion of life is constant change. It will be good for you to know that.

Now, when life, however, becomes disturbed by a disease, by an organic disease, then there is still life, and therefore there is still change. In a cancer, there is change. In an ulcer, there is change. But that is diseased life. And the life of a cancer is not the same as the life of a healthy tissue. But we will not discuss that. But you will understand that even in disease, where life is reduced but there is still life, this means constant change. And we simply know very few instances of diseases where the changes go down to a minimum. But there still are changes. But in the average disease, in cancer, in brain tumors, in abscesses, there is constant change. And, for instance, if [it] is a brain tumor, the headache develops. Well, the headache doesn't stay with the patient every day, all day. There are changes even there. But in nature, in dead nature—not in living nature, not in trees and plants—there is no change.

And when you watch, especially, such natural elements as a crystal, a salt crystal, that doesn't change, except if you moisten it. We know that. But if it remains as itself, it doesn't change. It may be preserved in all its qualities for millions of years. And if a thing doesn't change in life, then we say it is like nature, and especially like crystal, and we call that *crystallized*.

And this patient's symptoms became lifeless and crystallized because they didn't change. I hope you understand that. She could have spotted that and say, "That cannot happen in nature," in life, I mean. In life, that cannot happen. But then I would have told her, "But you must make one exception." There is in life, for instance in me, one thing that doesn't have to change. You see, my impulses constantly change. My feelings constantly change. Naturally, the tissues constantly change. I will not discuss that. They constantly move. The heart constantly moves. The lungs constantly expand and contract. The bowels propel the food in the stomach and the intestines. They constantly work. This means move and live.

One thing in human life can become crystallized, one thing only. And that is a belief or a thought, both ordinary thought and a belief. If you have the thought that two and two is four, that remains so for all your life and all eternity. That never changes. You can't change it. And if you have the thought that Columbus discovered America on a certain year—maybe I will not mention it because I might have forgotten it, might make a mistake and will not want to expose myself—if you say that Columbus discovered America in 1492—well, there it is—that is true for all eternity. That will never change. If it is a true fact, it will never change. And that a human being has two legs, that will never change as far as we know. Well, it may, but so far it hasn't changed, you know. And if I tell you that this is a table, be sure if the table is not destroyed, it will be a table for eternity, and so forth.

And I told you that is also true of beliefs. But the ordinary belief comes and goes. If I say I believe it's raining, then I know for sure in half an hour it most likely will not be raining, and my belief will be gone. And if I say that, let me say, the atomic bomb is a great invention, well, in a minute later I may change it and say it's a rotten invention—which is correct, by the way, in my opinion. But my opinion may change because it's a belief, too, you know. And if I believe that somebody is my friend, in five minutes I can change it after he may make a statement that shows me he is not such a good friend, you know, and so forth.

But there are certain beliefs that never change. For instance, if somebody has the belief that his mother is a great person, well, I presume he will never change that. In the overwhelming majority of the cases, he will not change it. And if we believe that people should be honest, well, let us hope we will never change that. You know, with certain principles, [they] don't change. They may change, but some of them don't change, you know.

And you see and that's what the patient does. Either he crystallizes his symptoms or he converts them into a mere thought, like Columbus discovered America, and that never changes, and his symptoms don't change. Or, he creates out of his symptoms a principle, an endorsed belief, a sacred belief. He defends it. If anybody slurs it, he defends it. He will fight, he's ready to fight anybody who will claim that his trouble is imaginary. Patients are ready to fight for their symptoms. So apparently they have endowed them and invested them with something that resembles a principle. For principle, human beings fight, and patients fight for their symptoms. They defend them. They stage battles with the members of their family. They try to convince them that their beliefs are wrong, that the relatives' beliefs are wrong, and their own beliefs are right. See, they make a crusade out of their suffering and crusade for the truthfulness of their symptoms or of their beliefs about their symptoms. And once a patient does that, what am I going to do about it? How am I going to help him? If he makes a sacred principle out of his symptoms and defends his belief about them, then there will be a running fight between him and me, and how can I get him well as speedily as I would like to?

And that thing that constantly moves in life, for instance, the heart, the intestines, the blood, naturally, constantly moves—my feelings, my thoughts, my thoughts if I let them move—if I don't make principles out of them. My impulses, my sensations, everything moves. And we call that *the life's pulse*. And we say everything within a human being pulsates. And if we find a human being crystallized, then we'll say, well, life ceased pulsating within him.

And that's what my patients do to themselves. They create rigid principles and apply them to their symptoms. And the rigidity of the principles excludes the pulse, the pulse of life, within that region of their symptoms. And this patient should have mainly spotted this item: that there is a fear, a panic, an emergency that has preserved itself for five solid years and has established crystallization. And that can never be done by anything except by thought, not by feelings, not by impulses. And once she would have spotted that, she would have known that's nerves. It's only thoughts, beliefs, that create nervous symptoms. They can't create organic symptoms. And that should have, of course, disabused her of the belief that these are real pimples, real bleedings, real discolorations. And if she had applied this principle of spotting, she would have been improved, or well, within a relatively short time.

[Continued in Lecture 68.]

444

LECTURE 68

IMPULSES, SELF-BLAME AND FATE

28 Minutes [Continued from Lecture 67]
Recorded Tuesday, May 4, 1954

I will then present to you another case, leaving out the inessentials. It was a young woman that I saw the day before yesterday for the first time, and so I cannot give you an account of whether she is improving or not. You can't expect anybody to improve noticeably in two days. I will merely discuss her case, and I will tell you what I am going to tell her in point of how to spot her symptoms. I haven't done that yet. Didn't have an opportunity. I just saw her once.

She reported that ten years ago, in 1944, she went on a vacation in good spirits. She had always been more or less a nervous individual. Well, who is not nervous these days? And she went on a vacation, and there she roomed with a girlfriend that was very sympathetic to her. There was quite a solid friendship between the two. And one day, while they took a walk, my patient felt the impulse to push her girlfriend against a tree. Then she got the impulse to knock her down, and for no reason. And my patient became scared. She developed a real fright. And she didn't like the vacation any longer, naturally. And she cut it short and returned to Chicago.

And she felt better until, before long, she felt the impulse on the street to strike people, strangers. Of course, she didn't do it. When she was in a party, she felt the impulse to yell. Well, you understand that this is a very disquieting and alarming experience for anybody, and she became

445

alarmed. And when I saw her the day before—oh, pardon me, it was yesterday—when I saw her yesterday, she added, "Well, I had all kinds of other silly impulses." And I asked her, "Tell me some." She wouldn't. So, she was ashamed of them. Now, mind you, those impulses that she mentioned, she was not ashamed of. She was ready to tell me. Of course, she wouldn't tell them [to] strangers. And the other symptoms she was ashamed to mention even to me. She knew a physician doesn't talk about any patient. And be sure I don't. You know that.

Well, I know these impulses, and I want to tell you something about them. I don't know exactly what kind of impulses, what specific kind of impulses she had that she called silly. But patients have a way of calling silly something that may impress them as more than silly, but they don't want to use a stronger term. Now, briefly, there are too many people—I think the majority of all people—that have all kinds of thoughts that one wouldn't like to speak of even to friends and perhaps not even to one's doctor.

First of all, people have the impulse, really, to grab things. They don't just do that, but they have the impulse. They pass by a jewelry store or a fine display in some window, and they feel the impulse, if they only could get hold of something there. And then you know that people actually have the impulse to steal, and you call them *the kleptomaniacs,* and I have seen quite a few of them from the finest families. It has nothing to do with morals. That's an impulse.

And then there are sex impulses. And among the sex impulses, particularly things that happen in [a] dream and people remember, and that is the impulse and the fact of sleeping with one's mother or with one's father. And people in general, if they have such dreams, are thoroughly ashamed of them. Well, there is nothing to be ashamed of. I remember distinctly having had such dreams, and at that time they scared me no end. Today, of course, I have gone through the mill of training and through the mill of symptoms, and I know there is nothing to it. And I am ready to admit that I had such dreams and had them frequently. But patients don't know that, and so I have to tell them that that's nothing to be ashamed of.

But at that time, ten years ago, that patient was not under my care, because yesterday I saw her for the first time. And you know that although she went to physicians for treatment and for relief, well, at any rate, the physicians didn't tell her anything about the fact that her impulses were nothing to be ashamed of. And for solid ten years so far, this woman has walked the earth constantly in an inner panic—not in an outer panic—that she was doomed, that her morals and her ethics were irredeemably lost. And along came a man and wooed her, and she liked him, and she held him off for years and finally married him. But you see, I mentioned that only in order to show you how handicapped such a person can be. She was afraid to get married, because she felt she was contaminated, morally contaminated.

And I have seen patients that had frightful impulses that they wouldn't talk about—but naturally some of them have talked to me—patients who entered a church and had to swear. That happens. I don't know how often, but it happens with people who would not call themselves patients, and with patients, naturally, too.

Well, this person could, of course, have spotted these symptoms, well, for instance, as something that is no danger. It's only distressing. The ordinary type of spotting that we practice in Recovery, that would have helped her. But then this patient would have told you, "Well, I know it's not going to kill me. I know it is not dangerous. You don't have to tell me that." Yes, she says, "I know." And I have heard that from patients. If I told them, "Well, spot your impulses as distressing but not dangerous," and they say, "Of course, I know this is not going to kill me. The impulse, whether sexual or immoral or otherwise or blasphemous, is not going to kill me. I know that, but I can't stand it."

So, I have to explain to them that when we speak of danger, we don't just think of those dangers that kill. We think of all kinds of other dangers. The danger that might kill is a physical danger. And naturally my patients, after having gone through some training in Recovery, ought to know— and many of them do know—that they are not in physical danger. But they will come back and say, "But how about psychologically speaking? Is my mind not in danger?" And then they say, "Well, there is a danger." Well, then I'll tell them, "Well, no, your mind is not in danger. I have examined you, and I ought to know whether you are a candidate for a mental disease or not. And if I tell you you are not, you better accept my statement." You know.

Then a patient may come up and say, "I know that there is no physical danger and no mental danger to my symptoms, but, after all, I don't like them." And by this they mean to say, well, there is some other danger. And there is. Or, at any rate, they say, "I knew that. What you tell me is nothing new to me." Then I tell them, "Well, there are other dangers, and you have to spot them."

There is the danger that we call *moral*. This means you are afraid that your impulses are—although they are not dangerous to your body and your mind—nevertheless they are impulses of which one ought to be ashamed. They're a disgrace. And whenever you call an impulse or a symptom a disgrace, then, of course, you fear it. That impulse, that symptom is a danger, because if somebody should know about this, it would be a social danger. People might misunderstand the meaning of that symptom, and they might condemn you. And if that happens, patients are stigmatized because of such symptoms. That, I am sure it is true, and I have seen it.

And I want you to know that if you want to spot a symptom, you must spot many kinds of dangers. Well, I have mentioned in my book three cardinal dangers: The fear of a danger that we call *physical collapse,* and another danger that we call *mental collapse,* and a third danger, *the fear of the sustained handicap,* the fear of incurability. But now I mention, for instance, the fear of the moral danger, the fear of the ethical danger. People are afraid, for instance, that they have some-thing on their body and somebody may see it. That's the aes-thetic danger. They will not undress in front of people. They will not take off their coats while others take them off at the permission of the host, and so forth. They have an aesthetic danger. There is the economic danger. There is the danger that a member of the family entertains because another mem-ber is ill, and so forth. There are all kinds of dangers.

And if I tell a patient that you are afraid of a danger, don't immediately pipe up and say, "No." Stop this silly *no* when you talk to me. Why should you contest my statements, if you come to me as an expert? And to you, I know I am the outstanding expert. I know how my patients happen to think of me. Why then do you engage in arguments with me? Well, I can only tell you, drop them. Then you will be a wise per-son. And I will be a comfortable person.

So, do you see, that patient could have spotted her symptoms as being due to the fact that she fears them, that she fears them to be dangerous. She could. On the other hand, she could have also spotted them as exceptionality. You know, everybody has impulses. Every patient certainly has violent impulses and nothing happens. So why was she afraid that something would happen with her? She could have applied that. She could also have applied our rule that she diagnosed, and she should have stopped that. She should rather accept my diagnosis of a harmless condition instead of her own diagnosis of something very serious, and so forth. She could have diagnosed it as a case of temper because be sure she became disgusted with herself, and that is inner tem-per. And as long as she is disgusted with herself because of these symptoms, she creates tenseness and tenseness and piles up tenseness, and therefore the symptoms crystallize. They don't disappear.

She could have done this spotting, but this we will not discuss. I will again, like in the foregoing case, discuss a type of spotting that is not well treated in my book. And I want to tell you something about it, although those of you that have

449

attended these classes frequently might have heard this matter already that I am going to discuss.

Look here. When I have an impulse, be certain I did not summon it. I did not call it into being. I didn't make any effort to get this impulse started, especially if it is an impulse that I hate, that I don't want. Then be certain I am not responsible for it. This means I didn't create it. I didn't do anything to bring it to the fore. So why should I blame myself? Why should I feel disgraced if I have any kind of symptom, whether it is the kind of symptoms that I mentioned that are blasphemous or disgraceful because they relate to your sexual affinity to your mother, and so forth? I didn't want this impulse. I didn't summon it forth. I didn't make any effort to put it into life. So, why should I call myself responsible for what goes on within me, and why should I blame myself? And that's what this patient, of course, did. That's what all of you do.

If you have something undesirable within you and you become ashamed of it—stigmatized, in other words—you blame yourself. You hold yourself responsible for having this condition. And if you do that, you distinguish between two spheres of life. And it would be good if you did that consciously, but you only do it intuitively. You distinguish between things in this world for which you are responsible and other things for which you are not responsible.

Of course, you know that you are not responsible, let me say, for rain and thunder. And even if the thunder strikes your home and destroys the home, destroys your prosperity, you will not blame yourself. You will say it was done by thunder, by lightning. And lightning we call *fate*. And whenever I'll tell you that you are responsible for something, then I mean to imply that you could have prevented that thing. And you can only prevent a thing if you exercise your will. And if I say that you are responsible for it because you could have prevented it, and then I tell you again that if you had prevented it, you would have exercised your will, then you will realize that here I contrast will with fate. These are contrasts.

The lightning strikes without anybody willing it, without anybody telling the clouds to strike. I presume that nobody [inaudible] that. But the human will does things because it wills. And if you want to do something, then you are responsible for what you are going to do or for what you did. And if it is an act that is disgraceful, you better feel ashamed of yourself.

And now it will be good for you to know this distinction between what happens by fate and what is done by will. It will be very good for you to know that consciously. You know it intuitively, but that will not help you. You must have it at your fingertips. You must know it consciously. You must always be able to present it to yourself, to view it, to know it. And merely knowing it dimly, that will not help you.

And every patient knows the distinction. For instance, the patient doesn't say, if he strikes his leg against the table, he doesn't say the table is responsible. That's nonsense. He might say that it was his fault, he is responsible, but he will never call the table responsible for anything. He knows this is fate, that a table is hard and just stands here. That wasn't done by my will. Even if it were, striking something against the table is not considered a will action. And if you are stricken with a pneumonia, that wasn't done by your will. That is fate, and so forth.

And be sure if somebody is born with a nervous system that is allergic to tenseness, that is fate. Take it from me. It is not true that you have developed your nervous condition through strain. Otherwise everybody would be a nervous patient. Where is there a person today that isn't under constant strain? There is no such thing. And to develop symptoms, well, we all develop symptoms because we are under constant strain.

But if you have a nervous system that is highly sensitive to tenseness, you react differently from what the ordinary person does. The ordinary person has symptoms galore, but they come and go. That's all. Because his nervous system is not as sensitive to tenseness as yours is. And if you are as sensitive as you have shown to be, then once you have a terrible scare, it will stay with you for a much longer period than with the average person. Your nervous system is too sensitive to absorb a shock easily, and once you are shocked, it's likely to stay on with you for some time. Either for ten minutes—but then with the non-sensitive person, it would have only have stayed on for one minute or a few seconds—or it stays on with you for two days or for three weeks. That's usually what happens in the beginning, and then it disappears. And if it then comes back and stays on longer, well, then you will know that is because your nervous system is so sensitive to tenseness. And you were born with this nervous system. That's the difference between you and somebody else who was not born with such a nervous system.

But then it is your duty to train your nervous system in such a manner that it gains resistance to tenseness. And that's what we do in Recovery. And you who go through this train-ing, strengthen the resistance of your nervous system and reduce its sensitivity. If you cooperate, then you will get your nervous system straightened out very soon, and if you don't cooperate, well, it will take longer. That's the difference between the cooperative patient and the less cooperative patient.

And if you begin to spot your nervous condition under the heading *will or fate,* then you naturally should immedi-ately spot it: That is fate. You have been born with a nervous system that is too sensitive for its own good. But now, in Recovery, you can go on spotting. You are being trained to develop resistance, to reduce the sensitivity of your nervous system. So, spot your nervous symptoms in two ways: First, you are not responsible for them. They have been created by fate. You are not even responsible for treating them right, because nobody has shown you how to do it until you came to Recovery.

Now, this patient that I've mentioned had gone for ten years suffering from her nervous system. And she could not have changed the situation, because nobody had trained her how to strengthen the resistance of her nervous system. Well,

I can't say anything as yet about this patient, but I have told you that that's how I am going to train her. That's what I am going to induce her to accept from me, to learn that her symptoms have been given her by fate. No matter how terrible her impulses were, they were given her by fate. She couldn't have called forth such impulses. It wasn't her way of doing that. It was against her nature. But fate gave her these symptoms.

And she will be trained to strengthen her resistance with our methods, so that henceforth when such an impulse comes—and it always comes by fate—I get such impulses, much more dreadful impulses, but my nerves have been steeled and trained to develop resistance. And [when] dreadful and mischievous and lascivious and blasphemous impulses reach my brain, I look away and wait till they depart. And they depart in no time, because my resistance has been strengthened. And fate is not strong enough to break my resistance once it is strengthened through training.

And what I am going to tell this lady, when I see her next week, I felt I should tell you, because this lady suffers from the same condition that you are suffering from, or have been suffering from. And the finest way of spotting such a condition of impulses, particularly that are repulsive to the person, is to remember: These impulses have [been] given you by fate. Your will has nothing to do with them. You will be responsible for these impulses if somebody comes along and shows you the way to get rid of them, how to strengthen your nervous system, and you refuse to accept what he tells you. And that's what I call *sabotage*. And I want to stress it here, you are never responsible for your system, but you are responsible for not accepting the training that I give you. That means, you are responsible for sabotaging my authority.

Thank you.

LECTURE 69

FEAR CAN CREATE A PSYCHOLOGICAL DISORDER (PART 1)

30 Minutes

Recorded Tuesday, November 17, 1953

The patient whom I will discuss tonight is a man [in his] late forties, and he was examined by me in March 1951. I will quote a statement or two that he made at that time. He said, "As far back as I can recall, I have always worried about every pain and ache I felt." Well, that doesn't mean a great deal. It means, well, that he was a complainer or a worrier. He may not have complained, but he certainly worried. This means he felt unsure of himself, self-conscious, and suffered most likely, and became restless, for sure. And he made another statement, saying, "I feel like jumping out of my skin."

Well, I mention these facts because he obviously was not a well-adjusted person at any time in his adult life and maybe since childhood. To illustrate the restlessness he suffered from, I will quote another statement. He couldn't stand waiting for trains or for elevators and became edgy whenever he had to wait for anything. For instance, let me say, he had to wait for somebody who was expected to come to the house at some hour and was late. Well, if somebody can't wait, and has to wait, well, that's frustration. And it is frustration because the person does not manage to bear discomfort. Now, don't misunderstand me. I don't like to be kept waiting either, and nobody perhaps does. But this patient was extremely restless under such conditions. Well, I mention all these things in order to tell you about what kind of a personality the man was before he developed symptoms. All of what I mentioned were not symptoms. They were personality traits.

Then, in 1948, that means three years before I saw him, his mother had a stroke. And she lingered on for another three years. Two months before I saw the patient, she passed away. And now the patient told me, during the three years, he attempted to find a suitable home for the mother, but somehow he couldn't. What that means does not matter, that he couldn't find a home. Presumably, there were only unsuitable homes, or too expensive homes. I know the situation, and this is most likely the case.

Two weeks after his mother passed away—and remember she had a stroke; I'll return to this feature—two weeks after the mother passed away, his brother-in-law collapsed suddenly and died. And at the same time, a close friend of his died suddenly on the street. That was a collapse. So, you will understand that this man had witnessed, either close by or at some distance, three cases in which the heart had given out. And he began to worry about his heart, but the worry was prepared. He did not just begin to worry about a heart condition three months or two months before I saw him. The mother had a stroke three years before I saw the patient. And a stroke used to be conceived by the lay people as a stroke and nothing else. Today, the situation has changed, and it has changed because of a most unfortunate development.

Today we live in an age where certain people—professional, semi-professional, and lay—have suddenly conceived the idea [that] they want to get rid of disease. They want to prevent disease. They want to do everything to create a happy humanity, which is, of course a very laudable enterprise. But the way these people go about it is deplorable.

There are associations today—all over, not only in this country—that set themselves the goal to prevent heart disease, or to find everybody conceivably suffering from a heart disease and get him to the doctor's office for treatment. And there is perhaps no objection to such an endeavor. But it's remarkable that if people become enthusiastic about an issue, they tend to make a crusade. And there are now going on dreadful crusades for the prevention of heart diseases, of cancer, of leukemia.

One nice young lady approached me the other day on the street telling me about leukemia, holding in front of my nose a container to drop money in. And I tell you this development, which I don't want to criticize otherwise, has been a bane to my patients. This development spreads terror into the population, because of the statements that these associations make; because, second, of the insistency and the eagerness with which they try to scare the population into a fear which will make them come to the doctor's office or to these screening—well—squads I guess I'll call them. And too many patients come to me with a scare that has been inflicted on them by the health crusaders. What they do is simply unbelievable.

This patient of mine saw a poster, which I saw too, which had the audacity and the unscrupulousness to state that two out of three die of heart diseases. There is not a scintilla of evidence for such a thing; the evidence points exactly the other way. And I want to explain that to you, so that you do not fall victim to this crusader instinct that is spread all around you. I want you to know the following things:

Everybody is likely to die of his heart—not of a heart disease, of his heart. If I will die without an infection, then I will die of an old-age heart, but not of a heart disease. Naturally, if somebody dies what we call a natural death, if he is not carried away by a severe infection, by a bullet wound, by an accident, then, of course, he dies of his heart. The heart gives out. If you want to find out whether somebody is still living, you examine the heart, whether it still beats. And out of this fact that everybody—or at any rate the majority of humanity—naturally dies of the heart, these crusaders have made the slogan that two out of three die out of heart disease. That's a falsification, a brazen falsification. And the men that are on the board of these organizations ought to know that. They ought to know that only a relatively small proportion of humanity dies of a heart disease.

Well, I could say something else that I will not say; it would lead us far afield. But this is an extremely irresponsible statement. And I will advise you, whenever you are approached by these organizations with pamphlets, with pronouncements, with posters on the street—well, I guess you have to see the posters; you may want to read the pronouncements, but be very careful—and I will advise you: Don't believe what they tell you. You shouldn't believe certain facts that they tell you, but since you can't discriminate between the facts that are correct and those facts that are monstrously exaggerated, I will advise you to take everything these associations say with a pound of salt, not a grain.

Well, plenty of my patients have suffered from the audacious statements sent forth by these organizations into the population. This patient did likewise. He was surrounded by an atmosphere in which vicious suggestions were fired at him by newspapers, by magazines, by the pronouncements of these well-meaning but ill-advised societies. I presume they are well-meaning. I don't think they are commercial. I am sure they are not. But they are crusaders, and crusaders are dangerous, because they have no sense of proportion. And so my patient—largely through the experiences that he had, naturally, with the three deaths that occurred in quick succession, but to a great extent abetted by the crusader spirit of these organizations and the newspaper health columns and the magazines that write about health and frequently make again exaggerated statements—developed a fear that he is doomed to collapse from a heart disease.

And the next thing that he knew, he had a dizziness— well, whatever a dizziness means—but he felt unsure on his feet. His gait was unsteady; he swayed; he thought he swayed. He developed a condition that many patients develop, a so-called light-headedness. And he became unsteady and dizzy, on the street and in his place of work—

he has a store—but not at home. Not at home. You understand what that means. I have told you about these distinctions that patients make.

Now this patient thought that he has a damaged heart.
What does a damaged heart know about the difference
whether it beats now at home or on the street? The heart
doesn't know the distinction between home and street. And
you will understand that the patient could reason. This particular patient has a good intellect, a sharp intellect, indeed.
He could have easily reasoned that a damaged heart will beat
and have skipped beats and palpitations, and will cause chest
pain—if it ever does—both at home and on the street. But the
patient doesn't want to reason. He immediately becomes convinced, although he is not really convinced, but he sticks to
his shaky conviction for some reason that I have described in
the Recovery News. But will you realize that every patient is
contradictory, and I have recently described a case to you in
which the contradictions teemed, were teeming. And there
were not too few contradictions in this patient's case.

And I will repeat: Whenever a patient makes for his
symptoms these strict distinctions of having a dizziness on
the street but never, or seldom, at home, then you will understand that such a symptom cannot come from a damaged
organ. And whenever you have such a distinction, then you
could be sure that this is nervous. Only the brain can make
such a distinction, not the heart, damaged or undamaged. It's
good for you to know that.

And he developed a fear of driving his car, but he could
ride in it. Now, how does a damaged heart know whether the
owner of the heart is a driver or a rider? If it was dangerous
for the damaged heart to sit in the automobile, then it was of
no consequence whether he was a driver or a rider. And this
patient of ours, and countless thousands of other patients,
could easily make this distinction, the distinction between the
brain that can conceive a difference between two localities,
and the heart that cannot.

And he developed a fear of being alone. Well, we will
not discuss that. Anybody can develop the fear of being

alone, with or without disease. And since my office is on the seventeenth floor, he was afraid to come up to the seventeenth floor, because he had [a] fear of heights. And he had the fear of heights because he was afraid [that] when he is somewhere up on the seventeenth or twentieth or fifteenth floor, and should a window there be open, he might be close to the window and begin to sway and flop on the street. Well, that sounds ridiculous, but why should symptoms be serious or wise? Symptoms are naturally ridiculous if they are nervous symptoms, but they cause so much trouble that you can't speak of ridicule.

He had, of course, all kinds of common symptoms. The ones I mentioned are closely related to the heart. The others, which I will mention, are partly related and partly not. For instance: blurring of vision, fatigue, lowered interests, and so forth. So many patients have them. But he had them mainly in the morning. In the evening, he felt fine, frequently or [inaudible]. On Sundays, he never felt good. Sundays were his worst days, as they are with most patients. And I'll ask you again: A damaged heart doesn't know when it's Sunday and when it's a weekday; why should a damaged heart—if his symptoms were due largely or mainly or exclusively to the damaged heart—how can a damaged heart know when it's Sunday or holiday or Wednesday? And the patient could easily convince himself that when he is face to face with such contradictions, that it can't be organic diseases. Diseases are not contradictory.

If somebody has a headache due to a brain tumor, that headache will never stop precisely on Sundays. It's all nonsense. And if somebody is paralyzed, he can't get up and jump around on a holiday. You see, organic ailments are never contradictory. Nervous ailments are frequently or usually contradictory. And if you keep that in mind, then it will not be difficult for you to discover that your condition is definitely nervous; this means no damage to any organ.

Well, we want to ask how the patient got well, our famous question that we always attach to the discussion of a case. How did he get well? The patient is here, together with his dear wife, and they listen. I hope they listen. What happened to a patient of this kind is this: Ordinarily our body, including the nervous system, but particularly the organic part of the body, is in order. Keep this term in mind. Everything in the body is in order, unless there is a disease. Then there is disorder, the disorder of a disease. And what is disordered in a disease is, for instance, if the body is paralyzed, then naturally—I mean if the body suffers a stroke and there is a paralysis—then be sure the total action of the individual is disordered. He can't make a visit, socially disordered. He can't raise his hand to eat. He must be fed. He is physically disordered. He is psychologically disordered, too, not only socially and physically, also psychologically. For instance, he can't speak if he has a stroke in a certain part of the brain. He has perhaps twitches. That's a disorder, disordered function of the muscles. So health means order, and disease means disorder. In disease, it is disorder due to damage, but there is another disorder.

While I am sitting here, I can easily create a disorder in myself. All I have to do is to remind myself that this afternoon I was exposed to the heat of the November sun to an unfortunate degree, and I was for some reason. And I had a topcoat on and carried a heavy load for some reason. And all of a sudden, I felt a pounding in the head. And I can assure you that I am a tolerably healthy individual, and there is no reason in the world why my head should have pounded, no reason of an organic nature, no damage that would explain it. So, why did my head pound? Well, you can say exertion and advancing years, I must admit. Well, I could now work myself up over this experience. I could say my years are advancing, so I can't carry on as I used to. I can try to persuade myself—or accept the suggestion without persuading myself—that things are not so well-ordered on my ledger. Then I could begin to worry. I could look ahead to the coming years and remember that my work is not completed yet. And will I not be snatched away without knowing anything about it? I could conceive all these ideas. Then I would not create a damage in my body but a psychological disorder, not a physio-logical disorder, at any rate no damage.

And that's what our patient did. He accepted certain suggestions from his environment: First, he got the sugges-tion that it's very easy for people to collapse either at home or on the street. And once he got this suggestion, he could con-ceivably have shaken it off. In former years, in former decades, people got suggestions the same as we get now. But they shook them off in the overwhelming proportion of cases. But I want again to tell you that today things have changed. There is too much talk about collapses and the danger of heart diseases and the danger of cancer. Cancer is dangerous. I don't deny that. Heart diseases are dangerous. But if you constantly talk and think and hear about the danger of organic diseases, you will not develop an organic disease from this. That will not cause any damage in you. It will, however, cause fear, and the fear will cause a psychological disorder of everything, of the blood vessels particularly. And I want to tell you something about what fear does to the blood vessels. Fear doesn't do anything to the bones. I doubt it.

[Continued in Lecture 70.]

FEAR CAN CREATE A PSYCHOLOGICAL DISORDER (PART 2)

24 Minutes [Continued from Lecture 69]
Recorded Tuesday, November 17, 1953

While fear doesn't do anything to the bones, it does something very disastrous and deleterious to other structures in the body. And I want to tell you, briefly: Fear, or emotions in general, act on those structures in the body that are in the form of a tube, the so-called *[hollow] organs.* First, the blood vessels, and particularly the small blood vessels, the capillaries that are in touch with every particle of the body; but second, the stomach, the esophagus, the bronchi, the intestines, the gall bladder, and so forth. Fear, as far as we know, does no harm to the solid organs, to the liver, to the spleen, in other words. But wherever there is a hollow organ, either blood vessels, capillaries, and so forth, and the other organs that I mentioned, it does something to the tubes.

These tubes work in a very precise manner. They constantly contract and dilate. They narrow the tube and widen it. And that is their function. And so we get from the blood vessels, when they narrow themselves and widen themselves, the so-called pulse, the heart pulse, the blood vessel pulse. And when the bronchi widen or narrow, then you get the breathing rhythm, inspiration and expiration. And so it goes with the intestines, with the rectum, with all the hollow organs. They are innervated by two sets of nerves. The one nerve narrows them, the other widens them. That's all you have to know.

And if it's, for instance, with regard to the heart, one set of nerves widens the heart, and then blood flows in. The other set of nerves narrows it, and blood flows out. And these two sets of nerves, both of them or one singly, are subject to the influence particularly of fear or anger. They are subject to the effect of the so-called *antisocial feelings,* that's fear and anger mainly. And whenever you become angry or fearful, you do something to the heart, that means to the nerves that go to the heart. You don't cause any damage. But you throw the nerves that go to the heart, to the lungs, to the gall bladder, and so forth, intestines, you throw them into disorder, not damage, into disorder.

They don't work in an orderly fashion, and for this [one-]minute or ten-minute period that you work yourself up emotionally, you work up the nerves that go to the organs. And you either produce too much widening of these organs or too much narrowing. And if you do that for ten minutes, this short period of disturbance has no effect. If after ten minutes you calm down, then the nerves get a rest, and they are as refreshed as ever. You can't do any harm to nerves. If you give them some sort of a rest, even for one fraction of a second, for this fraction of a second, they are relaxed, and their function is restored. No damage done. You can't do damage to nerves. And through nerves, you can't do damage to the organs. It's good for you to know that.

But if the emotional upset goes on and goes on and never stops or hardly ever stops, then you upset, not the organs, but the function of the organs. It's one thing to speak of the stomach and another thing to speak of its functions. The stomach cannot be damaged by any disturbance that you produce in the nerves, even if you produce it all your life, every day of your life. But the function of the stomach can be disturbed. You can disturb the production of hydrochloric acid. You can disturb the movements of the stomach. You can disturb your appetite, your eating function. And then you suffer. And you can, of course, produce the empty feeling in the stomach, vomiting, nausea. Then you suffer. And let me tell you, briefly, what you can produce is suffering. No damage. Intense suffering, but no damage. Or, let me say, you can produce disturbance to the functions of the organs but no damage to their structures.

That's all very well, but we want to know more about this thing of the disorder. When you develop a fear, and you disturb the function of your organs—their function only— then in all likelihood you will stop fearing sometime, in all likelihood. But if you are exposed to a concerted effort on the part of great organizations to strike fear into your head, well, that may go on for endless years and all your life. And let me tell you, there are too many efforts made today, systematically, continuously, first, to strike fear into the population, to constantly warn them of dangers without any visible use, and perhaps, let me tell you, without any visible advantage. To me, there is [no] visible advantage [for] these associations that scare the population systematically. And that's why I want to discuss that. Whether they produce good results, I don't know. The literature is very confusing, and nobody has ever been able to demonstrate that these associations do any good, except for one association. I don't want to mention it, because the others will be howling if they know about my effort here with my patients—if I mean anything to them. I don't know.

Mark it: If you scare yourself, that's not dangerous. If you are gullible and accept some suggestions that come from the inside, or from the outside—scary suggestions—if the suggestions don't come systematically, if they are not organized by some group that is then addicted to the spread of fear suggestions, then the average individual reaches a point where he changes his attitude, and the fears drop out. Remember that a hundred years ago, nobody knew of a nerve specialist. That wasn't known. Surgeons were known, internists were known, but not nerve specialists. Psychiatrists were unheard of. A hundred years ago, nobody knew of a phobia. The term hadn't been formed. It is now eighty years that the first phobia was described by a professor in Berlin. Up to that time, nobody knew of phobias. They existed, I guess, but they were insignificant in number; otherwise we would have known of them. Remember that.

That means plenty of people a hundred years ago conceived dreadful fears, but they faded away in time. But today you are not permitted to let your fears, when you are gripped by them, to fade away. There is an organized, systematic effort all over to scare you. And I have to talk to you about it because it scares particularly my patients.

Second, nerves are not only subject to the influence of fear and anger, but also to the influence of continuous, or more or less continuous, excitement. Whether it is gruesome excitement or funny excitement does not matter. And there is an organized, systematic attempt all over to constantly treat you to excitements. Well, I can't say anything about that, because I am sure it is not done by professional people. I am particularly against the deleterious effort of fear and hopelessness spread by organizations founded for the purpose of benefiting humanity. And if they scare my patients, I must do something about it with you, or with you only.

The excitements that are also very dangerous to the functions of the nervous system—no damage, again I must always tell you, but dangerous to the function, no damage to the structure—these excitements are usually produced by commercial elements, and I can't speak of them. We know that these commercial elements are sometimes not very responsible. But professional people should always be responsible.

Now, I remember—and with this I'll strike a personal note—that when I took my final examination for the purpose of getting my degree, I was given a case to diagnose, a middle-aged man who suffered from a certain heart disease. And I had to tell the professor at the end of the examination what I had found. And I told him, and everything was lovely. Apparently, my diagnosis and my comments on it pleased the professor. And in the end he flunked me. It was many, many years ago. And so I went up to the professor and asked him, "Well, what happened? You seemed to be pleased with my answers, with my diagnosis." He said, "Yes, I was very pleased. You did well." So, I asked him why he flunked me. So, he said, "There is a simple reason. I asked you what was the prognosis of this patient, and you said it was hopeless. And you said that in front of the patient, and therefore I flunked you." That was the general principle thirty-five and forty years ago. Well, I shouldn't have told you the number of years. You can draw conclusions from that. But that was the general principle. Whether you knew your medicine or not was naturally important for examinations. "But in addition, you must know how to talk to patients," the professor said. "If you don't know how to talk to patients, if you scare your patient, then you can't deal with patients. You must not be permitted to get a diploma." And I had to take the examination again. I was furious and did something to my hollow organs, but I learned a lesson, the lesson that patients must, under no circumstances, be scared, even if you think you do them good. "The end does not sanction the means," my professor told me. "Even if you think you have made a good diagnosis, don't go on talking and gabbing before the patient."

And there has been, for ages and for centuries, a principle that was binding on anybody that was professionally taking care of patients. And that principle stated that a patient must have only one physician. Two physicians were bad. A thousand physicians for one patient were, of course, a disaster. One physician, a patient must have. That one physician may confuse the patient, may treat him wrong, but he will not do him any damage. He will give him only one confusion. But two physicians will give him two confusions, and that's bad. One physician may give the patient a wrong diagnosis and a wrong opinion. That will not do great harm, provided the condition is not serious. But let the patient have a mild condition, and the one doctor tells the patient it's a severe heart damage, the other says, "Well, I don't find any condition of heart damage," and the third comes and says, "It's nerves," and the fourth gives another diagnosis. That patient is confused fourfold. That's bad. He doesn't know where to turn.

Well, briefly, in my days when I studied medicine, this so-called Hippocratic—not the "hypocritic"—tenet, principle, that a patient must have one physician only, that stood and held good for two thousand five hundred years almost. And today we don't see it any more. Today the health columns make diagnoses; the associations which I mentioned spread terror into the population with their diagnoses. They teach the patients how to watch themselves, and naturally the patients watch themselves with fear, not with joy. And they teach the patients how to make diagnoses. For instance, in cancer of the breast, they teach the patients to become expert diagnosticians of the most pernicious sort, fear diagnosticians.

And all I wanted to tell you was that here in Recovery, a patient of the kind that I described, has been purged of his fear. And that's how he got well. And in order to purge him of the fear, I had to train him to listen to me only. Or, if he wanted to consult somebody, to consult somebody, some one only, and not two, three, four and five consultants. But that's not enough. On top of it, I have to train my patients not to listen to those circles that initiate an organized, systematic terror campaign which they call an effort to eradicate diseases, to benefit humanity. Well, I don't know much about humanity, but I know a great deal about my patients. And I don't want you to benefit by this organized, systematic fear campaign.

After this patient that I discussed had first imbibed the principle that a patient must have one physician only, then I was sure he wouldn't go around shopping among doctors. Then he had to be trained in the manner that you know: not to self-diagnose and not to indulge in temper. But, third, he had also to be trained to listen to the radio, to television, to read posters in the streetcars, in the buses, emanating from these societies that I mentioned, and to discard them immediately, eliminate them from his attention, from his brain. And after he had learned that, he got well gradually. Nobody can get well in two days or in two weeks or in two months. I have not seen that.

And this is our technique, as you know, except that

467

today I wanted to talk about those fear suggestions that don't emanate from your own inner suggestions, nor from haphazard suggestions that you pick up from the street—from somebody collapsing and somebody else having a stroke—but also from the vicious suggestions offered you by organized, systematic, well-wishing crusaders.

Thank you.

Appendix

New Titles and Former Titles
of Lectures

Abraham Low's lectures were titled by the Recovery staff when the tape recordings were made available within the Recovery organization. The exceptions are lectures 55 through 64, which Low titled himself. In preparing this book and making the tapes available to the general public, the Low family has renamed some of the lectures to reflect their content more accurately. Following is a list of the recordings that were renamed:

1 There Are Two Choices: Security and Insecurity
  Formerly The Will to Bear Discomfort

4 Exceptionality
  Formerly Exceptionality and Averageness

9 Frustrations, Emergencies and Beliefs
  Formerly External and Internal Environment

11 The Patient Is an Apprentice
  Formerly Wait with Patience

13 Self-Blame, Exceptionality and Averageness
  Formerly The Principle—Don't Try To Be Exceptional,
  but Average

16 Convictions and the Setback
  Formerly Order, Beliefs and Convictions

17 A Sense of Humor Instead of Self-Blame
  Formerly Self-Approval Instead of Self-Resentment

19 The Purpose of Life Is to Maintain Peace
  Formerly Leadership and Fellowship—Your Attitude

20 Leadership and Muscles
  Formerly Leadership and Fellowship

21 Perfectionism Versus Human Limitations
  Formerly Total View and Partial Viewpoints

22 The Patient and the Physician Form an Intimate Group
  Formerly Total View and Partial Viewpoints

24 Temper, Temperament and Self-Blame
  Formerly Temper and Temperament

25 Exceptionality and Control of Impulses
  Formerly Tenseness Creates Symptoms